House by House, Block by Block

Also by Alexander von Hoffman

Fuel Lines for the Urban Revival Engine:
Neighborhoods, Community Development Corporations,
and Financial Intermediaries

Form, Modernism, and History:
Essays in Honor of Eduard F. Sekler (editor)

Local Attachments: The Making of an
American Urban Neighborhood, 1850–1920

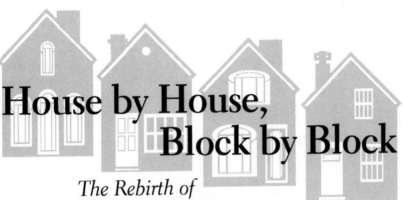

House by House, Block by Block

The Rebirth of America's Urban Neighborhoods

ALEXANDER VON HOFFMAN

OXFORD

UNIVERSITY PRESS

2003

OXFORD
UNIVERSITY PRESS

Oxford   New York
Auckland   Bangkok   Buenos Aires   Cape Town   Chennai
Dar es Salaam   Delhi   Hong Kong   Istanbul   Karachi   Kolkata
Kuala Lumpur   Madrid   Melbourne   Mexico City   Mumbai   Nairobi
São Paulo   Shanghai   Taipei   Tokyo   Toronto

Copyright © 2003 by Alexander von Hoffman

Published by Oxford University Press, Inc.
198 Madison Avenue, New York, New York 10016

www.oup.com

Oxford is a registered trademark of Oxford University Press

Library of Congress Cataloging-in-Publication Data
von Hoffman, Alexander
House by house, block by block : the rebirth of America's
urban neighborhoods / Alexander von Hoffman.
p. cm.
Includes bibliographical references and index.
ISBN 0-19-514437-6
1. Urban renewal—United States.
2. Community development, Urban—United States—Case Studies.
3. Inner cities—United States.
4. Urban policy—United States.
I. Title: Rebirth of America's urban neighborhoods.
II. Title.
HT175 .V66   2003
307.3'416'0973—dc21   2002151543

1 3 5 7 9 8 6 4 2
Printed in the United States of America
on acid-free paper

To Thomas N. Brown,
generous teacher, profound scholar, and good man

CONTENTS

ACKNOWLEDGMENTS

Researching and writing a book about community development was a little like community development itself. It was a gradual process—fact by fact, story by story—whose success depended upon the support, assistance, and advice of scores of people. I am deeply grateful to all of them for their help and apologize in advance to those whose names have been inadvertently omitted from the following list.

Let me begin by heartily thanking those without whose help the book might never have seen the light of day. These include Jack Beatty, Cullen Murphy, and William Whitworth, the editors of the *Atlantic Monthly*, who back in 1997 saw fit to publish my article on community-based housing, which became a springboard to the current work. Paul Grogan, author of the insightful *Comeback Cities*, gave crucial early encouragement to my idea for a book on the subject of inner-city rebirth and community development. In this he was assisted by others then at LISC, including Rick Cohen and Susan Shapiro, and also the late Mitchell Sviridoff. The Atlantic Philanthropies, and Joel Fleishman and Suzanne Gaba Aisenberg in particular, provided support for the research and writing of the book. Bill Apgar first and Nicolas Retsinas later invited me to pursue the project under the auspices of the Joint Center for Housing Studies of Harvard University. Literary agent *extraordinaire* Richard P. McDonough found it a home at Oxford University Press.

I greatly appreciate those who took the time to read and respond to the manuscript at various stages in its development. Richard McDonough, Robert Laubacher, and the anonymous reviewers of the early draft offered sage advice about how to improve the manuscript. Lawrence Anderson, Marc Jahr, Anita Landecker, Andrew Mooney, Susan Motley, Matthew Thall, and Melissa Turner carefully scrutinized individual chapters dealing with the cities about which they are experts.

I am beholden to the many, many people who spent the time and effort to describe their work, explain the history and conditions of particular inner cities, and connect me to other informed persons. For help with New York, they include Carol Abrams, Joseph Bodak, Peter Bray, Genevieve Brooks Brown,

Ed Chambers, Lucille Clark, Paul Crotty, Bill Frey, Louis Gaccione, the Reverend Louis Gigante, Paul Grogan, Mary Beth Guyther, Edward Koch, Michael Lappin, Richard Manson, Felice Michetti, Anita Miller, Janet Munch, Ralph Porter, Tony Proscio, Julie Sandorf, Michael Schill, the Reverend Monsignor William Smith, Lee Stuart, Kenneth Thorbourne, Mark Willis, Kathryn Wylde, and especially Jill Jonnes for sharing her research and expertise.

For Boston, there were John E. Avault, Katharine E. Bachman, Richard Carlson, Patrick Clancy, Pat Cusick, Jeanne DuBois, William Edgerly, James Ferris, Lewis Finfer, Ada Focer, Evelyn Friedman, Charles Grigsby, Robert H. Haas, Mossik Hacobian, William H. Jones, Willie Jones, Charlotte Kahn, David M. Kennedy, Langley Keyes, Gail Latimore, James P. Luckett, Edward H. Marchant, Peter Munkenbeck, Pat Riddick, Frank Sepulveda, Matthew Thall, Kenneth D. Wade, William J. Walczak, Gregory Watson, Eleanor G. White, Robert Whittlesey, and Sally Williams.

For Chicago, David E. Baker, Bishop Arthur Brazier, Peter Bynoe, Cecil Butler, Susan Campbell, Dirk Denison, Andrew Ditton, Patricia Dowell, Tyrone Galtney, Earnest Gates, Cornelius Goodwin, Bruce Gotschall, Ron Grzywinski, Elzie Higginbottom, Kevin Jackson, Phillip Jackson, Phillip Johnson, Connie Jones, William H. Jones, Sokoni Karanja, Leroy E. Kennedy, Harold Lucas, Larry Mayer, Leonard McGhee, Mary Nelson, Charles Orlebeke, Howard Pizer, Paula Robinson, Timothy Samuelson, Joseph Shuldiner, Gregory Sills, Dorothy Tillman, Richard Taub, Patricia Titus, the Very Reverend Richard Tolliver, Richard Townsell, Penny Walton, Wilma Ward, Francine Washington, Gregory F. Washington, Eric Wright, and Susana Vasquez, and, of course, the inimitable Bob Squires.

For Atlanta, Frank Alexander, Lawrence Anderson, Clara Axam, Bob Begle, David Crane, Maxwell Creighton, Douglas Dean, Michael A. Dobbins, Hattie Dorsey, Leon Eplan, Brenda Gammage, Michael W. Giles, Gregory J. Giornelli, Renee Glover, Douglas Greenwell, John W. Heath, Karen Huebner, Young T. Hughley, Jr., Larry Keating, Ray Kuniansky, Kate Little, William McFarland, Lorraine Mills, Eric Muschler, Carol Naughton, Mark O'Connell, Randall Roark, Deborah Schupp, Jane J. Stratigos, Craig Taylor, Marvin Toliver, Robert Upton, Sheila Vertino, LaToya Vezia, Rick White, Douglas Young, L. Mtamanika Youngblood, and, in particular, Melissa Turner for sharing her insights and reporting.

For Los Angeles, Norma Alvarado, Arlene Anaya, Yadira Arévalo, Ozabe Banks, Karen Bass, Marva Smith Battle-Bey, Neelura Bell, Stephen Cauley, Maggie Cervantes, May Cheung, Steve Clare, Michael J. Dear, Rocky Delgadillo, Sister Diane Donoghue, Melody Dove, Nevada Dove, Denise Fairchild, Eve Fisher, David Friedman, Linda Griego, Wendy Gruel, Greg Hise, Joel Kotkin, Anita Landecker, Tom Larson, Jacqueline Leavitt, Louise Manuel, Dean Matsubayashi, John Mutlow, Yvette Nunez, Virginia Oaxaca, Paul Ong, Debra Parra, Manuel Pastor, Jr., Anthony Scott, Jill Stewart, Beatrice Stotzer, Edwin Sundareson, Juanita Tate, Arturo Vargas, Arturo Ybarra, Kenny Yee, and Linda Yeung.

Among those who were sources for information about community and economic development in other cities and in general were John Blatt, Robert

Bolter, Conrad Egan, Gayle Epp, Ann Habiby, Daniel Hernandez, John Kromer, Paula Krugmeier, Stephanie O'Keefe, Michael Pyatok, and Peter Werwath.

I am grateful to all those who helped put the pieces of the book together. These include everyone who provided photographs for this book, and especially Ed Callahan, Monica Chadha, Glenna Lang, and Fred Stafford, who hit the streets to take pictures. Jim Carpenter, Elise Ciregna, Michael Collins, and Sondra Schwartz helped conduct research, James DeNormandie prepared demographic tables and the handsome maps, and Gary Fauth collected and compiled HMDA data.

At Oxford University Press, Peter Ginna, brought his exceptional editorial skills, knowledge, and enthusiasm to this work. Thanks also to Furaha Norton, Joellyn Ausanka, Tara Kennedy, Anne Holmes, Patterson Lamb, and to everyone else at Oxford University Press who transformed the raw manuscript into a fine-looking finished product and sent it out to the public.

Fellow scholars John Bauman, Robert Fishman, Marilyn Gittell, Scott Henderson, François Pierre Louise, Kathe Newman, Gail Radford, Patrick Simmons, Sara Stoutland, Thomas Sugrue, and Margaret Weir imparted their insights into urban issues.

Long-time friends and associates at Harvard's Graduate School of Design who helped this project include Dean Peter G. Rowe — an inspirer as always — Carol Burns, Lee Cott, John Driscoll, Alex Krieger, Edward Robbins, Russell Sanna, Jim Stockard, and François Vigier. At the Kennedy School of Government, Xavier de Souza Briggs and Howard Husock shared their keen interest in community development although from widely divergent viewpoints.

I am indebted to all my colleagues at Harvard University's Joint Center for Housing Studies, in particular, director Nicolas Retsinas, executive director Eric Belsky, and also Bill Apgar, Kermit Baker, Pamela Baldwin, Mark Duda, Josephine Louie, Nancy McArdle, and Natalie Perkins for their counsel and enthusiastic support.

Friends, many of them who know first hand the challenges of the writer's calling, offered sympathy and encouragement. Fred Bayles, Tom Brown, Maureen Foley, Perri Klass, Rob Laubacher, Katherine Powers, and Larry Wolf were among those who helped see this through to the end. With his boundless enthusiasm for this project, the late and sorely missed Timothy White inspired me as he inspired countless others to pursue their art.

Closer to home, my father, Nicholas von Hoffman, bestowed his gusto and knowledge of the ways of urban communities. My wife, Glenna Lang, advised, edited, took pictures, and generally pushed me to the finish line with spectacular patience and good grace. My daughter, Esmé, amiably tolerated the excursions to housing developments and inner-city neighborhoods — including her first trip to Los Angeles that began in Watts rather than Hollywood — and always cheered me on and up.

Merci beaucoup, y'all.

ACRONYMS

ACOG	Atlanta Committee for the Olympic Games
A.M.E.	African Methodist Episcopal
ANDP	Atlanta Neighborhood Development Partnership
ATF	U.S. Bureau of Alcohol, Tobacco and Firearms
BHP	Boston Housing Partnership
BRA	Boston Redevelopment Authority
BURP	Boston Urban Rehabilitation Program
CARECEN	Central American Resource Center
CDBG	community development block grant
CDC	community development corporation
CD Tech	Community Development Technologies Center
CEDAC	Community Economic Development Assistance Corporation
CHA	Chicago Housing Authority
CODA	Corporation for Olympic Development in Atlanta
DEA	U.S. Drug Enforcement Agency
DSNI	Dudley Street Neighborhood Initiative
EBC	East Brooklyn Churches
EDC	economic development corporation (appended to a name, as in Dorchester Bay EDC)
FIBR	Food Industry Business Roundtable
GBCD	Greater Boston Community Development, Inc.
HDC	housing development corporation (appended to a name, as in Codman Square HDC)

HPD	New York City Department of Housing Preservation and Development
HUD	U.S. Department of Housing and Urban Development
IAF	Industrial Areas Foundation
IIT	Illinois Institute of Technology
IOC	International Olympic Committee
LCDC	Lawndale Christian Development Corporation
LISC	Local Initiatives Support Corporation
MBD	Mid-Bronx Desperadoes
MHFA	Massachusetts Housing Finance Agency
MIT	Massachusetts Institute of Technology
NAFTA	North American Free Trade Agreement
NDC	neighborhood development corporation (appended to a name, as in Summerhill NDC)
NHSC	Neighborhood Housing Services of Chicago
RLA	Rebuild Los Angeles
SCBC	Southern California Biomedical Council
SEBCO	South East Bronx Community Organization Development Corporation
TASC	Toy Association of Southern California
TELACU	The East Los Angeles Community Union
WLCAC	Watts Labor Community Action Committee
WPIC	Woodlawn Preservation and Investment Corporation

House by House, Block by Block

INTRODUCTION

On a sunny day in August 1980, California governor Ronald Reagan, campaigning for the presidency on the Republican ticket, stopped on Charlotte Street in New York's South Bronx—the epitome of America's desolated inner-city neighborhoods and the place where President Jimmy Carter had famously visited three years earlier. Reagan stepped out of his limousine and took in the scene. He declared that it looked like London after the Blitz.

The candidate stood amidst the rubble and empty shells of buildings and delivered a speech. He attacked Carter for failing to keep his promise to rebuild the South Bronx and proclaimed that he would bring it back by attracting private businesses through tax incentives.

A small crowd of people across the street would have none of it. "You ain't gonna do nothin'!" they shouted. "Go back to California!"

Undaunted, Reagan crossed over to speak to the hecklers. "If you'll just listen," he began, "I'm trying to tell you—I know now there is no program or policies that a president can come in and wave a wand to do this."[1]

The message did not go over well, and Reagan drove off. Yet, however unwelcome the notion was, history seemed to support the idea that government was powerless to save areas such as the South Bronx.

Since the end of World War II, few great issues have perplexed Americans as much as the decline of central cities. For decades the federal government tried one program after another to stop the inner city from deteriorating. All in vain. First white upper- and middle-class households fled, then African American and Hispanic working families departed. As the inner city became the dominion of the poor and the pathological, city-government agencies withdrew like a retreating army.

The destruction of the inner city took on an inexorable quality. Buildings were deserted, vandalized, and burned. Epidemics of violence, gangs, and drug addiction swept through the streets. The wail of police and fire engine sirens provided background music to an endless stream of television and newspaper stories about sordid crimes and calamities. Most Americans dismissed the inner city as a dismal place given over to crime, gangs, and arson and to be avoided at all costs.

Yet today the inner city is no longer the lurid nightmare portrayed for so long on the local eleven o'clock news. From Newark to San Francisco, empty shells of buildings have been rebuilt, and real estate developers are constructing new homes and stores. Crime rates have plummeted to levels not seen in forty years. The fire engine houses are so quiet that in some areas they have been closed. As crime dropped, investors have begun to put money into the ghettos and slum areas—Washington's U Street, San Antonio's Skyline Park, Miami's Overtown and Liberty City, and New Orleans's Irish Channel.[2]

In the 1980s a scholar examining inner-city neighborhoods found only "islands of renewal in seas of decay." Today researchers write of "islands of decay in seas of renewal."[3] As startling as it may seem, across the United States inner-city neighborhoods are being reborn.

Not government but a myriad of small private groups has led the drive for community development, a term that encompasses the many and diverse efforts to save the inner city. During the darkest hours, citizens, clergy, and businesspeople have banded together in local nonprofit organizations to halt population flight, abandonment, and capital disinvestment. They have worked not only through churches, government anti-poverty agencies, or schools but also through a new kind of association: community development corporations, or CDCs. Operating out of storefronts and sometimes living rooms, the nonprofit organizations ran anti-crime programs, developed new homes and retail businesses, instituted job training and day care, and established health care centers. They sometimes failed, but they often succeeded triumphantly.

Workers in the field of community development have served as midwives for the rebirth of America's inner cities. An array of economic and social forces—such as prosperity, immigration, and gentrification—has helped rejuvenate inner-city neighborhoods, creating both opportunities and problems. Community development practitioners adjusted to the new conditions in a variety of ways. They helped the unemployed find jobs and renters buy houses. They helped immigrants learn the skills needed to survive and thrive in American society. Where upper-class professionals moved in, community development workers strove to preserve the homes for low-income residents and create mixed-income neighborhoods. More than anyone else, the individuals and storefront organizations in the community development field have taken the destiny of our urban areas upon themselves.

Local community development groups by themselves could not have survived without money or expertise. Numerous governmental and private institutions supported the small groups that marched in the forefront of the community development movement. Government agencies—city, state, and federal—assisted and promoted community development operations by providing money, land, and simple cooperation. Philanthropic foundations and nonprofit financial institutions conferred funds in the forms of loans and grants and technical advice and services. The leaders of the most successful organizations learned not only what programs succeeded in their neighborhoods but also how to win over government officials and nonprofit financiers and work with them to apply their insights.

House by House, Block by Block recounts the struggles and accomplishments of the people and organizations, small and large, devoted to revitalizing urban neighborhoods in five American cities: New York, Boston, Chicago, Atlanta, and Los Angeles. Culled from numerous interviews, published works, newspaper stories, official documents, and statistical analyses, narratives drawn from selected neighborhoods illustrate the social forces and practical methods that are reviving the inner city. Because the book is not a comprehensive or "best practices" survey, many low-income neighborhoods and worthy organizations were reluctantly omitted.

The cities examined here convey the scope and strength of the widespread movement to revitalize inner-city neighborhoods. Boston, New York, Chicago, Los Angeles, and Atlanta represent different geographical regions, depend on different kinds of economies, and have their own unique political cultures and traditions. Each metropolis exemplifies different stages of the community development movement—ranging from Boston and New York, where long ago grassroots organizations won the support of local government and foundations, to Atlanta, where the neighborhood groups are relatively young and the civic establishment only recently began to support the cause of community development. Each urban place described here is in its own way unique, yet reflects demographic trends and approaches to community development that can be found to greater or lesser degree in large cities across the United States.

The stories told herein emphasize the rebuilding of homes and stores—because the physical reconstruction of a neighborhood is a first step in its revitalization—yet they also report policing, economic development, health, education, and recreation programs that helped build functioning communities. The subject here is not the campaign to eradicate poverty—which has by no means disappeared—but the efforts to fix the places that have long been associated with poverty and help the low-income people who live there.

Before setting off to visit the five cities, we need to understand a little of the history of our subject. The book begins with a brief account of how inner cities were built in the first place, why they collapsed, and the repeated failures of the federal government to save them.

Our inner-city tour starts in New York City, where the South Bronx, the most infamous slum district in the United States, has undergone a miraculous transformation. Despite the enormous problems there, religious clerics, neighborhood leaders, and some plucky city government officials believed the Bronx could be saved. They boldly fought landlords, drug dealers, bankers, and indifferent bureaucrats. The most successful efforts, often led by street-wise priests and ministers, were those that did the best job of organizing the people to salvage their neighborhoods. At a crucial point, New York's government launched the largest housing program ever undertaken by an American city. To get around the obstacles of government bureaucracies and regulations, the program was set up so that hundreds of private organizations and contractors rehabilitated and built the new homes. For the first time in memory, the South Bronx became a livable place.

In Boston, a city that lacked the financial might of New York City, people in nonprofit community groups, business, and government discovered the power of collaborating with one another. Through a series of audacious experiments, unlikely alliances of Bostonians established community development systems in Boston by the early 1980s, before most other cities. They learned to work together to develop new housing and stores where others had failed repeatedly and devised a new set of policing tools to throttle gang violence. As a result, the locals were able to stay a step ahead of a rocketing real estate market and take advantage of it.

In the midwestern industrial metropolis of Chicago, the defenders of historic African American neighborhoods on the near South and West Sides first had to fight complete neglect and then the double-edged sword of upscale development—promulgated by, among others, the city's popular professional sports teams. The campaigns to save the inner-city neighborhoods often took the form of David and Goliath battles. The victories have been impressive, including a unique partnership between a local community development corporation and the Chicago Bulls to rebuild the near West Side. The old ghettos at last have attracted the interest of developers, and now community advocates must strive to protect long-term residents of the inner city against the full force of gentrification.

Atlanta has always been a quintessential southern boom town. For years the city all but ignored the plight of inner-city residents while "good old boy" white businessmen and canny black politicians avidly pursued development deals in outer areas such as the Fulton County airport or the burgeoning Buckhead district. The coming of the 1996 Olympics, however, threatened to expose the city's slums to the world and so galvanized the city's leaders—and former president Jimmy Carter—into supporting a series of showcase urban renewal projects. Some of these efforts succeeded and others dissipated, but taken together, they show that this pro-growth Sunbelt community where God and business go hand in hand has begun to take neighborhood redevelopment seriously.

In Los Angeles, revival rode in on a giant wave of immigration that is Latinizing traditionally black neighborhoods in South Central Los Angeles and Watts. The workers from Central America resuscitated the flagging inner-city real estate market but too often found themselves in sweat shops and overcrowded homes. A cultural gap emerged among the immigrant nationalities and between them and the African American community leaders. After the police beating of Rodney King, the worst riot of the twentieth century exposed the ethnic tensions and led to a massive effort to "Rebuild L. A." The crusade flopped, however, and only afterward did a few perceptive leaders realize that South Central was in fact an economic riptide which, if properly channeled, would raise all boats. Community development leaders devised a strategy of assisting mom-and-pop manufacturers and, in the process, put Los Angeles in the forefront of a national movement to revive the inner city by helping small businesses multiply and grow.

Each of these cities has different tales to tell, tales that are in turn inspirational, exciting, and above all instructive. There are stories of colorful individuals who took up the cause when it seemed hopeless, who audaciously challenged the powers-that-be, or who devised new ways to improve the world around them. They tell of those who aimed high, of those who hit their mark or came close, the few who missed, and those who are still trying. The tales from the cities teach lessons of democracy, struggle, organization, enlightened use of power and money, and the role of government. The stories vary from place to place, but they have one thing in common. They are all a part of a momentous change, the rebirth of America's urban neighborhoods.

THE QUEST TO SAVE THE INNER CITY
A Historical Perspective

1

In the beginning, inner-city neighborhoods in the United States were not disaster areas, but vital parts of the cities to which they belonged.

America's great cities, perhaps excepting Washington, D.C., arose as places where goods were shipped, processed, and traded. With their accessible ocean harbors, east coast cities such as New York and Boston became great ports. Goods moved to and from Chicago via Lake Michigan and the Chicago River and later by rail. Atlanta, located not on a body of water but at the site of a railroad junction (one of its early names was Terminus), became a central trade depot for the South. Los Angeles at first used the Los Angeles River, then acquired an ocean port, railroads, and finally a highway network to become the dominant port of the Southwest. To finance, sell, and distribute the goods the port brought in, each city developed business districts whose main streets—Wall Street, State Street, Peachtree Street—became synonymous with finance and commerce. Along the water and near railroad depots entrepreneurs built factories to process the goods streaming in and out of the city. Industrial areas, such as the stockyard district in Chicago and the Alameda corridor in Los Angeles, became almost as famous as the downtown business districts. After all, the commercial and industrial businesses that grew out of the port trade were the lifeblood of the country's lusty young urban centers.

Neighborhoods developed around the city's core to house the people who worked in commerce and industry. In the nineteenth and early twentieth centuries these districts—the inner-city neighborhoods—ranged from the elegant to the humble. Inner-city luxury districts such as Boston's Beacon Hill, San Francisco's Nob Hill, and Chicago's Gold Coast were known far and wide for their gentility and tasteful architecture.

At the other extreme were the lowly areas which, although inhabited by all sorts of people including shopkeepers and factory workers, were identified with the poor, the destitute, immigrants, and African Americans. Demand for homes ran high in congested working- and lower-class neighborhoods, and thus the poor crammed into cellars, alley shacks, and cheap tenement buildings. These abodes—damp, dark, and lacking rudimentary plumbing—were dubbed slums. By the end of the nineteenth century, the inner-city areas that contained slum buildings—such notorious neighborhoods as the Lower East Side of Manhattan, the North and West Ends in Boston, and the near West Side of Chicago—were also referred to as slums.

For most of the nation's history, Americans accepted the inner-city slums as an inevitable if unfortunate fact of life. The few people who thought they posed a problem were earnest reformers, and only after a shocking event— such as the publication of Jacob Riis's *How the Other Half Lives* or the disastrous Triangle Shirtwaist Fire of 1911—did the public and lawmakers pay the housing reformers any attention. For more than a century, any efforts to get rid of the slums or remedy the health and safety hazards they created were sporadic, local, and limited.

Starting in the 1920s, however, civic leaders came to feel that the slums menaced the well-being of the entire city. Local officials, downtown businessmen, and large real estate owners watched with growing anxiety as the upper-class residents departed for newly built suburbs and once-affluent neighborhoods and downtown commercial districts lost their radiance. Experts labeled the economic decline of neighborhoods "urban blight," which they said preceded a total degeneration into slum conditions. If the blight and slums continued to spread, government and business leaders worried, they would take the cities down with them.[1]

In fact, changing settlement patterns caused blight to spread from the central city. Instead of concentrating in a central area as in European cities, American urban areas fanned out from the core, and technological breakthroughs reinforced this pattern of decentralized urban growth. With the invention of the electric engine and the truck, commerce and industry began to move out of the central city into the surrounding countryside. The automobile, aided by a suburban building boom in the 1920s, accelerated the outward movement of families. In addition, industries that left an urban region—for example, the textile industry's departure from New England for the South—left factories quiet. Gradually, the loss of jobs and people in the central city caused the houses to become vacant and stores to close. Making matters worse, the United States government effectively cut off immigration in the 1920s, which deprived inner-city neighborhoods of a new supply of residents that would keep them vital.

The civic and real estate industry leaders who decried inner-city blight, however, paid little heed to these long-term trends and called for "urban redevelopment," which meant replacing the slums with more attractive structures. Since urban redevelopment was too expensive for private developers or local governments, they turned to the U.S. government and, after a long political struggle, achieved the Housing Act of 1949.

The Housing Act of 1949 was the first major federal program designed to rebuild the inner city. Its fundamental purpose was to acquire and demolish slum buildings and construct something better in their place. The act authorized the federal government to lend cities money to buy slum land and allocated a hundred million dollars to help pay public agencies or private companies to redevelop the land. The law also authorized federal loans and grants to build hundreds of thousands of new low-rent public housing apartments to replace inner-city slum dwellings.

The slum clearance program had trouble getting started, so five years later Congress passed another act that targeted not only slums but also blighted areas, and even potentially blighted areas. Instead of simply bulldozing neighborhoods, the law allowed buildings to be renovated but also gave more latitude to build nonresidential projects on the sites where people used to live. Since the term *urban redevelopment* smacked too much of wholesale demolition, the program was renamed "urban renewal."

Whether by urban renewal or any other name, the strategy of urban redevelopment embodied in the federal laws failed to recognize the profound population turnover in American cities. At first it was easy to miss the signs. The year 1950 represented a high-water mark in the population size and economic vitality of large cities in the United States. The crowded neighborhoods and downtowns bustling with well-dressed shoppers and striving businessmen proved to be temporary, however—the results of World War II and its immediate aftermath.

With most industry devoted to the military effort, few homes or businesses were built during the war. At the same time, the need for workers in the wartime industries prompted millions more unskilled southern blacks, Appalachian whites, Puerto Ricans, and Mexicans to seek employment in America's large cities. The newcomers settled in the industrial areas and inner-city neighborhoods—the old slums and ghettos—and sometimes spilled into formerly affluent neighborhoods. When the war ended, G.I.s returned from overseas to reclaim their jobs and start families, and the migration of low-income people from the southern regions continued to grow. Across the country, the population of cities swelled like a flooding river, and the scarcity of housing reached crisis dimensions.

The population logjam began to break about 1950 when the American economy adjusted, and suburbanization resumed in earnest. The decline of the central city resumed as well. The diversion of affluent and middle-class shoppers to the new suburban subdivisions and shopping centers led stores in downtowns and along the main commercial boulevards of the cities to close their doors or go downmarket. As the inner-city population became increasingly poor, apartments were overcrowded and undermaintained, crime and delinquency increased, and the social fabric began to fray.

Imposed from the top down, urban redevelopment programs neglected the social problems of the expanding ghettos and ignored the value of the stable working-class communities that remained in the city. Instead, the urban renewal program proposed a physical solution to urban decline: eliminate unsightly slums and replace them with attractive modern facilities. Well-planned and well-designed new structures, the reasoning went, would encourage the poor to assimilate and lure upper-middle-class people back to the central city.

The supporters of urban renewal, including many big-city mayors and downtown businessmen, were delighted to unveil the civic centers, luxury apartment buildings, and high-rise public housing that were built on urban renewal sites. They boasted that the program created glittery downtown projects—such as the

New York Coliseum and Lincoln Center in upper Manhattan—and helped resuscitate historic neighborhoods—such as Society Hill in Philadelphia.

Critics vehemently attacked the program, however, for benefiting private real estate developers, wantonly uprooting tens of thousands from their homes, and destroying vibrant working-class neighborhoods. They pointed to Boston, where the government demolished the city's predominantly Italian American West End neighborhood and then handed it to a private developer to build luxury housing, and Los Angeles, where officials cleared Chavez Ravine, a 315-acre village of poor but working Mexican Americans, for a public housing project, only to give the land to the Los Angeles Dodgers for a baseball stadium. Urban renewal dislocated so many African Americans that some took to calling the program "Negro removal." Local residents increasingly resisted redevelopment schemes by staging mass rallies, taking over redevelopment authority offices, and turning out the anti-urban renewal vote.[2]

The public housing program fared little better. In large cities such as New York, Chicago, and St. Louis, housing authorities used the money authorized by the Housing Act of 1949 to build sleekly modernistic, high-rise public housing projects that would better the living conditions of the low-income populace. Because white middle-class people objected, sometimes with rocks and bombs, to the presence of housing projects in their neighborhoods, the new projects were usually built in the old ghettos of the inner city.

Stigmatized as a kind of welfare housing, public housing projects attracted a growing number of so-called problem families, plagued by alcoholism, delinquency, and unemployment. By the late 1950s Harrison Salisbury, Moscow correspondent of the *New York Times* who compared American conditions to those in Russia, argued that some New York housing projects, such as Fort Greene in Brooklyn, were "monsters, devouring their residents, polluting the areas around them, spewing out a social excrescence which infects the whole of our society."[3]

Conditions in the giant projects continued to worsen as the number of crimes rose and rental revenues fell. During the 1960s the government spent millions of dollars to bring back Pruitt-Igoe, a massive high-rise housing project in St. Louis, before giving up and demolishing the project in the early 1970s— the first time a public housing project had ever been destroyed. Public housing, which was supposed to rescue people from the inner city, had itself succumbed to the slums.

Despite the troubles besetting urban policies, dramatic events during the 1960s put inner-city slums and ghettos in the national spotlight. The publication of Michael Harrington's *The Other America* in 1962 helped publicize the destitution that existed in the cities and countryside of an otherwise affluent society. In 1964 President Lyndon Johnson declared the federal government's War on Poverty. When the civil rights movement began to tear down the Jim Crow system in the South, movement leaders launched a crusade to improve the racial ghettos of the North. In 1966 the Reverend Martin Luther King, Jr., and his lieutenants arrived in Chicago and started a loud campaign that at one point included seizing a slum building in the city's West Side ghetto.

This was also the era of the long hot summer, four consecutive years when the nation's black ghettos exploded in violence. It began in New York in July 1964, when residents of Harlem went on a rampage for five days after a white policeman fatally shot an African American youth. The following summer the arrest of a young black man for drunken driving in the Los Angeles neighborhood of Watts touched off four days of looting and arson, leaving in its wake thirty-four dead, 1,000 injured, and a new slogan, "Burn, baby, burn!" Even worse violence occurred in 1967 in Detroit, where the toll reached forty-three deaths and at least $50 million worth of property destroyed. The assassination of Martin Luther King in April 1968 sparked major riots in Washington, Chicago, and Baltimore and minor conflagrations in more than one hundred other communities.

The riots of the 1960s devastated the neighborhoods where they took place. Rioters burned and looted hundreds of stores, many of which never opened again. Most white storeowners, who were frequently a target of the rioters, left the areas, whether they were struck or not. With fewer places to shop, many residents also left. Decades later one could still see storefronts that had been boarded up after the 1960s riots.

Mainstream opinion indicted the inner-city slums for the violence and poverty plaguing America's cities. In March 1968 the National Advisory Commission on Civil Disorders, chaired by Otto Kerner, placed much of the blame for the riots on the concentration of poor blacks in inner-city ghettos which, it said, racism and discrimination had created. "The urban problem can be described as the big-city slum," reported members of another presidential commission, the National Commission on Urban Problems, in December the same year. Showing prescience, the commissioners observed, "Slums in our big cities, which are now in the midst of social decay, may well become social and economic disaster areas."[4]

Under President Johnson, the federal government made an unprecedented effort to root out violence and poverty by uplifting the inner-city ghettos. To begin, Johnson recognized the importance of urban issues by establishing the Department of Housing and Urban Development (HUD) as a cabinet-level agency. Because Johnson's vision of a Great Society included better homes for the urban masses, his administration increased the money to build public housing—which despite its problems was still seen as the best alternative for very poor people—and started new programs designed to help low-income families buy houses and encourage real estate developers to build low-income rental apartments.[5]

Besides housing, the president's War on Poverty generated an array of programs—such as job training centers and the Neighborhood Youth Corps jobs program—aimed at individuals living in the slums. The Community Action Program located such efforts as Head Start preschools, legal services, and community health centers in inner-city neighborhoods.

The Community Action Program also started a novel type of organization, the community action agency, in which ordinary inner-city residents would work with representatives of social service agencies and institutions to plan and carry out anti-poverty measures for their communities. In part this approach was a

11

reaction to the top-down administration of the discredited urban renewal and public housing programs. When community action agencies helped organize protests against the local political establishment, however, big-city mayors attacked the agencies and the federal regulation that required "maximum feasible participation" of the poor. Although political opposition forced a retreat from activities under its aegis, the Community Action Program helped popularize the idea that people with low incomes should help determine policies and programs that affect them.

Finally, Johnson rolled out the most ambitious anti-slum program ever devised. The Model Cities program resembled the community action scheme except that it was designed on a grander scale, and in order to avoid political opposition, it explicitly included local government officials. Originally conceived as an experiment, Model Cities was supposed to induce social service agencies, government departments, and schools to coordinate their efforts and invent new ways to improve troubled neighborhoods and lift their residents out of poverty. Funds for the program were spread over many more cities than originally planned, however, and it lacked practical means to make institutions cooperate on projects. Almost before the Model Cities program was started, it was criticized for being an overly ambitious waste of money.[6]

Johnson left office just as his housing and neighborhood development programs were being launched, so it was up to his successor, Richard Nixon, to carry them out. Despite Nixon's lack of enthusiasm for the Great Society programs, his administration took a pragmatic approach and for a time continued anti-slum programs started by his predecessor. Then in 1973 Nixon responded to growing criticism—including accusations of corruption and mismanagement—of some of Johnson's housing programs by imposing a moratorium on the funding for all federal housing programs. The moratorium lasted until the end of a long struggle with Democrats in Congress, when the Nixon administration hammered out a new urban policy based on Nixon's new federalism philosophy.

Like Johnson, Nixon had no chance to supervise what he started. The Congress and the administration agreed on a compromise in August 1974, just two days before Nixon resigned in the wake of the Watergate scandal. Gerald Ford signed the Housing and Community Development Act of 1974 into law.

The 1974 Housing and Community Development Act marked another turning point in the federal government's urban policy. The law ended funding for the controversial urban renewal and Model Cities programs and replaced it with community development block grants (CDBGs) to local governments, which administered them under HUD's supervision. A provision in the law that the grants should help low-income families ensured that a good portion of the federal monies went to the inner-city slum areas. The inner-city focus was strengthened in 1977 when the administration of Jimmy Carter enacted the Urban Development Action Grant program, which sent additional federal funds to areas in extreme economic distress. By the 1980s block grants were used for a range of projects—including public facilities, planning, and most often low-income housing. As with the old urban renewal program, city-government agencies oversaw the redevelopment schemes that the block grants funded, but unlike the earlier program, they often contracted the work to neighborhood nonprofit organizations, some of which had been created by Johnson's War on Poverty community action program.

The 1974 law also introduced new low-income housing programs that ultimately would play a role in rebuilding the inner city. Section 8 of the 1974 act, which replaced and to some extent built on Johnson's housing programs, authorized the federal government to provide money to private landlords to lower the rents that low-income tenants paid. Section 8 also allowed developers who constructed or totally rehabilitated apartment buildings for low-income families to use tax-exempt bonds for financing. By combining Section 8 subsidies with tax savings from accelerated depreciation and the deduction of mortgage interest, the savvy developer could make out well in the low-income field.

Yet nothing seemed to work. As one federal program followed another, the inner-city neighborhoods just got worse. From the 1960s onward, the number of crimes in the inner-city soared. Street gangs and drugs, sometimes alternately and other times simultaneously, invaded the neighborhoods. Buildings were abandoned and burned. Storekeepers either barricaded themselves behind metal grates or shut down altogether. Except for the police and fire departments, which never seemed to show up in time to prevent a calamity, local governments seemed to withdraw from the inner city completely.

Inner-city neighborhoods suffered a demographic collapse, losing up to two-thirds of their populations. The advances in civil rights and the increasing availability of housing across the metropolitan area allowed aspiring inner-city residents—those stable working families who could serve as role models

A foggy day on Fox Street in the South Bronx, 1979. Courtesy of Carlos Ortiz.

of how to get ahead in society—to move out. First, middle-class residents departed for outer-city neighborhoods or the suburbs. Upwardly mobile working-class families soon followed them out. Then the working poor began to leave. Bustling communities came to resemble busted mining towns. The Summerhill neighborhood, adjacent to downtown Atlanta, at its high point had been home to 20,000 people, but by the 1990s only a few thousand hung on there. On Chicago's South Side, the population of Oakland shriveled from 24,380 in 1960 to 8,200 in 1990. Eventually, in such inner-city neighborhoods, it seemed that hardly anyone remained at all.[7]

For all practical purposes, the inner-city neighborhoods had lost their function. They had long since ceased to serve as residential areas for the downtown and port industries, which were now but shadows of their former selves. Now the old neighborhoods no longer acted as a reservoir of housing and springboard for in-migrant racial minorities.

If anything, the neighborhoods at the urban core had become, like the large public housing projects, a last resort for the aged, the afflicted, and the poor. Americans began to think of the inner-city residents as indigents who passed their dependency on government welfare checks to their many children. Expressing an abiding sense of pessimism, people referred to the inner-city poor by the term popularized by Ken Auletta in the early 1980s, *the underclass*.[8]

Ronald Reagan used to say that the government had fought a war on poverty, and poverty had won. Three decades of federal programs had done little to rescue the slum. On taking over the presidency, Reagan responded almost perversely to the ruination of the inner city. He drastically cut back the amount of money the federal government provided for social services and urban programs. The chief innovation of the Reagan administration was to promote Section 8 rental vouchers for tenants as a housing program, but it did so in part to avoid spending public monies on construction of low-income housing. Adding insult to injury, Reagan allowed the Department of Housing and Urban Development to sink into a mire of corruption.

Just as inner-city neighborhoods reached a nadir of misery, sprouts of life began to appear. Hardly noticed at first, a wide variety of small nonprofit organizations emerged to take up the cause of the beleaguered communities. Some were born of battles against urban renewal and highway projects, others were founded by churches to help the impoverished, and still others were started as neighborhood improvement associations. They included traditional social service agencies, hard-nosed power-oriented community organizations affiliated with the Industrial Areas Foundation, and community development corporations or CDCs whose explicit aim was to rebuild the neighborhoods. The groups were mostly small storefront operations, but they were led by talented and determined local people who struggled, sometimes at considerable personal risk, to save their communities.

The small inner-city organizations would do almost anything to improve the desperate situation of their neighborhoods. They pressed the government to provide the city services that had been withdrawn. They organized crime watches and coordinated community policing with the local precinct. Many built new homes or took over and fixed up old buildings, threw out drug dealers, renovated apartments, and rented to low-income tenants. Some groups helped to start or expand businesses. Others set up programs for child care, job training, and drug rehabilitation. Some groups introduced medical clinics to their neighborhoods. A few even operated schools.

Spurred to some extent by Reagan's budget cutbacks, a variety of large institutions helped the new organizations. Churches and church-related organizations such as Catholic Charities provided great amounts of money and sometimes carried out projects themselves. Philanthropic foundations bankrolled many of the projects undertaken by the community groups. The Ford Foundation was an early backer—it assisted the Bedford-Stuyvesant Restoration Corporation, a Brooklyn CDC prototype organization founded with help from Robert Kennedy—but others, such as Pew Charitable Trusts, Eli Lilly, Rockefeller, MacArthur, and Surdna foundations, also wrote checks. Certain large corporations, including the Prudential Insurance Company, gave and lent money to CDCs.

A new kind of institution known as a financial intermediary emerged as a mainstay of this community development movement. The Neighborhood Reinvestment Corporation was the first of the type, and like others it was inspired by local efforts. In the late 1960s a group of Pittsburgh residents in a fight with mortgage lenders who refused to make loans in their blighted neighborhood devised a successful program with credit unions and a local foundation to give home repair loans and guidance to homeowners. The model of the nonprofit Neighborhood Housing Services organization spread around the country—in large part due to William Whiteside, an urban specialist for the Federal Home Loan Bank Board—and expanded to include home purchases and apartment building renovations. To strengthen and replicate the operations of Neighborhood Housing Services organizations, the U.S. Congress in 1978 established the Neighborhood Reinvestment Corporation. The Neighborhood Reinvestment Corporation supports and administers a revolving high-risk loan fund to Neighborhood Housing Services (now called NeighborWorks) affiliates—of which there were 220 in 2002—in order to revitalize deteriorated areas, primarily through the rehabilitation of owner-occupied houses.[9]

The Ford Foundation helped start the Local Initiatives Support Corporation, or LISC, as a private national intermediary. The late Mitchell Sviridoff, then Ford Foundation vice president, had noticed the small community nonprofit groups and became convinced that they could be a catalyst for the economic and social revival of the inner-city neighborhoods. With a grant of $9.3 million from the Ford Foundation and six major corporations, Sviridoff established the Local Initiatives Support Corporation in 1980 to make loans and grants to CDCs across the country. Four years later LISC had obtained more than $70 million from 250 corporations and foundations and three federal agencies and had set up thirty-one branch offices, which raised funds from local sources. By 2002, LISC had raised over $3 billion from over 2,200 investors, lenders, and donors which it distributed to hundreds of CDCs in thirty-eight cities and sixty-six rural areas.[10]

Real estate developer James Rouse and his wife Patricia became involved in community development after helping two women from a church in Washington, D.C., salvage two badly run-down apartment buildings in the Adams-Morgan neighborhood. With James Rouse's financial backing, the church members formed Jubilee Housing, a community development organization, to renovate run-down properties and preserve housing for poor people in Adams-Morgan. The Rouses then decided to create a national institution, and in 1981 founded the Enterprise Foundation to work with any entity, from non-profit community groups to municipal governments, to develop or help develop low-income housing. Like LISC, the Enterprise Foundation grew quickly. In 1982 the Enterprise Foundation supported six nonprofit organizations in six locations. Twenty years later, its network included more than 2,200 groups in 800 places.[11]

By acting as broker, credit rating service, and rich uncle, the large private intermediaries became major financiers to the community development movement. LISC and the Enterprise Foundation allied with housing advocates in 1986 and wrested out of the Reagan administration and Congress the Low-Income Housing Tax Credit. Replacing the rapid-depreciation tax shelter, the Low-Income Housing Tax Credit allowed nonprofit and for-profit developers of either new or rehabilitated low-income rental housing to earn credits that could be sold to investors.[12] Nonprofit organizations had no need for tax credits (as tax exempt organizations) so the trade of immediate financing for tax credits advantaged them greatly. The intermediaries helped sell large corporate investors on the housing deals, created large capital pools, and directed them to local nonprofit organizations. LISC and the Enterprise Foundation each formed syndication corporations, which by 1998 had raised $2 billion in equity for CDCs and other nonprofit housing developers.[13] Nonprofit community development had become a big deal.

During the last fifteen years, the community development organizations emerged as an important part of the nation's urban policy. The federal government, under president George Bush, officially recognized its contribution in the 1990 Low-Income Housing Preservation and Resident Homeownership Act, which provided monies for a variety of housing programs. The law specifically allotted a proportion of its funds to nonprofit community organizations. Meanwhile, the number of CDCs proliferated. A recent survey found approximately 8,400 organizations carrying out community development programs in the United States, with about half of these founded since 1990. The community groups developed housing at an ever-increasing rate. In the late 1980s, nonprofit organizations produced more than 20,000 dwelling units per year. In the early 1990s, the production rate reached about 40,000 units, and between 1994 and 1997, more than 60,000 units.[14]

The efforts of nonprofits aside, major social changes again influenced the fate of inner-city neighborhoods. Immigration resumed during the 1980s at a scale not seen since the end of the nineteenth century. Millions of people from all over the globe have come to the United States during the last two decades, and, as in earlier immigration waves, most of the new arrivals took up residence in urban regions. At the same time, a small but increasing number of upper- and upper-middle-class Americans rejected the suburbs to settle downtown and in nearby neighborhoods. Attracted by the historic houses, neighborhood life, and cultural offerings of the city, affluent professionals brought an upscale tone to the places where they lived. Both types of newcomers, immigrant and urban gentry, found their way to forgotten sections of the central city.

In the waning years of the twentieth century, all these developments—the nonprofit community groups, the new wave of immigration, and gentrification—had converged. And lo and behold, the neighborhoods of the inner cities at last began to show visible improvements—in crime statistics, employment rolls, and physical appearance.

Such progress, however, was unpredictable and never came easily. Helped along by many hands, the long awaited rebirth of America's inner cities took place in different ways at different times in different places. Here follows a closer look.

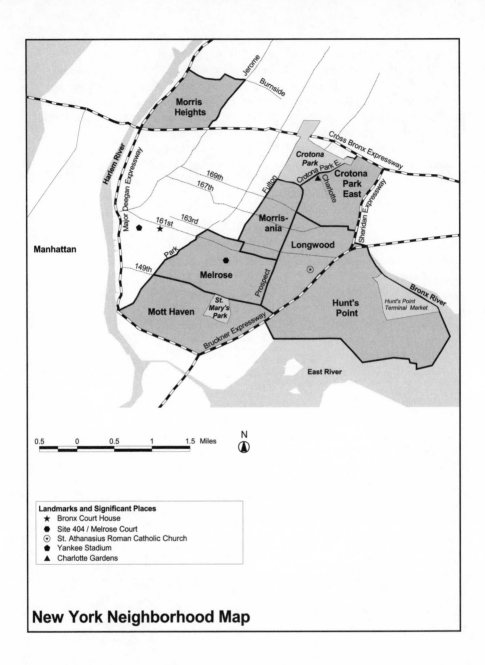

Morris
Heights

Jerome

Burnside

Cross Bronx Expressway

Crotona
Park

Crotona Park E.

Crotona
Park
East

Charlotte

Fulton

169th

167th

Harlem River

Major Deegan Expressway

Morris-
ania

Sheridan Expressway

161st   163rd

Longwood

Manhattan

Park

149th

Melrose

Prospect

St.
Mary's
Park

Mott Haven

Bruckner Expressway

Hunt's
Point

Bronx River

Hunt's Point
Terminal Market

East River

0.5   0   0.5   1   1.5 Miles

N

Landmarks and Significant Places
★ Bronx Court House
⬟ Site 404 / Melrose Court
⊙ St. Athanasius Roman Catholic Church
⬠ Yankee Stadium
▲ Charlotte Gardens

New York Neighborhood Map

MIRACLE ON
174TH STREET

2

In seven days during early October 1977, the South Bronx became the most notorious inner-city neighborhood in the United States. It had fallen into the abyss long before and languished — except for occasional hell-on-earth exposés — in disreputable semi-obscurity.

The fateful week began when President Jimmy Carter, in search of an urban slum, came to the South Bronx and stood among the rubble and ruins of Charlotte Street, shocked by the devastation that surrounded him. That night an announcer on the CBS network news declared the South Bronx the worst slum in America.

A few days later, network television delivered the message to those who preferred sports to news. During baseball's World Series at Yankee Stadium, ABC filled the slow moments in the game with views from a blimp above the stadium. The shots of scenery below displayed flames rising from various buildings and licking the night sky. As the camera returned over the course of the game to follow the progress of the raging fires, Howard Cosell, the renowned sportscaster, intoned in his trademark nasal voice, "The Bronx is burning!"

The South Bronx went on to become first the national, then an international icon of America's worst slum. Memoirs, novels, and movies used the South Bronx as the setting for depraved underclass violence and struggle for survival. A major film, *Fort Apache, The Bronx* (1981), turned the New York Police Department's besieged 41st Precinct headquarters into a melodrama, and Tom Wolfe in his 1987 novel, *Bonfire of the Vanities*, indelibly stamped the South Bronx as the underbelly of the materialistic excesses of the 1980s. In British and European cities as far away as Prague, neighborhoods beset by crime and drugs came to be called "the Bronx."[1]

While the image of the South Bronx spread around the world as an ultimate symbol of the urban hellhole, the neighborhood was coming back to life. Starting in the early 1980s and accelerating after 1986 when the city of New York undertook an unprecedented ten-year endeavor to rebuild its housing, deteriorated and abandoned apartment buildings were fixed up and rubble-strewn vacant lots were filled with new row houses. In the 1990s, the population rose and crime rates plummeted. The urban disaster zone became the emblem for inner-city revival.

It seemed a miracle had occurred. It was fitting then that religious clerics and faith-based organizations—of the type that President George W. Bush has championed—were prominent among those who spurred the revival. Yet what separated the clerical and secular leaders of the Bronx from other religious and not-so-religious citizens of New York was not faith in God but faith in their fellow men. They believed that through persistent struggle they gradually could reclaim their neighborhoods—house by house, block by block—and eventually prevail against all odds.

Indeed, the men and women of God who toiled to bring back the South Bronx acted more like precinct captains than spiritual visionaries. Tough-minded and street-smart, they organized the desperate to fight back for their neighborhoods. The foes were many and varied: bad landlords, drug dealers, callous bankers, indifferent police and fire officials, and ultimately a poisonous apathy that encompassed the South Bronx.

Anyone who cared about the South Bronx soon discovered the large influence government exerted on neighborhood life. By withdrawing services and ignoring crime and widespread arson, the government had allowed the borough to descend into a kind of urban hell. To save the South Bronx, therefore, usually involved fighting or winning support from city hall, the state capitol in Albany, or even, on occasion, the White House. Caesar, as well as God, would have to help the besieged inhabitants of New York's infamous inner-city neighborhood. In the drama of the South Bronx, the part of Caesar was played by the city's flamboyant mayor, Edward I. Koch, who at a critical moment decreed the largest, most expensive building program ever carried out by an American city. As important as its scale was, the broad scope of Koch's housing plan—involving everyone from nonprofit community groups to small private landlords—may have provided the key to its success.

Eventually the grassroots groups with help of real estate and building operators, government agencies, and an array of philanthropic institutions reversed the downward momentum and created an upward trajectory of expectations and accomplishments. As they reconstructed neighborhoods, livable communities—incredibly—once again blossomed in the South Bronx.

The Worst Slum in America

In contrast to what it became in the latter twentieth century, the Bronx at one time was a promised land to New York's aspiring working classes. At the turn of the century, New York City's enormous population, much of which was packed into lower Manhattan, cried out for more living space. The farms, towns, and estates of the nearby Bronx held great potential. Elevated rail lines were extended to the Bronx, and its streets became lined with five- and six-story apartment buildings that offered more room and the latest conveniences at lower rents than were available downtown. Gracious green spaces, such as St. Mary's Park, Crotona Park, and Bronx Park famous for its zoo, were bestowed on the burgeoning borough to prevent it from becoming an unrelenting tenement district. To such an enticing place came Irish and German working families, later joined by Italian and Jewish households—many of whom had moved there from the crowded Lower East Side—and in lesser numbers, Greeks, Poles, and African Americans. The Bronx by 1930 was home to more than a million and a quarter people. It had become a city within a city.[2]

For those masses of people who grew up and lived there, the Bronx was an exciting, important place. It had great boulevard thoroughfares, such as Southern Boulevard, 138th Street, and Bruckner Boulevard. In a category of its own was the Grand Concourse which sported such gaudy jewels as the Concourse Plaza Hotel where the high and mighty stayed and the Bronx County Building and Court House, where polished and pressed lawyers, judges, and politicians carried on their business. A few blocks away stood Yankee Stadium, "the House that Ruth Built" named after the mighty Babe, where decade after decade the greatest teams in the game of baseball headquartered.

Politically, the Bronx was the fiefdom of the nationally known Democratic kingpin, Edward J. Flynn. Flynn's political machine provided not only patronage but also city services to ensure that Bronxites were a satisfied lot. Such was the importance of the Bronx that presidents Roosevelt and Truman campaigned there to harvest the borough's rich crop of Democratic votes.

The population of the Bronx reached a high-water mark after World War II, and from thence began to recede. Through the 1950s and 1960s the enormous housing boom in New York's suburbs—highlighted by the creation of Levittown with its mass-produced houses—lured away the Bronx's Jewish, Italian, and Irish residents. Superhighway projects—most noticeably the seven-mile-long Cross-Bronx Expressway—promoted by Robert Moses, the city's construction czar, destroyed neighborhoods and uprooted people on a massive scale. Close to half a million white people departed the Bronx between 1950 and 1970.[3] The exodus left the borough with empty apartments and storefronts and dwindling congregations in churches and synagogues.

At the same time, African Americans and Puerto Ricans, part of a new migrant stream to America's cities, came to the Bronx, like the old immigrants before, in search of better housing and neighborhoods. They had settled in small numbers in the southern Bronx neighborhoods of Mott Haven and Hunt's Point by the 1940s, and after the war the population of blacks and Puerto Ricans swelled, pushing north into Morrisania, Melrose, and East Tremont during the 1950s. Their numbers had reached a point by the early 1960s that African American and Puerto Rican professionals routinely ran for political offices in the Bronx. Herman Badillo, for example, who held degrees in accountancy and law, was elected borough president in 1964 as a Democratic reformer and became the first Puerto Rican to hold such a high office.

Many of the racial minority migrants to the Bronx were aspiring middle- and working-class people like their predecessors, but following close on their heels came poorer people whose desperation bred a host of social ills. During the 1950s and 1960s neighborhoods began to look run down as garbage and litter collected on the streets, and the apartment buildings crowded with large families deteriorated. The numbers of crimes rose slowly at first, but assaults

21

and thefts shocked the older residents who remembered a time of relative safety. Gangs of young men fought bloody battles over turf. Initially, during the 1950s, gangs belonged to rival ethnic groups, with bands of Italian and Irish combating newcomers—the kinds of battles memorialized in the musical *West Side Story*—but from the 1960s on Puerto Rican and black gangs fought gangs of similar ethnic mixes.[4]

Heroin junkies appeared and multiplied during the 1960s until, as Father Gigante of Hunt's Point observed, "We had addicts up the ass."[5] With the drug dealing and addiction came a flood of crimes from muggings to murder. Eventually, at different times in different places, the disorder reached a critical mass and started a panic.

Sometimes a single event would serve as a catalyst of fear. On Jennings Street in Crotona Park East (near Charlotte Street, which Jimmy Carter would make famous) the brutal murder of Jacob Shertzer, a retired shopkeeper, in June 1963 brought a surge of store closings and a stampede of fleeing residents. For forty-five years the abrasive Shertzer, known to one and all as Jake the Pickle Man, had dealt his pickles to the neighborhood. He was found inside his apartment with the gas on, his hands tied behind him, and his mouth stuffed with a rag. That was the final straw for many in Crotona Park East.[6]

The police department's 41st Precinct, which included Hunt's Point, experienced a stratospheric rise in crime. Between 1961 and 1971, the number of murders increased from 18 to 102, robberies jumped from 183 to 2,632, and burglaries rose from 667 to 6,443. The policemen who lived the knife-edge existence of this corner of the Bronx dubbed their headquarters Fort Apache. One of the 41st Precinct cops wrote of their exploits in a sensational memoir, which in 1981 was made into a movie, *Fort Apache: The Bronx* starring Paul Newman. Thus did the South Bronx become the stuff of evil legend.[7]

Just as dramatic and almost as appalling were the fires. New York Fire Department Engine Company Number 82 covered Park East, including the Charlotte Street neighborhood. In 1967, Engine Company 82 answered 3,000 calls, twice the number it had ten years earlier, and became the busiest firehouse in the city. In 1970 the firefighters of Company 82 made 6,204 runs to 4,246 fires, or 11 runs a day! Neighborhood children fell asleep to the sound of the fire trucks' sirens.[8]

There was arson, arson, and more arson. Landlords burned their buildings to collect insurance payments and ditch their ruinous investments. Some owners or their hired arsonists were often considerate enough to notify the occupants prior to the torching. Firemen responding to an alarm in the middle of the night sometimes arrived to the disconcerting sight of fully dressed families standing on the sidewalk with their belongings carefully packed as they watched their former home blaze. Arsonists included welfare recipients who could qualify for a better apartment if they had been burned out of their homes, junkies and vandals who wanted to strip buildings of salable metals and fixtures, firebugs and kids who burned for kicks, and vengeance-seekers who burned to hurt and kill.[9]

What was frightening was that the pattern repeated itself over and over, spreading from one neighborhood to another. The early sign was a general

South Bronx rubble and empty shells of buildings, mid-1970s.
Courtesy of Carlos Ortiz.

seediness, accompanied by the arrival of people lower on the economic ladder than the current residents. It was hard to notice until some large building would be sold to a landlord who would bring in raucous tenants, ignore the graffiti that appeared on the walls, and allow trash to collect all over the property. Soon the crimes became too frequent and immediate to ignore, more buildings would deteriorate, an evacuation and more empty buildings would follow. Then came the fires, more crime, and more people fleeing the disaster. Eventually there would be streets of apartment buildings in various states: relatively normal-looking occupied edifices; empty shells known as "seethroughs" whose missing windows, walls, and roofs displayed the adjacent structures and the sky above; and the final state, piles of bricks on an empty lot. What started in Hunt's Point and Mott Haven spread north and west through Crotona Park East, Morrisania, and Melrose until it reached the places that had always been gold plate, the Grand Concourse and Morris Heights. Nothing, it seemed, could stop this scourge, nor once it struck, bring back a semblance of the stable community that had once thrived there.

A crew of Neroes fiddled while the Bronx burned. For years mayors, borough presidents, police and fire chiefs resolutely looked the other way. For years plucky leaders watched in horror as their neighborhoods collapsed and tried in vain to get city officials and the press to pay attention. Still trying to stop the fires, crime, and abandonment of East Tremont in February 1974, a neighborhood group pressured two hundred city officials, bankers, real estate businessmen, and newspaper reporters to take a bus tour to Charlotte Street. Local leader Genevieve Brooks displayed pictures and charts to illustrate the damage and proposed laws to stop the onslaught. The power brokers and newspaper reporters, however, ignored her and instead focused on Herman Badillo, who was running for mayor. Another local leader, Eae James Mitchell, grew so frustrated that he grabbed the bullhorn and screamed epithets at the visitors, but even this they disregarded. How were they to know that the South Bronx had just entered the Twilight Zone?[10]

Going beyond neglect and abandonment, some now spoke of eliminating the South Bronx altogether. In 1973 Robert Moses, retired from his master builder posts, proposed demolishing the South Bronx, which he deemed "unrepairable," and corralling its residents into new high-rise towers next to the Bronx-Whitestone bridge. In January 1976, Roger Starr, the head of New York's Department of Housing, audaciously suggested a policy of "planned shrinkage" to a B'nai Brith audience in which the city should close all the subway stations and institutions in the worst sections of the South Bronx, remove the residents, demolish all the buildings, and turn it into a national park. Heartless as they sound, the proposals only took official indifference to its logical conclusion.[11]

A graduate student at Columbia University named Richard Manson came to the South Bronx in the late 1970s and was introduced to the otherworldly quality of the collapse and the official reaction to it. As he walked up Prospect Avenue to attend a community board meeting, he saw open fires burning with no fire trucks in evidence. Most of the buildings he passed were abandoned.

Manson had come to observe a meeting of a subcommittee of the local community board, a quasi-government body, as part of his graduate education in planning. On his arrival he heard the chair telling ten nonplussed people that the way to rescue the South Bronx was for residents to manage their cash better. To the graduate student's astonishment, the man explained that people in the Bronx wasted their money by calling their relatives long distance during the day or not buying the most efficient utility plan. "My God," Manson thought to himself, "look outside—this has nothing to do with the issues here, Mister." Just then two teenagers ran into the room and yelled, "Get out of here, a gang is going to firebomb the place!" The subcommittee members shrugged it off. "Oh," the others explained to the alarmed young man, "they come in all the time." The meeting lasted an hour, without any bomb explosions, and the Bronx continued its downward slide.[12]

Giganteland

In the late 1970s, an audacious sign of hope arrived amidst the shells of apartment houses occupied by drug addicts and prostitutes in the Hunt's Point section of the Bronx. A proud banner appeared at the top of the apartment buildings visible from the Bruckner Expressway that proclaimed, "REBUILDING THE SOUTH BRONX SEBCO HOUSES—FATHER LOUIS GIGANTE—CHAIRMAN."

Even more remarkable than the banner were the buildings below, which actually functioned, giving decent shelter to paying renters.

"Rebuilding the South Bronx" banner seen from the Bruckner Expressway, July 1977. Courtesy of Tom Cunningham, New York Daily News.

Their existence was all the more impressive to those who knew the South Bronx because Hunt's Point was a gritty, industrial area that had been among the first to be affected by the urban plagues. Even as hard times hit the rest of the borough, people who wanted to show that there was still hope, that the South Bronx was not irredeemable, would say, "Come see what Father Gigante has done, come see the SEBCO houses, come visit Giganteland."

The Roman Catholic priest who helped save Hunt's Point hardly behaved like the modest, self-sacrificing saints from the catechisms. Lou Gigante spoke bluntly, swore, and acted tough. He ran for political office. He smoked cigars. He lived the high life, said his critics, dining, drinking, and going to the theater with friends. He owned a house in a leafy Hudson River valley town where he spent much of his time. Some people working for foundations worried that he earned more money than a director of a nonprofit organization was entitled to. A few even wondered—to themselves—whether he was connected to the mob.

Whatever the criticisms, no one has ever denied that through the worst of times, Father Louis Gigante dedicated himself to his Saint Athanasius parish. His formula for rebuilding was unusual, perhaps unique. Combining street moxie with intense discipline, Gigante won the support of parishioners and neighbors, used his leverage to pry any available funds out of the government, aggressively acquired properties, and ran his real estate operations on a strictly no-nonsense basis. Before anyone else in the South Bronx, the priest demonstrated the possibilities of a nonprofit organization working with the government.

Louis Gigante was the youngest son of Italian immigrants. He grew up in New York's Little Italy, which he would always remember as an ideal urban village with its bakery, fishmonger, candy store, and butcher shop. On Thompson Street, where Gigante's family lived, only Neapolitan was spoken. As far as politics went, Gigante knew very little except that sometimes his father or uncle would go to the local political club to get something done.[13]

Louis was a studious youth. He became the first in his family to attend college and chose Georgetown University. Tall and athletic, he excelled at basketball and was named captain of the team. Following graduation, Gigante studied to become a priest, and after his ordination, he went for further study in Puerto Rico where he mastered the island's local Spanish. Upon his return, Gigante was named to a parish on Manhattan's Lower East Side, the old slum district where large numbers of Puerto Ricans were moving. Gigante devoted himself to the neighborhood's rowdy teenagers and won their respect with his prowess on the basketball court and street-tough way of talking. In one incident that received attention in the daily newspapers, Gigante stepped into the middle of a crowd of two hundred gang members spoiling to fight with clubs and broken bottles and sent them on their way.[14]

Father Gigante was assigned to Saint Athanasius Church in Hunt's Point in 1962. Again he threw himself into work with the local youth, bringing them sports and social events to keep them out of trouble. "G brought a lot of love to that area," one of the kids of the time reminisced. Soon Gigante expanded his efforts. He met with landlords and city officials to try to save buildings on nearby Fox and Simpson Streets from the junkies who were tearing out the boilers and leaving the tenants without heat. In 1965, Gigante used War on Poverty funds to found the Simpson Street Development Association in which priests, nuns, and laypeople assisted residents in getting help from the social security agency, public housing authority, or welfare department.[15]

Saint Athanasius parishioners greet Father Louis Gigante
upon his release from prison for refusing to testify before a grand jury,
October 1979. Courtesy of Carlos Ortiz.

To take advantage of the Model Cities program, Gigante founded the South East Bronx Community Organization Development Corporation or SEBCO in 1968. The thirteen local parishes and affiliated groups used the federal money to draw up a complete plan for rebuilding Hunt's Point but for several years did little else. As yet there was no federal money available for rehabilitating buildings for low-income people.[16]

Another problem was that South Bronx's black and Puerto Rican leaders — including Ramon Velez, a political hustler who aspired to be a Puerto Rican version of Harlem's Adam Clayton Powell — engaged in a bruising political struggle to gain control of the local Model Cities program. The climax came when one of Velez's subordinates killed a rival's supporter in a brawl. Despite the violence, Gigante refused to cede any political control of his parish and after one meeting in which Velez called him a "maricon" (a derogatory term for homosexual) punched Velez in the face.[17]

Gigante jumped into politics to make the government pay attention to the quickly deteriorating situation in the South Bronx. In December 1969, the priest gathered three hundred residents of East 163rd Street to burn wooden objects taken from nearby abandoned buildings in an enormous bonfire and march to protest the lack of heat in their homes and the infestation of junkies and rats in their neighborhood. After schoolteachers' petitions to save their students were ignored, Gigante burst into the city council chambers and began yelling at the councilors to save Hunt's Point.[18]

The following year Gigante ran for a seat in the House of Representatives — attracting enthusiastic crowds of Hunt's Point residents to his rallies — and placed a respectable third, behind New York's preeminent Puerto Rican politician, Herman Badillo, but far ahead of poverty hustler Velez. Lowering his sights, the priest then won a race to become the Democratic district leader and went on in 1973 to capture a seat on the New York City Council. Having learned the ways of New York politics, Gigante was able to deliver city, state, and federal housing funds to the St. Athanasius neighborhood and SEBCO in particular. He considered himself an important political figure, although a *New York Times* reporter thought, "As the city's many public egos go, Father Gigante is only a minor patriarch." The priest never held a higher office than city council member, although he continued to aspire to government offices.[19]

In fact, a shadow hung over the battling priest's political career. It was Gigante's public connection to his three elder brothers. Father Gigante insisted that his brothers were merely gamblers, whose activities were illicit but otherwise harmless. Prosecutors and police had a different view and repeatedly arrested the Gigante brothers for racketeering as well as for more serious charges such as murder. They charged Vincent "the Chin" Gigante, said to be the head of the Genovese crime family, with ordering multiple killings even as he, out of real or feigned mental illness, wandered about the streets of Little Italy wearing his bathrobe. Father Gigante felt highly aggrieved that the press convicted his brothers and then found him guilty by association. Still, it did not help when he delivered a long eulogy at the funeral of Joseph Columbo, whom the Federal Bureau of Investigation considered a leader of organized crime, and spent several days in prison for contempt of court after refusing to testify about his efforts to ease the prison living conditions of an alleged mobster.[20]

Negative publicity did not stop Father Gigante from making deals to save the South Bronx. When a private developer named Herman Krause showed up in the South Bronx in 1975 looking for ways to use a new federal housing program called Section 8 to rehabilitate apartment buildings, Gigante negotiated with him to make SEBCO the assistant sponsor. The deal gave Krause the necessary local political support to operate in Hunt's Point and gave SEBCO an entry into the field of housing.[21]

The Section 8 program was one of the first government tools that could be used to rebuild depressed neighborhoods like Hunt's Point. Part of the sweeping Housing and Community Development Act of 1974, Section 8 offered private firms (commercial or nonprofit) rent subsidies if they built, rehabilitated, or maintained buildings for low-income tenants. (The law was later drastically modified during the Reagan presidency.)

Moreover, as Gigante and his staff at SEBCO learned from Krause, Section 8 could earn urban redevelopers money. They could raise funds by selling interests in the rehab project to private investors who wanted tax shelters. It was simply a matter of drawing up the terms of the deal to ensure some return for the developers above the cost of construction. With revenue from the deal, even a nonprofit organization such as SEBCO could help pay its own operating costs.[22]

From the beginning, Gigante insisted upon controlling whatever went on in his corner of Hunt's Point. The priest considered Krause "an excellent business man" but feuded with him over earnings. "He wouldn't give us anything for our labors and our work," Gigante explained, so "I told him, you'll never build again in this neighborhood. And he never has."[23]

Having learned the secret of financing low-income housing, Gigante quit politics and embarked on his real estate development career in earnest. When the federal government put up money for Section 8 rehab projects, Gigante teamed up with another developer, Jerome Chatsky, who would work extensively with nonprofits in the South Bronx. Father Gigante's years of haranguing and working with city officials paid off. In 1975 the city and HUD allotted 361 units in five buildings around the corner from St. Athanasius Church to SEBCO and Chatsky. The priest had learned from the earlier deal with Krause and found a good lawyer to draw up the investment terms for the projects he dubbed SEBCO I and II. With the money earned from selling shares of the project for tax shelters, Gigante opened a SEBCO office in one of the rehabilitated buildings and hired a secretary and assistant, the organization's first paid staff members.[24]

Over the next four years—until the Reagan administration all but shut down federal housing subsidies—Gigante repeated the SEBCO I and II formula. SEBCO, in partnership with Jerome Chatsky, developed a half-dozen projects, comprising 1,070 units in twenty-six buildings near St. Athanasius, between 1977 and 1981. When SEBCO opened up the last of the projects, almost 5,000 people lined up in the rain to apply for one of the 236 apartments. Since then SEBCO has added to its portfolio by developing residences for the elderly and apartment buildings and selling hundreds of single-family houses, co-op apartments, and even condominiums.[25]

Father Gigante worked tirelessly to expand SEBCO's operations and income. In its real estate deals, SEBCO graduated from the position of junior partner, earning a third of the revenues, to that of equal partner, and finally to that of principal developer. When the priest insisted in 1980 that SEBCO get the management contract for the newly developed properties, Chatsky and Gigante broke up their partnership. SEBCO started building management and security businesses to help maintain its properties and bring revenue to the organization. Gigante also recognized the importance of tenant participation and in 1978 started a social service and tenant organizing unit; within a few years it had helped get each of SEBCO's buildings to select building representatives and floor captains.[26]

Whatever means Gigante and his staff used to save them, SEBCO buildings stood out among the ruins and boarded-up buildings in Hunt's Point. The baby-blue walls were unblemished, their tile floors sparkled, and their elevators actually worked. "He presided over impressive renovations of dilapidated slums," wrote Jill Jonnes, the foremost authority on the South Bronx, "and then ran them with an iron hand. No one could spray graffiti on his walls or 'air mail' garbage in his buildings without risking eviction."[27]

Gigante did not escape criticism for his way of running the operations at Hunt's Point. Some complained of the priest's high style of living. The compensation Gigante received for services rendered to SEBCO, a *New York Times* reporter wrote, enabled him to support his mother and relatives, to drink and dine out, and to go to the theater. "I didn't take a vow of poverty," Gigante responded. "People think I don't get paid and that I'm a saint for doing it. That's their problem."[28]

Others wondered, without evidence one way or the other, if the priest kept an arms-length distance from the transactions that spun off SEBCO's management and security companies as independent businesses. Yet Felice Michetti, who has observed all the important community groups in the South Bronx, points out that unlike other New York nonprofits that were the darlings of the foundation world, SEBCO's companies delivered the services they were supposed to, did not inflate their fees, never were subject to any investigation of impropriety, and hired only community residents to boot.[29]

The proof was right there to be seen in what insiders took to calling "Giganteland" out of respect and awe. People who worked in government and the nonprofits began to take visitors to the redeveloped island around St. Athanasius Church in the midst of the disaster of the Bronx. Anita Miller, then working for the Ford Foundation, brought her boss, MacGeorge Bundy, and corporate executives to see. "Look," Miller told her guests, "here you have the kernel of a revitalized neighborhood. It can be done."[30]

"In the old days," Michetti explains, "when anybody had to show some success in the South Bronx, they went to Hunt's Point. They went to Father G. He succeeded with programs that other groups weren't successful at."

Gigante's success began with learning how to use a government program to redevelop and manage apartment buildings and build single-family houses in a poor neighborhood, but his vision encompassed more than just property development. Inspired by his memory of New York's Little Italy, the priest worked toward creating an urban village in Hunt's Point. He worked to establish youth groups and other social service organizations, community centers, parks, and neighborhood fairs and parades in his corner of the South Bronx. Gigante's understanding of his parishioners, skill in deal making, and knowledge of how to make things happen in New York City all helped him carry out his plan. "And," as Michetti points out, "he was relentless in pursuing it."[31]

Giganteland offered the earliest successful example of a nonprofit group using government programs to restore order and normalcy in the South Bronx. Gigante spread his method not only by setting an example but also by offering exhortation and advice to others who wished to emulate what he had done. With his work at St. Athanasius parish, the South Bronx took its first steps back.

Visionaries, Prophets, and Saints

As the South Bronx's infamous reputation spread in the 1970s, Gigante found that he was not alone. All sorts of saints, prophets, and lunatics appeared to save the Bronx. Mother Teresa herself slipped into the South Bronx in 1978, the year before she won the Nobel Peace Prize. She paid a quiet visit to St. Rita's parish where members of the Missionaries of Charity, the religious order that she founded in Calcutta, ran a soup kitchen and shelter for abused women from what had been a burnt-out apartment building.[32]

There were secular efforts as well. An unlikely pair—Jack Flanagan, a big, bearded Irish cop stationed in the 41st Precinct, and Erma Fleck, a Jewish activist and housewife—started the Bronx Frontier Development Corporation to plant gardens on the South Bronx's four hundred acres of debris. Working with other green space organizations, they managed to persuade the Department of the Interior to finance an effort to turn fifteen vacant lots into mini-parks. Fleck proposed combining waste from the wholesale produce market at Hunt's Point with manure from the Bronx zoo to create compost for the gardens she and Flanagan envisioned blooming throughout the Bronx. Improbably, the idea caught on, and Bronx Frontier sold the product known as Zoo Doo, which initially received great acclaim in national publications such as the *Wall Street Journal* and *New York Times* before eventually going under.[33]

Ramon Rueda, a Bronx native who had turned politically radical in college during the 1960s, got the idea from a street gang in Harlem to take over a city-owned abandoned building, known in its glory days as Venice Hall, renovate it, and inhabit it along with ten comrades who banded together as the People's Development Corporation. Rueda and the People's Development Corporation staged noisy demonstrations—wearing construction hard hats and boots, they laid siege to the New York City housing agency at one point—and persuaded the government to give them hundreds of thousands of dollars in loans for the homesteading project.

The most unconventional of the South Bronx's would-be saviors were fifteen hippie adults and twenty children who had been dispatched from the

Farm, a large commune in Tennessee. Costumed in long braids, headbands, and tie-dyed shirts, the Plenty Commune, as they styled themselves, cleared out a pack of wild dogs from one floor and four feet of garbage from another in a four-story apartment building located a few blocks from Rueda's homestead project. From their new home, they provided an ambulance and trained the locals as emergency medical technicians—both in short supply in the South Bronx. With characteristic dramatic flair the commune employed a used hearse to carry the sick and wounded to the hospital.[34]

In the summer of 1977, not far from Gigante's turf, the Banana Kelly Community Improvement Association was begun when about thirty families attempted to repair three dilapidated apartment buildings and got into a standoff with the city government, which had sent wrecking crews to demolish their homes. The families prevailed and started Banana Kelly, so named because Kelly Street has an unusual curved shape within Manhattan's street grid. In its early years it planted a community garden and rehabilitated buildings, and it would eventually develop some 1,500 dwelling units.

Perhaps lifting an area as prostrate as the South Bronx requires a lot of different people trying all sorts of ideas. The surge of energy and experimentation leads sooner or later to the discovery of ways to succeed. Most of the groups started in the South Bronx during the late 1970s and early 1980s eventually dissipated for one reason or another, but a few—including a number of community development corporations (CDCs)—survived to become more or less permanent institutions.

The ones that made it were blessed with inspired leaders. The leaders possessed a deep faith—which was almost absurd, considering the circumstances—that they would eventually rebuild the Bronx. Given that it was necessary to have this faith in order to persevere, it is not surprising that so many of the rebuilders were devout, either members or ministers of churches.

Desperadoes Waiting for the Train

No one was more stubborn than Genevieve Brooks, the driving force behind the Mid-Bronx Desperadoes Community Housing Corporation. At the age of seventeen Brooks left her family's farm in South Carolina for New York City. Eventually she came to live in a handsome apartment building on Seabury Place near Charlotte Street. When Brooks arrived, middle-class whites and blacks still lived in the neighborhood, but as they began to leave she was shocked to see that her building superintendent had stopped cleaning the hallways. When Brooks complained about the grime on the marble trim and the litter in the hallways, the landlord told her to move to Queens. Brooks was offended by the filth accumulating inside and outside her Seabury Place building—in the South, she liked to say, she had been brought up to keep her home and yard clean.[35]

While others fled, Gennie Brooks organized. A warm and intelligent woman, she inspired confidence. When her building started to go to seed, she joined with other tenants, such as Lucille Williams, to organize a tenants' association.

31

Genevieve Brooks, a founder of the Mid-Bronx Desperadoes, June 1992. Courtesy of Larry Racioppo, New York City Department of Housing Preservation and Development.

Then, to force the city to clean up the burned out cars and stop the dealing of drugs in broad daylight, she and her neighbors organized a block association. Worried about the fate of the neighborhood's small children, she organized the Seabury Day Care Center. To increase the power of the local residents, she registered voters and joined the community planning board. Year after year she and her neighbors tried to get the city's officials and politicians to recognize the arson that was destroying everything in its path.[36]

After arson had virtually annihilated the 174th Street area of Crotona Park East, Brooks called on the leaders of the surviving local institutions who wanted to rebuild their neighborhood. In 1974 representatives of nine local bodies — including the New Zion and Tried Stone Baptist Churches, two Catholic churches, the Hoe Avenue Boys and Girls Club, and the three organizations to which Brooks belonged — plotted how they might unite to form a strong coalition like Father Gigante's SEBCO.[37]

Not everybody had joined willingly. Father (now Reverend Monsignor) William Smith, a Catholic priest at the St. John Chrysostom church at 167th Street and Hoe Avenue since 1961, refused at first. Smith had never gotten over the accusation of racial bigotry by an employee at a War on Poverty organization, even after an investigation showed that he was innocent. Gennie Brooks, however, knew Bill Smith better than he knew himself. She knew that despite what he said, Father Smith worked tirelessly with local teenagers to keep them away from violence and drugs, even working out an exchange of homemade zip guns for oversized rosaries. Brooks told Smith that he had to help because the 174th Street neighborhood was getting wiped out. Smith agreed because, he explained, "you just don't say no to Brooks." Not only did he come to the meeting, Smith would become — along with the leader Gennie Brooks — the other half of the powerful team that would lead the new organization.[38]

At that first meeting, the assembled survivors ruminated about a name. Someone, perhaps it was Brooks, pointed out that the 174th Street neighborhood was located, in fact, in central not South Bronx. By the mid-70s, any blighted area in the Bronx below Fordham Road was considered to belong to the South Bronx. "We are desperate," Eae James Mitchell, a housing manager who had struggled alongside Brooks, suggested, "so let's call ourselves the Desperadoes." The others agreed, and thus was born the Mid-Bronx Desperadoes.[39]

Whether intended or not, the name Mid-Bronx Desperadoes attracted a lot of attention. When their lawyer applied to the State of New York for a nonprofit charter the following year, the functionaries sent back word that they would not accept the name because it sounded sinister. To mollify the state bureaucrats, the group reapplied for incorporation using its initials as the MBD Community Housing Corporation.[40]

Brooks and Smith set out to introduce themselves and the organization to the politicians and agency officials with whom they would need to do business. Brooks would call to make appointments with the local big shots for "skinnin' and grinnin'," as Brooks referred to the ritual pleasantries. "This is Gen Brooks from the Mid-Bronx Desperadoes," she would tell the official on the phone. "We'd like to set up a meeting to sit down and talk to you." Invariably the person on the other end of the phone line would pause, and sometimes gasp, imagining he or she was talking to a representative of a violent street gang. Brooks would insist, however, and get the appointment anyway. When the two of them arrived, a beautifully dressed black woman with a flower in her hair and a white priest dressed in black tunic with white collar, they could almost hear their surprised host sigh in relief.[41]

In the beginning the leaders of the Mid-Bronx Desperadoes, or MBD as it was often called, had little besides determination. About 1982 a bright-eyed twenty-four-year-old, Julie Sandorf, traveled through complete devastation on the Number Two train from Manhattan to 174th Street to see Brooks and Smith about a job. "How in the world are you going to rebuild this neighborhood?" she asked them in disbelief. "You've got one block, and everywhere you look for miles it's abandoned or vacant lots. How are you going to do this?"

With supreme confidence, Brooks and Smith proclaimed they would do it "building by building, person by person, block by block." Sandorf was so impressed that in spite of better offers elsewhere, she took the job.[42]

Brooks dreamed up all sorts of ideas in those early years. She eyed properties and thought up novel ways to use them. One year the Desperadoes tried to buy the defunct Palace Movie Theater to be the home of a new South Bronx Art Center. Like a lot of the schemes, this one did not go far, but the tiny staff kept plugging away.[43]

The first large success the Mid-Bronx Desperadoes scored was modeled on the work of Father Gigante, who counseled the group at critical points. Working with Jerome Chatsky, the developer who been Gigante's partner, and using tax shelters and federal Section 8 subsidies, as Gigante and Chatsky had done, the organization was able to rehabilitate four abandoned buildings on Vyse Avenue between 173rd and 174th Streets, containing 185 dwelling units.

Besides giving the old buildings a useful life, the project gave the Desperadoes office space on the first floor of one of the structures and a little revenue
in the form of development fees.[44]

Since the organization could now afford to hire a director, Fathers Smith
and Gigante carried on a six-month crusade to persuade Gen Brooks to take
the helm of the Mid-Bronx Desperadoes. At the time, Brooks was working
downtown as an accountant, making fairly good money. After work, however,
she ran the 1555 Seabury Place building and tenants' board of directors and
the Seabury Day Care Center, where she served as chairperson of the board of
directors. When she finally made up her mind to accept the post, Smith remembers her saying, "I have thought about it, I have prayed about it, and you
know, I finally decided, what the hell. I was working downtown, but I couldn't
wait to get out of work to go back up here to the Bronx to do all of the stuff I
was doing."[45]

Although Chatsky and a local lawyer did much of the development work
for the Desperadoes, the organization took responsibility for leasing the apartments in the renovated Vyse Avenue buildings. Brooks threw herself into this
task with her characteristic flair for organizing. After interviewing applicants,
she met with every tenant whose application had been accepted. She gently
but firmly explained the rules and signed each and every tenant to do some
community service, be it help the Girl Scouts, join a block watch, or take part
in tenant patrol.[46] Gigante's executive director at SEBCO, Mario Tolisano,
used a similar approach with SEBCO's tenants.

Like Father Gigante, Brooks instinctively knew that encouraging people to
participate in collective activities was a key element to success. By imposing
such discipline in the midst of chaos, the emerging community development
leaders helped an orderly sense of community to take root again in the South
Bronx.

Turning Point: Charlotte Gardens

Soon after the Vyse Avenue rehab was under way, the Mid-Bronx Desperadoes became involved in a controversial and loudly publicized undertaking
in Crotona Park East on Charlotte Street on the rubble where Jimmy Carter
had stood and shaken his head in dismay. However shocking the image of
Charlotte Gardens was, the publicity it garnered spread the word both inside
and outside the South Bronx that something new could emerge from the ruins of the old.

A twist of fate had made Charlotte Street—just one of many wretched city
blocks in the Bronx, Brooklyn, and Harlem—famous. In October 1977 President Carter was scheduled to address the United Nations, and he thought his
trip to New York could be an opportunity to show his support for beleaguered
urban neighborhoods by visiting a slum. New York City was awash in slum
neighborhoods in the late 1970s, and any one would have done nicely. As it
happened, however, New York's planning commissioner, Victor Marrero, was
the former director of a South Bronx housing organization. When Marrero

heard of Carter's idea through the grapevine, he privately persuaded the president's aides to take the president along a route through the South Bronx.

The presidential entourage, which included a bewildered Mayor Abraham Beame, happened to stop at Charlotte Street, by now the epicenter of the disaster zone that had moved north from Hunt's Point and Fort Apache. Surveying the ghastly ruins of the once-thriving Bronx, Carter turned to Patricia Harris, the Secretary of Housing and Urban Development (HUD) who accompanied the president, and ordered, "See which areas can still be salvaged. . . . Get a map of the whole area and show me what could be done." No great plan resulted from the president's momentary urge, but the federal government would eventually send money to the Bronx. In the meantime, with all the newspapers, weekly newsmagazines, and television news programs displaying the ruins of Charlotte Street, local officials at last realized they had to take action. The South Bronx had become a national scandal.[47]

Not long after Carter visited Charlotte Street, Edward I. Koch, a flamboyant reformer, defeated Beame in New York's mayoral election. Koch named as one of his deputy mayors Congressman Herman Badillo, which was something of a bold stroke since Badillo, the city's leading Puerto Rican politician, had also run for mayor and lost to Koch in the primary. In his new post, Badillo took charge of redeveloping the Bronx. HUD was in a mood to entertain proposals, so in April 1978 Koch and Badillo publicly proclaimed a massive plan to rebuild the South Bronx, primarily through housing—including the development of some 26,500 dwellings—at a cost of $1.5 billion. The New York politicians sought to have the federal government pick up the whopping tab. No doubt with that thought in mind, Koch declared that the rebuilding of Charlotte Street, where Jimmy Carter had alighted, would be the linchpin of the redevelopment of the South Bronx.

Badillo hired Ed Logue as head of the city's new South Bronx Development Office to carry out his expensive plan. Logue had made his reputation as a redevelopment czar first in New Haven, then in Boston, where in the 1960s he oversaw the rebuilding of a major section of Boston's old downtown and undertook innovative attempts at neighborhood renewal. In the 1970s Logue had led Governor Nelson Rockefeller's New York State Urban Redevelopment Corporation, which in its heyday built more subsidized housing than the rest of the country combined.[48]

As one of the last of the big-time government spenders—à la New York's own Robert Moses—Logue was the ideal man to head up a massive reconstruction effort. Logue got things done, whether it meant bellowing at bureaucrats, manipulating high government officials, or spending like a sailor on shore leave. By his own estimate, he was a con artist. "It was hard to get a straight answer out of him," remembers former mayor Koch who admired Logue. "He'd tell you ten times more than you had to know, but not necessarily on point."[49]

Unfortunately for Logue, Badillo, and Koch, the Carter administration immediately lost its appetite for a big reconstruction program in the South Bronx. The White House preferred a much smaller project—that emphasized not housing but employment and social services (when he visited the Bronx,

Carter had heard residents cry out to him to bring them jobs)—in which only about $55 million came from the federal government. According to Koch, Carter's domestic policy adviser, Jack Watson, backed away from the promise of support during a meeting at Badillo's apartment in the Riverdale section of the Bronx and later reneged on it altogether when in 1979 the city's Board of Estimate voted the project down. Koch blamed Badillo for fumbling the Board of Estimate vote, and Badillo blamed Koch for not supporting him. In either case, the city lost out on massive amounts of federal dollars.[50]

Carter, as it turned out, did not leave the South Bronx completely high and dry. The next year, 1980, was an election year, and the White House, desperately trying to keep traditionally Democratic urban and liberal votes, announced it had poured about $200 million into the South Bronx since the president had sojourned there. As the presidential campaign roared to a climax, the president grew generous, bestowing large sums on Bronx community groups. Ed Logue and his South Bronx Development Office received a hefty $1.5 million, which, combined with local government funds, put him in business. (The White House also sent $800,000 to Father Gigante, which enabled the priest to build a Spanish courtyard in front of St. Athanasius.)[51]

On the jobs side, Logue pushed for industrial parks. In 1980 he persuaded Koch, the Carter administration, and the New York Port Authority to put up the millions of dollars to develop an industrial park on a twenty-one-acre site at Bathgate Avenue. In years past, the city's leaders, believing that New York's economic future lay in becoming an administrative center, had been indifferent to the plight of manufacturing. Yet, after it opened in 1982, the Bathgate Industrial Park did surprisingly well. Light industrial, trucking, office, and educational firms rented space there, and today it employs about 1,350 people, most of them Bronx residents. Yet in an era of de-industrialization and increasingly global distribution, large-scale employment schemes were not going to transform the Bronx quickly, if at all.[52]

Logue looked for other ways to jump-start the process of renewal. Unlike the dictatorial Robert Moses, who forced his bridges, highways, and redevelopment projects down the throats of New York's citizenry, Logue liked to work with local groups. He felt this was democratic and made good political sense. Working in the heart of their territory, he naturally sought out the Mid-Bronx Desperadoes as a partner.

Somewhere along the line Logue got a wild idea. He would instigate the Bronx revival by developing and selling single-family houses. Then, going further, he proposed buying manufactured houses and shipping them to Charlotte Street.

He turned to Anita Miller, the Bronx officer of a new philanthropic organization called the Local Initiatives Support Corporation (LISC) for money. Over lunch in the South Bronx, Logue laid out his scheme. "Anita," he said, "I can see the white picket fences right now." "You're crazy," she replied. "How much money do you need?" They figured that Logue would need about $125,000 to build a couple of houses as models of those that would eventually line the street. Although sometimes they argued about the project—Miller remembers convincing Logue to add another bathroom because a single bathroom on the first floor was not enough for a three-bedroom house—she eventually put some $300,000 of LISC money into Charlotte Gardens.[53]

Logue's little project flew in the face of most people's preconceptions of what New York City should look like. Urban planners who only a few years earlier had called for completely emptying the South Bronx now criticized the project for putting too few people on urban land.[54] The population density of rubble-strewn lots was zero, but apparently that counted for little in the face of nostalgia for the Bronx's old six-story flats.

Logue nonetheless wanted to do something dramatic. He had noticed around the Bronx that even in the midst of complete chaos, homeowners persisted and carefully tended their homes. Logue's supporters agreed that making people homeowners would be like dropping anchors for the rebuilt community. Genevieve Brooks of Mid-Bronx Desperadoes told Logue that many locals—southern blacks, Puerto Ricans, and Caribbean immigrants who had enjoyed back yards in their old homes—would be enthusiastic.[55] At the official dedication of Charlotte Gardens, a heckler at the back of the crowd yelled, "These houses will be torn down in a week!" Koch, who always reveled in a fight, gestured at the new homeowners and shouted back, "These people will defend their houses with their lives!"[56]

It turned out that plenty of people were interested in buying a home at Charlotte Gardens. When the first ten ranch houses were sold in 1985, they went for only $52,000, about $30,000 less than the development cost. (Federal and New York State subsidies and state below-market mortgages knocked down the cost to the buyer.) During the first six weeks of sales, the Mid-Bronx Desperadoes acting as the sales agent received detailed applications from more than 500 families.[57]

Yet the Charlotte Gardens project had a surreal quality from start to finish. The prefabricated suburban ranch houses were dropped like alien beings among the shells and remnants of the Bronx's traditional six-story apartment buildings. Because of the size of the buildings, Logue's outfit and the Mid-Bronx Desperadoes had to transport the manufactured houses, through the good graces of the powerful Port Authority of New York and New Jersey, from New Jersey at night. For weeks, at about ten o'clock at night, a strange cavalcade would drive over the George Washington Bridge and into the Bronx wilderness. First came the vehicles of the Port Authority officials, then large trucks carrying the houses, and finally, pulling up the rear, a car or two conveying some MBD staff members to make sure everything went smoothly.[58]

On one of the first of these odd processions, Julie Sandorf went along to represent the Desperadoes. She brought her husband, Michael, a medical resident who had never been to the Bronx, to witness the laborious process of moving the houses into place. As they drove into the Charlotte Street neighborhood, he looked at her bewildered and said, "There are no lights. Why is it so dark up here? Where is everybody?" Sandorf explained patiently, "Michael, nobody lives in these buildings, they're all abandoned." Still not comprehending what sort of environment he had stumbled into, he said again, "Where are all the lights?"

"Honey," she replied, "I told you. No one lives here."

Charlotte Street, South Bronx, March 1981.
Courtesy of Camilo José Vergara.

Charlotte Gardens on Charlotte Street, October 1994.
Courtesy of Camilo José Vergara.

They pulled onto the site on the block where the two model ranch houses were located and stepped out of their cars. Members of the Nighthawks gang approached them and demanded suspiciously, "What are you doin' here?"

"I work for MBD," replied the good Jewish girl from Manhattan.

The tough young men looked at her and said, "Well, we work for MBD, too."

"What *are* you doing?" Sandorf's flabbergasted husband demanded of his wife. "There are no lights in this neighborhood. There are gangs. You're not doing this job anymore."

"Michael," Sandorf replied patiently, "they are the Nighthawks. They work for us."

Ed Logue had hired local gang members to patrol the site and keep it secure. It was one of the strategic moves in the South Bronx of which the old planner was most proud. If left to their own devices, the gangs would likely have vandalized the ranch houses. Logue figured that if he hired them to protect Charlotte Gardens, they would not rip up the houses or let anyone else do so. Playing it safe, Logue chose a gang with whom Father Gigante's SEBCO was working.[59]

Logue's cleverness aside, the Charlotte Street project was riddled with delays and cost overruns. Despite his long career in government, Logue could not believe the maze of government regulations and glacial pace of the city's bureaucracy. Early in the project, Logue estimated that each house required as much paperwork as a two-hundred-unit apartment building, except it did not need elevator permits.[60]

Ed Logue himself deserved some of the blame for the slowness in developing Charlotte Gardens. By all accounts, he was a poor project manager who paid little attention to the costs. He was woeful at negotiating with New York's rapacious contractors. Logue first hired an inefficient contractor who caused long delays and forced Logue to change contractors. When Logue grew worried that the government might not build the remaining eighty ranch houses, he ordered that concrete foundations be poured, but because the work was done in winter, the foundations cracked on freezing and had to be redone.[61]

In the spring of 1984, the federal government, now under control of the Reagan administration, took Logue's funds away and distributed them to several community groups. The Mid-Bronx Desperadoes was given the job of finishing Charlotte Gardens. Bloodied but unbowed, the veteran planner resigned. Given a free hand and some more money, he was confident that he could have completely recreated the South Bronx.[62]

As far as Logue was concerned, Charlotte Gardens had succeeded magnificently. From the moment the first two model houses were built, the Bronx received more press coverage than at any time since Jimmy Carter had dropped by, and this time the news was positive. The news media could not resist the images of the Charlotte Gardens project. The city's newspapers and national newsmagazines reproduced before-and-after photographs and published articles about rebirth in the Bronx. Architecture journals discussed the meaning of ranch houses and picket fences among the apartment-house craters. Even as he left New York, Logue knew that thanks to his efforts, the word had gone out that the Bronx was still alive.

Parish Priests against the Tide

Among the miracles of the Bronx, one must count the extensive organizing campaign led by dozens of Roman Catholic priests to hold back the rolling ruination that threatened to engulf the entire borough. In trying to understand what was happening to them, the priests and their allies put the spotlight on the financial institutions whose decisions influenced—some would say determined—the fate of neighborhoods and discovered the power of federal government regulation to change their destiny.

In the early 1970s Paul Brant, a brash young man studying for the priesthood, got himself appointed community liaison for Fordham University, the Jesuit school that was the borough's foremost educational institution. The real purpose of Brant's job was to halt the tide of deterioration moving north from the South Bronx.[63]

Brant sought allies among the local pastors, but it is worth noting that none agreed to work with him. Priests are no different from anyone else, and those whose parishes seemed stable did not think it reasonable to try to stave off the inevitable deterioration of the Bronx. Save one. Monsignor John McCarthy, an old-style Irish priest in charge of the Church of the Holy Spirit in Morris Heights, agreed to work with the seminarian. Morris Heights, located on the west side of the central Bronx, had shifted from a Jewish and Irish middle-class ethnic neighborhood to one that was predominantly African American and Hispanic working class. "There were already pockets of trouble," Jill Jonnes writes of Morris Heights in those years, "unemployed men hanging out on the streets drinking, some junkies in evidence, a few buildings with ripped-out mailboxes and graffiti, others without heat or hot water."[64]

With McCarthy's support, Brant hired two young community organizers to help the residents of Morris Heights take control of their destiny. One of them, Roger Hayes, had been trained by the Industrial Areas Foundation in Chicago and reflected its principle that people had to help themselves. During one meeting with aggrieved tenants held in an apartment lobby, a man with a dog passed through, the dog stopping to defecate in the hall. Hayes looked at the tenants and said, "You can't blame that on the landlord." The tenants were quiet for a moment until three men stood and retrieved the dog's owner and made him clean up the mess.[65]

As the neighborhoods of the South Bronx collapsed, more and more pastors to the north became alarmed. They converted the Northwest Bronx Clergy Conference, their hitherto innocuous association devoted to such weighty matters as bingo games, into an organization bent on preventing wholesale flight from their parishes. Instead of opposing the arrival of low-income families or trying to prevent ethnic change, the priests tried to unite their parishioners to stabilize the neighborhoods. The pastors teamed up with Brant and McCarthy and the group decided to replicate the Morris Heights organizing campaign across eight Bronx neighborhoods. They proposed marshaling the forces of sixteen parishes in a swath of territory running north from the Cross Bronx Expressway in the central Bronx all the way to the border of the city of

Yonkers. The priests even recruited a bishop, Patrick Ahern, who helped them raise money from foundations and corporations.

In June 1974 the Northwest Bronx Clergy Conference kicked off its great effort with a three-day conference on strategies to save the Bronx. Sixteen Catholic parishes, covering almost a quarter of the county, were represented. Cardinal Terence Cooke, the leader of the Archdiocese of New York, attended and delivered an ardent speech in support of the effort. Father Gigante also addressed the gathering of clerics and laypersons, and in his own way was as inspiring as the cardinal. The priest from Hunt's Point showed slides of the destruction in his district to illustrate the destiny of the eastern and northern Bronx neighborhoods if their representatives failed to act. Fight back, he urged them, as the members of SEBCO had done in the southeast.[66]

Out of the conference was born the Northwest Bronx Community and Clergy Coalition. In a city where racial and ethnic turf battles sometimes turned violent, the coalition was unusually diverse. Blacks and Hispanics from the southern parishes joined Irish and Italians who predominated north of Fordham Road to fight their common enemies.

From the motley crew emerged a formidable leader in the person of Ann Devenny, a hearty grandmother and former president of the Altar and Rosary Society of Saint Brendan's parish. Quick to quip, Devenny would take on commissioners and deputy mayors by saying, "You only get the government you deserve . . . and I know I deserve better." "Don't move," she exhorted her Bronx neighbors, "improve!" Whether protesting on picket lines or twisting the arms of corporate and government officials, Devenny's charm and persistence was hard to resist.[67]

By 1976, the Northwest Bronx Community and Clergy Coalition had created a great chain of citizen organizations to stabilize the central and northern sections of the borough. The coalition had helped form 550 tenant associations, thirty-three block associations, and twelve anti-crime and anti-arson patrols. It had run 150 street cleanup events and forced more than 12,000 building violations to be corrected.[68]

Energized by their large numbers, the members of the multiracial coalition took on the administration of Abraham Beame and forced the city's emergency repair program and parks department to fix up dilapidated buildings and neglected recreation grounds.

One of the keys to getting people to act to save themselves was to identify their common enemy. The tenants of a building knew when they had a bad landlord, but why were the buildings and stores of the Bronx, solid and permanent fixtures, crumbling and disappearing? Bill Frey, a Wisconsin native and recent Fordham graduate who joined the coalition as an organizer, found an answer.

The villains of the South Bronx, Frey discovered, were its money institutions.

Using a recently passed federal law that forced banks to reveal their lending practices, Frey discovered that the number of new home mortgages issued in the northwest Bronx had plummeted in the past ten years to next to nothing. More galling, the Bronx's local savings banks—Eastern, North Side, and the fifth largest savings bank in the country, Dollar—collected hundreds of millions of dollars in deposits from Bronx residents but issued only a tiny fraction of this amount in mortgages to them. And even worse, the banks were selling off the local mortgages for a song to speculators and slumlords. Even as they shrugged off the Bronx as a hopeless cause, local bank officers were aiding and abetting its destruction.[69]

In their fight against the banks, Frey and the coalition members enlisted tenants who in this land of apartment buildings made up the majority of the population. The standard mortgages on properties in New York contained provisions—although routinely ignored—that stated if buildings were not kept up, the bank had the right to foreclose on the properties. The Good Repair Clauses, as they were called, demonstrated to apartment renters that they too were affected by the banks' lending practices.[70]

The Northwest Bronx Community and Clergy Coalition now launched a crusade against the local banks, demanding that they stop dumping buildings and enforce the Good Repair Clauses. The leaders of the coalition tried to meet with bank officials. When they were ignored or met with vague promises of good will, they picketed the banks and campaigned to get depositors to close their accounts. On April 1, 1977, one hundred fifty members paraded in front of a branch of the Eastern Savings Bank in a prosperous Bronx neighborhood and startled the locals and bank officers with signs that said "Let's give up Eastern for Lent."[71]

The Northwest Bronx Community and Clergy Coalition escalated its battle to make the banks responsible to their depositors. The leaders appealed to the federal government agencies that supervised the banks. The coalition's lever was the Community Reinvestment Act, a federal law just passed in 1977, that required the powerful regulatory agencies before approving any expansions or mergers to consider how well the banks had served their home communities. Most bank officers assumed the law to be a dead letter, so it came as a great shock when the Federal Deposit Insurance Corporation denied the Eastern Savings Bank the right to open a new branch in suburban Long Island. Suddenly the banks began to pay attention to the ragtag army of priests, parishioners, and tenants.[72]

When the insurance companies began canceling apartment-building insurance policies in the northernmost Bronx parishes, the researchers for the Community and Clergy Coalition became suspicious. Like the banks' pulling money out of the neighborhoods, the cancellation of insurance policies administered an invisible but deadly poison to the communities. As insurance policies became more difficult to obtain, landlords would have to pay extremely high rates for them or take on the great financial risks of owning without insurance. More likely, they would walk away from their properties.

As a test, coalition members called insurance brokers about buying building insurance in their section of the Bronx only to be told that none could be had. The northwest Bronx was going to be part of the South Bronx, the brokers explained, and the arsonists were, no doubt, already on their way. The coalition added insurance redlining to their list of targets and was pleased in

1979 when it convinced one major insurance company, Aetna, to issue policies in their neighborhoods.

In a pivotal meeting held in a church auditorium on January 12, 1980, Monsignor McCarthy, Bishop Ahern, dozens of black-robed priests, the organizers, and citizen leaders such as Anne Devenny turned out to invite the officers of all the local banks and the Aetna Insurance Company to make a full-hearted commitment to the Bronx. The Northwest Bronx Community and Clergy Coalition asked the financial companies to underwrite two hundred new building rehabilitation projects, vigorously enforce the Good Repair Clause, and broadcast the availability of loans. Aetna Insurance Company was ready to make the northwest Bronx one of six inner-city districts that could borrow from a special $15 million redevelopment fund. All the other banks were ready to sign on, save the mighty Dollar Savings, which had stubbornly resisted out of pique. During the meeting, the anxious official from Dollar Savings ran out of the hall to telephone his office for instructions. After all the others had signed on, the chairman had to call Dollar's representative forward and ask him whether they would agree. The banker spoke for some time, but finally got to the point: "The other institutions have shown Dollar a better way. We're a proud bank, and we'll sign this gladly." The coalition members went wild, hollering for joy over their long-awaited victory. They had demonstrated the power of organization coupled with government regulation.[73]

The Northwest Bronx Community and Clergy Coalition was a pioneer in its efforts to use the Community Reinvestment Act. After the law's mechanisms were strengthened in the 1990s, it prodded banks across the country to make what came to be called community development loans. Not all of these loans help low-income neighborhoods, but they make it possible for community groups to use them—as did the coalition in the Bronx—to stanch the financial bleeding in aging neighborhoods.

A Good Landlord

Despite the victories, the Northwest Bronx Community and Clergy Coalition could not prevent more territory from being classified as "South Bronx," a label that had come to describe not a place but a state of abject wretchedness.

One of the chief problems the coalition organizers faced was the instability of the real estate market. As real estate values went into free fall, most owners of apartment buildings wanted to sell, and almost all of those who purchased properties were irresponsible or venal. The new owners flipped properties for a quick profit, milked buildings while they fell apart, or worst of all, burned them to collect fire insurance.

Then there was Joe Bodak.

In an apartment building on Valentine Avenue in the South Fordham neighborhood, conditions were so bad that the tenants had banded together and declared a rent strike. Almost all the building's thirty-three households took part. The head of the tenants' association, Milton Mejias, had convinced his fellow tenants to withhold their rents and use them to run the building themselves.

The tenants paid the oil bills so that everyone had heat, improved the building by fixing the lock on the front entrance, and had emergency repairs done on the apartments. Bill Frey, who was responsible for organizing tenants in South Fordham, was pleased that the beleaguered tenants and their talented leader had found a way to survive and fend for themselves.

One day Mejias, the tenant leader, called Frey in a panic to tell him that a man who said he was the new landlord was in his apartment. The Valentine Avenue building had been sold. The system that the tenants had so carefully put in place was in jeopardy.

"This can't happen, Milton," Frey said in dismay, "this is terrible." The young organizer rushed over to Mejias's apartment. There he confronted the new landlord, a short, middle-aged Polish Jew named Joseph Bodak.

"You can't do this," the organizer and the tenant leader indignantly told the landlord. "You know you're not going to get the rent money."

"Oh, I don't want the money," Bodak replied—in his heavy accent *want* sounded like *vant*—"just tell me what I'm supposed to do. I'm going to make the repairs."

"Well," said Frey, still suspicious, "you're not going to get the money."

Not long after Mejias reported to Frey that, sure enough, all the building repairs had been made. "The building is really improving," the tenant leader told Frey, "and you know, I want to work with this guy." And so he did, and the tenants, pleasantly surprised to see that their apartments were taken care of, began to pay Bodak his rent.

A couple of months later Frey was working in his South Fordham office when he received a call. "This is Joe Bodak," said the voice on the line. "I wonder if you'll do me a favor?"

"What's that?" Frey asked.

"I wonder if you could come over and organize the tenants in this other building I bought."

"Well, I mean," stammered the surprised organizer, "why are you doing this?"

"Because I found it very important to have a tenant association to work with me on my building."[74]

Bodak had concluded that organizing tenants was the only way to ensure that a building was safe, clean, and occupied by rent-paying tenants. He also appreciated the stately edifices of the South Bronx and lavished care on their renovation. He spent $2,000 restoring the Art Deco mural in the lobby of one of his buildings on 183rd Street. "Sure I want to make money," he explained to the *New York Daily News*, "but I also want to be proud of my buildings."[75]

Joe Bodak became a great resource for the Northwest Bronx Community and Clergy Coalition. If the group could not organize the tenants in a building and it looked as if it was going to be abandoned, Frey would call Bodak and say, "Joe, this building is in a critical area for maintaining the neighborhood, and the tenants really need help. Eastern Savings Bank has the mortgage on this building. Are you interested?" Bodak would acquire the property, and after a time the building was fixed up, running well, and filled with tenants. To Frey, it seemed like magic.[76]

*Joe Bodak, landlord, at the Thomas Garden Apartments, which he restored,
840 Grand Concourse, January 1988. Courtesy of Sara Krulwich,* New York Times.

The young tenant organizer got to know the landlord. Before World War II Bodak's family had moved to Berlin where they had been successful businesspeople. When the Nazis came to power, Bodak fled to the Soviet Union and during the war served in the Russian army to avoid concentration camps. After the war, Bodak came to the United States. He arrived in the Bronx in 1952, worked for a time in house construction, then in the South Bronx bought a large cold-water flat and a luncheonette, which he ran for many years. As the Bronx real estate market sank to the bottom, he bought buildings one at a time.[77]

Frey was so taken by Bodak that in 1983 he went to work for the landlord. Bodak, Frey discovered, never used a bank to finance his building purchases and improvements. Instead of financing, Joe had relationships. He cultivated a relationship with the owners of a hardware company and persuaded them to advance him merchandise in return for a share of his building. It's going to take me five years, Bodak would tell them, to pay back what I owe you on this building. He did the same with the lumberyards. The landlord ran up several hundred thousand dollars worth of debt from the oil company. He ran his buildings so well that he had no debt other than what he owed the vendors, and he eventually paid them off. After several years, Bodak turned to Frey and said, "Look, all my oil bills are paid off! Isn't this wonderful?"

In the end, Bodak built up a portfolio of thirty-five buildings, containing some 2,500 dwelling units, whose worth rose as the South Bronx revived, in Frey's estimate, to a figure between $25 and $30 million. The landlord improved the lives of his tenants and their neighbors, but he did more than that. Like Charlotte Gardens, the buildings that Bodak renovated and managed—and the newspaper articles acclaiming them and their owner—advertised a different South Bronx, a going concern rather than a dysfunctional community. Joe Bodak, in short, helped to push the Bronx toward the tipping point of revival.[78]

Life Lines

No matter how fanatically devoted the members were, the community groups that dotted the blighted landscape of the South Bronx and inner-city New York could not survive or carry out their rebuilding mission without money.

First and foremost, the local groups needed the help of the government of New York City. Besides disbursing the city's own funds, local authorities acted as gatekeepers for federal funds and held the power of approval over state programs carried out within the local jurisdiction. The city either turned a blind eye to the fate of the inner-city neighborhoods or heedlessly threw money away. The fiscal crisis that brought the government to the brink of bankruptcy offered it an excuse for refusing to provide basic services, let alone find city funds for rebuilding. Yet the city often sent federal monies to politically connected operators such as Ramon Velez whose organization did little if anything to save the Bronx. On the other hand, New York's housing preservation and development commissioner, Roger Starr, stymied community groups such as the Northwest Bronx Community and Clergy Coalition from carrying out rehabilitation projects on a large scale by refusing to release federal community development monies.[79]

Slowly and erratically, New York City's government roused itself from its lethargy and indifference and began to support community efforts. In the summer of 1977 a blackout brought a record 307 fires. Major looting and rioting in the Bronx demanded some response from Mayor Beame, especially since he was locked in a tight (and ultimately unsuccessful) primary race for reelection. Years after Bronx community leaders first pleaded with the government to help, the city put together an arson suppression unit and, not surprisingly, arson rates immediately dropped.[80]

City agency officials still disdained the nonprofits, however, except for a maverick officer of the Department of Housing Preservation and Development who was put in charge of a satellite office on Grand Concourse and 175th Street in West Tremont. Under Starr the agency had distributed few of the federal government's community development block grants, and this particular office, whose directors had been replaced every year for the last six, had done nothing at all. When the new director of the West Tremont Neighborhood Preservation Office, Felice Michetti, arrived in 1979, the Northwest Bronx Community and Clergy Coalition greeted her with a demand that the city close the office. The organization's members then boycotted the West Tremont office because they considered it to be a waste of time.[81]

They underestimated Felice Michetti. She had grown up and gone to school in the Bronx, where she had many relatives, and as a young planner she had watched with dismay the spreading abandonment and ruin. Michetti wanted fervently to help the neighborhoods and sympathized with the quixotic community activists. She dusted off a modest loan program for rehabilitating buildings and concocted the idea to combine it with bank loans to obtain a much larger sum. Michetti realized that the city's housing agency could work with the Northwest Bronx coalition to get the banks to make the loans and to carry out the rehabilitation projects. After Koch's election, the bosses at the Department of Housing Preservation and Development noticed that in the midst of despair and inaction, its West Tremont office was the most productive in the city. They brought Michetti downtown, where she would help design the Ten Year Plan in which the agency finally collaborated seriously with the community nonprofits.[82]

First among the private institutions trying to stave off disaster in the Bronx was the Catholic Archdiocese of New York. The church refused to close its parish churches and schools, no matter how desperate the situation became. New York's cardinals Terence Cooke and later John O'Connor gave their blessings and church funds to an array of maverick priests—from Father Gigante to the leaders of the scrappy Northwest Bronx Community and Clergy Coalition—who fought for the neighborhoods of the Bronx.[83]

In the philanthropic field, a new kind of nonprofit organization, the financial intermediary, had recently been established to help the little storefront groups in the South Bronxes of urban America. The Neighborhood Reinvestment Corporation, the Enterprise Foundation, and the Local Initiatives Support Corporation or LISC were experimenting with ways to funnel money and lend professional expertise to local nonprofit organizations. Eventually the intermediaries became national organizations, but in the early 1980s no one was certain whether or how any of this would work.

In the pioneer days there was no more adventurous philanthropist than Anita Miller, a field officer for the Ford Foundation who became the director of the South Bronx program for LISC. During the late 1970s and early 1980s, Anita Miller put money into all sorts of endeavors. Miller was among the first philanthropic officials to fund SEBCO, Banana Kelly, and the Mid-Bronx Desperadoes as well as Logue's Charlotte Gardens project. She got the Ford Foundation to pay the Northwest Bronx Community and Clergy Coalition to organize residents—something philanthropies were reluctant to fund—by applying for a grant to pay anti-arson experts, who were in fact ordinary citizens lobbying the political leaders to stop the fires. There were some spectacular failures, especially in the business sector—where Zoo Doo and an aquatic herb garden enterprise sounded better than they actually were. But Miller bet on many horses and several came through in the long run.[84]

In the mid-1980s the rebuilding of the South Bronx entered a new phase. Miller resigned in 1984 and handed the reins of the Bronx office of LISC to her assistant, Richard Manson. As he made the rounds to present himself as the new program officer, Manson, a well-scrubbed cheerful sort, received something like a hazing from the old hands in the field. On Manson's visit to Father Gigante's operation, one SEBCO staff member, a swaggering Bronx-born Italian American, displayed a gun in his car glove compartment, which he claimed helped him keep the tenants in line. At Banana Kelly, the director took the new LISC officer to a building that the organization was about to renovate. Manson stepped inside a dark apartment that had no floorboards—only joists—and was suffused with an unbelievable stench. As Manson adjusted to the gloom, he made out an elderly woman and her mentally retarded adult son staring blankly at a television and what seemed like hundreds of cats. The Banana Kelly director, no doubt smiling inwardly, led the relieved neophyte program officer away to view a recently finished apartment.

Manson was not fazed. He knew that the operatives were dedicated, even fanatic, about rescuing the South Bronx. "It's tough up here," Manson interpreted their message, "but we do God's work."[85]

The City's Big Push

God's work in New York still needed a big push, however, and in April 1986, Ed Koch, the city's voluble, showboating mayor, gave it one. In the wake of his recent reelection, the mayor announced a Ten Year Plan to rebuild the decayed physical structure of the metropolis. Over the next decade, he declared, New York City would spend $4.2 billion to build 250,000 units of housing for poor and working-class New Yorkers. The scale was breathtaking, especially for a city that had been on the verge of bankruptcy only a few years before. By the time the city was through—long after Koch had left Gracie Mansion—expenditures had risen to close to $5 billion. It was not only the biggest building program any city had ever taken on; it was larger than those of all other cities combined.[86]

A number of political circumstances induced Koch to concoct the Ten Year Plan. For years city officials had ignored or done little about the increasing number of abandoned and burned buildings, but during the mayoral campaign, the issue of housing—or more precisely, of housing the homeless—came to the fore. The numbers of homeless people had risen noticeably during the Reagan years, partly due to the release of the mentally disabled from institutions and partly to increasing numbers of very poor people. Many observers began to wonder why the city tolerated the vacant buildings that lined the avenues and expressways of the Bronx when pedestrians had to step over sleeping bodies on the streets of Manhattan.[87]

In New York the city's subsidized housing policy aggravated the situation. The government gave priority to homeless families waiting for apartments in city-owned buildings. Large numbers of poor people, many of whom were unemployed and lived with family members moved out and declared themselves homeless in order to be placed at the top of the waiting list for an apartment. The practice was patently unfair to the working poor who had waited for years for a subsidized apartment. The mayor heard about the problem and sympathized with the people who worked hard but earned little.[88]

At the same time, the Reagan administration drastically cut the amount of funds that the federal government had supplied and on which the city had come to rely. With the federal government out of the picture, any serious action on the housing front would have to be taken by another branch of government. As luck would have it, the city's finances had improved dramatically. By the mid-1980s, New York had come back from the brink of bankruptcy and could borrow on the bond market again. More money became available when the city government stopped issuing bonds for water and sewer projects based on the city's property taxes and created the Water Finance Authority, which could issue bonds based on its own revenues. Moving the water bonds off the city's real property books raised the number of bonds based on property taxes that the government could issue for housing. Finally, the revenues from Battery Park City, a large luxury real estate development at the tip of Manhattan, generated about $1.2 billion for housing projects.[89]

In fact, Koch's Ten Year Plan was not really a plan as such but a declaration that the city was about to spend billions of dollars on housing. When Roger Starr, then in charge of urban affairs for the *New York Times* editorial page, was shown the plan, he blurted out, "Well, this is not a public program. This is a finance document."[90]

Starr missed the big news: for the first time in decades, the city had money in its pocket and was going to rebuild the housing in New York's broken-down neighborhoods. Eventually the Plan became a broad attack that employed an array of old and new government programs to develop or redevelop apartment buildings and single-family homes, aimed at improving isolated sites, clusters of buildings, or entire neighborhoods.

But at first, the big pile of money Koch had placed on the table raised the question of who would build all these new homes.

One of Koch's first ideas was to let the Real Estate Board of New York, which often complained that the city's building regulations prevented new construction, develop large-scale high-rise apartment buildings. In several sites in the Bronx and Queens, the board's own nonprofit organization would build the kind of big, splashy projects associated with Robert Moses and Nelson Rockefeller and grandiose ribbon-cutting ceremonies.

This effort, however, quickly bogged down in the quagmire of New York politics. At one of the Bronx sites in Kingsbridge, near the upscale Riverdale neighborhood, a bitter fight broke out in which neighborhood residents, some of whom Koch and his deputies considered racist, fought tooth and nail to stop the project even though it was aimed at housing middle-income families. Despite Koch's personal intervention, the big project was stymied.[91]

On the theory that the large construction companies could achieve economies of scale that smaller outfits could not, the Koch administration gave large firms a chance to develop many apartments at once. The Housing Preservation and Development agency (or HPD) identified groups of vacant apartment buildings located near one another so that the big companies could produce units efficiently. When the large firms finished the apartments, they turned them over to New York's public housing authority.

This program—dubbed Construction Management—also flopped. The big companies did not save money; they were expensive.[92] Large-scale operations, it turned out, created large-scale overhead, boosting costs. The large construction companies had little experience fixing up buildings and ended up, in effect, building from scratch. And they used union contractors whose union workers were little interested in gut rehabilitation and small jobs.

Paul Crotty, Koch's new Commissioner of Housing Preservation and Development, concluded that the city needed a better method if it was ever going to build the promised $4.2 billion worth of housing. Time was of the essence. "You didn't have to be a genius to figure out," Crotty observed, that the housing program was "started because of the mayoral campaign in '85 and the accomplishments were going to be judged by no later than '89," the year of the next election.[93]

Crotty looked for properties that HPD could acquire and develop relatively quickly. The solution, he realized, was close at hand. The city owned more than 50,000 occupied units and more than 40,000 units in what were known as *in rem* buildings acquired through aggressive tax delinquency foreclosures.[94] These properties were attractive for many reasons. One important reason was cost. In New York, unlike many other cities, it is usually less expensive to renovate an existing building than to build anew. Second, the *in rem* buildings were frequently some of the worst in struggling neighborhoods, so unlike the Kingsbridge episode, local residents would support, not fight, their redevelopment. Some of the city-owned buildings were inhabited by the very poor who for one reason or another had been declared homeless. Many of the buildings, however, were unoccupied, obviating the knotty and costly problem of relocating tenants.

After debating whether the city government itself should redevelop the buildings, Crotty and his aides decided to let a thousand flowers bloom. The staff at Housing Preservation and Development would work with any housing producer who came to them with a reasonable offer—which included putting money into the deal. The city would put up $5 billion, but private developers, large and small, nonprofit and commercial, would rebuild New York. This was a crucial decision—to support many varied efforts—that ensured a more successful program than would have resulted from a giant one-size-fits-all approach.

Letting outside parties do the development had great advantages. Housing Preservation and Development could avoid the laborious and restrictive contract bidding process and work rules required when the city government developed properties. The agency could rely on parties outside government who knew the field to identify the effective developers and certify their work.

To deal with its diverse partners, New York's housing development agency would use any program it could. Ed Koch's Ten Year Plan grew to resemble the old rhyme, "Something old, something new, something borrowed, something blue." There were dozens of programs . . . programs for the homeless and for those with special needs, programs for renters with low incomes and for others with moderate incomes, programs for home buyers, programs to fix up the old apartments, and programs to build anew. To keep track of it all, Crotty and his deputy commissioner, Mark Willis, created a war room at the

Housing Preservation and Development headquarters. On the wall they hung huge charts with the names of all the different programs, in what parts of the city they were being run, and what stage they had reached.[95]

It wasn't easy, however, getting results from the trenches of the city bureaucracy, which created all sorts of friction with the outside groups who were supposed to carry out the real estate deals. Even at HPD, one former official estimated, only a third of the personnel enthusiastically embraced the mayor's housing plan. Another third were inefficient but teachable, and the last third of the workers hardly worked at all. And as usual, other governmental departments had little incentive to cooperate with the housing agency.

Through a simple trick, Koch himself motivated the bureaucrats to make his Ten Year Plan work. "If the civil servants and the policy people that you appoint conclude that the mayor is particularly interested in a program," Koch observed, "they will lend their best efforts to the commissioner in charge of the program."[96] Koch told Paul Crotty to meet with him in his office every Friday afternoon. Crotty was to bring Willis and other top aides who would report what they had done in the prior week to advance the plan and tell the mayor what he could do to eliminate problems they had encountered. As Koch intended, the word soon spread throughout city government that Crotty had the mayor's ear every Friday afternoon from three to four. Any opposition in the ranks melted away when Crotty and Willis said, "Look, if you're not happy, we'll raise this with the Mayor."[97]

Little Guys Do a Big Job

Crotty and his crew first turned to Michael Lappin and the Community Preservation Corporation, with whom they had worked before. The Community Preservation Corporation had been founded back in 1974 when David Rockefeller, Nelson's brother and head of Chase Manhattan bank, persuaded officers of New York's major commercial banks that they could stop the abandonment of neighborhoods and avoid criticism for "redlining" inner-city neighborhoods by pooling their money to help apartment house owners repair and remodel their buildings.

The Community Preservation Corporation was an unusual housing organization. It aimed its efforts not at government agencies or wheeler-dealers who fed at the government trough, but at small private entrepreneurs who operated for themselves. Across the nation, there are few organizations like it. One is Chicago's Shorebank, which has helped stabilize neighborhoods in Chicago and Cleveland by lending money to and otherwise helping "mom and pop" landlords. The Community Preservation Corporation attempted to get apartment owners in New York City's lower- and working-class districts to take advantage of a number of incentives, such as mortgage insurance and tax breaks, to upgrade their buildings. Although often ignored, the clientele of such groups are of enormous importance: the small-scale property holders own the great majority of buildings in the inner city and as such play a great role in maintaining their vitality.

Early in its history the Community Preservation Corporation had hired a staff member who made an important discovery. Michael Lappin, who was in charge of the organization's operations in Harlem and upper Manhattan, realized that, unlike large real estate players who were practiced in the arcane mysteries of government housing schemes, most of the landlords he dealt with knew little or nothing about government programs that could help them. Nonetheless, the local landlords were able to renovate their properties at about half what it cost the large developers—"the big boys," as Lappin referred to them.[98]

Lappin, a veteran of the civil rights movement in Buffalo, New York, a War on Poverty agency in Kentucky, and New York's Neighborhood Preservation Office under mayor John Lindsay in the 1970s, devised a "one-stop shop" approach that would make it easy for small entrepreneurs to borrow money and benefit from tax incentives. He helped coordinate with New York City's government a small but successful program that lent money to and guided landlords to fix or replace windows, roofs, and boilers in neighborhoods that might otherwise have gone the way of Charlotte Street. He went so far as to write some of the technical specifications for the program, even going to a Long Island window manufacturer to get the details right. Among the program's interesting features was a requirement that owners put their own money into the project—a minimum of 10 percent equity—as opposed to government housing programs that allowed developers to borrow and receive subsidies for their projects.[99]

Just as Bill Frey had learned to respect Joe Bodak, Lappin, who eventually became president of the Community Preservation Corporation, came to admire the urban landlords and investors who renovated apartments and buildings with their own money and at low cost. His clients, however, were a far cry from the types liberal reformers usually work with. They were not idealistic professionals or community activists. They did not speak the lingo of government programs and social improvement. When they wanted to evict drug dealers from their buildings, they would say, "I gotta throw out the garbage." If they felt they had to, they carried guns.[100]

These were the hard-bitten survivors of the world of inner-city real estate. They had a little money to invest and for one reason or another had decided to buy a building. Some were plumbers or building superintendents who acquired the building where they worked. Others were storeowners, like Joe Bodak, or retired cops. Some owners inherited their properties from their families who had owned them for generations. Many were immigrants or children of immigrants—Greeks, Jews, Russians, Chinese, Albanians, Dominicans—and American minority groups such as Puerto Ricans.

To survive, the inner-city landlords scoured the New York region for the best price for hardware, fixtures, and appliances. They tenaciously negotiated with contractors, who were sometimes connected to the mob or the unions or both. In general, they saved money by not paying union wages. Yet they hired locally, building in the process small employment engines of the type policy makers dream of creating. When organized groups came to shake them down during construction projects—demanding in one case that they hire three African Americans even though close to 90 percent of the workers were black—

they dealt with it by paying off the extortionists, hiring the workers, and hoping the employees might actually do something, or refusing—and suffering the consequences of broken windows and having cinder blocks thrown at them and their partners.[101]

The landlords in the South Bronx, Harlem, Washington Heights, Bedford-Stuyvesant, and other poor and working-class sections of New York did not question the conditions in which they worked. They accepted the drugs, crime, abandonment, and racketeering as a matter of fact.

The owners did business in the inner city for the simple reason that they believed they could squeeze profits out of properties in neighborhoods that most bankers and investors avoided like the plague. True, some landlords were bad apples who would strip the building of its assets and then sell or abandon it; but most, in Lappin's observation, believed in giving a good product for a decent price.[102]

The secret of success for the honorable but tough urban landlords was to keep costs low and rental income, no matter how modest, steady. The urban landlords used their relatives to help them do the work. One Greek landlord, Steven Zervoudis, would acquire a vacant building in a rough neighborhood and secure the building by installing his father and some guard dogs in the property.[103]

The landlords would not rest until they found the best price. In the early 1980s, a Russian emigré bought a thirty-unit apartment house in Inwood, a working-class neighborhood at the northern tip of Manhattan adjacent to the Bronx. Lappin and the Community Preservation Corporation helped the owner finance the deal through a program of the federal department of Housing and Urban Development. Of course, the HUD money came with many strings attached, including the requirement that the renovation cost no more than $15,000 per dwelling unit. On top of this, the HUD agents looked over the building and declared that to meet their standards, it would cost $30,000 per unit. The owner went about rehabbing the building in his hard-boiled fashion, and the HUD inspectors visited regularly, poring over the renovation work. When he was finished, the emigré had renovated the apartments at a cost of $13,000 each, well under the HUD maximum. As for the bureaucratic oversight, the Russian landlord was unperturbed. "This is just like Russia," he commented. "For every worker, there are two inspectors."[104]

The Community Preservation Corporation had figured out a good approach for saving and lifting up inner-city properties, but in its early years it had a limited effect. Until the mid-1980s the organization covered only a few neighborhoods. In the Bronx, it worked in the far northern region, which had not suffered nearly as much as the southern precincts. In 1986, propelled by the city's giant housing enterprise, the Rockefellers' nonprofit corporation would vastly expand its efforts to buttress the owners of small properties in New York's inner city.

To launch Ed Koch's Ten Year Plan and restore the city's massive stock of *in rem* abandoned buildings, Paul Crotty and his deputy commissioner, Mark Willis, asked Lappin to invite the best local landlords to bid on a vacant building, repair it, and rent it to families. The Vacant Building Program used the one-stop shop of the Community Preservation Corporation to funnel bank construction loans and mortgages along with government subsidies to buyers who agreed to repair the abandoned buildings to specific standards and in some cases offer rents that low-income families could afford.

When they announced the first round of bids for the Vacant Building Program in late 1986, Crotty and his people were nervous. Were people going to bid? Would they be strong contractors? Would the contractors be able to line up the construction money? Would they start the construction on time? Only a small number of bidders entered the first round. More followed the next year, and by 1988 a crowd had jumped in. As the local landlords and investors saw that the rules of the bid were predictable, they embraced it.[105]

The program was wildly successful. Applications to rent the newly renovated apartments flooded in. Often more than a hundred people vied for a unit, which typically boasted hardwood floors, solid wood kitchen cabinets, and tiled bathrooms. The Vacant Building Program was the largest of those supported by the city government during the Ten Year Plan. It carried out the gut rehabilitation of 40,000 dwelling units in a mere seven years.[106] As they had in the past, the local landlords came in well under the cost of other programs. And by sending all the new business to Lappin's organization, the program helped Community Preservation Corporation grow into a major institution, which today operates in all five boroughs of New York City, across New York State, and in New Jersey.

Oddly enough, the Vacant Building Program encountered resistance from the ranks of New York's Department of Housing Preservation and Development, which was in charge of the program. Agency staff members resented helping landlords make money from low-income housing and decried them as "Long Island developers," a euphemism for white ethnics.[107]

Mark Willis rode herd on the recalcitrant bureaucrats who wanted to make life difficult for the Community Preservation Corporation and local landowners. To Willis, it was simply a matter of answering the question, "Who can fix the buildings up the cheapest?"[108]

Willis was all for letting the local landlords make as much money as they possibly could since they were producing housing at far less cost than anyone else.

The Nonprofits Move Up

It seemed unlikely at the outset, but the Koch administration's Ten Year Plan also helped nonprofits reach a milestone in the movement for community development. New York's nonprofit community groups clamored to be included in the great campaign to rebuild New York's inner city. Through years of fighting to save their neighborhoods, community groups such as the Mid-Bronx Desperadoes and the Northwest Bronx Community and Clergy Coalition had earned a moral right to help redevelop them. From a practical point of view, the groups were familiar with the neighborhoods and the people who lived in them and could avoid the bloody battles over sites such as Kingsbridge.

Without government support, however, the nonprofits could accomplish little. The problem was that the staff of the Department of Housing Preservation and Development did not believe the nonprofit groups were capable of developing property. The more experienced organizations usually played the role of *sponsor* and *building manager*, not *developer*. In their early days, for example, stalwart organizations such as MBD and Father Gigante's SEBCO had formed partnerships with operatives such as Jerome Chatsky who actually did the contracting. After the buildings were rehabbed, the community groups took over and ran them. Most CDCs had little or no experience in developing real estate and lacked the skills to do it.

As the city officials planned Koch's new housing production program in the spring of 1986, they searched for someone who could choose and assist the nonprofits the way Mike Lappin helped small property owners. Kathryn Wylde, the director of the New York City Housing Partnership, which worked with the city to build houses for sale, knew what the city was looking for and encouraged Mark Willis and Paul Grogan, who had recently left city government in Boston to succeed Mike Sviridoff as president of LISC, to meet with each other to see if they could do business together.[109]

Wylde was on target. In Boston, Grogan had pioneered a collaborative housing program between the government and local nonprofit groups, and, as he took the reins of LISC in New York, now sought a way to help the nonprofits boost the number and size of their community development projects. When Grogan first arrived in New York where LISC's national headquarters was located, most of the organization's local program dealt with the South Bronx groups. To begin, Grogan surveyed the leaders of the CDCs and asked them what he could do to help them. The reply of Genevieve Brooks at the Mid-Bronx Desperadoes struck Grogan forcibly.

"Please," she said, "can you do something about the city?"[110]

It was a long-standing complaint with the CDCs. The attitudes at the Department of Housing Preservation and Development, CDC leaders felt, made rehabilitating abandoned buildings a tremendously laborious experience. Brooks remembered the Mid-Bronx Desperadoes approaching the agency and being told, adopt a building, no, first redevelop a block, no, come back with a plan. If Grogan could strike a deal with the city government, he could help the CDCs—across the city, not just in the Bronx—earn respect in the halls of power and work on a much larger scale than they ever had.[111]

As it turned out, Willis and Grogan—the city and LISC representatives—hit it off. They agreed on a large package deal to develop one thousand units. To avoid laborious paperwork on each building and CDC, the deal called for New York's housing development agency to select the abandoned buildings it wanted developed and sell them all at once to the participating CDCs for a dollar each. For its part, LISC would choose ten CDCs for the program, train or hire people who had the technical skills needed for development, and give them the money they needed to do the paperwork to run the projects.

Money remained a sticking point. The housing development agency insisted that the city not pay all the development costs. As luck would have it, the Congress (persuaded by the leaders of nonprofits and city government

55

officials) had recently enacted the low-income housing tax credit. The new law enabled corporations to invest in low-income housing projects in return for tax credits that the sponsors of the housing earned. LISC promised to deliver $25 million in tax credit investments by selling the syndicated tax credits for the CDCs, which would receive 25 percent of their development costs. (Later, as the tax credit market grew competitive, the equity share going to CDCs rose to 50 percent.) The Koch administration, which only liked to deal with partners who placed serious cash on the table, now offered to cover the rest of the costs and offered mortgages at 1 percent interest for buyers.[112]

Like the Vacant Building Program, the nonprofit housing component of the Ten Year Plan took New York City out of the painstaking business of choosing and supervising developers and passed it on to someone else—in this case LISC. Now LISC officers shouldered the burden, which appeared all the greater because they believed that if the program failed, it would set back the community development cause for years.

Grogan and the officers at LISC hired Julie Sandorf to create a uniform, smooth-running system for the CDCs and the city government to develop the thousand units of housing. They had seen what she had done at Mid-Bronx Desperadoes, working on Charlotte Gardens—including screaming at Ed Logue when necessary. Now the LISC brass asked Sandorf to cut who-knows-how-much government red tape, line up the inexperienced community groups, and march them forward. It was a tall order.

Sandorf's first task was to identify the best CDCs in the city. To do so, LISC insisted upon rigorously inspecting each organization's finances. "We hired CPAs to go through people's books," Sandorf recalls; "we wanted this cleaner than clean." No mismanagement or scandal would tarnish New York's big nonprofit housing program.[113]

LISC invited only the most experienced and reliable nonprofit organizations to develop the city's abandoned buildings. In the Bronx, they chose such stalwarts as the Mid-Bronx Desperadoes, Banana Kelly, Mid-Bronx Senior Citizen's Council, and BUILD (Bronx United in Leveraging Dollars), at the time the development arm of the Northwest Bronx Community and Clergy Coalition, and in Brooklyn, the St. Nicholas Neighborhood Preservation Corporation and Brooklyn Ecumenical Cooperative's New Communities.

Even with dependable CDCs, LISC found it difficult to raise money. Most potential corporate investors knew little about the recently enacted tax credit program or were not interested in sinking large sums into an untested program, especially one that involved investing in the disreputable neighborhoods of inner-city New York. When a corporation that had pledged to invest $10 million in the tax credit pool unexpectedly pulled out, it appeared that LISC would not be able to deliver to the nonprofit program the $25 million it had promised. Just in time to save the deal, John Mascotte, the CEO of the Continental Corporation and also chairman of the board of LISC, came to the rescue by investing his company's capital into the program. Nonetheless, the officials in the participating companies were dubious and considered their investment to be a charitable contribution. Years later they would be surprised when they learned that the money they put into the deal had earned their companies a significant return.[114]

With the necessary financing lined up, Sandorf set about creating a uniform system for processing the building rehab projects. She wanted the assessment of the buildings, the specifications of the proposed work, and the process the CDCs went through all to be standard. She even wanted a financial underwriting package that would apply to each project.

The LISC staff people held weekly meetings with the people in New York's Department of Housing Preservation and Development to track the progress of every single project. Sandorf regularly fired off memos to Mark Willis that detailed what had been done on a particular building and what remained for the agency staff to do—which earned her the resentment of the people who worked under Willis. "I got away with being such a bitch," Sandorf, ordinarily a good-humored sort, recalls in disbelief.[115]

The department personnel in turn blamed delays on the CDCs. The CDCs' staff, they told Sandorf, lacked the skill, talent, and technical wherewithal to succeed at real estate development. "No," Sandorf replied, "you don't have a system. Nothing's predictable. You never know what you're supposed to do next." Create a system of ten steps that each CDC would take to advance the project, Sandorf urged, with the last step culminating in a construction deal.[116]

The LISC part of the housing production program proved to be a success. It demonstrated that ten of the best nonprofits could successfully fix up dilapidated buildings.

So far, so good, but far more buildings needed restoration than the ten CDCs could handle. And LISC would work with only the CDCs it had certified as honest and capable.

The city's Housing Preservation and Development agency had an additional problem. It had tried and failed miserably to take advantage of a program set up by the state of New York called the Housing Trust Fund. The city's housing agency had given numerous apartment buildings to community groups who had access to the state money, but the groups were unable to accomplish anything further. The Trust Fund program provided loans of a maximum of $33,000 to develop a dwelling unit when the cost of rehabilitating an apartment was close to $80,000. The program's authors assumed that any amounts above the state loans could be obtained from other institutions such as banks. The state insisted on being repaid before the banks, however, and no banks were willing to make loans that might leave them holding the bag. As a result, numerous properties the city had transferred to community groups stood in limbo.[117]

Fortunately for the nonprofit programs, Jim Rouse and the Enterprise Foundation had recently arrived in town. The Enterprise Foundation resembled LISC, except that it ranged wider in the kinds of work and the kinds of organizations it would work with. Jim Rouse gave his organization the mission to provide the very poor with respectable and affordable housing so as to help them escape poverty. Rouse was open-minded about the means for fulfilling the mission, and as an old real estate developer himself, he thought the Enterprise Foundation

James Rouse (left), founder of the Enterprise Foundation, and Bill Frey, director of Enterprise New York, at an announcement of the New York Equity Fund, a joint effort of the Enterprise Foundation, LISC, and the City of New York, in front of a rehab project in the Bronx, 1988. Courtesy of the Enterprise Foundation.

would work with anyone who would do a good job of developing properties or even build the housing itself if it had to. In January 1987 Rouse hired Bill Frey, the former organizer for Northwest Bronx Community and Clergy Coalition, to head his New York office.[118]

The staff of the city's Housing Preservation and Development asked the Enterprise Foundation if it would take on the array of nonprofit organizations that were unable to redevelop the sites under the state's Housing Trust Fund program. If Enterprise would bring in money by selling low-income housing tax credits and combine it with the state funds, the agency staff offered, the city would put up any additional funds that were needed to finish rehabilitating the buildings.

Frey and his staff happily took up the challenge. The Enterprise Foundation eventually supported seventeen different organizations of all types and sizes with financing—including enough for reserve funds to protect against possible difficulties in the future—and expertise and training as needed. The large, experienced groups, such as Phipps Housing Corporation (a citywide subsidiary of one of New York's oldest philanthropic foundations) and the development department of Catholic Charities in Brooklyn, were primarily interested in getting the financing. Others had never developed anything and looked for assistance in all phases of the project. Asian Americans for Equality, having acted for ten years as a civil rights group and advocate for Chinatown workers and tenants, had just become interested in developing housing. In the Bronx the groups included the Mount Hope Organization, which the Northwest Bronx Community and Clergy Coalition had recently helped put together.[119]

1485 Fulton Avenue, before rehab, March 1991. Courtesy of Larry Racioppo, New York City Department of Housing Preservation and Development.

1485 Fulton Avenue, after rehab by Phipps Houses, June 1993. Courtesy of Larry Racioppo, New York City Department of Housing Preservation and Development.   59

Some wanted only to do one project and were not interested in becoming development companies. The Simeon Service Foundation was a tiny nonprofit organization started by St. Simeon's Church located in the South Bronx on 165th Street just east of the Grand Concourse. The group had been awarded some state funds to rehabilitate three buildings it had long wanted to resuscitate, and the Enterprise Foundation brought them the housing tax credit investment funds. With the help of the Enterprise Foundation, they planned to build a 4,500-square-foot day care center on the ground floor of one building and use the vacant lot next to it as a play area for the children. As it turned out, the day care center won the approval of the neighborhood community board, which wanted to reject any more low-income housing in the neighborhood. After developing its twenty-seven apartments, Simeon Service turned its attention to other community work.[120]

For the city agency, it was a blessing to have different brokers with which to work. In its part of the program, for example, LISC chose not to work with Gigante's SEBCO—because Gigante refused to show LISC SEBCO's private financial records. Since LISC would not agree to work with Gigante's operation, officials at the city's Housing Preservation and Development agency considered using another nonprofit to rehabilitate apartment buildings in Hunt's Point, where SEBCO was located.[121]

Within the city's housing agency, Felice Michetti strenuously objected to leaving the priest out of the nonprofit program. She felt such a decision would wreak havoc among the neighborhood organizations. Michetti argued that the community groups had informally carved the city into territories in which one group usually operated. If the city sponsored a project by a community group in another's territory—and especially if that territory belonged to the established and successful Gigante's SEBCO—it would signal that community group territories were no longer secure from incursions by other groups, and all hell would break loose. Michetti carried the day, and Gigante came on board through the Enterprise Foundation's part of the nonprofit program.[122]

Fighting Politics in the Programs

Although government support is necessary to revitalize urban places, politics can easily undermine community development. It is a tenet of the community development field that political considerations sank the War on Poverty by allowing "poverty pimps" to "piss away money." Operating large programs without political interference was and is one of the great challenges of the movement to revive the inner city.

In the 1970s and 1980s, New York's city government was rife with corruption, which posed a threat to Koch's big rebuilding plan. Fortunately, for the Bronx, the widespread political contracting and bribery scandals that exploded in the mid-1980s swept the corrupt Bronx borough president, Stanley Simon, and Democratic county leader, Stanley Friedman, out of power and into jail. The heir to the Bronx borough presidency was Fernando "Freddy" Ferrer, part of a new generation of Hispanic New York politicians who had worked their way up the party ranks.[123] Even had he been so inclined, the intense scrutiny created by the glare of publicity resulting from the scandal would have prevented Ferrer from playing the sleazy patronage games his predecessors had.

In any case, the government agency officials and nonprofit leaders were delighted to find that Freddy Ferrer welcomed the efforts to improve his district. As a result, the Bronx projects sailed through the Board of Estimate, the political shoals under New York's old charter where many a program had been shipwrecked.[124]

Ferrer let the agency operate freely in his district, asking only that his office be able to recommend which neighborhoods received priority. It was a reasonable request for a borough president. Ferrer asked that the city begin its reconstruction program in the South Bronx with the abandoned buildings, visible from the Cross-Bronx Expressway, that the city had plastered with decals of flowers and other signs of domestic life. Mark Willis at the housing development agency thought Ferrer's idea was brilliant. "So simple but so straightforward," he explained. "Once those buildings were fixed up, people thought the borough was fixed up." As seen from the highway, the rehabbed buildings advertised the rebirth of the South Bronx.[125]

Ferrer's open-arms approach in the Bronx contrasted at first with the tight political control exercised in Harlem, which had one of the highest concentrations of abandoned buildings in New York City. According to Crotty and Koch, the neighborhood's African American political leaders—David Dinkins, who was then borough president for Manhattan, and other worthies such as former borough president, Percy Sutton, and Congressman Charles Rangel—liked to have a say on any building projects going on in Harlem. Harlem officials insisted on employment set-asides and preferences for minority firms and workers, promoting certain developers and contractors. Koch remembers the politicians even attempting to select the tenants. (Before the new charter was implemented, building contracts with the city had to be approved by the Board of Estimate; the borough presidents sat on this board and could, if they wished, exercise veto power over any contract the board considered.)[126]

Koch, however, refused to let the politicians dictate who the developers would be, and the long hassles and racial mau-mauing eventually wore out the patience of the Housing and Preservation Department officials. Rather than be caught in the stalemate, they avoided doing work in Harlem. Instead they spent money in the Bronx and Brooklyn. Eventually, according to the government officials, Dinkins changed his tune and encouraged the projects regardless of the developer, at which point the program returned to Harlem.[127]

First, however, the area needed competent nonprofits to rehabilitate the housing. For all its importance as a center of African American life, Harlem had few community development organizations. For years a politically favored, state-chartered agency, the Harlem Urban Development Corporation, had been in charge of social and economic projects, resulting in "paralysis and inaction."[128]

Averse to working with politically wired groups, Paul Grogan and Julie Sandorf decided to try to locate Harlem groups that would qualify for the city's nonprofit housing program. The first organization they found turned out to be relatively small and ineffective, but even so, the leaders of the Harlem Urban Development Corporation apparently felt the LISC support threatened their monopoly.[129] Its director summoned Grogan and Sandorf to a meeting in his office in Harlem which he opened, Grogan remembers, by saying, "I would like to know what *your* plans are for *our* community." It was a classic ploy to place outsiders, especially white ones, on the defensive.

"We have no plans for your community," Grogan said, deflecting the charge. "We're going to try to help Harlem organizations fulfill their purpose." There was little in that with which to quarrel, and the conversation soon ended.[130]

Vital nonprofit redevelopment organizations grew in Harlem outside the orbit of the Harlem Urban Development Corporation. Rebuffed by the old organization, the energetic young minister of Harlem's historic Abyssinian Baptist Church, the Reverend Calvin Butts, had started his own CDC. Grogan and Sandorf lined up seed money for Butts so that he could hire a talented parishioner, Karen Phillips, to build up the Abyssinian Development Corporation and enable it to participate in the city's Ten Year Plan projects. It has become one of New York's most successful CDCs—renovating 150 brownstone rowhouses, operating a Head Start center, and developing some 600 apartments as well as the celebrated 65,000-square-foot shopping center with a giant Pathmark supermarket. Similarly the Harlem Congregation for Community Improvement, the brainchild of another charismatic minister, Preston Washington, benefited from LISC seed money and training and went on to redevelop some 1,300 apartments in Harlem.[131]

As Harlem's ministers and church organizations made conspicuous progress, the unproductive Harlem Urban Development Corporation withered away, losing its state funds in 1994. Unhindered by political meddling, community development could flourish.[132]

New York's Ten Year Plan was a boon to the city's nonprofit community development organizations. The nonprofit groups gained expertise and experience and ultimately the respect of the city government that they had long craved. To build up the CDC system in New York, two LISC staffers devised a new program in which LISC hired and trained staff members for inexperienced community groups so that the fledgling organizations could qualify to develop the city's properties. The city also lent a hand. In arranging the city's contracts with the nonprofits, Mark Willis of the Housing Preservation and Development agency incorporated a developer's fee to be paid to each nonprofit for every rental apartment it produced. With this financial cushion, the nonprofit groups could afford to pay more and therefore retain their top officers. During the ten years of the city's housing venture, the number of viable CDCs in New York City grew from a handful to over a hundred.[133]

New York, and particularly the South Bronx, became a national showcase for LISC and the Enterprise Foundation. Both groups showed that they could raise large sums from corporations—largely through investments in low-income housing tax credits—and proved that small community development organizations could produce housing on the scale of government and large commercial developers. The New York projects became a model that each of the organizations worked to re-create in other cities.

A Rocky Partnership

In the business of rebuilding communities, nothing helps so much as homeowners. Owning your residence gives you a financial and emotional stake in not only your house but also the surrounding area. In low-income communities homeowners often led efforts to clean up streets and empty lots, get rid of drug dealers, and improve the services provided by the city government. Like property owners in economically better-off neighborhoods, they take a keen interest in protecting property values and sometimes will oppose the development of public or subsidized housing.

As Ed Logue had discovered at Charlotte Gardens, people in the inner city hungered to own their own homes. Such aspirations were not surprising: since before the Civil War social reformers and promoters of the real estate industry have endorsed the independently owned single-family home in the United States—"the American Dream." The problem was and is that the cost of buying a house is too high for most poor people. Down payments and regular mortgage installments are out of reach for the irregularly employed or inadequately paid, and even when inner-city residents could afford to buy, money lenders often refused to issue them mortgage loans.

In the 1980s New York City, known as a land of rental apartments, produced two innovative, but quite different, ways of building houses and selling them to low-income families. The architects of New York's Ten Year Plan incorporated both approaches by working with the nonprofit organizations that invented them, the New York City Housing Partnership and the Nehemiah church coalitions. The groups shared the relatively innocuous goal of homeownership, but, surprisingly, fought it out in the South Bronx in one of the most bruising battles associated with the Ten Year Plan.

The New York City Housing Partnership ran the New Homes Program, which used private builders to construct one-, two-, and three-family houses throughout New York. The gist of New Homes was that the Partnership would receive vacant sites owned by the city and find private developers to build houses on them. Receiving generous allotments from federal, state, and local governments to help pay development costs, the Partnership would lower the sales price to the level affordable by "moderate-" and "middle-income" buyers. In 1992, buyers of Housing Partnership single- and two-family houses in Crotona Park, Hunt's Point, and Melrose earned from about $30,000 to $42,000. Five years later the income of eligible buyers for two- and three-family houses in two Housing Partnership projects in the Bronx—one a few blocks from Charlotte Gardens—ranged from $28,000 to as much as $70,000.[134]

David Rockefeller, the banker who had founded the Community Preservation Corporation, also dreamed up the Partnership. He originally planned a "New York partnership" of the city's labor unions and Chamber of Commerce businesses to revive the city's lagging economy, but labor refused to join with the Chamber of Commerce. Rockefeller charged ahead anyway and, inspired by the Corporation for Community Preservation, with fanfare launched the New York City Housing Partnership in 1982 as a way to hitch business and government to build middle-income housing. Just how this would be done

Site of future housing, West Farms Road, July 1991. Courtesy of Larry Racioppo, New York City Department of Housing Preservation and Development.

New row houses built through the New York City Housing Partnership's New Homes Program with the Mid-Bronx Desperadoes, West Farms Road, December 1994. Courtesy of Larry Racioppo, New York City Department of Housing Preservation and Development.

Rockefeller could not say. Mayor Koch nonetheless endorsed the banker's vague program because he agreed with the goal and surmised that Rockefeller would bring large sums of money to the task.[135]

To run the Housing Partnership's development activities, Rockefeller named Kathryn Wylde, the community housing specialist for a Brooklyn bank and formerly the founder and director of a community development group. Articulate, keenly intelligent, and tenacious as a bulldog, Wylde spent a number of years hunting for money to put the organization on its feet.

There were numerous setbacks, including rebuffs from the Ford Foundation and New York's leading corporations, before the Housing Partnership was able to wring money out of the federal and state governments. Rockefeller had to intercede personally with Ronald Reagan's secretary of the Department of Housing and Urban Development to get a large grant out of the federal government. Wylde spearheaded a lobbying campaign aimed at New York's state legislature, the highlight of which was the annual elegant reception that she and Rockefeller threw for all the members. After four years the state's leaders provided them with a large pot of money with which to build houses.[136]

Even with the funds, New Homes, the Housing Partnership's key program, did little building until the Koch administration included it in the Ten Year Plan. In mid-1986, four and a half years after it was started, New Homes—much to Wylde's frustration—had completed only six projects totaling 171 units. After the city's Housing Preservation and Development department embraced the program, production skyrocketed. By 1997, the Partnership could boast of 10,092 homes in 118 separate projects and thousands more on the way.[137]

It was a great victory, but getting there was ugly. Meetings between the staff of the Housing Partnership and HPD frequently degenerated into shouting matches in which both sides blamed the other for delays of projects. Angry memos flew back and forth between Wylde's group and the city agency, and the fights sometimes made their way into the press. It was hardly the harmonious collaboration that David Rockefeller had envisioned.

Much of the static can be traced to Wylde's way of working. Wylde, a member of the militant Students for a Democratic Society back in her college days, often evinced radical impatience in pursuit of the moderate goal of homeownership. Civil servants who did not move her requests quickly through government channels felt the heat of her blistering criticism, in private and sometimes in public. HPD officials felt that Wylde held a double standard, insisting that the agency rush certain Partnership projects at the expense of other programs in the Ten Year Plan but explaining away delays on her end with developers and financing.[138]

Some in the New York housing field disliked Wylde's penchant for attacking people who differed with or criticized her. "With Kathy, it was either her way or no way," explained a housing official under Koch's successor, David Dinkins, who chose to remain anonymous, "and you got the feeling she could hurt you, that she would not only get mad but get even."[139]

What drove HPD officials really crazy was Wylde's complaining publicly of government logjams and then claiming credit when the logjams broke. Wylde admitted criticizing HPD in the press. "What am I supposed to do?" she explained blandly. "Reporters call me and ask me questions. All I do is answer them factually." Such public criticism of the agency may have been a way of prodding the government to deliver the goods, but it alienated HPD officials who, in the wake of the corruption scandals and during the mayoral campaigns, were especially sensitive to criticism.[140]

It takes two to tango, however, and Wylde's aggressive nature was not the only reason for friction. The city government's process was byzantine. Projects moved as slowly as cold molasses. Everyone who worked with New York's government—even inside the agencies—found it maddening at times. Just obtaining sites that the city owned could take an eternity. Sometimes Housing Preservation and Development could not deliver sites because they belonged to other government agencies, such as the Department of Real Property, which did not want to hand them over. HPD officials also felt obliged to consider community opinion, allowing antagonistic neighbors and landowners to delay approvals to develop. The scandals only made city workers more cautious, further slowing procedures almost to a standstill. And some staffers, reasonably or not, thought that they had more important tasks than fulfilling Wylde's requests for the Housing Partnership.

Even those who clashed with Wylde freely praise her work at the Partnership. Felice Michetti, with whom Wylde fought for the top job at HPD, says that the Partnership's New Homes succeeded well at providing middle-income housing relatively inexpensively. Paul Crotty, another former HPD commissioner, credits Wylde for studying the city's complex disbursing and housing development processes, working with them, and even improving the city's methods. Given the sluggishness of New York's government, perhaps it took a Kathy Wylde to get things done.

Personalities aside, the most telling criticism of the Partnership's New Homes program was that it cost too much. The high costs, critics charged, meant houses were sold to customers who earned too much to justify the high subsidies from the government. One study reported that the average income of a New Homes buyer in the South Bronx was $38,000, but only 13 percent of the area's residents earned over $35,000 a year. In the late 1980s, Crotty claimed, the prices of New Homes houses even rose above those of some houses in the private market. Defenders of the program pointed out that it was necessary to lure higher income families to avoid concentrating the very poor and noted that the Partnership sold mainly to African Americans and Hispanics who were often locked out of homeownership. The scattered location and small sites of the New Homes projects also raised their development costs. Ultimately one's opinion about the worthiness of New Homes depended on one's point of view.[141]

Nehemiah

The Nehemiah program could never be accused of producing housing too expensively or selling to people earning enough to buy on their own. In development costs, the Nehemiah homes beat those of the Housing Partnership, sometimes by tens of thousands of dollars. Yet the faith-based organizations that invented this inexpensive method of building homes in the inner city were not primarily interested in housing or any sort of physical rebuilding as the CDCs were. Nor were they interested in providing social services. The Nehemiah organizations were affiliated with the Industrial Areas Foundation (IAF) and, as such, were dedicated primarily to helping the politically disenfranchised fight to gain political control of their communities.

The IAF group that invented Nehemiah housing arose in the Brooklyn neighborhoods of East New York, Brownsville, and Bushwick, which were every bit as devastated as the South Bronx. (In fact, as one Brooklyn leader bitterly observed, if Jimmy Carter's motorcade had turned east into Brooklyn, then its neighborhoods would have gained the national attention that the South Bronx had.) In 1980 a group of African American ministers and white Lutheran and Roman Catholic clerics invited the IAF to help them organize East Brooklyn Churches (EBC)—as was the case in most places where IAF director Ed Chambers sent organizers. They then scored a coup by convincing the Reverend Johnny Ray Youngblood, the minister who had revived the flagging St. Paul's Baptist church, to join them. A keen strategist and fiery speaker, Youngblood became a leader and spokesman for East Brooklyn Churches.[142]

In 1981 East Brooklyn Churches commenced its work by targeting local grocery stores that committed such abuses as overpricing, short-weighting, and mistreating customers. Members inspected local markets, made lists of rotten food and unsanitary conditions, and asked the storeowners to sign a pledge to correct the problems. Not wishing to incur community disapproval, almost all the owners consented immediately. The three holdouts caved in at a meeting in which hundreds of EBC members stood as one to condemn them. From this victory, East Brooklyn Churches went on to force government officials to resume and complete the stalled renovation of a local park and swimming pool and demolition of three hundred derelict buildings that had become the haunts of drug dealers and violent criminals.[143]

The impact of East Brooklyn Churches impressed New York's police commissioner Ben Ward who in the late 1980s came to east Brooklyn to a town hall meeting, his first visit since he had been sent there as a young police officer in the late 1960s to quell riots. As Ward listened to the local citizens fire one question after another concerning sanitation, traffic lights, and school transportation, he repeated to himself, "I don't believe this." The citizens might have been poor in education and income, but not in civic engagement.[144]

With small but strategic victories under their belt, the leaders of East Brooklyn Churches and its organizer, Mike Gecan, tackled the housing issue. The people of East Brooklyn wanted some alternative to public housing projects, burned-out buildings, and high rents. The question was how to do it.

At IAF director Ed Chambers's suggestion, Gecan and the EBC leaders teamed up with retired homebuilder and first-class curmudgeon, I. D. Robbins. For years Robbins had written pieces for the *New York Daily News* that trumpeted his plan for producing brick row houses for families that earned as little as $12,000 a year. Even for the feisty Alinsky-style organizations, however,

Robbins was an irascible character. He had once berated a newspaper reporter for quoting him as saying a politician was an idiot; Robbins insisted he had called the man a *"fucking idiot."*[145]

Gecan, Chambers, and the East Brooklyn Churches leaders met with Robbins and worked out the premises of their housing program. To create an entirely new community with its own distinct character, they would produce thousands of units at a time. The new buildings would be single-family houses sold to buyers who would feel accountable for their own behavior and the success of the project. To keep construction costs as low as possible, the houses would be attached row houses.[146]

On the financing side, East Brooklyn Churches would maintain as little entanglement with government programs as possible. In practice, this meant that the houses would receive from the city or state vacant land at token costs, low-interest mortgages, a ten-year deferral of property tax, and an interest-free loan of $10,000 to each homebuyer who would repay the loan on sale of the house.

The program received its name when IAF organizer Mike Gecan remembered a moving sermon about rebuilding community that the Reverend Johnny Ray Youngblood had delivered one Sunday. Gecan suggested naming the program Nehemiah after the Old Testament prophet who rebuilt Jerusalem.[147]

To pay for construction of all the new Nehemiah homes, Gecan and the East Brooklyn Churches proposed a $12 million revolving loan fund, a perfect idea except that East Brooklyn Churches lacked the money. Banks, insurance companies, and progressive Protestant denominations spurned the group in the winter of 1981–1982. Desperate, two Lutheran pastors induced the elders of the Lutheran Missouri Synod, as rock-ribbed a conservative religious body as there is, to put up $1 million. The group then enlisted the Roman Catholic Bishop of Brooklyn, Francis J. Mugavero, who himself had grown up in Brooklyn's working-class neighborhood of Bedford-Stuyvesant. Although at first he thought that the clergy must be crazy, the reform-minded bishop scraped up half the $5 million the Brooklyn diocese eventually contributed to the loan fund.

More than that, Bishop Mugavero swung the support of the politicians, those in Caesar's house, as the Reverend Youngblood skeptically referred to them. In June 1982 the bishop headed a delegation, which included Gecan, Chambers, Robbins, and Youngblood, to convince mayor Ed Koch to give them city land, defer the property taxes and loans, and lend each buyer $10,000 at no interest. Koch had no reason to love either Robbins, who had lambasted him as politically corrupt, or the Industrial Areas Foundation, whose affiliate in Queens three years earlier had publicly clashed with him. Prior to the meeting, moreover, Gecan somewhat shamefacedly confessed to the bishop that he only had a fraction of the $12 million dollars he had claimed.

"You worry too much," laughed the cleric, who was a friend of the mayor.

In Koch's office, Mugavero made the case for low-priced home ownership that would cost a fraction as much as the ranch houses on Charlotte Street. "Well, Ed," the bishop wound up, "we've got twelve million and we're ready to build."

The members of the East Brooklyn delegation sweated for what seemed an eternity, wondering if Koch would question the figure. Instead, the mayor turned to his housing commissioner (then Anthony Gliedman) and asked if anyone had ever come to the city with that kind of money. Never, came the answer.

Mugavero made his pitch for city support. "If we could get money from you . . ." he started, but the mayor interrupted, "There's no money."

"Then steal it," the bishop replied, tongue-in-cheek, "and I'll give you absolution."

"You got it," Koch agreed.[148]

Two weeks later, the mayor's deputy announced to a mass rally called by East Brooklyn Churches that the city would provide thirteen blocks of vacant land, $10 million in mortgage loans, and ten-year tax deferrals. Soon thereafter the Brooklyn Roman Catholic Diocese, the Missouri Synod, the Episcopal Diocese of Long Island, and local churches, such as Youngblood's Saint Paul (which put in $100,000), created a $7 million loan pool to finance the home building.

In June 1984, the first couples began moving into the Nehemiah homes. Over the next twelve years, East Brooklyn Churches developed an urban Levittown comprising 2,400 single-family two-story row houses. The income of the Nehemiah families averaged a mere $25,000 a year. About half the new residents moved to their new homes from public housing.[149]

So successful was Nehemiah that it was emulated by other IAF organizations around the United States. The federal government enacted a program based on the Nehemiah concept. Youngblood and the other leaders of East Brooklyn Churches were happy with their achievement, but true to IAF principles, saw it as only one more step for the citizens of East Brooklyn on their way to achieving control of their communities.

Nehemiah Comes to the South Bronx

In 1986 the Reverend John Heinemeier, a Lutheran minister and founding member of East Brooklyn Churches who had been transferred to the Morrisania neighborhood—not far from Charlotte Street—prodded local church leaders to invite the Industrial Areas Foundation to help create a powerful community organization in the South Bronx. Aided by a top Industrial Area Foundation organizer, Jim Drake, the clerics started South Bronx Churches, which they hoped would duplicate the success of East Brooklyn Churches.

The South Bronx of the late 1980s, however, differed from Brooklyn or even from the South Bronx of ten or fifteen years earlier. The area once lacked institutions, but now was almost crowded with them. An outfit called People for Change, for example, had attracted most of the politically minded Roman Catholic pastors in the district, depriving South Bronx Churches—which was supposed to be a broad-based church coalition—of priests. People for Change eventually faded away, but its existence delayed the readiness of South Bronx Churches to take on community issues. Eventually the South Bronx Churches would encompass Baptist, Lutheran, and Roman Catholic churches as well as a Muslim mosque.

Nehemiah houses, the organizers and leaders discovered, were accepted more easily in Brooklyn than in the Bronx. Brooklyn's Nehemiah was started at a time when much of the old population had disappeared, and its row houses did not represent a radical break with the single- and two-family houses and low apartment buildings that characterized Brooklyn neighborhoods such as East New York and Brownsville. The Bronx, in contrast, had been built up with great apartment buildings. By the late 1980s, the Bronx was gaining people. Demand for housing was rising—which was why South Bronx Churches placed home building on its agenda.

In the Bronx, moreover, it was difficult—impossible, as it turned out—to acquire large vacant tracts of land where a few hundred single-family row houses could be laid out at one time as the Nehemiah project had done in Brooklyn. South Bronx Churches set its sights on Site 404, one of the land parcels in the Bronx that the city government had acquired for building on. Site 404 was particularly desirable. It consisted of three cleared blocks on level sandy ground—unusual in the hilly Bronx—located just north of St. Mary's Park and the major commercial artery of 149th Street and in walking distance of subway stations of two transit lines.

In late 1987, leaders of South Bronx Churches approached New York's Department of Housing Preservation and Development and asked for the rights to build eighty units on the site. The leaders and organizers insisted that only on the large site would they be able to build at a large enough scale to establish a viable new community. They argued that they could produce low-density Nehemiah single-family houses for lower income clientele at a lower cost and with fewer subsidies (only a no-interest loan of $15,000 per unit) than anyone else could do.[150]

The city's housing preservation and development agency had other ideas. Its planners wanted to replace the population at its previous density. In the 1960s and 1970s, New York's urban renewal planners had been infatuated with apartment towers which—even though they had been discredited by the awful conditions in public housing high-rises—still lingered as an idea in keeping with the Bronx's tradition of large apartment buildings. Noting that zoning regulations allowed up to 600 units, the housing agency proposed developing 350 dwelling units in multistory condominium buildings at Site 404. Agency officials were not enthusiastic about the rich subsidies that went into Wylde's Partnership deals but felt that in some cases there was no way around them.[151]

Behind the scenes, the South Bronx Churches pressured John Cardinal O'Connor to support their demand for Site 404 and persuade his friend Ed Koch and the housing agency officials to reverse the city's stand. Koch remembers a showdown in which O'Connor heard each side make its case and decided in favor of the city.[152] Despite the many Bronx priests in South Bronx Churches and the success in Brooklyn, O'Connor never publicly favored the Nehemiah project at Site 404. The city, from the mayor on down, never budged.

In the spring of 1989, New York's Housing Preservation and Development selected the New York City Housing Partnership—a second choice after the first nominee turned out to be in trouble with the law—to develop Site 404 with up to 350 for-sale units. This was an ironic choice since the government agency officials admired the accomplishments of the Industrial Areas Foundation organizations and detested working with Kathy Wylde.

South Bronx Churches now declared war. The organization staged numerous events at which its leaders freely attacked government officials and the New York City Housing Partnership. In April 1989, 8,000 members of South Bronx Churches met at Site 404 and declared they would never give up this sacred tract of land. Men and women from each of South Bronx Churches' forty congregations stepped to the microphone and mocked their absent borough president, Fernando Ferrer, with the cry, "Where is Freddy?" At a June rally, members of South Bronx Churches picketed the headquarters of the American Express company and denounced James Robinson, chairman of both the American Express Company and the New York City Housing Partnership, as well as the Partnership's executive director, Kathy Wylde. The dramatic rallies as well earned South Bronx Churches extensive press coverage, and the New York Daily News came out with an editorial in its support.[153]

The group made some progress. Abraham Biderman, then commissioner of the Department of Housing Preservation and Development, in August 1989 offered South Bronx Churches a large number of alternative sites in exchange for the church group's dropping its opposition to the Housing Partnership's development of Site 404.

In true South Bronx Churches' fashion, Manuel Colon and the Reverend Bert Bennett barked back. "Your letter of August 28th makes no sense . . . with smoke and mirrors, you play number games with the South Bronx residents and community." The leaders threatened more demonstrations and lawsuits and closed with "Get serious: either give us Site 404 or get us enough of a contiguous critical mass to begin construction."[154]

With borough president Ferrer, however, the contentiousness backfired. Ferrer preferred that the Bronx be rebuilt at high densities, which after all would increase the number of voters who could support him. (In 2001 Ferrer ran unsuccessfully for mayor of New York City.) The leaders of South Bronx Churches offered a compromise whereby in addition to row houses at Site 404 the organization would build condos at high densities in other locations, but Ferrer, enraged by the lambasting he had received at the church confederation's rallies, dug in his heels.

The leaders of South Bronx Churches felt they might get a better deal from HPD after David Dinkins became mayor in 1990, but their spirits sank when Dinkins appointed Felice Michetti to be the new commissioner of Housing Preservation and Development. Heinemeier declared it was "the worst news we ever got!" They considered Michetti to be an enemy, since in the negotiations over Site 404, she had faithfully carried out the wishes of the former commissioner Biderman.[155]

Michetti had worked with noisy neighborhood groups throughout her career, however, and, in fact, admired both the community organizing and the Nehemiah homes aspects of the Industrial Areas Foundation organizations. Once installed as commissioner, she proposed to South Bronx Churches that they work together. Although she could not give them Site 404—because of Ferrer's implacable opposition—she offered them the opportunity to develop more units than Biderman had offered and without any link to its actions on Site 404 (such as the lawsuit the South Bronx Churches filed). The city and South Bronx Churches agreed on a compromise, and not long thereafter Michetti appeared as a guest of honor at an Industrial Areas Foundation fundraiser.[156]

The New York Housing Partnership proceeded to develop Site 404 as Melrose Court—265 condominium apartments in three sets of three- to four-story buildings that enclosed interior courtyards. As the housing agency had planned, the development was relatively densely populated at sixty people per acre, and like other Partnership projects, it carried significant subsidies. Nonetheless, architectural critics recognized Melrose Court for the quality of its design, and, undoubtedly, it greatly improved its neighborhood.[157]

With Michetti smoothing the way within the city government, South Bronx Churches built more than 500 units in the first phase of Nehemiah in the Bronx. In February 1991, the organization celebrated the groundbreaking on land six blocks east of Site 404 at the Thessalonia Baptist Church. Mayor Dinkins, I. D. Robbins, Michetti, and even Fernando Ferrer all spoke at the occasion. By spring 1996, South Bronx Churches had completed 224 single-family row houses and 288 condominium apartments in a three-story configuration. As promised, the costs and subsidies were low, and the buyers were working people of very low incomes; the average single-family purchaser earned less than $30,000.[158]

South Bronx Churches never did build on Site 404, but its leaders learned from their experiences. In 1998 they started a second phase of South Bronx Nehemiah, which has produced 425 more homes but with basic designs that diverged from those of the earlier Nehemiah one-family house and the condominiums. The condos, built in response to the city's requirements for population density, were dropped because they proved difficult to administer. Instead, South Bronx Churches in its second phase built 190 two-family homes in three-story row houses—similar to, if less expensive than, those built by the Housing Partnership. The group adopted the new housing type in large part because their members had requested the extra unit to house their relatives. The new approach has decided advantages. Besides housing more people in less space—a re-

Nehemiah program two-family houses, phase two, St. Mary's Street, July 2001. Courtesy of Glenna Lang.

sponse to the increasing demand for housing in the Bronx—the rents from the extra apartment cut the owner's monthly carrying costs to almost nothing.[159]

Despite all the furor, Ed Chambers of the Industrial Areas Foundation, the lead organizer Jim Drake, and the leaders of South Bronx Churches shrugged off the losing campaign for Site 404. As far as they were concerned, the struggle united the members of the organization and taught them to seize control of their public lives, which was, after all, the ultimate goal of the organization.

Paradise Found?

As the physical structure of the South Bronx was repaired, it became clear that the borough's other problems had to be solved to truly restore its neighborhoods. During the 1990s, community leaders shifted their energies to the areas of education, employment, and health. In this respect, the comprehensive approach of South Bronx Churches pointed the way. Led by immigrant parents, for example, the organization has campaigned to improve the local public schools. Like the Nehemiah homes effort, this campaign too was arduous, but it came to a successful climax in 1993 when South Bronx Churches established a new public high school with a college preparatory curriculum. The fights, according to the Industrial Areas Foundation philosophy, were just part of the long drive toward a vital and powerful community.[160]

Meanwhile, Ed Skloot, an officer of the Surdna Foundation, also realized that building housing by itself was not enough. With funds from Surdna and other foundations, he hired veteran foundation officer Anita Miller to return to the Bronx in 1991 and launch a $10 million program to improve six neighborhoods. Working with CDCs, Miller nurtured a wide variety of projects including neighborhood-wide planning sessions to determine local priorities, employment training centers to teach basic job skills, and professionally run child care centers.[161] By patching together seed money from foundations and state programs, Miller helped each of the CDCs obtain and assemble facilities for primary health care clinics run by the city's large hospitals. When she heard the Department of Agriculture had an urban program, Miller again played matchmaker and showed the agency the bricks and rubble sites where Bronx CDCs wanted to create parks. Out of this came a community effort coordinated by the Mid-Bronx Desperadoes to create Rock Garden Park, which so impressed New York's parks department that it reversed its policy against creating any new city parks and included it in its maintenance program. The South Bronx, once a national disgrace, now became an example of innovative community development for cities across the country.[162]

Efforts for housing, education, or beauty would have gone for naught, however, if New Yorkers had not solved the crime problems that had pushed the South Bronx over the brink in the first place. To anyone who saw the wild South Bronx of the 1970s and 1980s, the transformation was palpable. "It used to be a war zone, unbelievable," Juan Rodriguez, a building superintendent near 174th Street, reminisced, "and now it's a paradise."[163] The 41st Police Precinct has become so safe that residents joke that Fort Apache has become the Little House on the Prairie.

Interestingly, the incidence of serious crime in the Bronx fluctuated before going into a final descent. As the population of the South Bronx declined in the 1970s, so did the number of major felonies. Crime rates fell slightly during the early 1980s, but toward the end of the decade, a wave of violence sent crime rates spiking upward again. In 1990 the number of serious crimes—such as murders, assaults, and robberies—recorded in the 42nd Police Precinct, a large district that encompassed the Morrisania neighborhood and Charlotte Street, had climbed back to the level of ten years earlier. After 1990 the crime rates in the South Bronx began to fall again—a 26 percent drop was recorded in the 42nd Precinct—and starting in 1995 they tumbled sharply. So acute was the decline that in July 1995 New York newspapers hailed the plunge in New York's murder rates with banner headlines. (In the Bronx, the *New York Times* reported, the number of murders fell 40 percent from the number in July the year before.)[164]

Criminologists credit the increasing safety of New York's streets to new methods of policing, especially those initiated by the administration of Rudolph Giuliani. Under David Dinkins, who took over the mayor's office from Ed Koch in 1990 just as the number of major crimes reached an all-time high, the city expanded its police force and instituted foot patrols and community policing. When Giuliani became mayor in 1994, he named former Boston police chief William Bratton as police superintendent. Bratton put in place a sophisticated computer system to identify high-crime areas and implemented an aggressive policy in which police officers tried to preempt violent criminal acts by questioning and frisking individuals they suspected of possessing guns, even if the nominal excuse for the search was a petty violation such as fare-beating or drinking on the street. At the same time, the police cracked down on petty offenders, such as the car window washers, known as squeegee men, who asked for money in return for their unwanted services.[165]

Other experts note that the rate of serious crimes directly correlates with the use of crack cocaine in New York as well as in other cities. As the use of crack cocaine spread in the late 1980s, the numbers of violent felonies, such as murder, rose. When crack fell out of favor in the 1990s, crime rates fell. The brutal wars between gangs of drug dealers sent thousands to state prisons and untold others to the morgue. Deaths from drug overdoses and AIDS, spread through needles, also rid the streets of violent characters and, more important, persuaded many of the surviving youth to abjure crack cocaine and the violence that accompanied it.[166]

In light of these trends, the improved policing techniques instituted by Bratton and his successors resembled a knockout punch delivered by a boxer whose opponent was already reeling.

The New South Bronx

By the late 1990s, the effects of the great project of rebuilding the South Bronx—including the Ten Year Plan—could be measured, and they were considerable. Ten thousand new dwelling units had been created. Of these, 2,500 went to formerly homeless families. More than 3,000 new houses for sale had been constructed. Thousands of occupied apartments were rehabilitated, the number of abandoned buildings had dwindled, and vacant lots were less plentiful. Property values rose in general in the Bronx and Brooklyn, but even more so in the areas immediately surrounding the owner-occupied houses developed by the Housing Partnership and Nehemiah church coalitions. As the population increased again—thanks to the arrival of immigrants from the Dominican Republic and elsewhere—the apartment houses filled up once more, yet with less overcrowding than before. The South Bronx attracted minority home buyers of diverse incomes. (See Appendix I.) As demand for residences rose, arson and residential fires abated and the neighborhoods became safer than they had been in decades. Indeed, the rebuilding program probably helped reduce crime in the inner-city neighborhoods by dissipating the atmosphere of lawlessness and eliminating the hangouts of addicts and rip-off artists.[167]

Today visitors to the Bronx do not see pathological urban conditions—abandoned buildings, fires left to burn, open drug markets—but rather healthy city neighborhoods. People live in archetypical New York apartment buildings or newly constructed single- and two-family houses, and on weekends, the boulevards teem with shoppers. Just as in the suburbs, Little League baseball teams, sponsored by local businesses, play safely in well-maintained parks. When residents of blighted inner-city Baltimore neighborhoods came to the South Bronx in 1995 to learn about community development, they declared that such a vital place offered no lessons for them. The renaissance of the Bronx was certified in December 1997—twenty years after Jimmy Carter was first shocked by its destruction—when another president, Bill Clinton, came to Charlotte Street to celebrate its rebuilding.

The makeover of the South Bronx, however, should not be mistaken for the eradication of poverty. For despite its miraculous revival, the South Bronx remains a home to poor people. As of 1996, a fifth of the residents of the sections that had experienced the worst destruction were unemployed and about 45 percent received some sort of public assistance. Since then the South Bronx has improved in both categories, but still lags behind the city as a whole.[168] The new homeowners in the houses built by the New York Housing Partnership and South Bronx Churches are offset by the homeless whom the city places in its *in rem* and public housing. The taking and dealing of drugs continues, although at lower rates than before or in places further north in the Bronx. The South Bronx, in short, has become a functioning, albeit heavily subsidized, home to the working and non-working poor of New York City. Given that fact, all hands will have to continue to exert themselves to preserve and extend the gains of the last fifteen years.[169]

Does the reconstruction of the South Bronx provide a model for saving other urban districts? Certainly other inner-city areas would do well to emulate the crucial elements of the community development revival in the Bronx.

The resurrection of the South Bronx began with a small number of dedicated individuals who, despite the dismal conditions and others' disbelief, clung stubbornly to the idea that the rebirth of their communities was both possible and necessary. Taking a "house by house, block by block" strategy, they learned what worked and what did not as they went along. These exceptional leaders eventually persuaded enough citizens and officials in government and institutions to share their faith that the rebirth of the Bronx became feasible. Faith in the importance of community development is itself a catalyst.

A key component of community development, the leaders of the South Bronx realized, is the ability to organize people. Organizing is fundamental whether it is done on the small scale—pulling together tenants, for example, as the CDCs and the Northwest Bronx Community and Clergy Coalition did—or on the large scale, like the South Bronx Churches. Just bringing people together to tackle their shared problems can help reverse the psychology of decline. Beyond that, however, effective organizing is essential to carry out programs successfully and convince people in authority to lend support.

Although other kinds of programs contributed to community improvement, the leading edge of the revival of the South Bronx was housing development. In Hunt's Point, Father Gigante showed the way in renovating apartment buildings and then going on to residential development of all types. The most influential organizations in the Bronx profited from his example. The reconstruction and good management of rental apartments and the introduction of homeowners first stabilized and then rejuvenated communities of the South Bronx.

To carry out housing programs, the cooperation and support of government is crucial. As in Edward Koch's Ten Year Plan of housing production, the government should support a variety of approaches. The municipal housing agency should seek out both viable community groups and small-scale property owners, both of whom can play important roles in saving communities. Nor should the regulation of financial institutions that make loans in neighborhoods be neglected. In all cases, cities should avoid arrangements that encourage patronage or other forms of political favoritism will distort and undermine operations.

Government, however, cannot carry the burden of supporting community development by itself. Cities need institutions that work with government agencies and support local groups the way that LISC, the Enterprise Foundation, the Surdna Foundation, and other organizations did in New York. Both government agencies and philanthropic financial intermediaries should help nonprofit organizations find ways to earn revenue to sustain their operations.

Of course, New York City is in some ways unique. Other cities lack the resources to mount anything on the scale of a ten-year $5 billion housing plan. Yet the powerful winds of change are blowing across their inner-city districts too, and the results are, in their own way, just as startling as the transformation of the South Bronx.

BOSTON AND THE
POWER OF COLLABORATION

3

In 1971, Bob Haas, a twenty-seven-year-old engineer and classical piano player, moved to a commune in a large broken-down Victorian house in a section of the Boston Dorchester district known as Upham's Corner. Haas loved the history and vitality of Dorchester—a streetcar-era place where first the Irish and then other ethnic groups had made their home in "Baahston"—and a few years later bought the old house from his roommates.

Upham's Corner, however, was a neighborhood in crisis. Many poor African Americans and Puerto Ricans lived there. Houses caught on fire and were abandoned. Stores, including the neighborhood supermarket, closed. During his first ten years in Upham's Corner, Haas's house was burglarized twenty-three times. Children on his street grew up, joined gangs, took crack cocaine, and murdered or were murdered.

At first Haas naively thought that if he repaired his house, others would do the same, and the neighborhood would come back. When that did not work, he organized a neighborhood association. That did not stem the tide either, and in 1979 he and members of three neighborhood associations founded the Dorchester Bay Economic Development Corporation (Dorchester Bay EDC). Excited by its potential, Haas in 1985 gave up his other careers to become a full-time staff member and spent sixteen years as director of planning.

It took a few years, but this last effort began to show tangible results. Since its founding Dorchester Bay Economic Development Corporation has developed more than 500 dwellings, restored a major commercial building, brought in a new grocery store, coordinated anti-drug and crime watch groups, started a children's summer camp, and instituted annual neighborhood meetings and festivals for the Upham's Corner neighborhood.[1]

Upham's Corner's revival is not unique. All over Boston's inner-city districts of Roxbury and Dorchester, neighborhoods are experiencing rebirth. Old apartment buildings sparkle, and newly built houses stand on formerly vacant lots. Businesses are returning to the empty storefronts. The areas of abandoned and graffiti-scarred buildings and vacant lots have shrunk, and crime has dwindled to pre–Vietnam War levels.

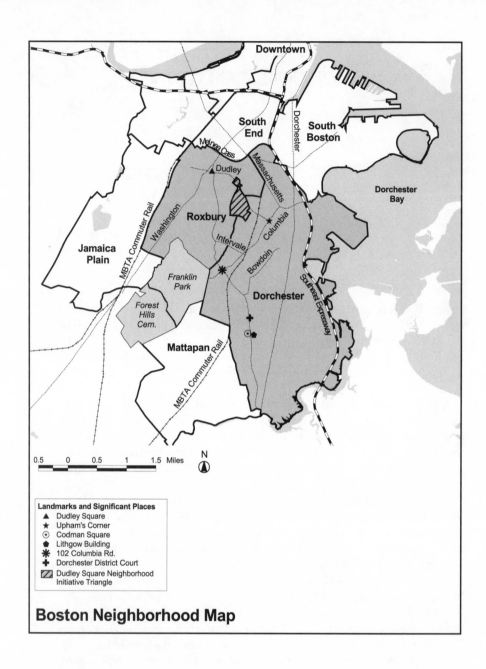

Boston Neighborhood Map

Downtown

South
End

South
Boston

Dorchester

Dorchester
Bay

Melnea Cass

Massachusetts

Dudley

Roxbury

Jamaica
Plain

Washington

MBTA Commuter Rail

Intervale

Columbia

Bowdoin

Franklin
Park

Southeast Expressway

Dorchester

Forest
Hills
Cem.

Mattapan

MBTA Commuter Rail

0.5   0   0.5   1   1.5 Miles

N

Landmarks and Significant Places
▲   Dudley Square
★   Upham's Corner
⊙   Codman Square
♠   Lithgow Building
✳   102 Columbia Rd.
✛   Dorchester District Court
▨   Dudley Square Neighborhood
     Initiative Triangle

(Facing page, top)   *House in disrepair, Monadnock Street, Upham's Corner neighborhood. Courtesy of Dorchester Bay Economic Development Corporation.*

(Facing page, bottom)   *Dorchester Bay Economic Development Corporation's Youth Arts and Crafts Summer Camp, August 1995. Courtesy of Dorchester Bay Economic Development Corporation.*

Some of the credit for the transformation of Boston's inner city must go to the thriving economy and real estate market. Boston, like San Francisco and Seattle, is an American city that has benefited from surging high-technology and service industries. And like other high-market cities, an influx of affluent professionals from the suburbs and elsewhere has created a real estate boom that has raised prices even in the inner city.

But in Boston, perhaps more than any other city, the community development movement took advantage of economic good times to shape an urban revival. Through years of trial and error, the city's nonprofit organizations and public agencies developed remarkable skills in collaboration. Sophisticated community development advocates and daring government officials—including some clever police officers—forged alliances to develop attractive housing, revive commerce, and end crime in the inner city. At first they measured progress in odd ways: a bewildering financial spreadsheet, calls to the Roto-Rooter company, and the silence of a policeman's pager. Eventually, their success became so obvious that now visitors from other cities and countries come to learn about Boston's spectacularly effective community development and anti-crime programs.

The Long Decline

Despite its grandiose nickname, the Hub of the Universe, Boston is small, compact, and old. Dating from colonial days, its streets wind through the town's rolling hills and valleys. Where three or four major roads converge, they form irregularly shaped "squares," which are the commercial and institutional centers of the neighborhoods around them. Isolated by topography, these neighborhoods, sub-neighborhoods really, inspire strong feelings of loyalty among their residents.

Boston's inner-city neighborhoods are located outside the city's colonial boundaries in the former towns of Roxbury and Dorchester, and parts of the neighboring South End. During the nineteenth and early twentieth centuries, Roxbury and Dorchester sprouted solid brick commercial blocks along the avenues, small factories in the lowlands, and houses—ranging from elegant mansions to working-class three-decker apartment buildings—everywhere else. Their population was similarly eclectic, including Protestant Yankees, Catholic Irish, and everyone from the well-to-do to the ne'er-do-well. As the century wore on, upwardly mobile white ethnics, especially the Irish and Jews, inherited these neighborhoods and filled them with small shops, pubs, delicatessens, churches, and synagogues.

In the late twentieth century, dramatic population shifts undermined the prosperity of Roxbury and Dorchester. Between 1950 and 1980, as the city of Boston lost more than 238,000 people, the population of Roxbury fell from 122,000 to 58,000 and that of Dorchester dropped from 118,000 to 83,000.[2] The vast majority of those departing the city were white working- and middle-class ethnics moving to the suburbs. In the 1970s, many fled to escape the federal court's school busing program, the rising crime rate, and the collapsing real estate market.

During this three-decade exodus, minority racial groups moved into the industrial belt of northern Roxbury, then into southern Roxbury and Dorchester. Roxbury experienced the greatest change in racial composition as its population changed from 80 percent white in 1950 to 10 percent white in 1980. Blacks had been living in Roxbury as early as the 1940s — when Malcolm X stayed there with his aunt — and by 1960 Roxbury became the capital of black Boston. In the 1960s African Americans began moving to western Dorchester. In the 1970s Puerto Ricans, and some Latin American immigrants, followed the blacks to northern sections of Roxbury, Dorchester, and the adjacent neighborhood of Jamaica Plain. In 1970, whites comprised almost 90 percent of Dorchester's population; twenty years later their share had dropped to just over half the population.[3]

Many of the newcomers were significantly poorer than their predecessors. By 1979 the percentage of people below the poverty line had risen to 30 percent in Roxbury and 17 percent in Dorchester. Single-parent households made up over a third of all households in Roxbury and over a quarter of those in Dorchester. Thirty-three percent of Roxbury's households received public assistance, as did 20 percent of the households in Dorchester.[4]

The transition to a poorer, more racially diverse population did not go smoothly. In the 1970s the school busing program, which required racial integration of the public schools, exacerbated racial tensions throughout the city. Increasing numbers of crimes in Roxbury and Dorchester contributed to a sense that order was breaking down.

As in other cities, where property values collapsed, buildings were liable to burn. For evening entertainment, people in Roxbury and Dorchester watched the fires from their porches and roofs and hoped that the blowing embers would not set their own houses ablaze.[5] Some fires arose from carelessness and even revenge. Others, perhaps most, were set intentionally to collect insurance or get rid of a property that was bleeding money.

Rapid change was particularly devastating to the south Dorchester neighborhood of Codman Square. The population west of Codman Square changed from middle-class Jewish to low-income African American during the late 1960s and 1970s, and the surrounding community all but collapsed. Real estate values plummeted to zero, vandals stripped the copper and radiators from buildings at night, and hundreds of houses burned. In 1969 fires emptied the Lithgow Building, the prominent commercial block of Codman Square. Once Codman Square had boasted 150 stores; by 1977 only thirty remained. Drug dealers shot out the branch library's windows because they suspected the librarian of snitching. One night someone attacked the gift shop with a chain saw. During the blizzard of 1978, which shut down Boston for a week, hundreds of rioters smashed windows and looted the remaining businesses, including the major supermarket, until the National Guard was called in. The supermarket closed soon afterward.[6]

By then, large stretches of Roxbury and Dorchester resembled the depressed mill towns of the New England countryside. The wooden shingles and clapboard on aged homes were faded and cracked or covered with cheap tar paper

Abandoned three-deckers and vacant lots in the Codman Square neighborhood, mid-1970s. Courtesy of William Walczak.

and asphalt shingles. Broken windows and tattered shades made many buildings look like haunted houses. Graffiti and boarded windows scarred apartment blocks and factories. Empty storefronts desolated the neighborhoods' once busy commercial boulevards and squares. Few, if any, banks would issue a house mortgage or business loan in these forlorn neighborhoods.

To make matters worse, the Hub's government seemed to withdraw from the inner city along with the grocery stores and bank branches. In his early terms as Boston's mayor, Kevin White had shown some interest in the problems of the neighborhoods, for example, by establishing Little City Halls and supporting the development of low-income housing. But by the mid-1970s, White concentrated on downtown development and tourist attractions, such as the Quincy Market development and the procession of the Tall Ships. Unable to solve the busing controversy that tore at the city's soul, White became preoccupied with building a political machine and allowed the city government to become mired in bureaucracy, patronage, and, in some cases, corruption.[7]

The Boston police department was slow to respond to inner-city calls in the White years, and when it did, it alternated between indifference and brutality. "You'd call the police when there was a housebreak," Bob Haas remembers, "and they would say 'You still live here?'"[8] Many officers used the term "maggots" to refer to youthful thugs, but some applied it to all members of racial minority groups and were easily provoked to violence. A few of the city's finest could be found on duty drinking in bars or sleeping in their parked cruisers.

Bill Walczak experienced the inertia of the city government in 1975 in a summer work program run by the parks department, a repository for patronage jobs. Walczak was a brash kid from New Jersey who dropped out of Boston University when he moved to Dorchester's Codman Square, where he would later become a community leader. Of four people in the program assigned to clean up Hemenway Playground, a badly neglected park in Dorchester, Walczak was the only one who ever showed up for work.

One day, in a burst of enthusiasm, Walczak raked the park, filled seven trash barrels with broken glass and litter, and rolled them to the top of the hill. He then walked over to the local park department field office and told his foreman, Mr. Dougherty, that the barrels had to be removed before the local kids rolled them down the hill. There was a big crisis at Ronan Park, another Dorchester park, Dougherty replied. Some locals had complained to the mayor's office, so the parks department sent all available workers to clean it up. Why didn't Walczak go there to ask for help?

When Walczak arrived at Ronan Park, he found seven people idling where fifty had been assigned. Walczak approached two men sitting in the cab of an empty dump truck and asked them to pick up the barrels in Hemenway playground. "Naww, we're assigned to Ronan Park," the men replied, "and we ain't moving outta Ronan Park."

Walczak, steaming mad, walked into the Town Field Tavern and called the mayor's office. "Hi, this is Jimmy O'Connor, I'm up by Hemenway Park," he rasped in his best working-class Boston accent. "There's some barrels that gotta be picked up or the kids are gonna make a mess."

Sure enough, when Walczak entered the field office half an hour later, Dougherty yelled at him to tell the guys at Ronan Park that the mayor's office sent orders to get the barrels at Hemenway Park. Walczak returned to the men in the empty truck. "Dougherty says, 'The mayor's office wants you down at Hemenway *now* to pick up the barrels.'" One man turned to another, shook his head disgustedly, and said, "We ain't gonna get no fuckin' break today."[9]

Searching for a Way Out

Boston's government might have slipped into lethargy, but a local tradition of social activism suggested that the citizenry would not succumb without a fight. Throughout the 1960s, residents of the South End and northern Roxbury, led by African American activists such as Mel King and Ted Parrish, had formed community organizations to obtain better education, stop landlords from exploiting tenants, and prevent urban renewal schemes. In 1964 the United South End Settlements obtained a grant from the federal government and founded South End Community Development, one of the first community development organizations in the country, to rehabilitate deteriorated row houses for low-income families. Under its first executive director, Robert Whittlesey, a World War II veteran with degrees in civil engineering and planning, South End Community Development began building new housing as well as remodeling old, expanded its operations to sites across the metropolitan region, and in 1970 was renamed Greater Boston Community Development, Inc. or GBCD. (Renamed the Community Builders in 1988, it is today a national organization.) From 1969 to 1982, GBCD helped South End and northern Roxbury community organizations develop more than twelve hundred units of low-income housing.[10]

During the difficult years of the 1970s and early 1980s, dedicated Roxbury and Dorchester residents fought the undercurrents that threatened to drown their neighborhoods. Some were natives, such as Ken and Juanita Wade, who stayed in Roxbury even as other middle-class African Americans moved away. Ken Wade helped lead the Roxbury Neighborhood Council and a successful campaign to get mortgage loans in the inner city—work that years later would lead him to become the New England district director of the Neighborhood Reinvestment Corporation. His wife, Juanita, took an interest in education and was elected three times to the Boston School Committee.[11]

Other activists, like Bob Haas, were newcomers. Adventurous young people—musicians, artists, and recent college graduates—moved to the inner city for the low rents and prime location. Some grew attached to their neighborhoods and remained to struggle for their adopted communities. Charlotte Kahn, for example, was a white photographer who moved to northern Roxbury and worked with African American leaders, Augusta Bailey and Mel King, to build a neighborhood garden and then helped establish a citywide organization of community gardens.[12]

The activists started dozens of nonprofit community development corporations or CDCs in order to rebuild the homes and revive the commercial life of Boston's inner-city neighborhoods. The CDCs were small storefront operations run by neighborhood volunteers and a few underpaid staff members. Some of the CDCs failed or accomplished little, but others—such as Dorchester Bay Economic Development Corporation in north Dorchester, Madison Park Development Corporation and Nuestra Comunidad Development Corporation in Roxbury, and Urban Edge Housing Corporation in Jamaica Plain—persevered to become significant real estate developers and service providers.

In Codman Square, newly arrived urban pioneers, African Americans, and some of the remaining middle-class whites organized a neighborhood association, a CDC, and a health center. When the residents founded the Codman Square Health Center in 1979, they made Bill Walczak, who had come to their attention by asking a lot of questions at the civic association's meetings, the director. Walczak was not particularly interested in health care; he simply felt that something had to be done for Codman Square. There was only one doctor left in the neighborhood, and the public library had announced it was moving up the street from its old building, opposite the abandoned Lithgow building. Walczak, whose motto is "better to seek forgiveness than permission," wangled a space for the health center in the basement of the old library and took over the rest of the building as a squatter when the city government was looking the other way.[13]

To stop fires from consuming their neighborhood, activists researched the arson around Codman Square. They discovered that the buildings most likely to burn had either been sold frequently or had no tenants. The Codman Square

The staff of the Codman Square Health Center (Bill Walczak at left)
on the day it opened, November 1979. Courtesy of William Walczak.

citizens systematically identified all these buildings and passed the information to state Attorney General Frank Bellotti who wrote a letter to the owners telling them that if their buildings mysteriously caught fire, his office was ready to investigate. The number of arson fires dropped noticeably, and some owners offered to give the buildings to the Codman Square CDC.[14]

But there were as many defeats as victories. In 1981 the Codman Square CDC opened a supermarket to replace the one that had closed, but the local people knew little about running a grocery business. The store quickly went bankrupt and took the CDC with it. A new CDC named the Codman Square

William Jones (left) and Bill Walczak in Codman Square. Behind them is
the old Second Church of Dorchester (left) and the vacant
Girls Latin School building, March 1983. Courtesy of Janet Knott,
republished with permission of Globe Newspaper, Inc.

Boarded-up Lithgow commercial building and empty stores in Codman Square, c. 1982. Courtesy of Codman Square Neighborhood Development Corporation.

Housing (later changed to Neighborhood) Development Corporation was formed; headed by Bill Jones, an African American who had grown up in a Roxbury public housing project, it spent years trying to redevelop the Lithgow commercial block. Sometimes Jones had financing, but no major tenant; at other times he had a tenant, but no financing.[15]

Meanwhile, a tree had grown through the roof of the boarded-up Lithgow Building, a visible symbol to those who sped through Codman Square on their way to somewhere else that the neighborhood was still a wilderness.[16]

Setting the Stage for Transformation

The CDCs clearly needed help, and it came in various forms. The activists built a pipeline from the state government when one of their own, Mel King, was elected to the state legislature. King also taught at MIT in the Department of Urban Studies and Planning and used his diverse occupations to bring together activists and academics at Wednesday morning breakfast meetings in an MIT conference room to figure out ways to bolster community development. Out of the well-fed assembly—King himself prepared the fish-fry breakfasts—came legislation, which King sponsored and Governor Michael Dukakis endorsed; it created two state agencies to provide loans, grants, and consultations to community and economic development projects and a line-item in the state budget that gave CDCs money for operations. As a result, Massachusetts became unusually hospitable to community development.[17]

The CDCs also received a giant boost from the Boston Housing Partnership (BHP), an early and conspicuous example of Boston's flair for collaboration in the cause of community development. Yet when it started, few would have predicted success for an alliance of downtown business people, city officials—who were traditionally suspicious of one another—and the ragtag CDCs.

The housing partnership was dreamed up by David Mundell, the head of the city's Neighborhood Development and Employment Agency. Mundell's agency administered federal programs such as job training and community development block grants, which allowed local governments to fund a variety of local improvement projects. The election of Ronald Reagan to the presidency in 1980, however, spelled doom for those federal programs. Reagan was a sworn enemy of big government, and liberal social programs were his favorite target.

But the idea of public-private partnerships was in the air, and Mundell looked to the business world to fill the gap created by the Reagan cutbacks. Mundell organized a Private Industry Council, in accordance with recent federal legislation that encouraged business-government collaborations to provide job training to the unskilled. Then Mundell had the idea to form a similar public-private partnership to develop low-income housing, and called on banker William Edgerly to organize and chair it.[18]

Edgerly feels unusually passionate about solving urban problems. He had helped establish Goals for Boston to rally the city's leaders to help different areas of city life. In the area of education, he convinced the Vault, a group of the city's corporate executives, to support the Boston Compact, an agreement that private companies would hire low-income youth if the school department gave them an appropriate education.

Despite his dignified Boston Yankee manners, Edgerly was a risk taker who had rescued the venerable State Street Bank and Trust Company. The bank had originally managed trust funds for old Boston families but during the 1970s had fallen on hard times. In 1975 State Street's board members conducted a nationwide search for a chief executive officer but turned to Edgerly, a fellow board member and an executive of the Cabot Corporation, even though he was not a banker. Edgerly embarked on what the bank officers called "the bold strategy," which took State Street Bank away from traditional banking and made it a highly profitable service provider for the mutual fund industry.[19]

Although the new housing partnership had a leader, troubles at the Neighborhood Development and Employment Agency almost killed the collaborative before it was born. A series of newspaper articles blasted the agency as corrupt, and the inspector general of the U.S. Department of Housing and Urban Development (HUD) launched an investigation into the agency's administration of the community development block grants. Relations between the agency and Boston's neighborhood organizations were badly strained because mayor Kevin White and his political operatives disliked any community organization they could not control, and most of the CDCs prized their independence.

Adding to the neighborhood development agency's troubles, its director, David Mundell, resigned. His deputy, Paul Grogan, a serious young man who had worked with Edgerly on the Boston Compact, succeeded him. Suddenly placed at the helm of an unpopular agency beset by corruption charges, Grogan decided to start funding CDCs. Years later as president of Local Initiatives Support Corporation (LISC), the national nonprofit lender and philanthropic organization, Grogan became a leading champion of CDCs, but at the time he knew little about them. Grogan just needed some time to solve his agency's problems and hoped that bypassing the city's controversial programs in favor of the CDCs might win back some of the trust of neighborhood residents.[20]

But to right the listing Neighborhood Development and Employment Agency, Grogan had to protect it from the mayor's lieutenants who wanted to use its funds for political operations. Grogan argued that the agency's critics and investigators would interpret such interference as evidence of the agency's corruption. For the most part, this strategy—based on what Grogan likes to call the "utility of trouble"—worked. At one point, the political operatives tried to reassert their control of the block grant program, and the mayor appeared to go along with them. Grogan, a controlled man who never throws tantrums at work, met with the mayor. "Tell them to back the fuck off," he angrily warned White, "or I'm out of here." The mayor sent the word, and the operatives never interfered with the city's community development program again.

Grogan actually used the neighborhood development agency's troubles to get the Boston Housing Partnership off the ground. Edgerly started the collaborative in 1983 by enlisting representatives of banks, insurance companies, and government departments, such as the Massachusetts Housing Finance Agency, to serve on the board of directors; but when he called the first meeting of the Partnership, he had no money or staff to plan, let alone develop, housing. Meanwhile, Grogan had learned from the federal investigation that his agency was inept, but not corrupt, and had funded numerous programs that were never carried out. Grogan rescinded the funds for the moribund programs and used some of the windfall of close to $50 million dollars, almost double his yearly allocation, to bankroll the Boston Housing Partnership. Ironically, this public-private partnership began life supported solely by government funds.[21]

Even with funds, Edgerly still needed to find someone to carry out the partnership's housing program, and in his search, he consulted with Bob Whittlesey's right-hand man and successor at GBCD, Pat Clancy. Whittlesey

Patrick Clancy (center) at a meeting with Mary Longley and others from the Tenants Development Corporation, Boston, c. 1974. Courtesy of Robert Whittlesey.

had hired Clancy back in the 1960s to research whether nonprofit low-income housing developers could use tax depreciation laws to syndicate their deals the way commercial real estate firms did. At the time, Clancy was a long-haired, radical law student working for Legal Services. Before long he became GBCD's principal deal maker, helping CDCs finance housing projects not only by garnering government grants but also by syndicating mortgage pools organized by for-profit subsidiaries. Clancy, who had become director of GBCD after Whittlesey stepped down in 1977, persuaded Edgerly that CDCs could develop the housing for the Partnership. Edgerly hired Whittlesey as director of the Boston Housing Partnership, and Whittlesey brought Clancy and GBCD on board to put the housing deals together.[22]

They were an unlikely but effective team. The zealous Clancy built the complicated financial deals for the development projects. Whittlesey, a button-down type, understood Clancy's financing arrangements and vouched for their soundness. And the persistent Edgerly kept the whole program moving. He pushed his board and staff to take care of their assignments—Clancy remembers meeting Edgerly one afternoon at 3:30 and agreeing to carry out three tasks. When he returned to his GBCD office at 4:00, he received a phone call from the banker asking him how he was getting along with his tasks. The executive used all the resources at his command, including the State Street Bank's financial analysts, to persuade investors that the Partnership's program was viable.[23]

Boston's First Collaboration

The Partnership largely improvised BHP I, the city's first great venture in community development collaboration. The leaders—Whittlesey, Clancy, Edgerly, and Grogan—were convinced that only a large-scale program would make a significant impact upon the neighborhoods. The CDCs would search for,

The power of collaboration: (left to right) Elizabeth Smith, executive director of the Hyams Foundation, Robert Whittlesey, executive director of the Boston Housing Partnership, and Anna Faith Jones, executive director of the Boston Foundation, 1985. Courtesy of Amos Williams.

acquire, and redevelop deteriorated and abandoned apartment buildings, and the Boston Housing Partnership would arrange the financing for the rehabilitation. Beyond that, the Partnership's leaders had little idea what would be possible. They set a goal of renovating a thousand dwelling units simply because the figure, according to Grogan, "had some zeros on it and seemed like a significant number."[24]

Through BHP I, ten CDCs would develop 700 units in sixty-nine buildings throughout Boston at a cost of $40 million, but with more than over thirty sources of funding, the financing was extremely complicated.[25] The lawyer for the Partnership, Katharine Bachman, went to Pat Clancy's office just prior to the closing of BHP I to get the details of the deal for the legal documents she had to file the next day. Bachman recalls that when she arrived at Clancy's office, she found the deal maker examining an enormous spreadsheet that covered his desk—in 1983 the computer and accounting software programs were not yet part of everyday life. Bachman began with simple but essential questions, "Who is the first mortgagee? Who is the second?"

Clancy waved at the figures spread across his desk and answered impatiently, "Here are the sources of the money, and here are the uses, can't you see? Here are the sources."

"Pat, when I record the mortgage," Bachman explained, "I need the names of the mortgagees . . ."

"Oh *that*," the finance wizard replied, "I haven't figured that out yet . . . what else do you need?"[26]

Eventually Bachman got the information, but the Partnership had underestimated costs badly. About 40 percent of the buildings, far more than the Partnership estimated, required complete rebuilding of the interiors. The decision of the Partnership to pay prevailing union wages raised costs, as did the passage of stricter and more expensive lead paint removal laws. CDCs were unable to rent to tenants with Section 8 vouchers as they had planned because the conditions of the rehabbed apartments were not up to HUD standards. To make matters worse, the Partnership had put aside too little reserve to absorb the unexpected costs. The shortfall required that the BHP I projects receive tax abatements from the government—which they got, thanks to the political clout of BHP board members—and kept Clancy busy for the first two years finding additional financing.[27]

In the neighborhoods, the CDCs that were designated to carry out the BHP I redevelopment projects encountered problems because inexperienced staff members bought properties that turned out to be disasters. As part of BHP I, the Dorchester Bay Economic Development Corporation acquired a building through foreclosure from a landlady known as Sarah the Torch. It was located across the street from the house of the organization's director, Jim Luckett. Luckett—a former economics professor who had given up an academic career to direct Dorchester Bay EDC—remembers the place as a madhouse. The grocery store owner on the first floor attacked and killed one of the tenants with a knife. In the cellar, tenants had attached garden hoses and wires to the gas and electric lines to avoid paying utility bills. Not surprisingly, the building caught fire. After the fire department left, Luckett started to board up the building, but he was shocked to find an invalid woman huddled on the top floor. The ambulance drivers he called refused to bring her out, so Luckett himself carried the woman down four flights of stairs.[28]

The shortage of BHP I funds also caused headaches for CDC staff members. Most compensated by cutting down the rehab work—ensuring they would have to do more work on the same buildings later. Dorchester Bay EDC, however, tried to complete the total renovation within the original budget in ways that Luckett years later characterized as "insane." To renovate one of the buildings, he hired a contractor who gave the lowest bid but could not post a bond and so instead gave the organization a letter of credit (which authorizes the bearer to borrow up to a certain amount of money). The contractor went broke. When Dorchester Bay EDC drew on the contractor's letter of credit to cover his costs, the man who had issued it sued (unsuccessfully) on the grounds that Luckett was stealing his money.[29]

Despite all the finagling it took to straighten out the deals, BHP I was a major accomplishment. It not only reclaimed 700 derelict units in Boston's low-income communities but it also made downtown government and bank officials believe in the CDCs. BHP I set the stage for later community development projects that would transform the image of inner-city Boston.

The Economic Tide Turns

In the 1980s the conditions for community development in Boston improved dramatically. Boston benefited from an economic boom—known as "the Massachusetts miracle"—which reversed the city's long-term population decline and prompted Governor Michael Dukakis to run for the presidency in 1988. Technology, medical care, and the mutual fund industry—Boston is the home of Fidelity Investments—drove the local economy and put serious money in the hands of the professionals in these fields. As in other large cities, it was the era of the free-spending Yuppies, the young urban professionals who helped set off the first big real estate boom the Hub had seen in decades. The city's foundations, corporations, and government would have money to spend on neighborhoods, if they saw fit.

The election in 1983 of a new mayor, Raymond Flynn, also boosted the cause of community development. Flynn, who came from the Irish neighborhood of South Boston, had run on a platform of helping the neighborhoods as well as downtown. He supported CDCs—the only official from the Kevin White administration whom Flynn asked to stay on was Paul Grogan—and channeled "linkage" funds from downtown development projects into low-income housing schemes in the inner-city.

Initially the economic boom concerned, rather than delighted, the residents of Boston's inner city. The boom helped turn the trickle of professionals who had been moving into the South End since the 1960s into a gush during the 1980s. As the renovation of nineteenth-century brownstones pressed forward, it pushed out low-income black and Puerto Rican residents, some to Roxbury and Dorchester. Residents of Roxbury looked at what was happening in the South End and became nervous about gentrification. The anxieties turned to panic in 1984 when the Boston Redevelopment Authority (BRA) prepared a plan for a $750 million complex of office towers, hotels, housing, parks, and light manufacturing in the Dudley Square area, the site of Roxbury's principal bus and train station.

The area did need improvement. Dudley Street crossed Roxbury between two desolate commercial centers—Dudley Square, once a business district second only to downtown Boston, and Upham's Corner in northern Dorchester. Toward Boston lay a belt of industrial buildings; inland were the winding residential streets that had been decimated by arson fires and subsequent demolition. By 1980, the Dudley neighborhood contained 840 vacant lots covering 177 acres.[30]

But Roxbury residents feared urban renewal projects, which in the 1950s and 1960s had demolished the vibrant ethnic West End neighborhood and a section of the South End where many blacks had lived. They did not think they could afford the new houses proposed in the BRA's Dudley area plan and doubted that the BRA would consult them in any meaningful way. The frightened residents enlisted in organizations to fend off the expected onslaught.

One of the new organizations became perhaps the most innovative community development collaboration in the Hub. The Dudley Street Neighborhood Initiative (DSNI) was founded in 1984 as an alliance of local social service agencies, CDCs, and churches. DSNI focused on a limited area (of approximately one and a half square miles) contiguous to Dudley Street and enjoyed the long-term financial backing of the philanthropic Riley Foundation.[31]

But for all its later success, DSNI got off to a rocky start. At its first public meeting, residents angrily challenged the right of the agency directors who lived outside the neighborhood to speak for the people of Roxbury. Unexpectedly, however, the meeting's leaders invited the dissidents to help lead the organization themselves. A number of the critics immediately joined the DSNI board, and one of them, Ché Madyun, a mother of three, was elected president.

Led by the former dissidents, DSNI emphasized local participation and community organization rather than social service assistance. The organization was highly democratic and multi-ethnic. Its by-laws required neighborhood residents to hold a majority on the board of directors and set aside three board seats for each of the four major ethnic groups in the Dudley Street area: black, Latino, Cape Verdean, and white. The DSNI board chose community organizer Peter Medoff, a Boston native who had worked in New York City and Hartford, rather than a social worker, to be the group's director.

Medoff and DSNI leaders gained local support by waging a Don't Dump On Us campaign to end the use of the Dudley Street area as a disposal district. The organization succeeded in forcing the city government to tow abandoned cars and close illegal trash transfer stations, both major grievances of Roxbury residents.

To counter the BRA's redevelopment plan, DSNI organized a series of community workshops to prepare a master plan to develop the area's abundant vacant lots. The residents devised a plan for developing an "urban village" of houses, parks, and shops by means of neighborhood control, possession of a critical mass of land, and simultaneous new construction and building renovation. But the vacant lots presented a major roadblock on the way to the urban village. The lots owned by the city, about half the total, were too scattered to develop in any coherent way. The rest of the lots belonged to private owners who were delinquent in paying taxes on the properties; foreclosing on each of them would delay development virtually forever.

To help them carry out the urban village plan until they hired a permanent director of development, DSNI's leaders turned to GBCD. Peter Munkenbeck, the GBCD consultant, suggested that eminent domain, a legal tool used by urban renewal authorities to force owners to sell their land for redevelopment, might solve their dilemma.

The lawyers who researched the issue for DSNI then made an intriguing discovery: Massachusetts law allowed the BRA to authorize an "urban redevelopment corporation" to exercise the power of eminent domain. Theoretically, DSNI could be that corporation. But would the city allow an upstart community group this coveted power?

In an unprecedented move, DSNI began to look for support for acquiring eminent domain authority. In March 1988 Medoff brought up the vacant lot problem in a casual conversation with Stephen Coyle, the flamboyant director of the BRA, and was startled when Coyle on his own suggested that DSNI form a separate corporation and apply for eminent domain authority. Convincing Lisa Chapnick, the hard-nosed boss of Flynn's neighborhood development agency, was not as easy. Chapnick was worried that the group had taken on too large a piece of land, but at the DSNI presentation, Medoff disarmed the agency officials by rolling out a map of the world and declaring this was the area DSNI proposed to take by eminent domain. After the laughter died down, Medoff, Madyun, and two other DSNI leaders made their case. Chapnick considered some of the DSNI plan completely unrealistic, "but the sincerity and honesty— I bought it. I just bought the people sitting in that room."[32]

The campaign to create an urban village in the Dudley Street neighborhood gathered momentum. In August 1988 DSNI organized Dudley Neighbors, Incorporated, to be the nonprofit urban redevelopment corporation that would exercise eminent domain. DSNI turned opposition to support by asking representatives of the Minority Developers Association, a group of predominantly African American real estate developers opposed to nonprofits, and the Roxbury Neighborhood Council, a district-wide planning body, to serve on the board of the Dudley Neighbors. The next month DSNI beat out the Boston parks department in a competition for a $1 million park development grant from the Massachusetts Department of Environmental Management to create Dudley Commons as a gateway to the district.

Meanwhile, Mayor Flynn enthusiastically endorsed DSNI's effort to acquire eminent domain authority. Flynn believed that city government existed to help communities control their destiny, and he thought that despite the obvious risks, DSNI could pull off the project. The city's development agency and DSNI negotiated a contract to work together to develop the Dudley triangle. On November 10, 1988, DSNI officers were invited to City Hall to meet with Chapnick and the mayor prior to attending the BRA board meeting

Dudley Town Common, a centerpiece of the Dudley Street Neighborhood Initiative's urban village plan, Dudley Street and Blue Hill Avenue, Roxbury, August 2002. Courtesy of Glenna Lang.

in which the board was expected to vote in favor of the proposal. Roxbury residents, DSNI members, and television camera crews waited at the BRA board room for the historic moment.

But at the last minute, the BRA board refused to approve the eminent domain deal. An irate Flynn asked his visitors to step out and called the BRA board into his office. BRA director Coyle marched the recalcitrant, glum board members in a single file past the DSNI people into Flynn's office. "It looked," Peter Medoff recalled in his history of DSNI, "like a scene out of the book *Make Way for Ducklings*."[33] Angry shouting could be heard behind the closed doors as the mayor, it turned out later, raged at the board members who felt only the government planners could decide what was best for a neighborhood.

After an hour, the board members emerged looking even glummer than when they entered. Chairman Coyle flashed a thumbs up sign at the DSNI representatives, and the board, two of whose members would shortly resign, returned to their meeting room and at last gave their consent. For the first time in the history of the country, citizens held the power of eminent domain to redevelop their own neighborhood.

A Face Lift for the Inner City

The Hub's community development alliances achieved their greatest successes during the 1980s and early 1990s when redevelopment projects, in the words of a Roxbury activist, "literally gave Boston's inner-city a face-lift."[34] The second Boston Housing Partnership drive had the most visible impact. In BHP II, as it was called, the Partnership and local CDCs redeveloped the Granite Properties, 51 three- and four-story apartment buildings in Roxbury and Dorchester that the government and private owners had tried and failed miserably to preserve for more than twenty years.[35]

The apartment buildings of Roxbury and Dorchester stood astride the residential boulevards like great ships sailing on the ocean waves. They filled entire blocks, with their walls of dark red brick spread flat or in undulating bays, punctuated by the arches over the entryways and the granite that crowned the entrances and windows. Once the envy of Boston's upwardly mobile Irish and Jews, from the 1960s their apartments were crowded with low-income African Americans and Puerto Ricans. Landlords cut back on repairs and set off a vicious cycle of deterioration, tenant resentment, and further deterioration.

In the wake of the urban riots of the 1960s, HUD officials in Washington gave developers low mortgages and rent supplements to buy and renovate inner-city apartment buildings in a new urban renewal program called the Boston Urban Rehabilitation Program or BURP. (An enthusiastic Boston Gas executive, who procured a contract for his utility company to serve the buildings, tried to get his public relations staff to publicize the company's role with the slogan, "When you BURP, think gas."[36]) But when vandals and thieves plagued the renovation sites, the cost of redevelopment spiraled upward. Having already taken their profits, the developers had no incentive—and little means—to maintain the BURP properties.

The Granite Properties (so named for the granite entrances) contained about two thousand units, the majority of the BURP buildings and the worst maintained. Located on main streets throughout Roxbury and Dorchester, these eyesores had a depressing effect on the surrounding neighborhoods. In the 1970s drug dealers moved into several of the buildings and terrorized their neighbors. A tenants' association, aided by legal service lawyers, filed suit to correct the terrible conditions, but meanwhile the number of empty apartments in the Granite Properties increased rapidly.

By 1984 HUD had taken possession of the Granite Properties. Following the free-market philosophy of President Ronald Reagan, HUD officials planned to sell the buildings to the highest bidder. But the leaders of Boston neighborhood and nonprofit housing organizations protested that this plan would bring a new set of absentee landlords, further deterioration, and more crime. They proposed that under the auspices of BHP and with the aid of the Massachusetts Housing Finance Agency, seven CDCs would purchase, renovate, and manage the troublesome buildings. After a long struggle, Mayor Ray Flynn, state officials, and neighborhood leaders convinced HUD officials to sell about half the Granite Properties—containing 958 dwelling units—to the nonprofits instead of the highest bidders.[37]

The BHP collaborators and CDCs swore that this time they would fix the Granite Properties the right way. Jim Luckett, the new director of BHP, remembered vividly his experiences at the Dorchester Bay EDC and insisted "with a spine of steel" that the CDCs get adequate reserves and subsidies to avoid the problems of BHP I and the disaster of BURP. The BHP II project also allowed CDCs to charge the Partnership development fees to pay for such expenses as staff salaries and office rents. For the first time, Boston's participating CDCs would have a little financial cushion.[38]

Nonetheless, BHP II put Boston's community development alliances to the test. In 1987 neighborhood groups—including Nuestra Comunidad and Dorchester Bay EDC—lined up to rehabilitate the Granite Properties. The Codman Square Housing Development Corporation (Codman Square HDC) won the right to redevelop 330 dwelling units in several apartment buildings on Columbia Road and Washington Street, several blocks from Codman Square. Invaded by drug addicts and dealers, the buildings were a nightmare. The management firm working for HUD had given up trying to maintain the Columbia-Washington apartments. To add insult to injury, on the day before the closing in which Codman Square HDC took over the properties, the firm removed the cores from all the locks that had not been destroyed.[39]

Sally Williams had moved to the second floor of one of the BURP-remodeled buildings, 102 Columbia Road, in 1969, but watched in dismay as shady characters took over apartments and hallways. They brazenly took drugs, rolled dice against her door, and left trash for the building's roaches and rats to feast on. Here, as in the other Columbia-Washington properties, drug users broke the locks on the doors to steal from and lounge in the apartments. A man upstairs dealt drugs and invited drug users to his apartment. "You'd think he was leading a train," Williams observed, as she watched groups of seven or eight march up behind him, stay for a half hour, and then leave.[40]

One day, some of the drug dealers argued, started shooting at each other, then ran into Columbia Road and continued firing even after the police arrived. The situation was no better in other buildings, such as 108 Columbia Road where the authorities regularly pulled out the dead bodies of addicts who had overdosed.

By the time Codman Square HDC took over her building, Williams did not want anyone to know she lived there. She was ashamed to let her friends see the boarded-up, abandoned-looking building. For fear of being assaulted, she tried to prevent strangers from finding out that she and another woman were the only tenants in the thirteen-unit building.[41]

Obviously the presence of drug dealers and users who had taken up residence in the Columbia-Washington apartment buildings spelled doom for any rehabilitation effort, but removing drug dealers is easier said than done. Some of the dealers knew that they could be evicted for nonpayment of rent and were scrupulous about paying their rent on time. Moreover, tenant activists, especially the Legal Service lawyers who provided free legal aid to low-income clients, fought all evictions as a matter of principle. Even if the neighborhood CDCs won, these court proceedings diverted precious time and energy.[42]

Getting criminals arrested was also difficult. Most of the law-abiding tenants in the Columbia-Washington apartment buildings and other Granite Properties were too intimidated to report the dealers and other wrongdoers. When people did call, the police took forever to respond, claiming that another police district had jurisdiction.[43]

Fortunately, the Massachusetts Housing Finance Agency (MHFA), which floated bonds to finance BHP II, spearheaded a multipronged campaign to restore law and order in the Granite Properties. Displaying Boston's unique capacity for effective collaboration, the state agency convened the Inner City Task Force—made up of representatives of government departments, the CDCs and managers of the Granite Properties, tenant organizations, and residents. The Task Force met with the leaders of the Greater Boston Legal Services and argued that the lawyers should first protect the rights of the low-income tenants who did *not* break the law and terrorize their neighbors. The argument convinced the Legal Service lawyers to cease representing known drug dealers and other scofflaws in eviction cases.[44]

The Massachusetts Housing Finance Agency also hired a private security firm run by Eric Straughter, a huge, formidable-looking man and a nephew of local Muslim leader Don Muhammed, to patrol the Granite Properties and ride herd on the bad guys. Not only did Straughter and his men look tough, they were designated special police officers who carried guns and made arrests, thanks to an agreement the MHFA reached with the police department. At the same time, the Inner City Task Force persuaded the police to settle their disputes over district jurisdictions and respond immediately to calls in the Granite Properties. A series of drug raids soon followed.[45]

The staff of the Codman Square Housing Development Corporation took steps to prevent the recurrence of drug problems in the Columbia-Washington apartment buildings. As they consulted with the tenants' association about the renovations, they enlisted the tenants' help in identifying drug dealers to keep them from returning. Using funds from the MHFA, the Codman Square organization also hired young men and teenagers who lived in and around the buildings to work with the contractors on the rehab project. Eventually the young people formed their own contracting company.[46]

A few weeks after the beginning of the push to civilize the Granite Properties, Codman Square HDC's new property manager reported that something strange was going on in the Columbia-Washington apartment buildings. The

102–108 Columbia Road, at corner of Columbia Road and Washington Street, after rehabilitation by Codman Square Housing Development Corporation, August 2002. Courtesy of Glenna Lang.

manager was paying large amounts of money to the Roto-Rooter company for cleaning the sewer drains. Old buildings often developed expensive problems with the heating and electric systems, but it was highly unusual to have sewer problems. The Codman Square staff eventually solved the mystery when they noticed that the Roto-Rooter calls always occurred soon after the police raids: tenants were flushing drugs down the toilet and blocking the drainage pipes.[47]

A Community Development Breakthrough

By 1988 Codman Square community organizations had revived enough to launch a neighborhood planning drive, but the local activists knew that as long as the Lithgow Building, Codman Square's most important commercial building, remained boarded up with a tree growing out of it, this corner of south Dorchester would never be anything but a place from which to escape.

A small but significant break occurred that year when Bob Mahoney, head of the Bank of Boston's Massachusetts division, told Ada Focer, a board member of the Codman Square Housing Development Corporation, of his plans to remodel the Codman Square branch the bank had tried to close ten years earlier. Mahoney, who would later become president of Citizens Bank in New England, was an unusual banker for the time because he believed that banks could earn profits in inner-city neighborhoods. Focer made the case that the Lithgow building would make a better site for a branch, and Mahoney signed on. Despite the patent riskiness of the Lithgow project, Mahoney persuaded the Bank of Boston not only to help finance the Lithgow building but also to become its first-floor tenant.[48]

Still, the Lithgow rehab project was bound to fail unless Bill Jones, director of the Codman Square HDC, found a tenant to rent the second and third floors. Fortunately for him, state officials of all persuasions respected Jones for having made good on a defaulted loan that the bank had all but forgotten. Codman Square HDC had taken the loan in the 1970s based on the state's written agreement to pay it fees for redeveloping a building, but officials under the conservative governor Ed King reneged on the fees and told Jones to "sue the state or suck it in and move on." In those days banks made loans to CDCs strictly as a philanthropy and wrote them off immediately. Most people in the nonprofit field would simply have dropped the matter.[49]

After Michael Dukakis was elected governor in 1983, however, Jones went to the new state officials and persuaded them to pay the development fees— not to profit the Codman Square organization but to pay a debt it had taken on in good faith. "While I don't think the bank is going to come after us and take our typewriters," he told them, "I would feel a lot better in life if I could pay them." So it was that two years after the bank's officers had written off his loan, Jones startled them by walking in and announcing, "Here's your money."[50]

Jones pursued the directors of the Dorchester Counseling Center, a locally run state-funded mental health clinic, who wanted to leave their present location in a former mental hospital, to be the anchor tenant at Lithgow. However, seemingly insurmountable obstacles soon appeared. First, the going rent for commercial space in an economically depressed area would not provide enough rent to carry the costs of the building. Second, Massachusetts authorized appropriations for state institutions only one year at a time, but local banks, reeling from the savings-and-loan banking crisis, refused to approve a mortgage unless the tenant leased the property for five years. It did not matter that, as Jones argued, once the Counseling Center moved into the building, "the likelihood that it would move out was slim or none."[51]

Because of his personal reputation and skill in building alliances, Jones was able to call on government officials to help seal the deal. He successfully lobbied the governor's office to locate the Counseling Center in the Lithgow Building at the prevailing rent for all of Boston, not just for depressed areas. Dorchester's state legislators, led by Paul White, a senator from a conservative white area, convinced a reluctant state legislature to approve a special long-term lease for the Dorchester Counseling Center.[52]

Finally, in another example of a successful community development collaboration, the Bank of Boston, Massachusetts state agencies, and the city of Boston put up more than $7.5 million to do the deal. The Codman Square HDC reconstructed the Lithgow Building—half of it was built anew—and immediately behind it developed thirty-one rental apartments, of which fifteen were subsidized for low-income tenants and the rest were let at market rates.[53]

The completion of the Lithgow Building project in 1991 had a dramatic effect on Codman Square. Within four years, over forty new businesses opened there, including the first pharmacy in more than two decades. Bill Walczak helped lead a multimillion dollar capital campaign for the Codman Square Health Center, with the result that in 1995 the Center created a shiny new

Lithgow Building renovated at last, 1995. Courtesy of William Walczak.

medical facility in a former nursing home across from the Lithgow Building. A McDonald's franchise opened in the former Smoke Shop where drugs had been sold openly. An annual historic house tour advertised the charms of south Dorchester. And suddenly, local inhabitants who for years had claimed they resided in other neighborhoods began to say they lived in Codman Square.[54]

Boston Fights Crime

Just as Boston's CDCs, government agencies, and individuals had begun to make progress in creating livable neighborhoods, a wave of youth violence engulfed the inner city. Characteristically, Boston responded to the surge of crime by forming partnerships, which became a successful model for cities across the country. Like the Boston Housing Partnership, however, the collaborations proceeded by trial and error, not predetermined strategy. "Boston's response," concludes John Buntin, a student of Boston's anti-crime programs, "evolved over a period of years out of the work done by a disparate group of people—police, probation officers, ministers, social workers, and academics— who sought each other out and jointly created something no single one of them had envisioned."[55]

In the late 1980s, Boston's inner-city street gangs began dealing crack cocaine and amassing guns and rifles to protect their share of the market. As police patrols picked up dazed "crack zombies," gang members fought with knives and guns over drugs, turf, girlfriends, and slights real and imagined. Gun battles killed not only gang members but also innocent bystanders including a grandmother sitting in her living room and a twelve-year-old girl standing on a sidewalk.

Fueled by the growing number of youth murders, the city's homicide rate skyrocketed. By 1990 the total number of homicides in Boston had soared to a record 152, over twice the figure of just three years earlier. Remarkably, seventy-three of these victims were twenty-four years old and under. The unprecedented bloodletting climaxed on Halloween night when eight teenagers pulled a twenty-six-year-old woman from south Dorchester into the Franklin Field athletic grounds and beat, raped, and stabbed her 132 times. "She was a loving person," the stunned father of the victim lamented, "and she didn't deserve to die this way."[56]

Bostonians improvised a wide variety of volunteer efforts to fight the crime wave. Often aided by CDCs, they formed hundreds of crime watches to monitor their streets. One man organized a group named Gang Peace to stop the fighting on Dorchester's Blue Hill Avenue. New nonprofit organizations such as Citizens for Safety and Drop-a-Dime targeted crime and drugs; others such as City Year, begun in 1988 and now a national organization, attempted to provide youth with alternatives to gang activities. A local television station, Channel 4, led its own campaign called "Stop the Violence."

The city government also took action. The director of the city's Youth Services created a new program called Streetworkers in which youth workers would build relationships with gang members who did not usually come to community centers, then try to get them involved in positive activities such as after-school recreation, midnight basketball, and summer jobs. Mayor Raymond Flynn also announced a Safe Neighborhood Initiative, which provided a forum for local leaders and government officials to discuss strategies for dealing with youth violence.

Unfortunately, few neighborhood residents trusted the Boston police. The police department's Citywide Anti-Crime Unit responded to violence by stopping and searching any youth they suspected of being a gang member, but Boston's blacks and Hispanics felt the unit harassed all minority youths. Many officers belonged to the "bang 'em up, lock 'em up" school of policing and thought that the Streetworkers and Eugene Rivers, a Pentecostal minister who was trying to reach troubled youth in Dorchester, were little better than gang members. Then in September 1989, in a crime that gained national notoriety, Charles Stuart, a white man, called the police from his car near a Roxbury public housing project and told them that a black man had just shot him and murdered his wife. Ordered to find the suspect, the police rounded up all young blacks near the project. Only later did they discover that Stuart himself was the murderer.

In 1990 the police department attempted to improve its image and effectiveness by disbanding the Anti-Crime Unit and forming a much larger Anti-Gang Violence Unit. After a slight improvement from 1990 to 1992, however, the problem of violence in Boston persisted. The number of total and youth homicides dropped to just under eighty and forty, respectively, approximately the levels where they remained, like a stuck gauge, for the following three years. In May 1992, several youths interrupted a funeral for a gang member of Morning Star Baptist Church in the Mattapan neighborhood and, in front of hundreds of mourners, attacked and stabbed a young man in the church. Another round of killings followed. In response, a group of black ministers, including Eugene Rivers, organized the Ten Point Coalition to mobilize churches to stop the gang violence. Several black clergy took to the streets to help gang members who were not violent criminals to stay out of trouble.[57]

Meanwhile, quietly and on their own initiative, some rank-and-file members of the city's law enforcement agencies began to build a new coordinated approach to the youth violence problem. Bill Stewart, a probation officer in Dorchester District Court, who had recently been shifted from the juvenile to the adult division, noticed that the same teenagers who had been on his case load were being re-arrested as adults. At his suggestion, the District Court established a new unit, Youthful Offenders Group, to deal with those aged seventeen to twenty-four as a single group. Stewart's cases were the youths who were being wounded and killed on the streets of Boston. "Our office looked like a war zone," Stewart described the scene, with "kids shot in the face. Somebody with a colostomy bag on. Somebody with their leg shot off below the knee . . ."[58]

To put some teeth into probation, Stewart and his colleagues at the Youthful Offenders Group convinced the Dorchester judges to impose strict curfews, a requirement to attend school or report weekly on their job search, and a prohibition against associating publicly with any group of three or more people. But there were too few probation officers to monitor and arrest wayward kids, and the police rarely coordinated with probation officers. Youths on probation continued to commit mayhem on the streets after curfew—three of those arrested in the Halloween murder case were on probation and under curfew orders. As far as Stewart was concerned, these youths were giving probation officers the finger.[59]

The police began to take probation officers seriously, however, after Stewart found that one of his probation cases had participated in the Morning Star Church attack and pressured him into identifying the assailants in front of a grand jury. Stewart now joined the monthly strategy meetings of the Anti-Gang Violence Unit where he explained that probation officers had the authority to arrest probation violators. The cops asked Stewart if he would actually accompany them on their rounds. Certainly, he replied, because right now probation is a joke.

Despite opposition from members of their respective departments, probation officers and police officers began to visit the homes of kids sentenced to probation. Surprisingly, most mothers who met them at the door were delighted to see them. "Probation?" Stewart recalled them saying, "What kept you? God bless you for being here." Sometimes the officers talked with the youths or counseled a mother who was unable to cope with her son. Other times, especially when kids were not home in violation of their curfew, the officers searched rooms for firearms and drugs and made arrests.[60]

Under pressure from a blue-ribbon panel to clean up the police department, Mayor Flynn in June 1993 appointed William Bratton, an ambitious former Boston cop, as commissioner of Boston's besieged police force. (Bratton would later serve as police commissioner of New York and Los Angeles.) Like Paul Grogan years before at the Neighborhood Development Agency, Bratton took advantage of the crisis. He announced he would rebuild the relationship with the city's minority population and meet with black elected officials and ministers such as Eugene Rivers. He transferred police with a record of complaints out of the inner-city neighborhoods and put officers on beat patrols. To demonstrate compassion for poor inner-city kids, Bratton started the Youth Service Program in which police officers visited schools to talk to students.[61]

At the same time, Bratton escalated the drive against Boston's street gangs by setting up a new interagency collaborative. The Youth Violence Strike Force included Boston police officers and personnel from such agencies as the parole board, the state Department of Corrections, the county prosecutors' office, and the housing and transit authority police forces. The Strike Force also worked closely with the federal Bureau of Alcohol, Tobacco and Firearms (ATF) and Drug Enforcement Agency (DEA). To command the Strike Force, Bratton appointed a tough veteran of the Citywide Anti-Crime Unit, Detective Sergeant Paul Joyce. An intense-looking, intimidating cop—he shaved his head, wore a goatee, and rarely smiled—Joyce proved to be an intelligent leader and a perceptive law enforcement officer.

Since the Anti-Gang Violence Unit already conducted nighttime intelligence and anti-drug operations, the Strike Force members chose to pursue people with outstanding arrest warrants, especially dangerous offenders who used firearms. In early 1994, Joyce contacted and offered to work with the Boston branch of the state's Department of Youth Services, the agency responsible for convicted criminals aged 17 and under. Since the outbreak of violence, the department had completely lost control of its charges, some of whom were the most dangerous youths in the city. The department accepted Joyce's offer, and the heretofore unhelpful district police turned out in force to hunt down young parole violators.

The Youth Violence Strike Force had made 750 arrests by spring of 1994, but its members also wanted to help the many young people involved in gangs who were, in Joyce's words, "just fringe players." Joyce and the head of the Anti-Gang Violence Unit thought up a new program, the Summer of Opportunity, to keep the fringe players out of trouble by employing them. The policemen enlisted the John Hancock Mutual Life Insurance Company and Northeastern University to train forty young people between fifteen and seventeen years of age during the summer. Those who completed the course would get part-time jobs at the insurance company for the rest of the year and a one-year scholarship to college. The Strike Force members also raised money for Kids at Risk, a program for young people aged seven to fourteen; they paid summer camp tuitions and YMCA memberships, and supported fall and winter sports leagues.

Superintendent Paul Joyce, chief of the Bureau of Special Operations, Boston Police Department, and former director of the Youth Violence Strike Force, left, shakes hands with Derrick Booth, 20, of Dorchester after the Youth vs. Police basketball game at Ronan Park (the Police team won 50–46), August 2000. Courtesy of Chitose Suzuki, Boston Globe.

The city's government and non-profits, including the Ten Point Coalition, also pitched in with jobs and recreational programs, but the personal efforts of the police officers to help inner-city youth impressed community leaders and neighborhood residents. In the past the Boston police had done little besides locking kids up. The volunteers and staff at the Ten Point Coalition and social service organizations, such as the Streetworkers, now felt they were allies of the police.

Having earned a measure of trust, the cops found they could crack down on violent gang members and drug dealers without angering local blacks. The police and the Boston Housing Authority decided to clean up the worst public housing projects, and in September Joyce and the Strike Force supervised a massive three-day sweep of the Mission Hill project in Roxbury (the same one where the Stuart manhunt had taken place). Hundreds of police arrested 135 people, most of whom had criminal records, for trespassing, yet they received no citizen complaints.

In July Bill Stewart and another parole officer obtained from a young parole violator the name of a Mississippi college student who was running guns to Dorchester. They passed the name to a detective on the Youth Violence Strike Force and soon the Boston police, the ATF, and the U.S. Attorney's Office launched Operation Scrap Iron to eliminate gun trafficking in Boston. The Operation Scrap Iron team conducted numerous campaigns, including one against a gun-running gang on Wendover Street in Dorchester that was so effective gang members came on their own to the police and handed in their weapons. The team gained confidence when the number of murders, including youth homicides, dropped in 1994.

But in the summer of 1995 a sudden burst of youth slayings raised the specter that violence would spiral out of control again. In August, thousands of Bostonians took to the streets to participate in a national night out against crime. In the bowels of the police department, a working group of law enforcement officers and researchers from Harvard University's Kennedy School of Government searched feverishly for a strategy to thwart the carnage. David Kennedy, a Kennedy School researcher whose shoulder-length pony-tail made him look a most unlikely consultant to cops, had instigated the working group in January to test his theory that the murderous violence in Boston was no longer connected to drugs and gangs. The Kennedy School researcher's investigation of homicide perpetrators and victims, however, confirmed what Joyce and the Strike Force members already knew: a small group of hard-core criminal gang members were responsible for most of the violence. More important, the Strike Force members could identify these violent youths.

As the violence mounted and the working group grew desperate, Kennedy returned to the Wendover Street operation to understand what could induce gang members to cease violence and turn in their guns voluntarily. Eventually he concluded that the key components of the operation were, first, warning the gang members that the Strike Force would disrupt all activity until the violence ended and, second, conducting a full-court press that included sending gang leaders to remote prisons, towing the gang's unregistered cars, and prosecuting wrongdoers under stiff federal laws. The working group concluded that conducting a few such operations simultaneously might effectively stanch gang-related bloodletting.

Using the Kennedy School's crime data to make their case, the working group convinced the police department to expand Operation Scrap Iron. In 1995 Police Commissioner Paul Evans, named by the new mayor, Thomas Menino, enlarged the Strike Force by folding the Anti-Gang Violence Unit into it. The Strike Force now contained forty-five Boston police officers and fifteen law enforcement officers from other agencies, and a new commander, Lieutenant Gary French, formerly of the Roxbury and Dorchester police district.

In April 1996 the Strike Force gave the new collaboration, known as Operation Ceasefire, a trial run in Dorchester on Bowdoin Street, the home of the Vamp Hill Kings and the scene of two recent murders. Officers of the Boston police, the state police, the probation department, the ATF, and the Department of Youth Services descended on the neighborhood and scoured the streets for lawbreakers. Even the Boston police animal control unit showed up to capture dangerous pit bull dogs. Despite the effort, a boy was killed on his front porch only minutes after French, Joyce, and Stewart had visited the home to persuade his mother to get him out of town.

The following month, the Strike Force held a forum for the Vamp Hill Kings at the Dorchester District Court to warn them that violence would no longer be tolerated. The fifteen gang members who sauntered into the meeting were surprised to see a powerful array of law enforcement agencies. The officials from the DEA, the ATF, and the U.S. Attorney's office especially disturbed them. The terms of federal prosecutions were harsher than those of local jurisdictions: often bail and pre-trial releases were not available, and federal laws produced "fed time," long jail sentences in distant penitentiaries.

The feds told the Vamp Hill Kings the story of Freddie Cardoza, one of the most violent gang members in the city. The previous year, gang unit officers had stopped Cardoza on the street, found a single bullet on him, and arrested him. Using a federal law that imposes severe penalties on armed career criminals, the U.S. attorney prosecuted Cardoza and sent him to jail for almost twenty years without parole. Apparently the Strike Force made its point. The killings stopped on Bowdoin Street.

The anti-youth violence units spread the word about the new law enforcement policy. Whenever conflicts between gangs threatened to erupt, the Strike Force moved in and reminded the gangs, we are the people who brought you Bowdoin Street. The police chose their quarry carefully. At times they overlooked drug violations and other offenses, but always struck against violent criminals.

The Strike Force and the DEA felt ready to take on one of the most feared gangs in the city, the vicious Intervale Posse, from Intervale Street in north Dorchester. For months the law officials had gathered evidence of drug trafficking by the core members of the gang. Then in August the Strike Force warned the chief of the Intervale Posse to stop the violence. When the gang members ignored the warning, the police and the DEA moved in and arrested twenty-one gang members. They busted fifteen of the Posse, including their leader, on federal charges, and took them into custody without the possibility of bail.

As the news of the jailing of Freddie Cardoza and the Intervale Posse raid spread, a most surprising thing happened. Calm fell across Boston's inner-city streets. The gang members who had flouted the authorities for so long now became paranoid about being busted. The kids on the street thought that the feds were lurking everywhere, even cruising the neighborhoods in vans with tinted windows. Gary French, who carried a pager to inform him of the latest violent gang incident, joked that he needed to take the pager to the repair shop to make sure it was working properly.

As violent crime statistics went into free fall, Boston became one of the safest cities in the nation. The tally of homicides of people under twenty-four plummeted from forty-six in 1995 to fifteen in 1997, a far greater drop than the national average. From June 1995 to November 1997, no one under the age of seventeen was killed with a gun. In 1998 the number of homicides fell to thirty-five, the lowest total since 1961.[62]

Boston's collaborative methods became a national model for fighting youth crime. In February 1997, President Clinton visited Boston to announce a $500 million anti-youth-crime bill based on the city's accomplishments. Other cities sent delegations to learn the secret of Boston's anti-crime programs. Today, deadly violence sometimes strikes Boston's inner-city neighborhoods, but the residents, and increasingly outsiders, view such crimes as exceptions in otherwise peaceful communities. The reign of terror has ended, and the neighborhoods are born anew.

End Game in the Inner City

With real estate booming through the 1990s, Boston's government and nonprofit organizations have begun to play a redevelopment end game in the inner

New infill housing, part of the Boston Housing Authority's Orchard Gardens development, along Dudley Street, Roxbury, August 2002. Courtesy of Glenna Lang.

city. After decades of losing buildings, Roxbury and Dorchester now led all other Boston neighborhoods in requests for permits for new construction and renovations. Blacks, whites, and Hispanics have been purchasing homes there at a brisk pace, and in 2000 the number of low-, moderate-, and high-income households taking out mortgages were close to parity. (See Appendix I.)[63]

In the Dudley Street neighborhood, DSNI has overseen the development of 300 vacant lots into 225 new homes, playgrounds, gardens, and community buildings. Working with government funds—including a recent federal grant of $10.5 million to restore Roxbury's Dudley Square—the city and the CDCs continue to redevelop historic commercial blocks and lend money to help small businesses. Through a program funded with government and nonprofit sources, the CDCs now focus on rehabilitating houses for one to four families.[64]

Under Mayor Menino, the city of Boston has been aggressively filling the empty spaces created by urban decline. The newly named Department of Neighborhood Development (formerly the Neighborhood Development and Employment Agency led earlier by Boston Housing Partnership founders Mundell and Grogan) sells vacant lots owned by the city at discounted prices to builders who will keep their house prices low and to adjacent neighbors who want to enlarge their yards. For abandoned houses, the Menino administration conducted several programs, including one called the House of Shame program in which the mayor personally calls on absentee landlords to repair

(Above, left)   *Celebration of the Ten Most Wanted Drug Houses Task Force seizure of 147 Bowdoin Street, Dorchester, July 1998. Courtesy of Dorchester Bay Economic Development Corporation.*

(Above, right)   *147 Bowdoin Street rehabilitated, October 1998. Courtesy of Dorchester Bay Economic Development Corporation.*

their abandoned properties or sell them. As a result, between 1997 and 2001, the number of abandoned residential buildings in Boston fell from 790 to a paltry 260. In the inner city, the number of vacant houses in Dorchester fell by two-thirds and in Roxbury by more than half.[65]

Boston continues to make good use of the collaborative approach. The Boston Metropolitan Housing Partnership now concentrates on maintaining the properties it helped develop. The Dudley Street Neighborhood Initiative works on different fronts, including efforts to strengthen local schools, help existing and new businesses, and experiment with turning local gardens into agricultural businesses that will serve the city's restaurants.[66] The Ten Most Wanted Drug Houses Task Force, a multi-agency collaboration like the Youth Violence Strike Force, identifies the worst drug-trafficking houses, shuts down the dealers, confiscates the property, and turns them over to a developer, frequently the local CDC, for renovation.

Collaboration Becomes Routine

The collaborations in Boston over the last twenty years created something all cities need to make community development work: a set of semipermanent relationships between neighborhood groups and private and public funding agencies. That is, Boston has created a support system for its grassroots neighborhood efforts. Generally speaking, cities that succeed at improving neighborhoods have some sort of community development system, but Boston's has become a paradigm for those who hope to start or expand neighborhood rebirth.[67]

The first and essential ingredients for a successful community development system are, of course, good grassroots organizations, and for a city its size, Boston benefits from a disproportionately large number of energetic and effective community groups. Among its thirty or so active CDCs are several that people in the community development field regard as among the best in the nation. The tradition of citizen activism helped cultivate a cadre of savvy practitioners to lead the nonprofit groups, and their successful experiences have helped recruit and train new talent.

So vital are community development groups in the Boston area that they can participate in two influential trade organizations. The Citizens' Housing and Planning Association is an umbrella organization for all parties, private or public, in the fields of housing and community development. The group's annual dinner is a must-attend social event for anyone seriously involved in community development in Massachusetts. The local CDCs also have their own specialized trade group, the Massachusetts Association of Community Development Corporations. Both organizations lobby the legislative and executive branches of state government on behalf of CDCs and community development programs.

The state and local governments have provided unusually strong and sustained support for housing and community development projects in Boston.

Within the government of Massachusetts, agencies, such as the Department of Housing and Community Development, the Community Economic Development Assistance Corporation (a quasi-public funding organization), and—as we have seen in the case of the Boston Housing Partnership—the Massachusetts Housing Finance Agency, not only provide funds but also participate in community development projects. Under mayors Raymond Flynn and Thomas Menino, the city of Boston has put money into a variety of community development programs and—with its share of federal community development block grant funds—CDCs themselves.

In Boston, the private sector throws its weight behind housing and community development groups and projects no less than the public sector. Local philanthropies, such as the Boston Foundation, the Hyams Foundation, and the Riley Foundation—which supported the Dudley Street Neighborhood Initiative—have contributed money to community development. Representatives of financial institutions, such as FleetBoston and Citizens Bank, and law firms, including the venerable Ropes and Gray, sit on the board of the Metropolitan Boston Housing Partnership. Sixteen Massachusetts banks in 1990 formed their own nonprofit housing finance institution, the Massachusetts Housing Investment Corporation; since then it has pledged or invested more than $500 million in 165 housing projects.[68]

Financial intermediaries aid the cause in most cities where community development thrives, and Boston is no exception. LISC opened a field office in Boston in 1981 and ever since has played a leading role in financing projects and assisting CDCs. Boston LISC backed the Boston Housing Partnership in the crucial early stages and helped lesser-known CDCs to get the recognition and money they needed to expand. With the help of local foundations and Boston-based corporations such as Cabot, Cabot, and Forbes and the John Hancock Insurance Company, LISC put up $13 million in loans and grants for community development projects between 1980 and 1996.[69]

In addition, the local LISC office worked with Boston philanthropies as well as the United Way to create a new organization that helps CDCs pay for their operating expenses, including hiring or training people with specialized skills. Reflecting the collaborative approach typical of Boston, the organization is named the Neighborhood Development Support Collaborative.

Boston's support system for community development brings a wide range of important political and business leaders into the field. This means that community groups have many places to turn for support. Just as important, when projects or CDCs run into trouble—as some inevitably do—the leaders of the institutions that back them will step in and help set matters aright. Even failures will not stop community development in Boston.

As people from cities across the country look to Boston for lessons to revive their inner-city neighborhoods, it is worth remembering that neither the city's collaborative schemes nor its community development system were planned or inevitable. Years of experiments and setbacks preceded the successes. Downtown business leaders and government officials had to discover community development and learn to coordinate with CDCs. And even community development advocates point out that the small size of the city works to their advantage.

The approach that worked in Boston might not work in a city of different size and circumstances—such as a mighty industrial metropolis. To take the measure of community development, then, let us travel to Chicago and discover what devices the defenders of the historic African-American ghettos employed to save their neighborhoods.

*Upham's Corner street festival, renovated Pierce Building in background.
Courtesy of Dorchester Bay Economic Development Corporation.*

IN THE RUST BELT
Can the Ghetto Be Rebuilt?

Come onnn, baby, don't you . . . want to go?
Come onnn, baby, don't you . . . want to go?
Back to that same old place . . .
Sweet Home Chicago

Robert Johnson

Earnest Gates, as hard-nosed and practical a person as you will ever meet, was walking through the luxurious apartment and deciding whether to buy it when a voice spoke to him.

"What," the voice asked incredulously, "are you *doing?*"

Here was Gates, who had grown up on the tough Near West Side of Chicago, built a successful trucking business, and now could take his wife and children out of his run-down neighborhood and live pretty much wherever they wanted. And what they wanted could very well be this apartment in the Americana Towers in the fashionable Old Town neighborhood.

But as Earnest Gates admired the fancy features of the rooms, the voice inside his head kept talking. "The neighborhoods are never going to get better as long as people like you continue to move out."

Then the voice stopped him in his tracks: "You know, you are doing the *exact same thing* that you criticized other people for doing."

That did it. Gates knew he had to make a decision. Do I pick up and go, or do I return home and try to bring the neighborhood back? He had an opportunity to escape the inner city and its problems and give his kids an opportunity to grow up in a nice apartment in a comfortable neighborhood. Or he could return to the old haunts, the empty lots and abandoned houses, the liquor stores, elderly people hunkered down in their homes, and the poor kids imprisoned in the Henry Horner public housing project—the one made famous by Alex Kotlowitz's grim book entitled *There Are No Children Here*. And Gates had no idea what steps someone would take to make such a place thrive.

The brass ring or the fool's errand? The choice was obvious. Throw aside all the common sense that he had used to succeed in his trucking business. Walk out of the luxury apartment and return to the 'hood. Gates followed the

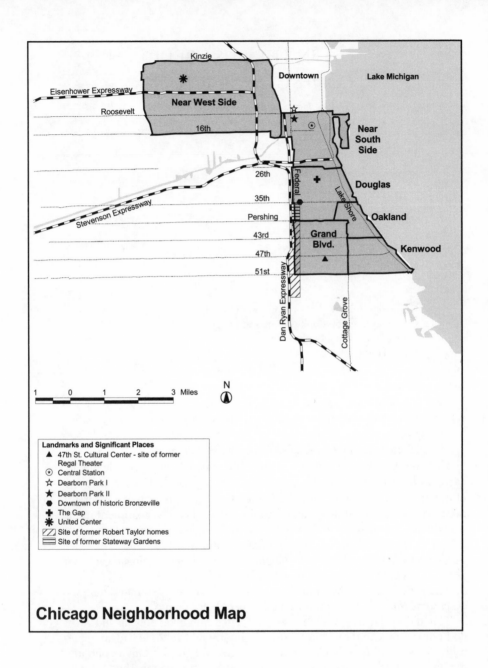

Kinzie

Eisenhower Expressway

Roosevelt

16th

Near West Side

Downtown

Lake Michigan

Near South Side

26th

35th

Pershing

43rd

47th

51st

Federal

Stevenson Expressway

Dan Ryan Expressway

Lake Shore

Cottage Grove

Douglas

Oakland

Grand Blvd.

Kenwood

N

1   0   1   2   3 Miles

Landmarks and Significant Places
▲ 47th St. Cultural Center - site of former Regal Theater
⊙ Central Station
☆ Dearborn Park I
★ Dearborn Park II
● Downtown of historic Bronzeville
✚ The Gap
✳ United Center
▨ Site of former Robert Taylor homes
▤ Site of former Stateway Gardens

Chicago Neighborhood Map

inner voice. Family and friends told him he was crazy, but he decided to work to make the Near West Side into a place where people of all incomes, ages, walks of life, and races could live and prosper.[1]

As foolhardy as his undertaking seemed at the time, Gates was not alone. All across Chicago's West and South Sides, people were dreaming of turning neighborhoods on the edge of extinction into stable mixed-income communities.

At first their efforts met resistance at every turn. On the South Side, an unlikely prophet of African American history wandered in the wilderness for years, preaching to no avail that the neighborhood possessed a priceless treasure, the historic artifacts and legacy known as Black Metropolis; at the same time, brave souls made homes in architectural-landmark houses as they tried to ignore the crime, abandoned buildings, and dreadful public housing projects that surrounded them. On the Near West Side, when Earnest Gates began to renovate houses in order to improve a neighborhood ravaged by urban renewal, a devastating riot, and massive population flight, the local branch bank refused to help and his neighbors, apparently accustomed to degradation, criticized him for showing off.

Gradually the neighborhood improvers inched forward, however, and today the change is palpable. Old homes are repaired and new ones built, housing prices continue to rise, and real estate speculators prowl the streets in search of properties they can turn around for tidy profits. Lately the city government has accelerated the resettlement of Chicago's urban population by tearing down the massive high-rise public housing buildings—beginning with Henry Horner Homes on the West Side and moving on to the South Side Goliaths such as Robert Taylor Homes and Stateway Gardens—and developing new mixed-income subdivisions on their sites.

The influx of affluent citizens into the South Side, a process known as gentrification, has propelled the improvement of Chicago's inner ring of old ghetto neighborhoods. Upper-middle-class African Americans arrived first. Then whites, who had long shunned such areas, started to move in. Historic houses and convenient access to downtown jobs and entertainment attracted the newcomers. Long-time residents thought, there goes the neighborhood. Indeed, too much gentrification can improve a place so much the original residents can no longer afford to live there.

Over years of struggling to start and then control the forces of neighborhood betterment, Earnest Gates and like-minded citizens on the West and South Sides of Chicago discovered the value of forming alliances with large institutions within or near their neighborhoods. Professional sports teams, universities, or hospitals pose a danger to their surrounding communities when their directors act only in their short-term interests. In those cases, the defenders of old ghetto neighborhoods must become latter-day Davids who best the institutional Goliaths and force them to the negotiating table. It gives them a chance to outrun the gentrification that is reshaping the inner city and create a community for citizens of all walks of life.

The surges of gentrification that are transforming the central ghetto neighborhoods are felt scarcely, if at all, in many of Chicago's outer ring of low-income neighborhoods. Nonetheless, an array of hardy grassroots organizations has brought redevelopment to these shores as well. They do not labor unaided. Chicago's innovative community development intermediary organizations — including the oldest commercial community development bank in the United States — provide nonprofits across the city with capital and professional support.

Inside and out, one way or another, the capital of America's rust belt was being reborn.

The City of Big Shoulders

In their lusty youth, America's great cities of industry exploded in size and raw power. Such places as Birmingham, Buffalo, Cleveland, Detroit, Milwaukee, and Pittsburgh churned out steel, cars, machines, and the machines to make the machines. They attracted people, businesses, and jobs in awesome proportions during the late nineteenth and early twentieth centuries. They also suffered from the effects of industrialization and growth: bloody labor wars, ethnic strife, overcrowding, and pollution. Located mostly in the Midwest, the industrial cities ruthlessly exploited the natural resources of their rural hinterlands and their workers.

Of these industrial powerhouses, Chicago is the metropolis. At the turn of the twentieth century, it was the country's shock city, a place whose spectacular growth made it a national phenomenon. The poet Carl Sandburg described its character and economy:

> HOG Butcher for the World,
> Tool Maker, Stacker of Wheat,
> Player with Railroads and the Nation's Freight Handler;
> Stormy, husky, brawling,
> City of the Big Shoulders[2]

More recently, historian William Cronon described Chicago as "Nature's Metropolis," the capital of a vast inland empire whose meat, lumber, and grain it rapaciously consumed. At its height, the city's occupants kept furiously busy slaughtering cattle and packing meat in and around its well-known stockyards; manufacturing farm machinery — in the wake of Cyrus McCormick of reaper fame; producing steel in the mills of south Chicago and Gary, Indiana; fabricating metal products — including the railroad cars at Pullman — and machine tools; turning out men's clothing, and moving goods and people by water, wagon, and, above all, train. And at white-collar business transactions — banking, issuing insurance, and especially selling; Chicago was, after all, the home of the Sears, Roebuck and Montgomery Ward department stores.[3]

Chicago, like its fellow industrial cities, acted as a magnet for people in search of jobs and business opportunities. American Protestants of British descent, Germans, Irish, Slavs, eastern European Jews, Italians, and black and white American southerners poured into the industrial city, divided it into geographic and political territories, and fought with each other to control their piece of the pie.

The Rise and Fall of Black Metropolis

Each wave of migration defined and redefined the industrial city, and none more so than the historic movement of African Americans to the urban north. Once concentrated in the rural South, the mass of African Americans moved to cities over the course of the twentieth century and in the process created such well-known neighborhoods as the Hill in Pittsburgh and Central Avenue and Hough in Cleveland.

Of all the northern industrial cities, Chicago was the most alluring. "The Promised Land," as Nicholas Lemann has termed it, beckoned the African American masses to leave the poverty and repression of the South. Mostly they came by rail, but later also by bus and car. From 1900 to 1940, the black population of Chicago climbed from 30,000 to 277,000, with the steepest increases between 1910 and 1930 when it leaped by 190,000 people. After the Second World War, an even greater surge of arrivals from the South boosted the number of African Americans in Chicago; by 1960 the black population was almost 813,000, which made up 23 percent of the city's total population.[4]

Most of the newcomers from the South landed in Chicago at the Dearborn Station just south of the Loop, at the Illinois Central Station, slightly further south at 12th Street and Michigan Avenue, and the bus station a block away. They settled near where they landed immediately south of the railroad stations in the area that became known as the Black Belt and from there fanned out gradually across the South Side. The wealthy whites of Prairie and South Park Avenues retreated from their elegant homes, but middle- and working-class whites inhabiting neighborhoods bordering the Black Belt resisted fiercely. They refused to sell to blacks, placed racial covenants on property deeds, and bombed and stormed African American homes outside the Black Belt. Hemmed in like no other ethnic group, African Americans transformed the South Side neighborhoods of Douglas, Grand Boulevard, and Washington Park into a city within a city. In their classic 1945 study, sociologists St. Clair Drake and Horace Cayton dubbed this Black Metropolis.[5]

Black Metropolis, or Bronzeville (the name popularized by a local newspaper) boasted several commercial areas—including its own downtown at 35th and State Streets—a host of major institutions, and predominantly upper-, middle-, and lower-class neighborhoods. One of the leading churches among many on the South Side was the Olivet Baptist Church. After acquiring the building of the white First Baptist Church, Olivet built its membership to more than 8,400 and by 1919 had become the largest Baptist church in the United States. Black Metropolis was the center of African American journalism, the home of the *Chicago Defender*, the most important African American newspaper in the United States, and later national magazines such as *Ebony* and *Jet*. The South Siders were free to vote and participate in politics (as they had not been in the South), and with their large numbers and close-packed settlement pattern, they sustained the path-breaking political career of Oscar DePriest, Chicago's first black alderman and the first black from the North to be elected to the United States Congress.[6]

Chicago's South Side made an indelible mark, or rather several, on American music. It was in Black Metropolis in the teens and twenties that the immortal Louis Armstrong, along with his sidekick Earl "Fatha" Hines, helped transform the sounds of New Orleans into a national music. In later decades, Chicago nurtured or sent forth such great jazz musicians as Dinah Washington, Nat "King" Cole, and Lou Rawls. It was on the South Side that in the 1950s, second-wave refugees from the Mississippi delta—including Muddy Waters and Howlin' Wolf—sang the blues that inspired the Rolling Stones and countless other rock and blues musicians. And it was in Chicago's black ghettos during the 1960s that Curtis Mayfield and the Impressions, Gene Chandler of "Duke of Earl" fame, and Fontella Bass—regular performers at the Regal Theater on the South Side at 47th and South Park Avenue—helped create the "Chicago sound" of soul music.

For all its vitality, the Black Metropolis was the scene of much suffering. Most of the African American refugees from the harsh life in the South were poor and unskilled, and so from its earliest days Chicago's South Side—as well as subsequent areas of African American settlement on the West Side—contained shocking poverty and appalling slums.

Efforts to remove the slums and revive the South Side began sixty years ago and have continued intermittently ever since. Government programs and millions of dollars scooped out thousands of dilapidated buildings and tens of thousands of their residents, often African Americans, but did little to stem and may have encouraged the exodus of middle-class people. The construction of highways—especially the Dan Ryan Expressway on the South Side, which in the middle of the old Black Metropolis widens to fourteen lanes, a rapid transit line, and six lanes of local access roads—removed more families than any other cause.[7]

The government cleared large tracts of ramshackle homes and gave the land to developers. Some built modernist-style high-rise apartment buildings with views of Lake Michigan for middle-class occupants. The government cleared more than 100 acres inhabited by 3,400 predominantly black and low-income families to make way for Lake Meadows, ten buildings with more than 2,000 middle-income and luxury units, developed in 1953 by the New York Life Insurance Company. The high-rises were intended to be racially integrated, but Lake Meadows became predominantly African American and Prairie Shores, a similar complex built in 1962 by Michael Reese Hospital, was inhabited mainly by whites. Carving up the South Side ghetto, the Illinois Institute of Technology (IIT) created a 120-acre campus, Michael Reese and Mercy Hospitals expanded their facilities, and the city built the McCormick Place convention center on the lake shore.[8]

For fifteen years, from 1950 to 1965, city planners and the housing authority erected along State Street the largest concentration of public housing in the country, a four-mile wall of high-rise buildings interrupted only by the IIT campus. The city's political leaders, in cahoots with the Chicago Housing Authority, supported the construction of these giant complexes of elevator buildings as a way to prevent the growing African American population from spreading into white neighborhoods.

Both the planners and the politicians failed utterly in their goals. Instead of containing the black population, they decimated their residential areas and forced many to seek shelter away from the old Black Belt. The number of people living in the South Side Douglas and Grand Boulevard neighborhoods—the heart of Black Metropolis—peaked in 1950 at more than 193,000 and fell by one-third over the next ten years to 132,360. By 1990 the population of these neighborhoods had plummeted to 66,550, about half what it had been in 1960 and only a little more than a third of what it had been in 1950.[9]

Setting out to build large projects that would be a catalyst for improvement of nearby slums, government planners and their developers created homogeneous enclaves of middle- and upper-middle-class households. The middle-class islands did not prove contagious as hoped. The public housing projects that replaced the slums became slums themselves, and the neighborhoods fell into greater poverty.

Indeed, Douglas and Grand Boulevard were among the six poorest neighborhoods in the city. In 1980, 43 percent of the families in Douglas and 51 percent of the families in Grand Boulevard earned income below the official poverty level; in 1990 the figures had risen to 49 and 64 percent, respectively, leaving an impoverished core population, which included many children.[10]

During the 1980s, the old ghettos were being cleared again, but not by government urban renewal programs. First, a building was abandoned or caught fire, then the city government tore it down. The process was relentless. Almost 19 percent of the 32,200 units in Black Metropolis neighborhoods—including 10,000 units in public housing—were vacant in 1990.[11]

"I'd be away from a block for a while," remembers Sokoni Karanja, "and come back and the whole block would be gone. Amazing!" He tried to stop the destruction.[12]

Dr. Sokoni Karanja, founder and director of Centers for New Horizons. Courtesy of Centers for New Horizons.

A soft-spoken intellectual activist, Karanja came to the South Side as a postgraduate fellow at the University of Chicago after earning a doctorate at Brandeis University and working on economic development in Tanzania. When he arrived in Chicago, he saw that most of the South Side's residents had departed or were about to, leaving behind collapsing communities inhabited largely by impoverished and suffering people. Inspired by the ambitious economic and social programs of Tanzania's leftist president Julius Nyerere, Karanja in 1971 founded an organization called Centers for New Horizons and set up learning centers in the public housing projects, using an African-centered curriculum aimed at young children and their parents. Since then

Karanja has gradually increased the programs of Center for New Horizons, making it perhaps the most important community educational and social organization in its area.[13]

As he worked to build his organization during the 1970s and 1980s, Karanja found himself attempting to stop the juggernaut of the city's building department from destroying abandoned or merely vacant buildings. Karanja and his associates went to court to stop the proceedings and gain time to notify the owners.

But it was difficult. Even buildings that Karanja's organization owned were demolished. "If you're not there when the bulldozer comes," Karanja warns, "they'll tear it down." He learned to watch the list of buildings with code violations from the Building Department to see where the demolition machine would strike next. He concluded finally that the city government pursued its voracious policy of building clearance because officials had decided that the South Side land was more valuable to the city if it were vacant.[14] Not until ten years later, in the 1990s, would Karanja begin to see new home building instead of demolition—in the revitalization of the Gap area of the South Side.

Until then, however, the South Side continued to decline. Over the years, the streets were emptied first of people and then, to a great extent, of buildings. By the 1990s empty stores and vacant lots lined the great commercial boulevards—35th Street, 43rd Street, 47th Street, 63rd Street—that had hopped with life as recently as the 1960s. The restaurants, fried chicken and rib joints, hair dressing parlors, barbers, music stores, hat and clothing shops, grocery stores, currency exchanges, blues clubs, jazz lounges, and just plain bars were

Residents walk through an unreal urban landscape dominated by empty spaces, South Side, Chicago, 1988. Courtesy of Camilo José Vergara.

almost completely gone. The Regal Theater burned down in the 1970s. Every mile or so, often next to an elevated train station, a few shops held on through the end of the 1990s. At the once busy intersection of 47th and South Prairie, a liquor store faced Shelly's Loan Company, which survived because, as a small sign announces, Paramount Pictures used it to shoot the pawnshop scene in the 1980 comedy film, *The Blues Brothers*. Elsewhere the shops hunkered down; the boards and bars on the windows and doors made it hard to tell whether they were open or closed.

The residential side streets told a similar story. Where once—eons ago it seemed—the six-flat apartment buildings and cut-up single-family houses stood filled to the bursting point with people who had fled the South, the lots are covered by grass and weeds and here and there a stand of buildings. Even the hulking public housing projects looked abandoned and alone; Fred Wiseman conveyed the sense of desolation that pervades them in his 1997 documentary film, *Public Housing*. The South Side contained so many empty, lonely streets that the overcrowded slums of yesteryear appeared a nostalgic joy. At the end of the twentieth century, Black Metropolis had come to resemble a ghost town.

To Save Lost Treasures

Even as old landmarks crumbled from neglect and the ruthless wrecking ball of the building department toppled once-elegant homes, individuals who saw something of value in Chicago's ravaged neighborhoods embarked on lonely quests to turn back the tides that were daily destroying what was left of formerly proud communities.

Of all the lonely crusaders, none was more quixotic than Tim Samuelson, who stumbled on Chicago's commercial and cultural artifacts of the historic Black Metropolis and tried to save them. As a teenager in the 1960s, he developed a lifelong passion for the city's architectural masterpieces, particularly the works of Louis Sullivan, the masterful designer and mentor of Frank Lloyd Wright. Samuelson, whose family lived in the far north side neighborhood of Rogers Park, took to wandering the city in search of Louis Sullivan's work—downtown and on the south side—photographing the handsome buildings. Sadly many of the landmarks were slated to be demolished, and, when they were, Samuelson faithfully recorded their images and even salvaged architectural ornaments amidst the rubble. His father forbade him to go to the South Side—with its reputation for crime and danger to white people—and became furious at his son for traveling there. Samuelson was undeterred, however, and found such gems as the synagogue, at 33rd and Indiana, designed by the famous team of Sullivan and Dankmar Adler, at which Adler's father had presided.[15]

As he grew older, Samuelson continued to roam the South Side in search of landmarks and history, and despite the South Side's fearsome reputation, always felt at ease there. He delighted in meeting and hearing the stories of neighborhood residents—especially old-timers such as Leo Montgomery who had been in his house since 1919 and could remember when upper-crust whites lived in the neighborhood. For their part, the South Siders enjoyed Samuelson's earnest enthusiasm and knowledge of the history of their homes and neighborhood. In all the years Samuelson visited the South Side, only once was he ever threatened. While he was working for an architectural firm in 1982, he went to the corner of 47th Street and Langley Boulevard to supervise the demolition of a large commercial building designed by Sullivan, attempting to save its ornamental features. The project was a seat-of-the-pants affair: the city's landmarks commissioner was too frightened to venture into the South Side and so sent Samuelson (who had discovered that the building was being torn down without the agency's required permission). The wrecking company was a small, cheap labor enterprise.

As Samuelson directed an effort by the wreckers to salvage a three foot square terra-cotta ornament on the front of a wall they were pulling down with a bucket and crane, the ornament slipped out of the crane to the back of the building. Samuelson rushed frantically around the corner of the part of the building that was still standing to save the piece before it was crushed by the rest of the wall. As he came around the corner, a man brandishing a knife stepped out of a door in the undemolished section and demanded, "Your wallet!" The distracted preservationist waved him off impatiently, "Not now, I'm busy!" and continued on his way. Only hours later did he realize what the man had said.

Sometime afterward, as he examined the building to see what more might be saved, Samuelson heard the laborers on the other side of the wall talking about him during their coffee break. "That Mr. Tim," he remembers one commenting, "he sure is one crazy white man." "Yeah," responded another, "he'd be the *original* crazy white man"—at which Samuelson stepped out and they shared a good laugh.[16]

Tim Samuelson may have been crazy, but he was passionate in his historical pursuits, which besides architecture, included ragtime, the genre that swept America's popular music in the years leading up to World War I. The best-known ragtime composer is Scott Joplin, but Samuelson's passion for the field soon led him to an accomplished but now largely forgotten South Side Chicago ragtime musician, Joseph Jordan. Jordan, Samuelson was fascinated to learn, had played at the Pekin Theater, which a gambling lord opened in 1905 at 22nd and State Streets, and in 1916–1917 used the money he had earned from songwriting and music publishing to develop Chicago's first major commercial building financed by African American capital.[17]

Soon Samuelson reconstructed the entire institutional landscape of the Black Metropolis whose downtown centered at 35th and State Streets—including the great Olivet and Pilgrim Baptist Churches which had welcomed the first wave of migrants from the South in the early 1900s and the Peoples Movement club that served as the headquarters for pioneering African American politico Oscar DePriest.

He found the sites of the music halls and nightclubs—the Dreamland Cafe, the Royal Gardens, and the Sunset Cafe—where King Oliver, Louis Armstrong, and Jelly Roll Morton created the Chicago style of early jazz that was listened to and imitated around the world. So much great music poured out of Black

The surviving remnants of Black Metropolis's downtown, with Jordan Building on the left, State Street and 36th Street, early 1980s. Courtesy of Timothy Samuelson.

Metropolis, Samuelson learned, that people used to say if you held up a horn on the corner of 35th and State Streets, the instrument would play itself.[18]

Samuelson discovered over a dozen buildings that were remnants of the ten-block business district that once boasted the most important concentration of African American enterprise outside Harlem. At 36th and State Street, the locale of the Jordan Building, Samuelson also found the Overton Hygenic Building, once the proud central office of three of Anthony Overton's businesses: a cosmetics manufacturing company, a life insurance firm, and the city's first state-chartered bank owned by an African American. Down the block was another building where Overton, who was born into slavery, had operated his own newspaper, the *Chicago Bee*.[19]

Samuelson also found the building, a former synagogue, that had served from 1920 to 1960 as the home of the *Chicago Defender*, the nation's first African American mass-circulation newspaper. Robert S. Abbot, the *Defender's* founder and editor, had purchased the building at 34th Street and Indiana Avenue after white printers refused to print his newspaper during the race riot of 1919 (in which working-class whites declared a war on the city's blacks). Just off 35th Street stood an imposing structure, the Eighth Regiment Armory Building, constructed in 1915 to house the "Fighting 8th." The black volunteer regiment, commanded by black officers, was formed to fight in the Spanish-American War and later served during World War I where it earned recognition for helping to drive the German forces from the Marne valley.[20]

Yet as excited as Samuelson was to locate these precious artifacts of history, he was disturbed to see that by the 1980s only a couple of the buildings were occupied and some of them—especially the Jordan building—were falling apart. Samuelson began a crusade to save the buildings he felt were too important to African American history to lose. He landed a job with the Chicago Landmarks Commission to review building permits in 1983, but carried out his real preservation work on his own time.[21]

Samuelson made a slide show to stir up interest and presented it to community organizations, churches, and anybody who would listen. He produced flyers and pamphlets telling the story of Black Metropolis. He wrote proposals to convert the buildings to housing and give job training to local youth in the process. Nothing came of it. Samuelson went to city agencies, including the Chicago Housing Authority, to see if they could use the buildings for offices, but they all turned him down. He compiled statistics on each building, showing how much their tax payments were in arrears and how the city could take them for no cost.

People said they loved the story of the buildings but could not see what they could do to save them. He tried to get help from well-known figures who could throw their weight behind the cause. After he worked for two months to get an appointment with Dempsey Travis, a noted author of books on jazz and a local real estate developer, Travis told Samuelson that the buildings would never be saved because they were next to the State Street public housing projects.[22]

Getting no place with community groups and city departments, Samuelson thought of a strategy to interest private investors in buying the edifices of Black Metropolis before they wasted away. If the buildings were designated as landmarks in a historic district, he reasoned, investors might become interested and preserve these important sites of black history. In 1984 Samuelson submitted a proposal for a Black Metropolis Historic District to the landmarks commission that approved the landmark designations—although Samuelson suspected that the members were more interested in reaching out to the black community than preserving a set of precious historical artifacts—and sent it on to the Chicago Planning Commission. The Planning Commission simply sat on the proposal, however, because its staff feared that the designation would give the city government responsibility for decrepit buildings that would have to be torn down or rebuilt at great expense. Once again Samuelson's efforts were stalled.

Meanwhile, the buildings continued to deteriorate. Samuelson grew desperate. He wrote brief histories of the buildings and made enlarged copies of the early twentieth-century advertisements that showed the buildings in the illustrations and posted them on the boarded up windows. He mounted signs on the Jordan building that said Please Do Not Vandalize.

Time was running out. The roof of the Defender building collapsed, although the owner fixed it. Overton was abandoned, and vandals stole its terra-cotta copings along the tops of the walls. Samuelson stumbled across the copings in a salvage shop and called the police. Twice he went to building court to save the Jordan building from imminent demolition. He tried in vain to get city officials to secure the site of the Jordan building to protect it from vandals. Finally Alderman Bobby Rush managed to get the city government to build a chain link fence around the building—an act not strictly by the rules since the land was private property. A few days later, nonetheless, somebody drove a truck with a chain and steel beam to the back wall of the Jordan building, hooked the steel beam horizontally inside a window of the building, and broke open the wall to get the bricks. Chicago's old bricks, it turned out, were in demand for chic-looking interiors of homes and restaurants in California.

Then, for political reasons having nothing to do with Black Metropolis, the city government decided to rewrite its landmarks ordinance and, in the mean-time, eliminate all pending landmark proposals.

Not for the first time, Samuelson, Chicago's most dedicated preservation-ist, lost heart. He wished he had never tried to save the buildings. "It would have been better to let them crumble in anonymous dignity," he decided, than to see them ignored.[23]

But Samuelson's determination, or stubbornness, pulled him just far enough out of despair for one last attempt to save the physical legacy of Black Me-tropolis. He nominated thirteen buildings and an outdoor monumental sculp-ture commemorating the black soldiers who fought in World War I to be placed on the federal government's National Register of Historic Places. Placing the Black Metropolis district on the National Register would bring the structures recognition, qualify their owners for historic preservation tax credits, and, he hoped, increase the pressure on passive city officials to save them. Although he feared city officials would see his motives and veto the nomination, they let it go ahead. The National Register removed two of the buildings from the proposed district, but approved the rest in 1986.

One person by himself, however, can do only so much to change the fate of a neighborhood. Two days after the National Register of Historic Places ap-proved the Black Metropolis Historic District, the front wall and the interior of the Jordan building collapsed.

Jordan Building collapses, 1986. Courtesy of Timothy Samuelson.

123

Gentrification

Yet the picture was not as bleak as it may have seemed. One of the great forces for urban revival, the migration of upper-middle-class people to inner-city neighborhoods, was beginning to stir in Chicago. Gentrification is nothing new; middle-class newcomers have been elevating the tone of old neighborhoods since the early twentieth century. Once highly respectable, Greenwich Village in Manhattan, Philadelphia's Society Hill, and Georgetown in Washington, D.C., became seedy immigrant and poor people's quarters, which then attracted bohemians and intellectuals who savored their old-fashioned buildings and old-world atmosphere. Eventually these neighborhoods became desirable and expensive again, but the transition took place so long ago many Americans assume they were always that way. In fact, affluent newcomers have been upgrading run-down neighborhoods almost continuously for the last hundred years.

The recent wave of gentrification started during the 1960s and 1970s, came to a roaring climax during the economic boom of the 1980s, and consolidated its gains and spread further during the long prosperity of the 1990s. Skeptics pooh-pooh the importance of the upscaling trend because the new urban gentry are few in number and have not reversed the ongoing movement to the suburbs, but the trend brought notable improvements to numerous urban neighborhoods such as Manhattan's Upper West Side, Washington's DuPont Circle, and Boston's South End, a district that had been down at the heels for a hundred years.

These gentrifying neighborhoods followed a similar evolution. Starting in the 1960s, young single people and couples, many of whom were homosexual, began occupying and painstakingly restoring historic buildings, often nineteenth-century row houses, with stoops and bow fronts, high ceilings, and elegantly crafted woodwork. In the 1980s young urban professionals, the fabled "yuppies" often disparaged for their materialism, joined the pioneers, expanding the zone of rehabilitated residences and raising fears of "displacement" of the earlier, less wealthy population. During the 1990s, even wealthier people, many of whom were riding high on the soaring stock market, arrived and helped drive real estate prices to heights beyond even the reach of the original rehabilitators. By the end of the century, the new urban gentry had all but taken over the old neighborhoods, and any remaining poor blacks or Latinos held on in small pockets and subsidized housing projects.

Writing in the mid-1980s, Brian J. L. Berry, the author of the most cogent explanation of the causes of gentrification, concluded that two factors were needed to trigger it. The first was a large supply of homes in a metropolitan area. The second was a significant growth in the central business district of the number of offices—or, in effect, jobs—which increased the number of professional and white-collar workers who would be interested in living in the city. When these two criteria were met, well-educated, usually childless, single people and couples found inexpensive, vintage homes in areas close to the downtown and the cultural and entertainment amenities—for example, art galleries, museums, theaters, parks, restaurants—of the city.[24]

Berry initially believed that gentrification had or would occur only in the large national or regional administrative centers—such as New York, Los Angeles, and San Francisco—that led the shift from an industrial to a service economy. More recently, as he and others have observed, the number of cities whose neighborhoods have been uplifted by an inflow of newcomers has increased, spreading to such locales as Milwaukee, Wisconsin; Hoboken, New Jersey; and Providence, Rhode Island.[25]

As a general rule, neighborhoods that gentrify possess advantageous locations and/or physical amenities. They frequently are situated in the inner city, close to the jobs and nightlife in and around downtown or in areas along transit lines that lead to the business and entertainment districts. Neighborhoods that attract urban pioneers and gentry usually have historic buildings, which may be either old commercial and warehouse buildings—that can be converted to the kind of residential lofts popularized in Soho in lower Manhattan—or houses, especially "Victorians" whose architecture ranges from the sedate row houses of Brooklyn Heights to the ornate "painted ladies" of San Francisco.

In its early stages, gentrification brings improvements—carried out by home and store owners and government agencies—to neighborhoods that have been going downhill for decades. Most old-time residents applaud this progress and the new arrivals who at first come in easily assimilable small numbers.

Uncurbed gentrification, however, threatens to displace or create hardship for less-affluent residents—often minority and elderly people—by raising their rents and property taxes. Indeed, when it reaches its logical conclusion, gentrification changes the preponderant population of a neighborhood—from a low-income to a high-income group—the reverse of the social transition that happens when an upscale neighborhood becomes a slum. Thus, in the 1970s and 1980s, community activists railed against the urban gentry by crying displacement. The arrival of the professionals and white-collar workers improved the physical character of the neighborhood at the expense of the existing population.

The city of Chicago was a prime candidate for the kind of gentrification that Berry described. Although it was hard hit by industrial restructuring—like so many rust belt cities—the Windy City enjoyed a robust economic base. It was a regional economic and administrative capital, home to the nation's leading commodities exchange, numerous corporate headquarters—including major finance, insurance, and real estate companies—and unparalleled transportation facilities, with one of the largest and busiest airports in the world. As the number of white-collar workers grew, the tough, hard-drinking, hard-hatted workers no longer personified the city. As early as 1968, Chicago's illustrious newspaper scribe, Mike Royko, took note of the city's emerging effete character by writing an acerbic parody of Sandburg's classic poem. No longer City of Big Shoulders, Chicago was now

Hi-Rise for the World
Partygoer, Stacker of Stereo Tapes
Player with Home Pool Table and the nation's Jets;
Dapper, slender, filter-tipped,
City of the Big Credit Card.[26]

Gentrification took firm hold in such a place. But it moved in an almost exclusively northerly direction, expanding the city's Gold Coast shopping and luxury district and transforming North Side neighborhoods such as Old Town and Lincoln Park. In the 1990s, the new affluence spread further into the North and Northwest Sides. Working-class Chicagoans watched with growing apprehension as real estate developers and boutique owners reinvented their old precincts as tony "villages" where when the going gets tough, the tough go shopping. "Hey, we've got a real problem," yelled a woman at a public meeting in an old working-class neighborhood on the northwest side, "I went to bed in Logan Square and I woke up in Logan Village!"[27]

South Side Rediscovered

As the North Side boomed in real estate and fashionable people, the process of rediscovery had begun, quietly and unbeknown to most Chicagoans, on the city's South Side. As it turned out, Tim Samuelson was not the only one who valued its old neighborhoods. Starting in the 1970s, a number of people ignored the danger and destruction and bought inexpensive buildings to renovate. These were the South Side's urban pioneers, counterparts to those hearty souls elsewhere who restored historic properties in dilapidated areas and sparked neighborhood revivals. In contrast to the young white urban professionals, black urban professionals—"buppies" as opposed to yuppies—began the revival of Chicago's South Side.

The South Side's intrepid urban pioneers were especially attracted to a section of the Douglas neighborhood called the Gap, a district of Victorian homes most of which miraculously had survived the afflictions of the previous decades. The neighborhood gained its peculiar name, according to legend, from the planners who in the 1950s and 1960s ordered the clearing of hundreds of acres for Illinois Institute of Technology (IIT), Michael Reese Hospital, and the Lake Meadows apartment complex. The planners, the story goes, referred pejoratively to the dozen or so blocks south of 31st Street between the giant land-eating institutions as "the gap" in their clearance efforts—they hoped to return and finish the job of clearance later.[28]

Where the planners had seen only blight to be obliterated, the newcomers—including salesmen, schoolteachers, doctors, and architects—along with a few resolute old-timers saw a treasure to preserve. They appreciated the Gap's proximity to the IIT campus and the Lake Meadows and Prairie Shores middle-class apartment complexes, and they downplayed the looming presence of the public housing projects beyond. They relished the Gap's connections to the city: the neighborhood was a ten-minute car ride from Chicago's downtown and had access to a rapid transit elevated train, commuter rail line, and two major highways.

The urban pioneers were bargain hunters, and the near South Side offered rock-bottom prices in the 1970s. Tom Gray, a manager of information technology at Amoco Corporation, paid $12,500 in 1977 for a house that had been cut up into twelve kitchenette apartments; only after he had reconfigured the building did he discover it had been designed by the great architect, Louis Sullivan. Cornelius Goodwin, a real estate broker, surveyed the properties in the mid-1970s and found that the average price for a masonry house and lot came to a mere $7,500; in 1999 he said a vacant lot cost $50,000 and one with a house that had not been rehabilitated went for around $100,000. A few of the braver souls picked up several old buildings in the hope of selling them someday; but for years no one wanted the ghetto properties, so most pioneers just rehabbed one—their home.[29]

Most of all, the rediscoverers of the Gap loved the houses. They were fascinated by the history of the structures, many of which dated from the 1880s. They admired the handsome gray stone and brick exteriors with the jutting gables and bays. As the newcomers renovated their old houses, they came to appreciate the sturdy construction of the buildings, and many cherished the decorative features—the oak mantelpieces, carved banisters, and pocket doors.

The newcomers lived like real pioneers, too, fixing their homes while they lived in them. For many of them, hazards and disorder were the rule of the day: holes in the walls and floors, exposed wires, stairs without risers, exposed rafters and lathing, lumber and tools underfoot, and everywhere, dust. Cornelius Goodwin lived for a time with but one electrical socket in the entire house and the bathroom with no door.[30]

It was good that the prices were low, Goodwin recalls, because on most of the South Side, mortgage money to buy or renovate homes was virtually impossible to obtain. Bank officials were scared to make home improvement loans in an area they considered dead. The Gap's new homeowners resorted to borrowing against their life insurance policies to finance their home improvements.[31]

Leonard McGee working on the exterior of his home in the Gap, December 1984.
Courtesy of Rochelle L. McGee.

Living together on an urban frontier in the South Side ghetto brought the rehabbing newcomers together. About a dozen young married couples met in each others' homes where they swapped stories about rebuilding their homes, shared the names of contractors, and reported the latest about properties around the neighborhood. They formalized their group as the Gap Community Organization.[32]

Within a few years the leaders of the Gap Community Organization realized that simply fixing up their houses would not by itself lift the neighborhood. The newcomers wanted to lure investors to the Gap to renovate the old houses and develop new homes on the area's more than fifteen acres of vacant land. The local leaders worked to involve other residents in their neighborhood improvement efforts, in some cases succeeding and in other cases merely uncovering the differences in perspective between themselves and certain of their financially strapped neighbors.

The Gap's new leaders looked outside the neighborhood for help. They lobbied real estate assessors to appraise property at their true market values and bank officers to make renovation loans. They canvassed politicians to help them clean up the vacant lots and streets and increase safety. Headed by the energetic and enthusiastic Leonard McGee, an information systems manager and leader of the Saving Grace Ministries, the group placed articles in the daily and weekly newspapers that highlighted the Gap's qualities and recent progress.[33]

Inevitably, conflicts arose between the interests of the poorer inhabitants of the Gap and the newcomers bent on improving the neighborhood. To protect the late nineteenth- and early twentieth-century buildings and help attract long-term investors, the Gap Community Organization campaigned in the mid-1980s to have the neighborhood declared a historic district by the city's landmarks commission. The group called on Tim Samuelson for information and support. The ardent preservationist was, of course, happy to see the effort to protect the old buildings, but he worried that some elderly homeowners lacked the money to repair their houses in the historically accurate way that the city's landmark law required. He suggested that the group instead apply to the National Registry of Historic Places, which imposed fewer restrictions and enabled property owners of landmark buildings to apply for federal tax credits. The Gap's leaders, however, were anxious to prevent any more demolition and felt the city's requirements would force new investors to preserve rather than demolish the structures that made the Gap distinctive. They prevailed, and in 1988 the Commission on Chicago Landmarks approved the Gap as a landmark district.[34]

Slowly the Gap began to attract others besides preservationists and rehabbers. During the home construction surge of the 1980s, a couple of adventurous African American architects showed up and developed a high-rise condominium on 31st Street and Martin Luther King Drive. Most developers were competing on Chicago's booming North Side and considered the South Side good only for rental apartment projects, but these architects saw an opportunity in the Gap. The neighborhood's location and growing popularity with professionals, they concluded, would make their new units easy to sell—and they were right.[35]

But the real breakthrough in the redevelopment of the Gap came when a large institution—the Chicago White Sox, of all things—began to develop local real estate. The South Side's venerable major league baseball club decided in the late 1980s to replace their old stadium—Comiskey Park, located west of the IIT campus and remote from the Gap—with a new one nearby. (The White Sox owners, it must be noted, had been negotiating to move to St. Petersburg, Florida, and decided to remain on the South Side only at the last moment after the city and state governments agreed to build the team a new stadium.) For those whose homes were slated for demolition and wanted to stay on the near South Side, the White Sox promised to build new houses. When the relocation families requested that their new homes be located in the Gap, the team obliged and in 1988 placed nineteen new houses on vacant lots there. It was the first significant house construction in the neighborhood in a century.[36]

Home building in the Gap began to seem plausible partly because an alliance of movers and shakers had brought about a startling transformation of a once oppressive landscape just two miles north. At the turn of the nineteenth century, the major railroad lines from the south converged south of Chicago's Loop to feed the factories and businesses there. With passengers pouring in and the adjacent printing industry booming, the Dearborn and Central Railroad Stations had spawned in the early twentieth century a thriving vice district that one observer described as the "borderland of hell." By the 1970s, however, both the passenger and freight rail industry had collapsed, the printing business had moved out, and what remained were lines of sleazy bars, blocks of empty industrial and commercial buildings, and 600 acres of idle railroad yards. Nearby, the Loop's entertainment district had become a hangout for outlandishly dressed young men—Super Flys—who attended the black exploitation films at the city's formerly grand movie palaces.[37]

To rid the city of this eyesore, several of Chicago's prominent business leaders and real estate developers—including in the latter category Ferd Kramer and Philip Klutznik who had helped promote the first slum clearance and redevelopment projects of the South Side—along with a few unconventional architects began a civic enterprise to develop first-class residential neighborhoods on this unpromising site. Among the formidable obstacles was the area's reputation. A marketing analyst told Klutznik in the early 1970s never to refer to the planned racially and economically integrated community by the proposed name of South Loop New Town. "*South* has a bad connotation in Chicago," explained the consultant, "and using the word with *Loop* is suicide." His survey reported that the overwhelming majority of every group—city dwellers, suburbanites, blacks, whites, and Hispanics—"pointed to some negative quality about the area."[38]

It was a torturous process—described vividly by Lois Wille in her book *At Home in the Loop*—but with the strong, if sometimes erratic, support of a succession of Chicago mayors, various developers and architects were able to convert the industrial buildings of Printers Row into residential lofts, recycle the old Dearborn Railroad Station into an office-retail building, and develop Dearborn Park, a combination of high- and medium-rise apartment buildings

Block of newly constructed row houses, South Loop, August 2002.
Courtesy of Monica Chadha.

and almost 200 row houses. And unlike Kramer's earlier attempts at integrated redevelopment on the South Side, the new community was racially integrated.

This remarkable wave of redevelopment during the 1990s pushed south below Roosevelt Road (12th Street) into Chicago's original Black Belt. Dearborn Park II was made up of a new public school, attached low-rise residences, and single-family detached homes, including a surprising subdivision of houses derived from Frank Lloyd Wright's Prairie-School architecture. Further south and east, the old Central Station site was redeveloped into row houses, one of which Mayor Richard M. Daley bought in 1994 for $450,000. The mayor's move from Bridgeport, the South Side Irish citadel where his family and other politicians had lived for generations, to Central Station was a significant cultural event in the city's history and a coup for the up-and-coming near South Side. After almost a half-century of trying, Chicago had managed to create a program of self-sustaining urban renewal.[39]

Once the development of the South Loop broke the barrier of Roosevelt Road, some enterprising real estate businessmen peered into the South Side and saw not the old bugaboos but the new frontier. Larry Mayer, a land broker and developer in Chicago and Florida who had helped sell railroad land for the Dearborn Park developments, had the idea to hold Chicago's annual Parade of Homes in the Gap. It would break tradition: Parades of Homes—those gala events in which construction and decorating firms demonstrate the real

Left to right, Leonard McGee, Mayor Richard M. Daley, and Lewis Collens, president of the Illinois Institute of Technology, talking at the ceremony celebrating the Parade of Homes in the Gap, the first to be held in an inner-city neighborhood. September 1992. Courtesy of Rochelle L. McGee.

estate potential of an area by building and selling several different types of model houses—were always held in suburbs.

Nonetheless, Mayer knew that IIT owned empty lots that were for sale and joined with Jack McNeil and Daniel McLean, two leading Chicago builders who had developed houses at Dearborn Park, to persuade the Home Builders Association of Greater Chicago and the City of Chicago Home Builders Association to sponsor the event. These industry folks were interested in profit but also in demonstrating the viability of building in the city for a racially integrated clientele. They had seen the possibilities of a new kind of urban community and wanted to extend the accomplishments at Dearborn Park.[40]

Within the Gap, some residents feared—accurately as it turned out—that the buildings would promote gentrification. Others—including Leonard McGee and Sokoni Karanja—were delighted at the prospect and pushed to get the model homes built. During the month of September 1992, more than 8,000 visitors attended the Parade of Homes, the first of its kind to be held in an inner-city neighborhood in the United States. Nine buildings, designed in a range of styles from modern to neo-Victorian-Gothic with interiors to match, trumpeted the potential for new development in the old ghetto. The houses, priced from $109,900 to $195,000, sold quickly—four during the first week of the event. In the aftermath of the Parade, one of the contractors, Whitman Architecture and Construction, was contracted to build ten copies of the three-bedroom Phoenix model—complete with spiral metal stairway, central living-room fireplace, and oak flooring—which visitors voted as their favorite building in the Parade. More important, the Parade of Homes started a real estate revival in the Gap that lasted through the 1990s and is still going strong.[41]

The Big Boys Get in the Game

Despite the renewed interest of home buyers and real estate developers in the South Side, the district's revival depends ultimately on the enthusiastic participation of powerful entities, in this case, IIT and the government. Little gets done in Chicago without the intervention of somebody or some entity with power, the access to or exercise of which the locals call "clout." It is pretty much the same everywhere, but Chicagoans, who follow local politics as avidly as they do sports, are particularly blunt when they speak about power. When a big project is announced in the city, which is often, the locals first ask if the deal involves somebody who "can walk on water," and only if the answer is in the affirmative do they believe anything will come of the announcement.[42]

It has been this way with the Gap and the near South Side. IIT has been the semi-invisible hand pushing the revival, an about-face for an institution that in the 1950s cleared thousands of homes for its campus and until very recently acquired and bulldozed old houses adjacent to its campus as a matter of course. A few adroit administrators orchestrated the change in the university's policy by running a sort of guerrilla operation on the inside until they got official backing from their higher-ups. Among the conspirators to make IIT a good neighbor, the one who has been at it the longest is Leroy Kennedy, a community organizer who has served as director of community relations since 1989 and associate vice president for community development at IIT since 1994. Kennedy jumped on the Parade of Homes idea, for example, and with the help of IIT's chief counsel, helped engineer the sale of the school's empty lots to the developers to build the new housing. They saw it as a great opportunity for the school to demonstrate that it could help rather than hurt the neighborhood.[43]

Further discussions between IIT and local leaders such as Leonard McGee of the Gap Community Organization led the university to organize the South Side Partnership, a permanent coalition of institutions—such as colleges and hospitals—and community groups—including the Gap Community Organization, Karanja's Centers for New Horizons, and the Grand Boulevard Federation, an organization dedicated to improving social and educational services for local low-income people—to identify local needs and find ways to fulfill them. The Partnership soon concluded that their South Side neighborhoods needed not just a few new houses but a complete strategy of redevelopment. Thus, Kennedy seized the opportunity when the McCormick-Tribune Foundation gave $8 million to IIT to renovate its campus and wheedled $300,000 from the foundation via the city government to establish in 1990 the Mid-South Planning and Development Commission. After three years of consulting local residents and organizations, the Commission produced the Mid-South Strategic Development Plan, a 130-page book that detailed an agenda for resurrecting three and one-half square miles, from 22nd to 51st Streets, of Chicago's South Side.[44]

"Make no little plans!" commanded Daniel Burnham, a founder of the city planning movement in the early twentieth century and author of an influential plan for Chicago. The Mid-South Commission took his advice to heart.

The Mid-South Plan calls for repopulating the district with 100,000 people—approximately 50 percent more than the current number—of all different incomes and for the construction of large numbers of single-family houses to raise the anemic rates of home ownership.

The way to generate this population and economic boom, the Mid-South Commission declared, was to create an African American historic and music tourist district. Inspired by Tim Samuelson's work on Black Metropolis and the historic preservationists in the Gap, the South Side planners revived an old name for the district, Bronzeville, and urged saving historic structures that had survived and marking the sites of those that had not. They called for the creation of visitor attractions, particularly an entertainment "Blues District" on 43rd Street, which would supplement the famous Checkerboard Lounge with additional nightclubs and tourist-oriented businesses. The planners also dreamed of a large hotel and entertainment complex, with 400 guest rooms, banquet facilities, and a 15,000- to 20,000-seat facility, located near the city's McCormick Place convention center, that would serve the conventions of black churches, fraternities, sororities, and professional organizations whose members would enjoy visiting the Black Metropolis historic sites and music establishments. A local resident, Harold Lucas, formed the Black Metropolis Convention and Tourism Council to develop sightseeing attractions and services with an African American heritage theme on the South Side.[45]

Yet even as IIT, led by Leroy Kennedy, won the trust of neighborhood residents and leaders by lending a hand with community planning, some officials at the school were seriously considering closing their campus and deserting the South Side, a move that would have dealt neighborhood redevelopment a severe blow and left behind enormous bitterness. The IIT officials who wanted to move argued that enrollment, particularly among undergraduates, had been declining at the South Side campus for several years, the once-modern Mies van der Rohe buildings were aging, and the school's younger branches in the suburbs and downtown were thriving.[46]

In 1995 the executive director of the national committee established to devise a strategy to give IIT a national prominence reported that, as he later said, it was time for the school to fish or cut bait. Either IIT should remain on the South Side and encourage undergraduates to attend by restoring and modernizing the campus and stabilizing the surrounding neighborhoods, or it should depart.

The decision to stay on the South Side, IIT officials reasoned, rested in large part on the city government, which they felt must help them if they were going to convince their alumni and supporters to donate money to make the campus a central attraction for the school. The situation was awkward because the mayor, Richard M. Daley, hated any bargaining position that smacked of coercion—such as threatening imminent departure. Even when word got out that certain IIT trustees thought the school should reassess its present location, he grew furious. There followed delicate negotiations, often done by proxy. IIT asked the city to move the elevated transit tracks, which ran right through campus. This the city refused to do. Yet when Daley changed the location of a proposed giant new police headquarters from the West Side to a nearby site on the South Side, university officials took heart. The police headquarters would help mitigate one of the area's drawbacks, its reputation for crime. In discussing the police station with the administration, representatives of IIT, including trustee Jay A. Pritzker, a founder of the Hyatt Corporation, convinced the mayor that the school sincerely wanted to enhance the campus at its present location and Daley in turn pledged to rebuild and plant trees along the public streets that ran through the IIT campus. Thus reassured, in 1996 Pritzker and another donor put up $120 million in the form of a matching grant to restore the main campus, build a new campus center, and endow scholarships.[47]

Having committed itself to staying on the South Side, IIT joined a national movement by colleges and universities to strengthen and revitalize the neighborhoods around them. For decades, many schools adjacent to declining areas ignored or turned their backs on their neighbors, but by 1994 enough institutions of higher education had reached out to neighboring communities that the federal department of HUD started a special office to encourage "university partnerships." Trinity College's announcement in January 1996 that it would spend $175 million to help renew a 15-block area surrounding its campus in Hartford, Connecticut, garnered headlines, but a diverse range of schools, including Yale University in New Haven, Connecticut, Howard University in Washington, D.C., Duquesne University in Pittsburgh, Pennsylvania, Arizona State in Tempe, and the University of California at Berkeley also conducted extensive programs to develop their home communities. South of IIT, the University of Chicago, which once literally walled itself off from next-door Woodlawn, now deploys its own police and funds nonprofit development projects in the neighborhood.[48]

At IIT, Leroy Kennedy and his boss, David Baker, the school's vice president for External Affairs, have begun to put the school at the service of the local community. With grants obtained from the MacArthur Foundation and HUD, IIT launched a plan to expand its volunteer tutoring and assistance program to help the public and Catholic schools in Bronzeville in the technology, math, and science fields in which the university specializes. It has also worked with public schoolteachers on computing, helped organize computer clubs for young people, and offered Saturday computer training sessions for adults. To increase the employment of community residents, the university coordinated with contractors and subcontractors to get jobs for local public housing residents, especially from Stateway Gardens. IIT has joined with other local institutions to help develop a new mixed-income neighborhood to replace Stateway Gardens and plan a rejuvenated 35th Street commercial corridor. And in a complete break with tradition, IIT built faculty and staff housing near its campus—120 townhouses and condominiums designed according to the guidelines laid out in the Mid-South Plan.[49]

Indeed by the late 1990s, the efforts by the planning commission, community groups, local politicians, IIT, and other institutions to resuscitate the South Side were generating a certain synergy. In 1997 the mayor declared his full support for the revival of Bronzeville. Daley's administration, which had adopted a general policy of encouraging community development with public facilities such as libraries, took the bold step of replacing an infamous Bronzeville motel—derided by locals as the "'ho' hotel"—with a new central police department headquarters building, completed in 2000 at a cost of about $65 million. The presence of the giant high-tech police command center at 35th Street and Michigan Avenue immediately improved the marketability of nearby real estate. The city government also built a new entrance near IIT for the Chicago Transit Authority elevated train.[50]

Having received the message from the mayor, the city council in 1998 approved a landmark designation for the Black Metropolis Historic District of eight buildings and one statue, fourteen years after Tim Samuelson first proposed it. With much finagling, legislators obtained monies from the state and federal governments to renovate three of the Black Metropolis landmarks. The historic Armory building, once headquarters of the black "Fighting Eighth" regiment, was renovated, appropriately enough, as an African American military and ROTC charter school. The city helped obtain $3.4 million to restore the Chicago Bee newspaper building as a new branch of the public library. The Wabash Avenue YMCA, built in 1913 as a result of a fund-raising drive by Sears, Roebuck and Company chairman Julius Rosenwald to develop a state-of-the-art facility for African Americans, has been preserved as a YMCA on the lower floor and redeveloped into a single-room occupancy hotel on the upper floors.[51]

There is still a long way to go. The African American preservationist Harold Lucas helped save the historic Supreme Life Building from the wrecking ball, but the building's fate was still uncertain, and at last report the city was seeking another developer with a viable plan for it. The near South Side does not yet generate enough commerce to make the remaining historic buildings financially viable. The era of neglect, however, had at last passed Black Metropolis.

Meanwhile, the Gap emerged as the cutting edge of gentrification on the near South Side. In 1998 the price of rehabbed homes in the Gap started at about $200,000, but could go as high as $350,000, and a commercial developer built Landmark Row, five townhouses that resemble the old buildings but are smaller, and sold them for $195,000 to $220,000. Since then developers have been busy filling in empty lots, no matter how narrow, with new condos and townhouses, and the prices have continued to climb. When Sokoni Karanja moved to the Gap in 1984, he could walk his dogs in the vacant lots, but some years ago he could no longer find such places to take them. So prosperous is the neighborhood's reputation that realtors and residents try to cash in by referring to the area below the traditionally accepted boundary of the Gap at 35th Street as the South Gap.[52]

For the most part, African American upper-middle-class professionals, businessmen, and bankers are buying the new and renovated homes in the Gap. One of Chicago's celebrities, Herb Kent, a radio personality and soul music disc jockey known as "the Cool Gent," has a home there and has come to be known as the mayor of Bronzeville. But Karanja was disconcerted to observe two "Caucasians" building $450,000 homes near his house.[53]

The new wave of commercially sponsored development started to spread here and there in the late 1990s. Close by the Gap, the owners of Lake Meadows are building, adjacent to the high-rise development, seventy townhouses

Bronzeville Pointe, 44th Street and Martin Luther King Drive, April 2002. Courtesy of Glenna Lang.

that sell for as much as $357,000. South of the Gap, at 44th Street and Martin Luther King Drive, one of Chicago's great old boulevards, a team of African American developers in 1998 built three single-family homes and Bronzeville Pointe, a gated community of eighteen attached two- to three-bedroom condominiums, most of which they sold for well over $200,000. On another corner of the same intersection a married couple, both college professors, built a 6,000-square-foot custom home said to be worth $400,000. Since 1998 several commercial and not-for-profit developers have built or announced plans to build in South Side locales—in the Douglas neighborhood, for example— that would have been unheard of just a few years earlier.[54]

Recent data support the observations of residents and visitors that the old South Side ghetto neighborhoods are attracting affluent residents, some of whom are non-black. Between 1994 and 2000, the number of home mortgages issued in the poor neighborhoods of Douglas, Grand Boulevard, and Kenwood-Oakland jumped by 330 percent. In 2000, the proportion of customers for these mortgages who earned close to the median income for the city of Chicago ranged from 25 percent in Douglas to 37 percent in Grand Boulevard, while the proportion of those who earned more than 120 percent of the median income ranged from 29 percent in Douglas to 42 percent in Kenwood-Oakland. The majority of mortgage borrowers were African American, but a noticeable minority—13 percent in Douglas and Grand Boulevard, 22 percent in Kenwood-Oakland—were white. In the same year in the Near South Side, an area that is located close to the Loop and includes the later phases of the trendy Dearborn Park developments, more than half the mortgage buyers earned more than 120 percent of the median income for Chicago, and more than 60 percent were white. Change has come gradually to the old South Side neighborhoods, but its direction is unmistakable. (See Appendix I.)

Vacant Lots and the Power of an Alderman

New construction projects on the South Side are as yet scattered and small in number, however, and vacant lots still dominate the landscape. The empty lots create an opportunity for development but also depress land prices and leave holes in the urban fabric. Their disposition will influence the kind of community that ultimately emerges on the South Side.

In the Third Ward that fans out south of 35th Street, the fate of the vacant lots lies in the hands of alderman Dorothy Tillman. Tillman is a tall, large-boned woman whose trademarks are flamboyant hats and a loud, passionate personality. She spent her childhood in Alabama and Florida, joined the civil rights movement and the Southern Christian Leadership Conference while in high school, and in 1965 followed Martin Luther King to Chicago. Tillman was an early and vocal supporter of Harold Washington, Chicago's first African American mayor, who in 1984 appointed her to fill a vacancy in the city council, where she has thrived in the tough world of Chicago politics. Re-elected easily ever since, she led community cleanup operations, has helped garner millions of government dollars to improve the ward, and bluntly advocates setting aside contracts and jobs for African Americans.[55]

Despite her background in the civil rights movement, the Third Ward's leader wields power like an old-time ward boss. Tillman uses her aldermanic prerogatives unapologetically to act as the arbiter of real estate development and urban design for most of her ward. It is the custom in Chicago city government that the aldermen have a privilege to veto any city action within their ward, although most representatives of inner-city neighborhoods decline to use it to stop new development projects. Ward Three has 3,300 vacant lots owned by the city—over a third of such lots in all Chicago—but their sale, through various city programs, is subject to the aldermanic hold, which in Tillman's case is a tight grip. Recently the newspapers blasted Tillman for denying some constituents the opportunity to purchase garbage-strewn lots where teenagers congregate and drink. To be fair, Tillman insists that she merely wants to use her influence to give African Americans an opportunity they will not get in white neighborhoods. In February 2000, for example, the alderman announced that she had lined up ten black developers to build homes on ten city-owned lots. She would like to reach her goal of 70 percent African American developers, although she has also worked with white builders. The effect of the aldermanic hold is to make Dorothy Tillman a sort of Robert Moses—the powerbroker who built the bridges and highways of New York—of Chicago's Third Ward.[56]

Tillman has all but ignored the work of the Mid-South Planning Commission and developed her own plans for reviving Bronzeville. Tillman's vision for the South Side, like the Mid-South Plan, involves new housing development and a music district, but its core is an African Village, a shopping bazaar of African, Caribbean, and African American shops. She also has in mind an immigration center where Africans or West Indian immigrants could obtain help, learn of employment opportunities, and meet one another. Speaking of the local planners whose ideas, such as the black historical theme, differed from hers, the alderman declared, "We take whatever they have that's good and use it, and if it's not, then we have to discard it."[57]

Tillman and the Mid-South Commission clashed repeatedly over the best way to exploit the South Side's musical heritage—indeed, she once questioned the executive commissioner's right to speak on community matters in a public meeting. The commission had helped make the city's blues festival an annual event, while Tillman organized her own annual music event, the Bring It on Home to Me Roots Festival.[58]

Since the 1980s South Side community groups had called for an entertainment Blues District on 43rd Street, an idea they incorporated into the Mid-South Plan. After all, the Checkerboard Lounge, one of the last of the great blues clubs, was located on 43rd Street, and the city recognized the street's importance by naming a section of it Muddy Waters Drive.

Alderman Tillman felt differently. She favored a music district located on 47th Street, which happened to be around the corner from her office. Furthermore, at the corner of 47th Street and King Drive, the site of the Regal Theater that burned down in the 1970s, Tillman spent years helping to raise more than $4 million of state and city funds to help a nonprofit organization develop the 47th Street Cultural Center and Lou Rawls Theater, which includes an 800-seat auditorium, roller-skating rink, recording studio, and radio and television broadcast and training facilities. Opposite the Lou Rawls Theater site, she let the city tear down an old commercial building—the last standing in the area—to build a statue honoring the famous musician Quincy Jones, who left Chicago with his family when he was eleven years old.[59]

In 1998 the city's planning department came out in favor of 47th Street, and the partisans of 43rd Street protested that the alderman had pressured the planning department behind the scenes. Agency officials cited their consultant, who made the reasonable argument that a blues district stood a better chance on 47th Street, which connected directly to two of Chicago's major highways and still had working stores on it. The officials also confirmed her opponents' suspicions that they had listened to Tillman, and given the custom of deferring to local politicians, the alderman's opinion would decide the issue.[60]

Yet for all her political influence, the alderman has been slow to develop her vision for Bronzeville. Her pet project, the Cultural Center and Lou Rawls Theater, ground to a halt in 2000, prompting the singer, who had come every year to the Bring It on Home to Me festival, to stay away. The following year he was further upset to find Tillman had dropped his name from the theater without telling him. By the summer of 2001 little more than a building shell stood on the site and little progress had been made on either the African Village bazaar or the 47th Street Blues District.[61]

As appealing as village bazaars and blues clubs sound, lack of demand for such outlets thwarts the planning dreams of both the Third Ward's alderman and the Mid-South Planning Commission. Relying primarily on African American tourists to patronize a blues district year-round, wherever it is located, seems unrealistic, especially since the blues is more popular among whites than blacks. In general, retail outlets and projects that depend on paying customers require a sufficiently large population living nearby to support them — which is why depopulated inner-city areas often suffer from a lack of stores. The key then is to bring in more people, which will happen when the alderman and the city government allow all those vacant lots to be developed.

Whither the Public Housing?

Even more important to the South Side's rebirth than Tillman's vacant lots is the fate of the mountain range of high-rise public housing projects. The city's mayor, Richard M. Daley, has made a cause of destroying the elevator public housing buildings over whose construction his father, Mayor Richard J. Daley, once proudly presided.

Chicago loves big deals, and so the schemes to demolish the projects are hugely ambitious. At the infamous Cabrini-Green project near the city's Gold Coast, the mayor declared a billion dollar development project that included demolition of the old buildings, construction of a new school, and development of hundreds of new homes as well. In February 2000 the mayor, HUD Secretary Andrew Cuomo, and the Chicago Housing Authority (CHA), signed a five-year $1.5 billion Plan for Transformation for Chicago's public housing projects. The plan called for the CHA to develop or rehabilitate more than 25,000 units on current public housing sites, destroy all fifty-one of the gallery high-rises — which contain more than 18,000 apartments — and provide all the current residents with either a new low-rise home in new mixed-income developments on the same site or a housing voucher to use in private housing elsewhere.[62]

The people who lived in the CHA apartments at first were skeptical of the grandiose plan to destroy the monoliths. Some doubted the CHA would ever demolish the buildings — until they saw it happening with their own eyes. Others thought the redevelopment would happen, but feared that it would put people who were better off in new homes and leave them out in the cold.

The residents of the public housing projects, especially the high-rises, could be forgiven their skepticism, in light of the history of the housing agency.[63] The city's obsession with high-rise public housing first emerged during the early 1950s as a way to confine public housing to slum neighborhoods; and long after the enthusiasm for tall public housing projects had cooled in other cities, Chicago continued to erect monumental slabs that came to be seen as monumental failures. On the Near West Side was Henry Horner Homes (920 apartments in 7 seven-story and 2 fifteen-story structures) completed in 1957. On the Near North Side, two projects, the 1958 Cabrini Extension (1,925 units in 15 buildings seven, ten, and nineteen stories tall) and the 1961 William

Green Homes (1,096 units in eight, fifteen, and sixteen stories), comprised the intimidating Cabrini-Green. Down State Street on the South Side the city built one high-rise building after another. The best known were Stateway Gardens, built in 1958, which contained 1,684 units in 2 ten-story and 6 seventeen-story buildings, and the monster of them all, Robert Taylor Homes. Approved during the first mayor Daley's reign and completed in 1962, Taylor's 4,312 units in twenty-eight identical buildings of sixteen stories made it the largest public housing project in the world.[64]

Once the object of pride, today this roll call of monstrosities raises the question: what were they thinking? Probably about making money. Chicago, after all, is the city—according to columnist Mike Royko—whose unofficial motto was Ubi Est Mea? or Where Is Mine? To the consternation of federal officials, public housing development costs in Chicago far exceeded those in New York where land and construction wages were higher. Nothing symbolizes the descent of the Chicago Housing Authority more than the rise to power of Charles R. Swibel. Daley the Elder appointed Swibel to the CHA Board of Commissioners in 1956 and then promoted him to Chairman of the Board in 1963 despite the controversies that swirled around him. Although the nominal purpose of public housing is to provide decent homes to low-income people, Swibel made his money as a landlord of skid-row hotels and investor in other slum buildings. Sensing the irony, local newspaper scribes dubbed the new chairman "Flophouse Charlie." Despite a series of scandals, Swibel managed to survive the end of the first Daley's reign and become a principal adviser to one of Hizzoner's successors, Jane Byrne.[65]

Not surprisingly, Swibel's reign at the CHA coincided with growing mismanagement of the CHA and its projects. Early on, the high-rises were plagued by elevator breakdowns, mechanical failures, poor maintenance, and lack of cleanliness. Then, as Chicago's public housing population grew poorer, the social problems escalated. The poster child for a sick public housing project was Cabrini-Green on the Near North Side. After ten people were murdered in Cabrini-Green during the first nine weeks of 1981, mayor Jane Byrne and her husband temporarily moved into the project, much to the delight of the local and national news media. So great was the wreckage of what once had been a model agency that the directors who followed Swibel—whose tenure at CHA mercifully ended in 1982—failed to tame the Chicago Housing Authority or the worst of its nightmare projects.[66]

The people who lived in Chicago's large public housing projects survived as well as they could, many running under-the-counter businesses that ranged from hair dressing and car repairs to prostitution. In the absence of the usual authorities such as the police, tenant leaders instituted their own system of social order. Using small payoffs and personal contacts, the leaders regulated the tenants' businesses, got CHA personnel to make repairs, found willing cops to investigate burglaries, or sent some muscle to lean on wife beaters and other miscreants. The tenants' informal social system broke down, however, in the late 1980s when the street gangs converted to full-time drug-dealing operations and took over the housing projects. Gang members shot each other and bystanders as they fought one another over market share, beat up the residents, and strong-armed the tenant entrepreneurs to pay them extra money.[67]

By the 1990s, high vacancy rates, intense poverty, single mothers, teenage pregnancies, violent gangs, and drug wars had come to characterize large-scale public housing in Chicago. Shocking violence—such as young children being killed—became a regular occurrence.

"The Folks," a descendant of the Gangster Disciples, one of two major gangs that once divided the territory of the ghetto between them, controlled the drug trade in the high-rises. Speaking in the spring of 2000, Connie Jones, a health technician at Stateway Gardens where conditions were the worst, reported that the gang members acted as if they owned the place, searching visitors and taking violent retribution on any who defied their will. The drug dealers shouted the names of their wares—such as "Titanic," a brand of cocaine—to their customers, many of whom appeared to Jones to be affluent whites from far away. The dealers hired older addicts to act as lookouts. The dealers' security guards pretended to sweep the sidewalk and cried "white and blue! white and blue!" when they saw the familiar colors of the police squad cars. The drug addicts and dealers, according to Jones, exploited the women in public housing, referring to them contemptuously as "project 'ho's."[68]

Patricia Titus, a resident of Robert Taylor Homes, probably spoke for many when she expressed her weariness and frustration with the life in the high-rise developments. To her, Robert Taylor Homes is a place where tenants throw their garbage in the hallways, drug dealers run open markets, and gangs recruit boys at an early age. Titus said that she avoided her neighbors and kept her children inside her apartment as much as possible. She and other residents and resident leaders were exasperated with the CHA for failing to enforce its own rules and screen applicants.[69]

Things had not been going well at the Chicago Housing Authority either. By 1995 mismanagement at the CHA was so bad that HUD took it over and installed at its head Joseph Shuldiner, a HUD deputy secretary who had earned a reputation as a good manager in New York and Los Angeles. Shuldiner began the work of renewing Chicago's troubled housing projects. Prying money out of his old agency, HUD, he oversaw the redevelopment of Henry Horner Homes on the Near West Side and the early rebuilding of Cabrini-Green. Shuldiner encouraged the tenants to help CHA draw up plans for what to do with the projects, and interestingly, they chose to save some buildings and demolish several others.[70]

Before Shuldiner could carry out the plans, however, HUD, under its new secretary Andrew Cuomo, transferred the CHA back to city control, and in April 1999 Mayor Daley put in his own team headed by Phillip Jackson, a former chief of staff at the public school department who had once lived in Robert Taylor Homes. The word around town had it that the mayor thought the first public housing redevelopment plans were too limited. The mayor, it was said, wanted to destroy all the high-rise projects and give the residents vouchers to live elsewhere.[71]

Sure enough, eight months later, Jackson announced the sweeping Plan for Transformation, which entailed the demolition of all Chicago's high-rise projects (except those for the elderly, not generally considered a problem). Making such an ambitious plan possible was HOPE VI, a multi-billion dollar HUD program begun in 1993, which aims to demolish the worst public housing projects in the United States and reconstruct them as well-managed, mixed-income developments. Jackson confidently predicted that the city's public housing stock would be completely overhauled and within seven years would be an asset to the city.[72]

Jackson's short tenure was marked by controversies: there were disputes with HUD officials and CHA board members, and key administrative personnel including the chief financial officer quit or were fired. In May 2000 Daley named another supporter, an African American alderman, Terry Peterson, to head the CHA and implement the Plan for Transformation.[73] Peterson, the third director of the CHA in as many years, brought a measure of stability to the CHA. He fervently believed in helping the poor and pushed the CHA to provide social services, which for years it had badly neglected. Peterson also got along well with people. Besides earning the loyalty of his staff and board, he won the trust of the public housing tenant leaders. This was no easy task, but it was important because the tenants were extremely anxious about where they were going to live.[74]

Through all the turmoil at the top of CHA, Chicago's high-rise buildings continued to come down — forty-two of the fifty-one would be gone by the end of 2002.

Their demise posed critical questions about what would happen after the demolition. The year it adopted the Plan for Transformation, the CHA guaranteed that it would provide 25,000 new or rehabilitated dwellings to accom-

Demolition of Stateway Gardens, 3615 South Federal Street, 2001.
Courtesy of Camilo José Vergara.

modate all the households then located in Chicago's public housing. The destruction and redevelopment required families to move to temporary residences, however, and that made tenants uneasy about whether they would in fact ever return. In addition, the CHA had committed to help find homes by the year 2007 for some 6,000 households that it estimated would choose to use supplemental rental vouchers to live in privately owned apartments. Yet when squatters who lived in the projects were included, which activists insisted on, the number of potential families taking vouchers far exceeded 6,000. Furthermore, Chicagoans of all racial and ethnic backgrounds were opposed to public housing residents moving to their communities. Advocates for the poor feared that many families would simply be lost in the process, either because they were disqualified by work rules or arrest records or because the CHA, known for its inefficiency in the past, would lose track of them. Their doubts were understandable: it took fifteen years under the court-ordered Gautreaux program to place 7,100 Chicago public housing families in homes outside the ghetto.[75]

For the inhabitants of Bronzeville, the crucial question was what would replace the projects. The Plan of Transformation calls for mixed-income communities—in which small numbers of public housing tenants live side by side with larger numbers of middle-income people. Nonprofit and commercial private developers would develop and build thousands of new single-family row and detached houses where the high-rises once loomed.

As attractive as the plan sounded, obstacles remained. Although the CHA looked to Atlanta's Centennial Place (described in Chapter 5) as a model of such a development on the site of a former public housing project, no city has developed so many large mixed-income subdivisions simultaneously. Then there was the matter of money. The CHA always knew that the $1.6 billion committed by the federal government was only a first installment on the entire cost of developing 25,000 low-income dwelling units. When the agency decided to draw down the sum faster than originally planned—to show some end products quickly—and worry about additional financing later, critics feared that it would run out of money and be forced to reduce the number of low-income homes.[76]

They need not worry. Mayor Daley's avid support for the massive redevelopment campaign makes it inevitable. City agencies such as Chicago's planning department, which might have been indifferent otherwise, realized that the mayor backed it and joined the effort. Even without having enough funds to finish the job, CHA officials are confident that when the time comes, the mayor will help them find the large sums needed to complete the job.

In short, the demolition of the high-rise public housing projects and the redevelopment of their sites is a done deal. Like the program that built the high-rise public housing in the first place, local political support and federal largesse made it possible. In the end, the government will put up billions of dollars to construct the new public housing units in the mixed-income developments, and the developers will borrow what they haven't received from the government to build the market units. Rather than nonprofits, commercial real estate firms and consultants—such as the teams that won the contracts to

143

develop the sites of Stateway Gardens and Robert Taylor Homes—will do most, if not all, of the development.

And if the scheme works—if the new houses that replace the public housing are attractive and well managed—the revival of the South Side will snowball. Perhaps then nonprofit community groups and government leaders, both of which have done little development so far, will help fill the empty tracts with housing for working-class people and create the balanced communities of which they have dreamed.

But so far the market for housing on the South Side indicates a different outcome. More likely, upper-middle-class professionals, black and white alike, will move in—attracted by the neighborhoods' excellent location, transportation, and historic heritage—rents and housing prices will climb, and private developers will enter the South Side *en masse* to rebuild the vacant land. Once the land rush begins, not even a Dorothy Tillman will be able to hold them off. The visions of African American mixed-income or working-class neighborhoods, like so many other visions of South Side renewal, will fade, and upscale gentrification will be the order of the day.

Chicago's West Side Story

If the South Siders want a good example of a community taking charge of its own redevelopment, they might well look to the West Side, which is ironic since the West Side had always been the poorer, tougher part of Chicago.

Indeed, the history of the Near West Side, the neighborhood that Earnest Gates' inner voice encouraged him to revive, gave few reasons for hope. Long ago, in the 1890s, the Near West Side was so poor and overcrowded that it was chosen by Jane Addams as the site of Hull House, the most influential settlement house in the nation. As immigrant Russian and Polish Jews, Italians, and Greeks progressed and moved away, they were replaced by African Americans.

Like the South Loop, the West Loop had a skid row of flophouses, missions, and bars. And like the near South Side, the West Side experienced slum clearance and the construction of public housing projects, including the first Jane Addams Homes and Henry Horner Homes, and waves of urban renewal, promulgated by an aggressive university (the building of the Chicago campus of the University of Illinois destroyed an old Italian neighborhood) and medical institutions. Unlike the South Side, the West Side had been an area of major African American settlement only since the 1950s, yet it was dominated by white ethnic politicians and still contained much old and run-down housing. Burdened by poverty, discrimination, and a relative lack of black institutions, the West Side bred more violent rage than did the older South Side communities. Twice in two years, in 1966 and again after the death of Martin Luther King Jr. in 1968, the West Side exploded in violent riots, destroying several blocks of stores and causing white residents and business owners to flee.

These events took their toll on the district. The Near West Side suffered a tremendous drop in population. In 1960 the neighborhood was home to 126,600 souls; by 1970 the figure had dropped to 78,700. In 1990 the U.S. Census counted 46,200 people there. One of the poorest neighborhoods in Chicago, the Near West Side's median household income was $9,336 compared to $23,902 for the city as a whole. About half the families earned income below the poverty line.[77]

Yet catalysts of transformation are at work on the West Side, too. Like the South Side, real estate development in Chicago's downtown is spilling into the old neighborhoods. Capitalizing on the growing popularity of the idea of living downtown, owners of old commercial and industrial buildings on the western edge of the Loop converted them into residences—"loft" condo apartments complete with small decks—for young working couples and single people with cash to spare. Soon stylish restaurants began to appear next to the hardware stores, plumbing supply shops, and warehouses of the industrial district west of the Loop. The prestige of the area shot upward when television star Oprah Winfrey built a studio complex for her productions there. But in the heart of the Near West Side, it was the opening of the United Center sports arena in 1994, followed by the Democratic convention held there two years later, that accelerated growth and revival.

Earnest Gates knew nothing of the future trends when he returned to try to breathe life into his depressed section of the Near West Side. All he knew was that he had to begin somewhere. Gates, perhaps listening to his inner voice again, decided to start on Leavitt Street with the house where he had been raised. If he could remake the image of this block, Gates believed, he would demonstrate to the neighborhood and the world beyond that here was a place worth saving and inspire others to join in. He completely renovated his house—inside and out—and stepped back to assess the situation. His building looked really great, Gates thought, "but the rest of the buildings looked like crap." There was plenty of work left to do.[78]

Gates bought up neighboring properties on the Leavitt Street block, sometimes by paying the back taxes on buildings that had been seized through a forfeiture process. Now I have all these junk buildings, he realized, and need somebody with whom to share them. He buttonholed a couple of old buddies, fellows he had grown up with, and described his vision of restoring the block. Surprisingly, they listened to Gates and bought houses and began to fix them up.

Gates encountered skeptics. The vice president of the bank where he had done business for years listened politely to his request for a loan to rehabilitate the house next to his. But when Gates mentioned the location of the house, she told him the bank was not interested in that location. "Why not?" Gates asked. It's just not a good area, came the reply.

Gates pointed out the address of the building he planned to rehabilitate and that of his own home. "They're right next door," he explained. "People do live in that neighborhood. I live in that neighborhood." The bank officer was unimpressed. Back and forth they went. Finally Gates said, if he didn't get the loan, he was pulling his commercial account from the bank. The vice president reluctantly agreed to the loan.

Leavitt Street block buildings, which Earnest Gates and his friends renovated, on the Near West Side, August 2002. Courtesy of Glenna Lang.

Even more shocking was the reaction of people who lived in the neighborhood. Instead of applauding Gates's renovation projects, the neighbors were suspicious and jealous. "What's he trying to prove?" they asked. "Who does he think he is?" Even residents of the Near West Side thought their neighborhood was beyond hope of redemption.[79]

Fighting Off Bears

Ironically, it was a threat to destroy the neighborhood that shook the residents out of their apathy and galvanized them into saving it. The city's football team—"Da Bears" as they are affectionately known in Chicago—had grown anxious in the late 1980s to leave Soldiers Field, the team's original home located south of the Loop on Lake Michigan. After a year of considering and rejecting suburban locations and failing to win support for a new stadium on the lakefront, the team decided on a site on the Near West Side close to the old Chicago Stadium, where the city's professional hockey and basketball teams, the Chicago Blackhawks and the Chicago Bulls, held their games.

With the support of the mayor at the time, Harold Washington, and the governor of Illinois, the Bears and their owner, Mike McCaskey, in 1987 announced a plan to build a new 75,000-seat football stadium and adjacent parking lots. Most of the land where the football stadium itself was to be located was vacant, and much of it was owned by William Wirtz, the well-connected owner of the Blackhawks and the Chicago Stadium. But the majority of land in the western part of the plan was occupied by homes and businesses. In total, the plan called for destroying 328 homes of up to 1,500 people, most of whom were elderly and low-income African Americans.

To compensate for the demolition of houses, the team and the city proposed one of those grand plans frequently announced in Chicago, but less frequently carried out. A 100-block tract of the Near West Side, according to the scheme, would be developed into the new football stadium; a refurbished Chicago Stadium; a sports medicine center run by the Rush-Presbyterian Hospital; a model neighborhood of renovated and new townhouses, parks, and stores; and an industrial park and economic development zone.[80]

The Bears' scheme, therefore, was to be a mix of urban renewal programs. It would use the old-fashioned bulldozer approach the city had pursued enthusiastically in the past, even though it displaced people from their houses, and combine this with the more recent economic development approach. Members of the city's establishment—including the *Chicago Tribune*—wanted the new stadium to be built and thought redeveloping the Near West Side, which they considered an eyesore, was a great idea.

But on the West Side, local community organizations were divided over the Bears stadium plan. Supporting the plan were the Midwest Community Council, an organization that represented a larger area than just the Near West Side, and its leader Nancy Jefferson, an ally of Mayor Harold Washington. Jefferson, according to people in the neighborhood, had been hired by the Bears to round up local support. The district's newly elected alderman also supported the plan.[81]

In vehement opposition was the Interfaith Organizing Project, a coalition of a dozen local churches and local residents, especially those whose homes were slated for demolition. The opponents of the football project believed that the number of displaced residents could reach 2,000, that much of the promised replacement housing would never materialize or be too expensive for the present occupants, and that the members of the community who had held on for so long would be scattered to the wind.[82]

The elderly citizens whose houses were threatened provided the backbone of the effort, the local ministers—especially the Reverend Arthur Griffin, pastor of the First Baptist Congregational Church—added spiritual fervor, while the creativity came from two "partners in crime," Earnest Gates and Wilma Ward. The two had become friends over a shared interest in reviving the Near West Side. Gates was involved in building renovation and quietly supported the young men of the neighborhood by donating to their basketball teams. Ward had grown up in a town outside St. Louis in a family whose deep commitment to the civil rights movement had imbued her with an unquenchable thirst for social justice. She worked in community nonprofits, first as a manager of a low-income housing development and later as an administrator of a home repair program for Chicago Commons, a settlement house. Gates and

Ward were both deeply perturbed by the stadium proposal and soon found themselves fighting it side by side.[83]

Led by the Interfaith Organizing Project, the stadium opponents staged colorful, attention-grabbing demonstrations that often made the evening news. They marched at city hall and the mayor's house, invaded an elegant fashion show sponsored by the hospital, and protested at the Bears' opening exhibition game in Plattville, Illinois. At the last protest, Ward says, Bears' owner McCaskey promised to withdraw his plan but later reneged on the promise. The West Siders went to McCaskey's posh home town, Winnetka, where they first staged a mock football game between the "Bares" and "West Side Residents" and then went door-to-door to gather support from McCaskey's neighbors by showing them a map that described the impact the stadium plan would have if carried out in the suburb. The noisy opposition forced the stadium planners back to the drawing board more than once.[84]

But for all their protests, the people who fought the massive redevelopment scheme sometimes felt isolated. The opponents of the stadium redevelopment plan could not understand why their leaders would side with white executives against ordinary black citizens. They felt especially wounded that Jesse Jackson, a Chicagoan and a national civil rights leader, never spoke publicly against the scheme in his hometown, yet traveled to Florida to crusade against the displacement of African Americans by the construction of the Joe Robbie Stadium in Miami. Gates approached Harold Washington to arrange a meeting to lay out the community's case, but the mayor died shortly afterward in November 1987. His successor, Eugene Sawyer, endorsed the stadium project.[85]

The fight got nasty. The *Chicago Tribune* ran a story that tried to discredit the leaders of the Interfaith Organizing Project as outsiders and extremists and attacked Gates as a wealthy speculator of the type he decried. Wilma Ward's supervisor insisted she leave her job if she continued her community work because the demonstrations against the mayor endangered the organization's funding. State officials harassed Gates's truck drivers, and his firm lost an account. They received harassing calls, even death threats.[86]

The local resistance led by Griffin, Ward, and Gates managed to delay the football stadium project just long enough for events to catch up with it. First the state legislature gave a cool reception to the city's request for $90 million in financing for the project. Then Bears' owner McCaskey enraged Chicago Stadium owner Wirtz by trying to push through the Illinois General Assembly a bill for stadium aid that would have allowed the city to take Wirtz's land through eminent domain.

Convinced McCaskey was trying to steal his real estate and then charge him for its use, Wirtz set a crack team of lobbyists against the bill and stopped the football stadium legislation dead in its tracks. The millionaire hockey team owner then announced that he intended to build another stadium for the Blackhawks hockey team on the very land, as it happened, coveted by the Bears but would still maintain the old Chicago Stadium for circuses and concerts. A plan for three stadiums on the Near West Side was too much even for Mayor Sawyer and Nancy Jefferson, leader of the conservative Midwest Community Council. They supported only the football stadium, which the Bears could not develop without the land of the wrathful Wirtz. Richard M. Daley was elected mayor of Chicago in 1989 and delivered the coup-de-grace to the project by opposing the use of any public money for a football stadium.[87]

Unity at United Center

The residents of the Near West Side had little time to savor their victory before the new stadium project again threatened the homes of neighborhood residents. The owners of the Chicago Blackhawks and Chicago Bulls unveiled a plan for a 22,000-seat arena and parking lots for 7,000 cars—the arena that would eventually become the United Center. Unlike the government-supported Comiskey Park venture, the teams would use private financing, based on revenue of luxury skyboxes, to pay for the new stadium project. They still wanted a lot of help from the city and local governments, however, including $18.5 million in state funds for public works improvements—such as rebuilding several streets and moving utility lines—and an exemption from the "local option" that allowed residents to vote to ban alcohol sales in their precinct.

In addition, the partnership wanted the state to give the city "quick take" condemnation powers so that tracts could be acquired before the price was determined. Wirtz already owned and had cleared land south of the stadium, but to create 500 parking spaces the plan called for demolishing seventy units of housing occupied, as had been the case in the football stadium scheme, by elderly, low-income African Americans. The demolition plan raised the issue, as a state senator put it, of "what we do with the people to be displaced."[88]

In this venture, Wirtz had a partner, Jerry Reinsdorf, the owner of the White Sox and more relevantly, the Chicago Bulls, the basketball team that rented the Chicago Stadium for its games and, thanks to its prodigious young star, Michael Jordan, was on the verge of becoming one of the most dominant teams in the history of American professional sports. In the wake of strong seasons by the Blackhawks and Bulls, the teams' owners tried to get the city to help them rush a stadium bill through the Illinois General Assembly, but failed to do so before the state legislature's session ended.[89]

The political equation had changed, however. Even though Wirtz had long been a friend of the Daley family, the mayor made it clear he would not jump on the bandwagon until the neighborhood received satisfactory answers to its questions, especially the matter of who would pay for replacement housing. It was an ironic turn of events for the Near West Side: once a black mayor had supported the white owner of a sports team against black residents; now a white mayor supported the black residents against the white owners of the sports teams.

In the fall of 1989, the United Center consortium, represented by Bulls owner Jerry Reinsdorf and his right-hand man and Bulls' executive president, Howard Pizer, came to the Near West Side to meet the neighbors and the Interfaith Organizing Project leaders and win their support. With the memory of the hard-fought battle against the Bears still fresh, the defenders of the Near West Side prepared for difficult negotiations. "Wilma, be careful," Ward remembers a sweet little old lady telling her. "You can't trust white people." This time the neighborhood, Ward said, was determined to "get something out of the deal, and get it in *writing*." As they entered a public meeting held at a West Side community college, the consortium representatives first encountered Earnest Gates, who some people said had a chip on his shoulder, standing in the doorway, scowling, arms folded, with a block of wood strapped to his shoulder.[90]

The stance the team owners adopted at the early meetings alienated the neighborhood representatives. Reinsdorf, who had a reputation for being a hard-nosed businessman, began one meeting by saying he wasn't there to rebuild the West Side and had no moral obligation to do so. Wilma Ward said we don't want you to rebuild the neighborhood, but we would like a partner in our efforts. To the requests of the Near West Siders, Pizer and Reinsdorf replied again and again, "No." Finally, after a couple of similar parleys, one of the spokesmen for the neighborhood said to the owners, "If you have that attitude, you won't get a stadium." Reinsdorf barked, "I don't need this," and he and Pizer walked out of the meeting. Later they were convinced to return, but Gates concluded that the team owners were jerks. "They think they can just walk in here," he remembers thinking, "throw a few dollars on the table, and take our land."[91]

For their part, Reinsdorf and Pizer looked at the project as a relatively simple transaction: money for homes and land. Representatives from the Interfaith Organizing Project insisted that in order to produce dwellings of equal quality, the United Center consortium would have to replace houses worth somewhere between $40,000 and $85,000 with new houses to cost over $200,000. The team owners objected to paying so much more than the properties were currently worth. Not only that, but the actual number of houses to be replaced was uncertain, and the sports teams' financial advisers said that if all the homeowners chose to have a replacement house—versus selling their current houses and moving elsewhere—ballooning costs would threaten the entire stadium project, which in any event could not get backing from any major United States bankers. And Reinsdorf and Pizer could not understand the deep skepticism of the representatives of the Interfaith Organizing Project, who feared that the team owners would not do what they said they would.[92]

But Mayor Daley made it clear that the team owners had to obtain local consent for their plans before he would do anything for them—including provide the public improvements the Center would need. Reinsdorf and Pizer came back to the Near West Side to meet with the neighborhood's representatives in the basement of St. Stephen's African Methodist Episcopal Church. This time the locals—led by the Interfaith ministers, Wilma Ward, and Earnest Gates—submitted to the team owners a list of points such as creating a revolving fund to develop new homes in the neighborhood. They insisted upon these points as a prerequisite for community support. The owners' staff took up and agreed to each of the points, and the local leaders voted to proceed.[93]

After meeting for a couple of months to hammer the points and conditions into a workable legal document, the negotiations came to an abrupt halt. Reinsdorf and his people became unavailable and no longer took or returned phone calls from the Near West Side leaders. It was as if the new arena agreement had just died.

"Well," Gates thought, "there was life before this. We'll just go back to work, try to get some housing built and see if we can help solve the social issues of the neighborhood."[94]

Gates and his allies on the Near West Side believed that the sports teams were trying to go around them. Gates heard later that Blackhawks' owner Wirtz advised Reinsdorf to break off negotiations and wait until some leader "came to the back door," as Chicagoans say, with a price, in the form of consultant fees, to swing community support for the deal.[95]

According to Pizer, the sports consortium simply wanted to make a deal and found itself caught between the two community groups that had clashed over the Bears' stadium. Nancy Jefferson, the Interfaith Organizing Project's old rival, had worked for years on and off with the Wirtz family, and her group, the Midwest Community Council, supported the new project. Jefferson told the sports consortium representatives that no one had elected Earnest Gates to be the neighborhood representative and suggested they make offers to individual homeowners who could decide for themselves. The team officials did so, and according to Pizer, many people took them up on the offer. But not everyone: a few refused—key elderly property owners who were aligned with the Interfaith group.[96]

The team owners went to Mayor Daley, according to Gates, to see if he would help by taking the dissenters' land through eminent domain. Even without that help, the deal depended on the city's willingness to provide street and service improvements and to donate its empty lots for replacement housing. Perhaps the mayor did not want to be held responsible for throwing old people out of their homes so two relatively unpopular sports owners could build a stadium. Perhaps he was influenced by Tom Rosenberg, a local real estate developer, long-time Daley supporter, and a friend of Gates, who helped the Interfaith group in the negotiations. Or perhaps the mayor just wanted neighborhood consensus before he spent public money on a private project. For whatever reason, Daley made it clear that until Gates and his allies were satisfied, there would be no new stadium for the Bulls and Blackhawks.[97]

For almost a year, nothing changed. No neighborhood leader showed up to sell out the group, and the senior citizens who owned the crucial properties held firm. Then one day Gates's phone rang. It was Jerry Reinsdorf. "I want to talk about your favorite project," he said. "Oh, what's that?" Gates replied coolly. "Don't be stupid," the sports mogul told him.[98]

The two sides went back to the bargaining table and eventually agreed on almost everything Gates and the Interfaith group originally had asked for, including the replacement homes that cost about $220,000 each. Still, the neighborhood people worried that the United Center consortium would not live up to its part of the bargain and placed elaborate safeguards for both sides in the agreement. Even so, the two sides continued to go back and forth. The elders

Earnest Gates and Wilma Ward, founders of the Near West Side Community Development Corporation, April 2002. Courtesy of Glenna Lang.

did not like the first house, which was built as a prototype for those that followed. They preferred a duplex house, with a basement and a garage. Fortunately, not all the owners wanted a replacement house and, as Pizer explains, the sports owners were too deeply involved to back out, so they agreed to the changes.[99]

When the sports teams finished building the first set of replacement houses, the mayor and the Interfaith Organizing Project held a large celebration in which Daley spoke in front of the new homes for the benefit of the media. Reinsdorf and Pizer were surprised at how elated the community folk felt at the completion of the buildings. They thought the time to celebrate would have been when they had signed the agreement, not after the buildings were constructed. "It wasn't that big a deal to us," Pizer later recalled, "because we said we were going to do it. But we didn't understand their experience," one which included broken promises and bitter struggles.[100]

In 1994, the consortium completed the construction of the United Center—known in Chicago as the "The House That Michael Built" and thirty-two dwellings in 16 two-flat buildings for the elderly homeowners who lost their houses. Gates and Ward started the Near West Side Community Development Corporation and used the $600,000 construction escrow account from the United Center consortium to build seventy-five new homes affordable to those earning between $41,000 and $62,000 a year.[101]

In the process of all that negotiating, something unusual happened. Reinsdorf and Pizer became more, not less, involved in the community. Pizer in particular became close to Gates and Ward, inviting them to his daughter's wedding and joining the board of the Near West Side Community Development Corporation. He and Reinsdorf helped the residents push the city government to put more money into the neighborhood by rebuilding a park and constructing a library. They took responsibility for keeping up the library and improving a local school. The Bulls built the neighborhood a new Boys and Girls Club at a cost of $4 million and named it after James Jordan, Michael Jordan's father who had recently been murdered. The two Blackhawks' and Bulls' owners, Wirtz and Reinsdorf, put $1 million into the United Center Community Economic Development Fund—Earnest Gates sits on the board—to help local entrepreneurs start or expand small businesses primarily with low-interest loans.[102]

When the Bulls fined one of its star players, Dennis Rodman, for swearing on television, the team called Gates to help them find a worthy cause for the $130,000 they had collected. Gates and the Near West Side Community Development Corporation devised the Rodman Fund to dispense grants for home improvements to elderly seniors who could not otherwise afford to repair their homes.[103]

In pursuing the vision of a healthy mixed-income community, the Near West Side Community Development Corporation took a keen interest in the Henry Horner Homes public housing project. When the Chicago Housing Authority began to reconstruct Horner as a mixed-income subdivision of brightly painted, quaint-looking, single-family row houses, Gates and Ward were dismayed to discover that the CHA had not kept out residents with serious criminal records and leaned on the agency to be more selective. After that, Gates became a member of the board of the CHA, and the Near West Side Community Development Corporation extended its services to the Horner development, instituting a home visitor program to help families adjust to life in their new homes.

Not all has gone smoothly. The United Center Economic Development Fund has made loans to small businesses but has had difficulty finding business projects that will create a significant number of jobs. After encountering a string of delays and obstacles, however, it helped bring a Walgreen's drug store into the area and a new grocery store across the street.[104]

Yet so far, the Near West Side has managed to stay in front of the upscaling trend that could transform the neighborhood more drastically than the residents and their leaders wish. As on the South Side, time is of the essence. Developers are buying lots and building homes, and whites are seen more often traveling and even buying into the neighborhood.[105]

The Strengths of Community Development in Chicago

As gentrification continues apace on Chicago's North Side and in a crescent of neighborhoods that surround the Loop, a few ripples of redevelopment, hastened by large projects such as Dearborn Park and the United Center, have traveled farther west and south. In general, however, urban rebirth has not reached the intensity in the more distant southern and western neighborhoods that is has closer to the city center. In the meantime, a number of excellent organizations operate in Chicago's next ring of lower- and working-class, African American, and immigrant areas.

One of them, Bethel New Life, Inc., has attained international recognition. It started in 1979 when members of a local Lutheran church began to develop housing in the tough West Side neighborhood of West Garfield Park. Even though Bethel New Life began small, its founders boosted its effect by working exclusively in a compact geographic area and ensuring that its projects met more than one need. For example, the senior citizens' residence developed by Bethel New Life contained a space for a health clinic on the first floor, and the organization rehabilitated the Guyon Towers apartment complex to include not only 114 dwelling units but also eight ground-floor storefronts, including a large corner space set aside for a branch bank. By 1988, with tens of thousands of residents in its housing developments and programs, Bethel New Life felt able to tackle large issues such as crime, drugs, and schools. Today, Bethel's "holistic approach" — in the phrase of its leader, Mary Nelson — embraces urban planning and design projects, the construction of new townhouses, local black history exhibits, arts festivals, a recycling center, as well as the economic training and employment programs.[106]

One of the most inspiring stories of a community development leader is that of Richard Townsell, executive director of a West Side organization, the Lawndale Christian Development Corporation. Townsell grew up in a public housing project in North Lawndale at a time when poverty and gangs dominated the neighborhood. While raising three sons, his mother suffered a debilitating heart attack that forced her to rely on a wheelchair to move around; he never knew his father. Townsell nonetheless persevered, attended and graduated from Northwestern University, and became a high school mathematics teacher in a suburban high school. He also trained as a wrestler, winning a spot on the United States wrestling team that competed in 1992. Richard Townsell was poised to escape his ghetto past forever when his pastor from North Lawndale, a man who had helped him rise above his circumstances, called him and persuaded him to return to North Lawndale to help others who were not so fortunate as he.[107]

The Lawndale Christian Development Corporation is one of three closely affiliated church groups. The Lawndale Community Church Recreation Center runs basketball games, aerobic classes, and weight lifting. Its body building room attracts young men to the facility; it was what first attracted Townsell himself to the church. In the same building, the Lawndale Christian Health Center is almost a small hospital. It employs more than 100 staff members, including twenty-two physicians, and offers a wide range of medical services.

The Lawndale Christian Development Corporation, established in 1987 by Lawndale Community Church, started by restoring houses. One of its early programs is a five-year college preparatory curriculum that offers academic classes, tutoring, training in standardized tests, college tours and advising, and assistance in college applications. Thirty to forty Lawndale students enroll every year. All of those who complete the program have graduated from high school, and 85 percent of these go on to attend college.

 Besides education, Lawndale Christian Development Corporation has emphasized real estate development and community organization. In the real estate field, the group has concentrated on producing homes for sale. It has rehabilitated single-family homes, and has renovated apartments, converting them to condominiums. The Corporation had produced fifty-four homes by 2000 and has begun to build more than twenty-five new single-family and two-flat houses on vacant lots. Under Townsell, Lawndale Christian Development Corporation has helped coordinate block clubs, school groups, and other organizations to pressure the government to improve neighborhood safety, schools, and infrastructure. The Lawndale organization has also joined United Power for Action and Justice, an Industrial Areas Foundation regional coalition that works to achieve affordable housing, health care for the uninsured, and better collaboration between African American and Hispanic organizations in Chicago.[108]

The Resurrection Project, which started in 1990, is headquartered in Pilsen, formerly associated with Czechs and other central Europeans and today a predominantly Mexican neighborhood. With the support of a large number of local churches, the Resurrection Project has become a powerhouse that serves about 2,000 people through community development and organizing programs for the Hispanics in Pilsen and adjacent neighborhoods. It has developed 121 homes containing 174 units overall, renovated 73 rental apartments, and is currently developing housing for more than 200 residents in 83 apartments as part of a $16.1 million project. In addition, the Resurrection Project runs two day care centers and an after-school center, which serves more than 400 children. The Resurrection Project celebrates culture and the arts as well, presenting performances at its annual anniversary galas; the Project converted an old church into a theater and arts center, which arts organizations such as the Mexican Folkloric Dance Company call home.[109]

On Chicago's South Side, an Episcopal priest, the Reverend Richard Tolliver, has led a revival in the Washington Park neighborhood that has received national acclaim. Before he arrived in Washington Park, Tolliver's career had taken him as a priest to New York City, the Boston Roxbury neighborhood, and Washington, D.C., and as a director in the Peace Corps to Kenya and Mauritania. When he became the rector of St. Edmund's in 1989, the number of parishioners had shriveled from 2,000 in the 1970s to only about 400. Trying to breathe a sense of hope into this dispirited community was lonely work in the first few years, but gradually Tolliver made headway. He started neighborhood block clubs, reopened the church's elementary school, and joined forces with the Chicago Police Department on a community policing program. The St. Edmund's Redevelopment Corporation has made its most visible impact on the neighborhood by rehabbing more than a dozen townhomes and apartment buildings—including a twenty-four-story high-rise that had become blighted—totaling nearly 500 residential units.[110]

Also on the South Side, a partnership of nonprofit organizations has initiated an effort to rebuild large pieces of the Woodlawn and Kenwood-Oakland neighborhoods. A CDC subsidiary of the Woodlawn Organization, which was started by Saul Alinsky and the Industrial Areas Foundation in the 1960s, has joined with the Woodlawn Preservation and Investment Corporation (WPIC) and the Fund for Community Redevelopment and Revitalization, formed in 1992. The common denominator is Dr. Arthur M. Brazier, pastor of the Apostolic Church of God, who was the founding president of the first group and chaired the board of the latter two. The Fund developed a large shopping center in Kenwood and rehabilitated hundreds of subsidized apartments in Kenwood and Woodlawn. In Woodlawn, the Woodlawn Organization and WPIC have built dozens of single-family and duplex homes and have undertaken an ambitious scheme to convert the virtually empty commercial boulevard of 63rd Street into a thoroughfare of houses. Rebuilding Woodlawn and Kenwood is difficult work, but much like the neighborhoods to the north and west of Chicago's Loop have benefited from the expansion of upper-middle-class housing downtown, they get some lift from a real estate boomlet in the adjacent neighborhood where the University of Chicago is located.[111]

These Chicago organizations, like their counterparts in New York and Boston, enjoy the advantage of a strong support system for community development. In Chicago, as elsewhere, a healthy community development system includes grassroots groups, trade associations for the nonprofits, and a range of private and public institutions willing to put in money and time to ensure the success of community development organizations and projects.

One sure sign of strength is the union of local nonprofits in an umbrella organization. In Chicago local groups came together in 1977 to share professional expertise, and today their coalition, the Chicago Rehab Network, includes more than forty organizations—from one-person to citywide operations—working in more than sixty Chicago neighborhoods. Confronted with the gentrification trend, the Chicago Rehab Network soon adopted its central theme of "Development Without Displacement" to prevent the resegregation by class and race of Chicago's neighborhoods. In keeping with its roots, Chicago Rehab Network offers staff and board members of community development organizations training classes in accounting, housing finance, project management, and property management. Just as important is the work of researching, educating, and mobilizing support for housing and community development legislation and programs. Because it represents so many organizations, the Chicago Rehab Network can get the ear of policy writers and lawmakers in the city, state, and federal governments.[112]

As in other cities, active financial intermediaries are a key component of an effective community development system. In this respect, Chicago is blessed. The Neighborhood Housing Services of Chicago, for example, is the largest member of the Neighborhood Reinvestment Corporation's network of more than 200 affiliates. Since it began operating in 1975 under the leadership of Bruce Gottschall—a former community organizer and CDC director—Neighborhood Housing Services of Chicago has run nineteen programs in low- and moderate-income, minority neighborhoods, stepping into the gap after traditional banking services disappeared and, in seven cases, closing programs once the lenders returned. As of March 31, 2002, Neighborhood Housing Services of Chicago had recorded making more than 13,000 loans totaling almost $285 million to low- and moderate-income families to acquire, rehabilitate, or remodel their homes. It helped 2,000 individuals and families become new homeowners. It financed the rehabilitation or building of more than 22,000 houses and apartment buildings, including 900 foreclosed vacant houses that were sold to first-time home buyers. In addition, Neighborhood Housing Services of Chicago trains first-time home buyers and organizes local residents to improve their neighborhoods.[113]

Philanthropic foundations and companies support the local branches of national intermediaries, such as Neighborhood Housing Services of Chicago and LISC (whose Windy City office helped fund the organizations described here), as well as run their own funding programs. In Chicago, the philanthropies include not only those known and active on the national scene, such as the John D. and Catherine T. MacArthur Foundation, but also local institutions such as the Lloyd A. Fry Foundation, Chicago Community Trust, and Polk Brothers Foundation. Heavy-hitting corporations that headquarter in the Chicago area—the Allstate Insurance Company, La Salle Bank, and Bank One Chicago, to name a few—also support community development.

In addition, Chicago is the birthplace of Shorebank, the first commercial community development bank in the United States. Today many banks make loans in urban areas, thanks mainly to the pressures of the Community Reinvestment Act, but Shorebank was founded first and foremost on the principles of community reinvestment. It began in 1973 when four friends—idealistic 1960s types—who wanted to do something practical in the cause of social justice, purchased a bank in South Shore, a South Side neighborhood whose population was undergoing a drastic racial and economic turnover. As other banks fled the neighborhood, the South Shore Bank, later Shorebank, settled in to offer banking services to one and all.

The bank lost money in its first few years. The small depositors the bank's founders solicited used their accounts like a coin jar on a dresser, adding and taking out tiny amounts, while most local residents continued to put their major savings in large downtown banks. Learning as others did of the extreme difficulties of economic development, Shorebank took a beating on its loans to small businesses, particularly stores. Only by attracting socially conscious depositors from outside the neighborhood was Shorebank able to turn a profit.[114]

Then the bank discovered—primarily through a no-nonsense mortgage officer named Jim Bringley—a profit center: lending to small-scale property holders. In the South Shore neighborhood, two quite different groups provided enterprising energy; these were African American married couples and Croatian janitors, both of whom, in the words of Shorebank founder Ron Grzywinski, "know how to squeeze a quarter's worth of rehab out of a nickel."[115]

By issuing mortgages to such mom-and-pop housing entrepreneurs—the same sorts given loans by Mike Lappin and the Community Preservation Corporation in New York and another successful lending operation started by Chicago's major banks, Community Investment Corporation—Shorebank's managers found they could do good and well at the same time. Shorebank continued to make small business loans, albeit carefully underwriting them, specializing in serving minority-owned firms, as well as offering a full range of banking services. As of 2002, Shorebank had lent about $600 million to 13,000 families and businesses on Chicago's South and West Sides. Shorebank has set up shop in Cleveland, Detroit, northern Michigan, and Washington state, and it has spread its gospel overseas by doing business in such far-flung countries as Poland, Pakistan, Kenya, and Bangladesh.[116]

Mortgage operations like Shorebank's, it should be noted, work best as a way of stabilizing neighborhoods that are receiving a low-income population— as South Shore had been—and are generally ineffective in areas that are already severely depressed.

Lessons from the Windy City

The ongoing transformation of neighborhoods on Chicago's South and West Sides has reversed the long-standing trends that first created the city's great black ghettos and then left them in ruins. On the South Side, the discovery of African American historic and architectural legacies, the devotion of neighborhood institutions, especially IIT, and the city government to neighborhood restoration, and the remarkable redevelopment of the adjacent South Loop area triggered the changes. On the Near West Side, personal attachments of residents to neighborhood and neighbors, solidarity and savvy gained in political campaigns to ward off external threats, and again the cooperation of large institutions—in this case, the city's professional hockey and basketball teams— combined with the spread of fashionable residences and entertainment businesses from the downtown to start a revival.

One of the lessons that Chicago's experience in community development teaches is the importance of collaborating with large institutions. Universities, hospitals, even professional sports teams can help contribute or procure the necessary financial and political support for programs and projects that have a long-lasting impact on communities. City government too is a large institution, and when it gets involved, it can have the impact of the proverbial six-hundred pound gorilla. The mayor's program to replace the city's infamous high-rise public housing projects with mixed-income subdivisions has the power to transform communities and elevate inner-city real estate markets faster than anyone can imagine.

Chicago also teaches the lesson that a system is necessary to the success of community development. As in New York and Boston, the grassroots organizations in Chicago would not have accomplished so much without a strong network of organizations that will provide money, expertise, and, when needed, political weight.

Finally, Chicago illuminates a central problem of community development work: improving a low-income neighborhood but not allowing a wholesale replacement of the population by high-income groups. Community nonprofits here have long sought to uplift the inner city through "balanced growth" and "development without displacement." If gentrification is left unchecked, the upper-middle-class will claim increasingly larger proportions of territory and population, pushing low-income groups into new ghettos further out. In Chicago, as elsewhere, neighborhood, institutional, and government leaders must continue to struggle to get in front of this powerful trend if they are ever to realize their golden visions of spirited communities inhabited by people of diverse incomes and races.

OLYMPIC EFFORTS
IN BOOMTOWN

As the busboys whisked the plates away, the diners pushed aside their desserts and coffees and directed their attention to the speaker's podium. The conventioneers always enjoyed the food and conviviality of this event at the annual October meeting of the National Association of Industrial and Office Properties—and the 1997 luncheon held in the Hyatt Regency in San Francisco was no exception—but they were curious to hear the man of the hour, the recipient of the association's real estate Developer of the Year award, Thomas G. Cousins of Atlanta, Georgia.[1]

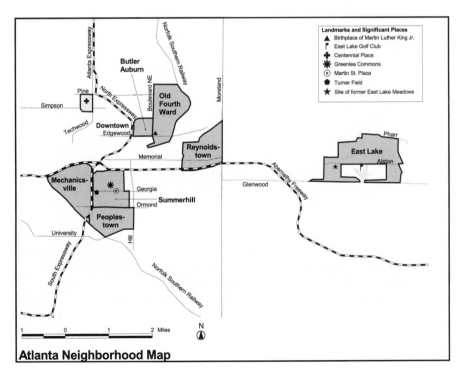

Atlanta Neighborhood Map

Tom Cousins surprised his audience of real estate developers and property owners. For one thing, his public speaking style was soft-spoken and awkward, not the charismatic manner that one would expect from a master developer. For another, Cousins ignored his firm's triumphs—the far-flung suburban residential office and industrial parks, the downtown Atlanta skyscrapers, and the highly profitable real estate investment trust he had created.

Instead, Cousins painted a picture of misery. The East Lake Meadows public housing project in Atlanta, Cousins explained quietly, was considered an urban war zone to both police and residents. The great majority of people living there had been the victims of a serious crime within the last year. Eighty-eight percent of the families earned less than $1,000 a year, only 16 of 450 families had fathers in the home, and the average age of a grandmother was 32. At the local school, gangs battled openly for the right to sell drugs and only 5 percent of fifth-graders passed the state math test.

Cousins further startled his audience when he told them what he was doing about the dreadful conditions at East Lake Meadows. Next to the housing project was an old golf course, where the golfing great Bobby Jones used to play. Cousins had renovated the golf course and its splendid clubhouse and was turning them into an "economic engine" that was fueling the resurgence of the East Lake neighborhood.

Cousins had founded a nonprofit foundation for East Lake and was amassing a fortune for it by selling memberships in the golf club to large corporations. The foundation, in cooperation with Atlanta's public housing agency, had begun to replace the housing project with a new mixed-income housing subdivision complete with its own golf course and swimming pool.

Nor was that all. The nonprofit was training and hiring the underprivileged African American youth of the neighborhood to be caddies at the historic golf course, running an after-school enrichment program centered on recreational golf, and organizing a charter school to supplant the old neighborhood school.

The men and women of the real estate profession listened intently as Tom Cousins, ever the salesman, exhorted them to try to do the same in their parts of the country.

"Face it. Governments don't know how to do this. It takes a developer to make things happen."[2]

When Cousins stopped speaking, the real estate professionals rose to their feet as one and gave Cousins a spontaneous ovation; even the food servers and busboys stopped what they were doing and joined in the applause.[3]

Though the notion of black caddies serving white tycoons may seem an odd way to combat poverty, Cousins's East Lake revitalization efforts represent one of the corporate approaches to inner-city revival that has emerged in boomtowns. As in other thriving capitals of the Sunbelt—such as Miami, Houston, and Dallas—the entrepreneurial class rides high in the saddle in civic matters in Atlanta. In such cities, enthusiasm for big downtown real estate deals usually outruns support for nonprofits and grassroots neighborhood redevelopment.

For years Atlanta's business fraternity alternated between neglecting the city's neighborhoods and demolishing them for some urban renewal scheme.

Likewise, the city government had done little to revive the old communities. That all changed in 1990 when Atlantans, who are chronically insecure about the status of their city, learned that their city would host the international Olympic games six years hence. That announcement set off a flurry of activity aimed at making Atlanta appear attractive and "world-class" to the millions who would visit and see it on television during the Olympics. All of a sudden, it seemed that everyone, even former president Jimmy Carter, was trying to revive Atlanta's inner city.

It was natural that Atlanta businessmen, who played a prominent part in civic affairs, would get mixed up in trying to improve inner-city neighborhoods. Add to this Atlanta's unique blend of southern politics, race, and religion, and you have a potent brew for community development. Although people in the community development movement make a point of adopting business practices, active business people rarely lead neighborhood revival efforts.

Perhaps it was the boomtown boosterism or the evangelical fervor of born-again Christianity, but whatever it was, it encouraged Atlantans to trumpet their urban revival schemes as the means of complete transformation. Expectations soared, and when the programs inevitably fell short of their lofty goals, disappointment, heartbreak, and sometimes bitterness followed.

Yet when the dust settled, Atlanta had begun to embrace community development. True, the city displayed a tendency to produce real estate showpieces and was taken by surprise by a powerful and sudden surge of gentrification. Atlantans nonetheless could point to a range of efforts from the unorthodox campaign of real estate king Tom Cousins to the humble house-by-house crusades of lesser known community advocates. The boomtown that for years cared about little else but private development and economic growth began at last to take neighborhood redevelopment seriously.

The Olympics Come to Atlanta

One day, out of the blue as he tells it, a successful Atlanta real estate lawyer and inveterate booster, William Payne, had a vision of bringing glory and honor to his city. He would make Atlanta the site of the international summer Olympic games. Payne, who goes by the name of Billy, became obsessed by his great civic enterprise. He signed up three Atlanta women who specialized in organizing fancy fund-raising events for charity. Payne's new team threw an impressive ball for visiting members of the United States Olympic Committee and, as their effort became credible, persuaded mayor Andrew Young and the city's money interests to back them. At first no one gave Atlanta much chance, but being a tourist and convention center with numerous hotels and facilities was a mark in its favor. Juan Antonio Samaranch, the president of the International Olympic Committee (IOC), surprised everyone in Tokyo in September 1990 when he dramtically announced, in his thick Spanish accent, that the site of the 1996 Olympic games would be "the city of Aht . . . lanta."[4]

Payne and his cohorts explained their victory by saying that Atlanta's bid team had won over the members of the IOC with large doses of southern charm and hospitality and some shrewd lobbying. Some years later, however, the investigations in the wake of Salt Lake City's bidding scandals revealed that the Atlantans had won the Olympics with the same sharp practices used by bid committees in other cities. Payne used all the hustling techniques of the real estate trade, the first of which is the ability to talk fast. He avowed to the IOC members, for example, that the average temperature in Atlanta in the summer was 75 degrees, an astounding idea. Later during the blistering Olympic summer of 1996, Payne coyly explained he had never stated what time of day the average temperature was taken. Payne and former mayor Andrew Young later asserted that they never violated their consciences, but the Atlantans nonetheless showered IOC members with antiques, china, and crystal, paid for their shopping sprees, provided them with free medical treatment, and even sent them to Disney World.[5]

Once Atlanta won the bid, Payne seized control of the Olympics project. In other Olympic cities people experienced in staging athletics took over after the bid committee completed its work, but in Atlanta Payne insisted that his bid committee run the Olympics. He converted his group into a new organization, the Atlanta Committee for the Olympic Games, or ACOG, and placed himself at the head. Ever the hustler, Payne paid himself a salary higher than what he made in real estate (to be fair, he felt it was his due for three years of unrewarded effort to win the bid). He also required that all vendors of Olympic-related merchandise provide his committee with a sample (to display in a future exhibition devoted to Atlanta's Olympic experience) and after the conclusion of the games, he claimed it as his property and sold it—together with his personal Olympic memorabilia collection—for nearly $1 million to a foundation he created and led. Although Payne might have been deemed crass elsewhere, his activities were acceptable in booming free enterprise Atlanta.[6]

One of Payne's most important early decisions was to choose the sites for the Olympic events. In other cities that held the Olympics, the athletic events and the housing for the athletes were located some place remote from the central city. Payne had originally envisioned a far-flung set of sites, but the IOC wanted the tournaments held in a relatively compact area. In response, Payne declared that most of the Olympic events would be held at downtown and inner-city arenas, a choice that would have a profound impact on Atlanta's neighborhoods.[7]

With the announcement that Atlanta would host the 1996 Olympics, the city's leaders and residents suddenly realized that millions of visitors and television watchers would be looking at their city. It was an unsettling thought for Atlantans who suffer from a chronic sense of civic insecurity. The superhighways and mega-projects that were the pride and joy of the city's elite chopped the capital's downtown into separate pieces that would bewilder any pedestrian who happened to wander into them. The sidewalks and streets were in bad shape. The city's many bridges had deteriorated so much that they were deemed unsafe for buses, and buses would be an important means of transporting the millions of visitors to the Olympic sites.

Worst of all was the deplorable condition of the city's neighborhoods. For years white business executives and politicians who dreamed of Atlanta becoming a magnificent "world-class city" pushed through civic improvements that inflicted untold damage on the city's neighborhoods, particularly the African American neighborhoods. In the 1940s Atlanta's business leaders lobbied for construction of two expressways to link the central business district with the suburbs and then had the original plan altered so that the north-south expressway would remove parts of three low-income black neighborhoods and create a buffer between downtown and the remainder of the black areas. Starting in the 1950s the business elite pushed for a series of urban renewal projects, one of which in the 1960s cleared an old black residential area known as Buttermilk Bottom for a new civic center and auditorium. The civic improvements dislocated thousands of residents and left acres of vacant land behind.[8]

The neighborhoods were almost powerless to fight back. For decades, the mayors of Atlanta took orders directly from the downtown businessmen, especially the executives of the city's first great corporation, the Coca-Cola Company. The white businessmen were even able to win support from African American businessmen and college officials who had an interest in renewal and new housing plans. The neighborhoods, black and white, gained a voice in 1973 when maverick politician Maynard Jackson was elected mayor, the first black person to hold the post. As vice mayor Jackson had cast a tie-breaking vote against a new expressway project and as mayor he loudly refused to kowtow to the businessmen. He and his planning commissioner, Leon Eplan, set up a strong local planning system, but because Jackson alienated the downtown business leaders, they could do little else on behalf of the neighborhoods.[9]

Jackson's successor as mayor, Andrew Young, if anything was less effective on behalf of the neighborhoods. Formerly an aide to Martin Luther King Jr. and United Nations ambassador, Young returned the city to a pro-development policy. Andy Young, it was said, never saw a building permit he didn't like. As mayor, he seemed more interested in securing government contracts and jobs for African Americans than sorting out the complicated problems of the neighborhoods.[10]

It did not help that the neighborhoods were growing poorer, especially in comparison to the vibrant sections of the city—such as Buckhead in northernmost Atlanta—and the far-flung suburbs. From the 1950s many of the city's blacks were able to climb into the middle and upper-middle classes, and as they prospered, they moved out of traditionally black neighborhoods and into the outer city and the inner suburbs. At the same time, impoverished African Americans remained behind in the old neighborhoods that degenerated into places of crime, drug trafficking and addiction, and broken homes. Occasionally the city attempted an urban renewal project to clear out some particularly bad section, but for the most part, the free-enterprise tradition and the seemingly intractable problems led the city fathers to neglect the inner city. Neglect it, that is, until they saw the Olympics coming.

Jimmy Carter's Big Project

A number of influential individuals who cared about Atlanta's people and neighborhoods saw that the approach of the Olympic games created a golden, if brief, opportunity to transform their city. They knew that the business and political elite who ran the city were going to be anxious to clean the place up in time for the Olympic games, and that this civic pride could be used to pursue improvement schemes, the like of which the town had never seen.

None of those who wanted to transform Atlanta had more renown than Georgia's first citizen, the former president of the United States, Jimmy Carter. Carter possessed an almost magical power to capture people's imagination and enlist them in a cause. The former president's efforts at improving health and promoting democracy and peace in Africa and Central America were touted as great successes, and by 1990 he felt strongly that he should turn his attention to his own country.

The arrival of the Olympics provided Carter a way to channel hometown pride into a crusade to help the poor and afflicted. Carter dreamed of launching a project that would do domestically what he had done internationally. It would tap the volunteer spirit of church members, the wealth of civic-minded corporate executives, and the authority of government officials to create or strengthen institutions that benefited poor people. Ultimately, Carter hoped, the people of Atlanta would learn to continue the effort on their own. Unlike his foreign ventures, which he helped to start and then moved on, in Atlanta Carter hoped to be involved intimately for the duration of the project.[11]

As with many of the efforts to uplift Atlanta, a religious feeling suffused the former president's campaign. As a born-again Christian, Carter felt a missionary impulse to help people, and in this he received encouragement from James Laney, the president of Emory University and himself a former missionary, and William Fahey, the director of his Carter Center and former head of the Centers for Disease Control. The three men saw a similarity between the depressed sections of Atlanta and the parts of the Third World where they had worked.[12]

Enthralled by a powerful vision, Jimmy Carter and his comrades-in-arms were disinclined to examine closely the actual situation. The former president held a dinner at the Carter Center for a small group of civic and philanthropic leaders to enlist their help. The fare was meager—ham sandwiches; the former president meant business. He laid out his ideas, then went around the room and asked the participants for their reactions. A few screwed up their courage and asserted that however admirable the project was, its goals were too ambitious to achieve. That piqued Carter. "I didn't invite you here to ask your permission or get your opinion," one participant remembers him snapping at them. "I presented it to you and want to know if you are going to join us." Years later Carter would admit his goals had been too ambitious.[13]

In late October 1991 Carter went public with his campaign. He announced that he was beginning the Atlanta Project, as he named it, to take on a wide range of urban ills. In the following weeks, Carter attracted attention by publicizing problems in inner-city neighborhoods. He brought news reporters to see a child born prematurely to a crack-addicted mother, which the hospital nurses named Baby Pumpkin. The pathetic infant, small enough to fit in an adult's hand, "brought tears to our eyes," said the ex-president. "It still doesn't have a home, it still doesn't have a mama. I think we ought to do something about it."[14]

The former president visited tenants in the notorious East Lake Meadows housing project where an eight-year-old boy recently had been killed by police during a gunfight with the child's stepfather. "We want to get several thousand volunteers to come in and adopt families and be grannies to help with children, make sure the housing authority mows the grass, make sure the tenants have enough pride to pick up the trash, maybe reopen some units," Carter declared. "I'd like to see the increased police presence be permanent, not just after a little boy gets killed in his bed," he said.[15]

Carter was vague about what exactly his approach would be, but he seemed to want a coordinated, holistic effort. "All the problems—crack babies, teenage mothers, juvenile delinquency, dropouts—are related," he declared. "There are programs all over dealing with these issues, but I don't think it works to deal with them separately." In the Summerhill neighborhood, he suggested that schools could become community centers where residents could pick up their food stamps and get medical care, counseling, and other services.[16] Like other comprehensive community efforts such as the Dudley Street Neighborhood Initiative in Boston and the Surdna Foundation's campaign in the South Bronx, the watchwords for the Atlanta Project were collaboration, empowerment, and system change.[17]

Enthusiasm ran high for Carter's Atlanta Project, even though no one knew exactly what it was. Carter's exhortations and ruminations left many with the impression that he intended to wipe out or at least begin to break up the pernicious poverty and related social problems that had plagued the city for decades. One newspaper reporter caught the spirit of the city's feeling of anticipation when he wrote of the impending Atlanta Project, "Atlanta may never be the same."[18]

When the former president came calling, Atlanta's civic and philanthropic leaders were unable to resist. "I have never been more excited and frightened," Atlanta United Way director Mark O'Connell remarked at the time. "Carter just might have the ability to carry this off, in which case it will be the most exciting urban change process America has ever seen." The possibility that Carter's idea might work could not be ignored; O'Connell signed up for the Atlanta Project.[19]

O'Connell was not alone. Responding to Jimmy Carter's powerful appeals, the Atlanta establishment coughed up an extraordinary amount of money for the Atlanta Project. By July 1992, it had garnered pledges of more than $11 million from the southeast region's major banks, large corporations—such as United Parcel Service, Coca-Cola, Home Depot, J. W. Marriott, Delta Air Lines, and Georgia Power—local philanthropic groups, including the Robert W. Woodruff Foundation (the fund started by the long-time CEO of Coca-Cola), and out-of-town foundations and television celebrity Oprah Winfrey. Over the next four years, the former president's crusade raised almost $34 million: $18 million in cash and the rest in in-kind contributions such as loaned officers, office space, and computer equipment. Indeed, the Atlanta Project raised so much money that the directors of some local nonprofit organizations feared that it would divert contributions from their groups and force them to go out of business. Their fears were unfounded: Carter elicited contributions that otherwise would never have been given.[20]

In the six months following Carter's announcement in October 1991, the Atlanta Project took shape, or rather became manifest; it was too amorphous to map precisely. In November Carter chose an executive director to run the project. Undoubtedly on the advice of Atlanta's leaders, the former president turned to Dan Sweat, a man who had made a career of administering the civic and philanthropic institutions of Atlanta's business elite. Sweat had directed the Central Atlanta Progress, the powerful downtown business organization, from 1973 to 1988 and more recently had gone to work for real estate developer Thomas Cousins as the president of Cousins's private philanthropy, the C. F. Foundation. With Sweat installed as executive director of the Atlanta Project, Carter began to develop a hydra-headed entity that spawned operations from both central headquarters and the neighborhoods.[21]

Carter called for a full-time "secretariat," much like the presidential cabinet over which he used to preside, consisting of prominent professionals to head committees in areas such as health, housing, and education. The committees were supposed to run their own programs as well as assist the Atlanta Project's neighborhood operations. The secretariat (later renamed the Resource Group to avoid sounding too authoritarian) also had diverse administrative responsibilities—deploying the thousands who volunteered to help the Atlanta Project, coordinating the corporations' participation, running an information system, and helping to plan and train people for central and neighborhood programs.[22]

The cluster organizations were the heart of the Atlanta Project. Following Carter's belief that the local school should be a center of neighborhood life, Atlanta Project officials set up small organizations to operate in twenty high school districts in Atlanta and nearby counties that had high rates of social problems such as single-parent families and school-age pregnancies. They called these organizations "neighborhood clusters" because each school district encompassed numerous neighborhoods of various and sundry characters. The neighborhood clusters varied greatly—their populations ranged from 8,000 to 58,000. For each cluster, the Atlanta Project hired a coordinator whose job was to organize local residents to come up with a list of worthy projects and form committees to carry them out with the help of volunteers and corporate and university employees.[23]

In August 1992—almost a year after Carter had announced the Atlanta Project—the Crim cluster, which included the East Lake neighborhood, held the campaign's first major event, a large fair with food, music, health screening, and more than 130 agencies' exhibits of their services for low-income families. The Crim fair was a great success: hundreds of people attended, including ex-president Carter and his wife, Rosalyn, whose presence ensured that it was well publicized. Just as Carter had hoped for the Atlanta Project generally, private companies—including the Marriott Corporation—helped out, paying for the tents, tables, chairs, food, and toilets. "There was so much I saw," Sandra Mundy told a reporter as she stopped by on her way home from work. "The income tax help. The legal aid. It's good, and it'll bring the community together." The Atlanta Project seemed to be off to a great start.[24]

The Crim Cluster's fair set a pattern over the next few years of one-time or short-term public events that left a good feeling but little in the way of tangible, long-term accomplishments. Across the city the more efficient cluster organizations held health and social service festivals, housing expositions, and business forums. These usually were day-long affairs in which agencies distributed information or delivered services, such as health screening, on the spot. The cluster groups celebrated local communities through arts fairs ("Art from the Hood" one was called), multicultural festivals, and mural projects—such as the one in which local students depicted life in their inner-city neighborhood—and exposed their youth to culture through field trips to museums and theaters and artists' visits to schools. The organizations also sponsored discussion forums for young people—on problems ranging from high school detention to single parenthood—and for adults, including Words to My Sister, a meeting to raise the morale of black women held in October 1993 at which Rosalynn Carter showed up to listen.[25]

The Atlanta Project clusters carried out less ephemeral projects as well—cleanup and beautification projects and special extracurricular instruction for children, such as tennis camps and African dance and music classes. In the Grady Cluster, a particularly active group, music teachers donated their time to give about thirty children musical instrument lessons, and Georgia Tech students conducted an after-school family history project to teach research and writing skills. At least four groups, including the Carver Cluster in south Atlanta, held training sessions for high school students about to take their SAT tests. At the Crim cluster, a "Professional Elegance After School Program" somehow combined homework tutoring and discussion of self-esteem and life experiences for about 100 children. The clusters' projects did well by their participants, but by and large, they did not become permanent programs, and years later it was hard to say how they helped solve the big problems that had so worried Jimmy Carter.[26]

Despite the cluster organizations and talk of grass roots, the Atlanta Project scored its largest victories out of the home office. To many people, the Children's Health Initiative was the Atlanta Project's signature program. Its chief goal was to create a massive data base of the health records for very young (five years and younger) inner-city children for use by medical practitioners, public health departments, and community health centers. The Atlanta Project used an immunization drive to kick off the campaign. First, thousands of volunteers went door-to-door to 54,000 households, passing out information on immunization and recording information. Then with great festivity medical teams set up shop at forty-three sites for eight days. They examined about 16,000 children and inoculated 6,000 of them. The event received extensive publicity in the local media—several well-known entertainers helped the cause—and became the best known, and sometimes the only known, program of the Atlanta Project.

After the hoopla died down, an analysis showed that the health campaign accomplished less that first appeared. Only 400 of the children who had been

Former president Jimmy Carter visiting a public housing family as part of the Atlanta Project's immunization project. Courtesy of The Carter Center.

immunized, it turned out, had never received an inoculation at a health clinic before, and 160 of these were newborn infants. The need for the program was apparently less acute than it seemed, and therefore the drive introduced only a small number of people to the health system.[27]

In perhaps the Atlanta Project's greatest public success, Jimmy Carter personally spearheaded an effort to simplify and streamline the process of applying for government social programs. Carter observed that reams of red tape stood in the way of people who tried to sign up for food stamps, Medicaid, housing assistance, the Women, Infant and Children Program, Aid to Families with Dependent Children, and Supplemental Security Income. Carter personally lobbied presidents George Bush and Bill Clinton and pushed for a special task force of representatives of these government agencies. In the end, his efforts condensed sixty-four pages of applications into an eight-page form that allowed someone to apply for all six programs at once.[28]

Housing was one area in which, as Carter had hoped it would, the Atlanta Project fostered collaborations to solve neighborhood problems and strengthen anti-poverty efforts. Under guidance of the Atlanta Project's housing expert, Frank Alexander, volunteer students from Emory Law School wrote and distributed brochures about building codes, and cluster directors led a campaign to clean out abandoned cars and salvage derelict buildings. The housing committee also cajoled Atlanta's reluctant housing organizations to start a Housing Resource Center, a long-standing goal of the city's reformers, to inform and assist neighborhood groups.[29]

Much of the Atlanta Project's work consisted of quiet lobbying and support for community projects. The Project helped Atlanta's city government prepare its application to the federal government to be designated as an Empowerment Zone,[30] for example, and worked with the Metropolitan Atlanta Chamber of Commerce and six banks to create an $11 million fund for loans to inner-city businesses on favorable terms. The Atlanta Project also discreetly helped local groups: almost any time a community group threw a party, a long-time staff member recalled, the Atlanta Project paid for it.[31]

Despite all the fairs, enrichment, and help in delivering social services, the Atlanta Project fell into the abyss of racial mistrust that regularly opened between Atlanta's civic-minded white executives and black leaders. In September 1992, one of the three African Americans originally appointed to the six-member secretariat, a professor of education at Georgia State University, resigned in a public letter to the former President decrying racism in the top echelon of the Atlanta Project. He made it clear he did not mean Carter was racist, but left the question open in regard to Sweat. Carter and Sweat quickly appointed another African American professional, but work commitments forced another member to resign, leaving only two African Americans on the secretariat. The next July, the director of the Carver cluster delivered a bluntly critical speech, complaining that no blacks held key positions in the Atlanta Project and that neighborhood leaders had too little say in spending the millions of dollars it had raised.[32]

Carter and Sweat took the charges seriously and expanded the numbers of high-ranking blacks in the Atlanta Project. Most notably, they hired Jane Smith, the director of development at the Martin Luther King Center (the institution established to commemorate and continue the work of the slain civil rights leader), as budget and program administrator, second only to Sweat in the chain of command.[33]

Whatever his faults, Sweat, who died in 1997 at the age of sixty-three, was not a racist. Prominent African Americans such as Andrew Young and Hattie Dorsey, the founder of the Atlanta Neighborhood Development Partnership, worked with him and admired his efforts. Even Sweat's critics acknowledge that he worked hard for numerous good causes throughout his career.[34]

Sweat may have been the wrong person to start the Atlanta Project, however. He did not like to share authority. Although Sweat kowtowed to the elite, he was gruff and autocratic when dealing with those beneath him. While working at the Atlanta Project, Sweat kept a coffee mug on his desk that read: "Me Boss, You Not." Moreover, this long-time chief executive of Atlanta's civic and philanthropic institutions initially resisted the idea of strengthening local organizations—which was considered "empowerment." For a man who was impatient to get things done, attending interminable meetings where everyone is allowed to speak must have been a trial. Not surprisingly, some local leaders came to view him as another arrogant white man insensitive to the needs of the people.[35]

So determined to exercise tight control of operations was Sweat that he not only kept Atlanta Project board members at a distance, but he also kept Jimmy Carter at a distance. This was unfortunate: Carter had a vision of what he was trying to create; Sweat did not. What Carter needed to be effective—as he had been in the political work in Nicaragua and Panama, for example—was a knowledgeable aide who could translate his vision into specific goals by preparing the field and could give the former president a course of action. Sweat's experience was in boardroom politics.[36]

On January 1, 1995, Jimmy Carter tapped Jane Smith to direct the Atlanta Project and asked Sweat to help him organize a national version of it. Yet people inside and outside the Atlanta Project do not feel that Jane Smith had the organizational abilities to run such an operation. Her great skill was political—an ability to communicate, get good press, and get along well with people. If so, the Atlanta Project would have done better by first hiring Smith to get the project underway and later turning to Sweat to run it.

The Atlanta Project suffered a critical blow in February 1995 when an evaluation conducted by a political scientist at Emory University became public. No matter who ran the Atlanta Project, the report made clear, the contradictory goals of decentralized empowerment and centralized service delivery were sure to make life difficult.[37] Furthermore, the Project created new organizations—the clusters and headquarters—without seriously considering how they would fit with existing ones. Despite its goal of collaboration, the Atlanta Project left most of the city's nonprofit organizations in the dark about its purposes, and cluster staff members rarely coordinated with neighborhood groups.[38]

Overall, the Atlanta Project seemed to be everywhere and nowhere. According to the evaluation, all the activity and the enormous sums of money had neither changed Atlanta's social service and community organizations nor helped them meet their goals. Even where it had done well—as in the health and housing areas—the Atlanta Project suffered from the sky-high expectations that Jimmy Carter and the project's directors had raised at the outset. Worse yet, more than three years after the Atlanta Project was founded, it lacked a coherent plan for implementing Carter's vision in a coordinated way. The grand goals were laudable, the work on the ground was pursued in earnest, but there was little attempt to harness latter to the former.

The evaluation of the Atlanta Project crystallized growing doubts about the program. The head of the city's United Way and several cluster leaders publicly agreed with the findings, and rumors abounded that behind the scenes the heads of corporations and foundations felt uneasy. Jane Smith declared that the Atlanta Project would fix its problems, but time was not on her side. In September 1995 four of the cluster coordinators declared that their organizations were seceding from the Atlanta Project, and Jimmy Carter was forced to ask others not to follow suit.[39]

In 1996, the year the Olympics came to Atlanta, the year by which some thought the Atlanta Project would eliminate or significantly diminish poverty in Atlanta, Carter and Smith drastically reduced the Project's scale. With a fifth of the budget it had once enjoyed, a smaller staff, and only four local offices instead of twenty, the project narrowed its focus to helping children and families.[40]

By then the newspapers were delivering the postmortems of the Project, and analyzing why it failed. The Atlanta Project, wrote the local pundits contradictorily, had tried to do too much and underestimated the difficulty of solving the problems of the inner city.

As he distanced himself from his brainchild, Jimmy Carter said it was better to have tried and failed than not to have tried at all. He might have added
that for all its faults, the Atlanta Project had helped provoke corporate Atlanta
to face the problems of the inner city and try to do something about them.

Atlanta Dresses Up for the Olympics

When Atlanta was announced as the site of the upcoming Olympics, Atlanta's
mayor, Maynard Jackson, grew worried. Jackson, who had returned to the
mayor's seat in 1989 after Andrew Young completed his term, was concerned
about the impact of the games on the city. Three weeks after the city was
named the host of the 1996 Olympics, he called Leon Eplan, the city planner
in his earlier administration, to return to the post and help get the city ready.
Eplan was one of those who saw the upcoming Olympic games as a unique
opportunity for the city. During the next two years Eplan took whatever spare
moments he could find to draft and build support for an ambitious program of
civic improvements.[41]

In October 1992 Jackson acted on Eplan's recommendations and announced
the creation of the new agency, Corporation for Olympic Development in
Atlanta, or CODA, which would plan, raise money for, and coordinate city
improvement and neighborhood redevelopment in areas near the Olympic
arenas.

*On the left, a tower and bridge with sculptures of the Olympic flame and the
Olympic rings commemorate Atlanta's great event near the former site of the Fulton
County Stadium, and on the right, new housing, whose development the games
helped inspire, in Summerhill, January 2001. Courtesy of Glenna Lang.*

Jackson and Eplan thought big. They envisioned a broad Olympic Boulevard stretching from the Capitol southward to the stadiums, a blockwide string of parks originating at the entrance to the Atlanta University Center, and the revitalization of "Olympic neighborhoods" such as Summerhill and Mechanicsville. The city officials estimated that CODA might spend $500 million to $1 billion to beautify and rebuild the city for the Games, possibly eclipsing the cost of construction projects—such as the new Centennial Olympic Park built downtown—carried out by Billy Payne's Atlanta Committee for the Olympic Games (ACOG). The announcement of CODA, in short, followed the pattern of presenting impossible goals that later provided irresistible fodder for critics.[42]

Jackson tried to enlist the business leaders in the cause of improving the city. He kept the new agency outside the government so as to allay fears of political interference. Jackson named Billy Payne and prominent business people to CODA's board, along with foundation officers, government officials, and neighborhood and labor leaders. He wanted a prominent businessperson to join him as co-chair of the organization, but had difficulty finding one willing to serve. The former and present chiefs of Coca-Cola, BellSouth Telecommunication, and SunTrust Banks reportedly turned Jackson down before the mayor persuaded the chairman of the Georgia World Congress Center Authority to take the position.[43]

In order for CODA to have accomplished all its goals, the agency would have had to work with clocklike efficiency every moment of its existence, and even then it probably would not have had enough time. In any event, the organization stumbled at the gate. Its first director, Shirley C. Franklin, a former city government administrator and vice president of ACOG (and future mayor of Atlanta), quit after a few months. Franklin returned to work for Payne for a significantly larger salary, but perhaps she was daunted by the growing list of large projects that yet lacked funds to pay for them.[44]

Maynard Jackson and his predecessor, Andrew Young, approached Clara Axam, who had served both mayors, to take the helm of CODA. Axam, whose family had long roots in the historic African American Auburn Avenue area, was reluctant to accept the job. As far as she could tell, Atlanta's major institutions and power brokers did not support CODA. Worse, Axam suspected that CODA was intended to fool people into thinking that the city was going to help the neighborhoods when in fact it had no real program. The mayors beseeched Axam again and again, but she refused until Young challenged her by saying, "I'll tell you what—let's assume CODA's a subterfuge. It's the only game in town. Are you going to play?" In July 1993 Axam took the job.[45]

When Axam arrived at CODA, the assignment seemed more hopeless than she imagined. She was installed in a tiny office with file cabinets and an answering machine and no clerical staff. Franklin handed her a notebook with a list of what everybody thought the agency ought to do. Axam began adding up the costs of each item, but when she reached $500 million, she gave up in exasperation. Furthermore, CODA's board of directors was unenthusiastic. The members told Axam that they were serving out of a sense of civic duty or personal obligation to the mayor, not because they thought that CODA would succeed.

Conservative financiers advised Axam not to "get stuck in the neighborhood stuff" and never get anything done. To accomplish nothing for the neighborhoods was, of course, her greatest fear. On the other hand, the city's elected officials, led by the mayor, wanted her to improve fifteen neighborhoods. Randy Roark, an architecture professor at Georgia Tech whom Axam hired, commented that it was as if the city council handed the neighborhoods to CODA, and said, "Here. We haven't been able to fix these in 50 years, but could you please fix them in the next three?"[46]

With only the city's slim budget, Axam immediately faced a financial dilemma. Until more cash came in, she had to choose between paying CODA's employees or proceeding with the ambitious plans they were developing. Yet if the staff did not start work, no projects would be completed. She called a meeting and asked her staff members, "Are we going to try to pay ourselves for the next eight or nine months, or are we going to take all the money we've got and stick it in design and try to get going?" The staff members surprised their boss by voting to use the meager funds to design the projects. For the first time Axam began to feel that CODA might work. "Well," she thought to herself, "maybe Andy was right."[47]

Axam chased any available pot of money she could. She managed to persuade skeptical officials at the Woodruff Foundation to put up $1.5 million. Georgia Institute of Technology, known locally as "Tech," agreed to lend faculty and facilities. In the end, she obtained most of her money from the government, including a hefty portion of a public works bond. Despite Maynard Jackson's vision of a grand civic enterprise, the fault line of Atlanta's politics—the mutual distrust felt by white businessmen and black government officials—prevented a broader effort to fund the transformation of the city. By 1995 CODA had received $32 million from the bond issue, $25 million in federal matching grants, and another $14 million in private donations.[48]

Clara Axam divided the CODA into its component parts: public spaces and neighborhood revitalization. She placed Randy Roark in charge of the public spaces. Roark aggressively tackled the job of making Atlanta into a comprehensible place that the millions of visitors could enter by subway or bus and find their way on foot through pleasant thoroughfares to interesting and even inspiring public parks and plazas as well as to the sites of the games.

Although it took a good deal of wrangling with old-fashioned highway engineers, Roark and Axam persuaded the Atlanta Regional Commission and United States Department of Transportation to spend $15 million in federal transportation funds not just on highways but on all manner of transportation—including bicycle paths and an electric shuttle bus system.[49]

Roark's ultimate and unstated goal was to restore the relationship between the neighborhoods and downtown, so whenever possible he obtained infrastructure improvements for the redevelopment areas. He started with six pedestrian corridors that connected Olympic athletic sites to subway stations and expanded the number to twelve thoroughfares by adding likely tourist destinations such as the King National Historical Site in the Auburn Avenue neighborhood. On these corridors and along important automobile routes,

CODA—in cooperation with the city's public works department—widened and rebuilt sidewalks, planted new trees and lawns, hung street banners, installed ornamental street lamps, and placed historic district markers. Roark improved Woodruff Park downtown but also created several new parks and plazas in the neighborhoods. Going well beyond CODA's original mandate, Roark and Axam managed to institute Atlanta's first program of public art, sponsoring sculptures, monuments, and artistic works in the name of infrastructure improvements.[50]

Redeveloping neighborhoods, everyone knew, was a far thornier task than improving public space. On the recommendation of Ed Logue, the well-known veteran city planner with whom Maynard Jackson had consulted, CODA hired Logue's former aide in Boston, David Crane, to assess local conditions, an essential first step in planning neighborhood revival. In the summer of 1993, Crane assembled teams of college and graduate students to carry out a forced march survey of the Olympic neighborhoods. The students traveled in rental cars, which they ruined by driving slowly with the air-conditioning running full blast. "I think we went through 20 or 30 rental cars," a team captain remembered, "even though we only needed eight." The young planners had plenty of adventures. A woman wearing nothing but a raincoat walked up to a car of surveyors and threw open her coat. Dealers of crack cocaine mistook them for police informers or customers and confronted them, sometimes with firearms. By the end of the summer, almost all the surveyors had been propositioned by either a prostitute or a drug dealer.[51]

Despite their travails, in twelve weeks the CODA workers surveyed fifteen neighborhoods covering eight and a half square miles and 14,000 parcels. They analyzed land uses, real estate values, tax delinquencies, building vacancies, and the conditions of buildings, sidewalks, and streets. They compiled neighborhood histories and demographic statistics and evaluated community institutions. All the information was poured into a massive digitized database complete with maps, which Crane used to create methodical schedules— including sources and amounts of revenue—to implement each neighborhood plan over the next fifteen years.[52]

In mid-October 1993, CODA issued a comprehensive plan for revitalizing fifteen neighborhoods and creating twenty-four pedestrian corridors, civic spaces, and parks. It would cost, reported the *Atlanta Journal Constitution*, more than $220 million, less than half the original estimates but still a breathtaking sum. As for an agenda that could be completed in time for the games three years hence, Clara Axam announced a goal developing five neighborhoods and seven corridors and parks at a cost of $100 million. CODA, however, never raised the $100 million and only began to redevelop the neighborhoods.[53]

Bob Begle, Crane's assistant, grew dismayed as he watched the neighborhood redevelopment program become the ugly stepsister in the CODA family. Neighborhood planning remained a small operation with a few people camped together in one room. CODA officers spoke of accomplishing its goals in decades, not by the time of the Olympics. Meanwhile, Roark's department added new projects, hired additional staff members, and received commendations from the press and officials. Finally the infrastructure division grew so large that it moved across the street to better accommodations—with individual offices—taking CODA chief Axam with it and leaving the neighborhood group behind.[54]

One reason that the neighborhood redevelopment efforts were slow was the painstaking process of organizing local residents to formulate and support the neighborhood plans. In each neighborhood Crane and Begle presented the results of the survey and then carried on a series of meetings with neighborhood residents and leaders to carefully devise an acceptable plan. The CODA representatives had to persuade angry and suspicious residents that designating their neighborhoods as slums—in order to use urban renewal powers—would not result in wholesale involuntary clearance of their homes. The CODA team then had to submit each plan to the City Council for approval, which involved the council members asking the residents whether they supported the plans. An anxious Begle would wait breathlessly until neighborhood residents spoke in favor of the plan and was delighted at times to hear the residents explain the plan's features in detail.[55]

When all was said and done, CODA could claim credit for helping complete only five neighborhood redevelopment plans, and one of these, the plan for the Summerhill neighborhood, had already been written before CODA was started. Looking back, even Mayor Jackson felt somewhat disappointed. "On a scale of one to 10, we'll probably hit around six or seven," the former mayor said. "I've never been satisfied entirely with neighborhood development." CODA's greatest problem was that it never earned the whole-hearted support of Atlanta's business leaders. Where government provided most of the funds—in building the public spaces and amenities—CODA succeeded. Without great sums of money and enthusiastic press, it was difficult to gain momentum to rebuild neighborhoods. Persuading residents to participate and negotiating the inevitable differences of opinion took even longer than usual.[56]

On the other hand, Clara Axam feels that CODA did as much as it could given the short amount of time it had. When she worked at CODA, Axam adopted the idea of what she originally called "planting bombs," preparing improvements that would be completed eventually. (After an actual bomb exploded in the new Olympic park, Axam changed metaphors and spoke of planting seeds.) The plan for the Peoplestown neighborhood, for example, paved the way for the Peoplestown Revitalization Corporation, led by Richard McFarland, to replace a forbidding apartment building filled with drug addicts, criminals, and broken glass with a handsome residential development. Similar cases of subsequent developments in Peoplestown, the Old Fourth Ward, and Mechanicsville buttress Axam's belief that CODA's influence may take time to be felt.[57]

By enhancing the streetscape, planting trees and greenways, and connecting downtown to the inner "Olympic ring" neighborhoods, and by pushing inner-city residents to plan and improve their neighborhoods, CODA contributed to an urban revival in Atlanta.

Behind CODA, of course, were the Olympic games, which spurred numerous efforts to improve and beautify the central city. In Atlanta's downtown, for example, Billy Payne and ACOG created an Olympic park, and

New house built by Peoplestown Revitalization Corporation next to boarded-up house, Peoplestown, June 2000. Courtesy of author.

Central Atlanta Progress, the business interest's civic organization, was able to stir up interest in restoring the turn-of-the-century commercial buildings in the historic section of the business district. The International Brotherhood of Painters and the Sherwin-Williams Company joined the city government to paint more than 250 houses located near the Olympic event sites.

The Olympics also prompted the Atlanta chapter of Habitat for Humanity to go on a building binge. Habitat for Humanity, an international organization, uses approximately 17,000 local affiliates to bring volunteers and low-income families together to build simple, inexpensive houses that the families can then buy at very low cost. Habitat is resolutely nondenominational, but founder Millard Fuller—who came to his calling through something like a conversion experience—was inspired by the Christian concept of service to humanity and made the work of volunteers fundamental to its mission. Headquartered in Americus, Georgia, Habitat for Humanity attracted the support of fellow Georgians Jimmy and Rosalyn Carter, who became the organization's most famous volunteer house builders. The year before the Olympics were scheduled to begin, the Atlanta chapter declared a goal of constructing 100 new houses before the start of the games. The building blitz triumphed, placing twenty of the new homes in Peoplestown. Fueled by the volunteering zeal of such churches as Peachtree Presbyterian in Buckhead, the chapter pushed forward, and upon completing its 500th home three years later, was declared Habitat for Humanity's "Most Productive U.S. Affiliate."[58]

The Olympics and all the concomitant ventures—such as CODA—advertised and propelled a back-to-the-city movement in Atlanta, a place best known for unrelenting suburban sprawl. Even as the leafy suburbs boomed during the 1990s, a small but significant stream of Atlantans took up residence in central Atlanta. Artists, professionals, and young singles moved into newly developed lofts downtown in old commercial buildings and nearby in old factories. Increasing numbers of young couples of both races purchased Victorian houses in inner-city neighborhoods. The majority of people taking out home mortgages earned income at or above the median for the metropolitan area. (See Appendix I.) Suddenly, in town living became cool, and gentrification, like that in northern and western cities, took hold in inner-city Atlanta.

Summerhill: A Revival Runs Off Course

The Olympics and the interest in urban living came to Atlanta in such a rush, however, that even having the support of CODA, civic leaders, and business interests was no guarantee of success. In the years leading up to the Olympic games, Atlanta's business leaders took a direct hand in promoting the renewal of Summerhill, a neighborhood located just south of downtown. Foundations, businesses, and government agencies poured money into Summerhill. All the funds and plans fostered renewal of a sort but also brought angry disagreements, charges of racial prejudice, and the squandering of millions of dollars. Once touted as a model of community development for other neighborhoods to emulate, Summerhill became a model of mistakes instead.

Summerhill was flat on its back when Billy Payne hatched his plan for bringing the Olympics to Atlanta. Its population had shriveled from about 20,000 in its heyday in 1950 to perhaps 3,500 in 1990, many of whom were elderly, poor, or unemployed. The main commercial drags sported empty stores. The neighborhood had suffered a series of blows at the hands of various government agencies. In the late 1950s and early 1960s, construction of interstate highways had taken a large piece out of the community. Soon thereafter urban renewal programs razed another section, eliminating businesses, churches, and homes. The government built Fulton County stadium in 1965 to bring the Milwaukee Braves baseball team to Atlanta and in the process carved up large chunks of the Summerhill and Peoplestown neighborhoods, displacing thousands of people. After the team moved in, the stadium blighted the adjacent territory by encouraging land owners to turn their lots into makeshift parking lots. There were plenty of lots: out of a total of 1,200 residential lots, more than 700 were vacant in 1991. "Summerhill," a newspaper reporter gloomily concluded in December 1990, "has been in the dead of winter for more than 25 years."[59]

However dismal its state, many people still took pride in Summerhill and its modest bungalows and southern shotgun-style houses. A group of present and former residents, who had run into each other at funerals, in 1987 decided to plan a neighborhood reunion so they could socialize under more pleasant circumstances. Much to their surprise, when they held the event the following year, thousands of people showed up. The excited organizers, led by Douglas Dean, decided to make the reunion annual and use it as a springboard to restoring the neighborhood to its former glory.[60]

Summerhill's leader, Doug Dean, was the last of four generations of his family to live there. At the time of the reunion, he had represented the neighborhood in the state legislature for a dozen years and had moved to the nearby

177

Pittsburgh neighborhood. A religious man with political skills and a down-home accent, Dean made the revival of Summerhill his cause and career. To draw up a redevelopment strategy, in 1989 he helped organize and became the head of Summerhill Neighborhood, Incorporated.[61]

While Summerhill residents were taking their first steps toward redevelopment, Atlanta's downtown establishment took an unusual interest in Summerhill. Central Atlanta Progress conducted a survey of the neighborhood, much to the surprise of Summerhill leaders; they only learned of it by asking the college student they noticed walking up and down their streets what she was doing. Doug Dean then approached the downtown business organization for help, and Joe Martin, director of Central Atlanta Progress, assigned the organization's African American vice president to the task. Central Atlanta Progress then induced the Urban Land Institute—a national think tank funded by the real estate industry—to send its strategic planning panel for low-income neighborhoods to help Summerhill start its community development effort. Dean and his colleagues asked few questions; they were only too happy to receive such help.[62]

The Summerhill folks soon discovered why Atlanta's business leaders had become so solicitous of their neighborhood's interests. In July 1989 Billy Payne and his Olympics bid group publicly announced their plan for staging the Olympics at different sites in Atlanta. The centerpiece of the scheme was an 80,000-seat stadium to be constructed in northwest Summerhill, near Fulton County Stadium. The stadium was to hold many of the main Olympic events and afterward be converted to a baseball stadium, replacing the existing stadium. The leaders of the adjoining neighborhoods of Mechanicsville and Peoplestown protested loudly that a new arena and parking lots would devour their neighborhood's streets and homes, just as the baseball stadium had. Although he too was shocked by the announcement, Doug Dean soon welcomed the stadium in the belief that he could parlay support for the stadium into money for redevelopment projects.[63]

Dean, however, knew little of business or real estate development and turned to Robert Lupton for help in launching redevelopment projects. Lupton was white, a trained psychologist, and a devout Christian. In the mid-1970s, he founded Family Counseling Services Urban Ministries to serve inner-city Atlanta and moved his family to the then-depressed Grant Park neighborhood. Since about 1980 he had worked in Summerhill, administering youth and elderly programs and, through an affiliated organization called Charis Community Housing, building modest houses for low-income people. An engaging and energetic man, Lupton was more than glad to assist his friend, Doug Dean. Lupton felt that God had sent a vision of Summerhill physically rebuilt and spiritually reborn, and in 1991 he helped Dean organize the Summerhill Neighborhood Development Corporation (Summerhill NDC) as a nonprofit real estate development organization.[64]

For all his spirituality, Bob Lupton is a man of action whose motto is "Lead, follow, or get out of the way!" Lupton thought it would be a good idea to invite successful white businessmen to help the redevelopment effort. During his years of missionary and social uplift efforts in Atlanta's neighborhoods, Lupton had come to know several such businessmen (including real estate magnate Thomas Cousins); he admired them for their acumen and effectiveness, and they in turn had helped finance his programs. To serve on the board of the Summerhill Neighborhood Development Corporation, Lupton enlisted Joe Martin, a one-time real estate developer who had presided over Underground Atlanta, the city's festival marketplace, before taking the helm of Central Atlanta Progress.

Lupton also persuaded William "Billy" Mitchell, president of Carter and Associates, one of the southeast's largest real estate companies, to serve as chairman of the board of the Summerhill Neighborhood Development Corporation. Lupton and Mitchell both attended the downtown North Avenue Presbyterian church and had worked together in Grant Park to redevelop an old stockade building into low-income housing. As he got involved, Mitchell became convinced that the only way to complete the projects in time for the Olympics was to take direct control of operations. With Lupton's and Dean's approval, he became the executive director of the Summerhill Neighborhood Development Corporation.[65]

At first Dean and his Summerhill allies embraced Lupton and Mitchell because they believed the white men would bring expertise, contacts, and money that would help them revive their neighborhood. "We came into this as friends and those that wanted to be friends," Lupton recalled. "We wanted to be reconciled across the race and class lines that had divided us historically. It was a blissful marriage from everybody's point of view."[66]

The organizations that represented the neighborhood, however, were divided along racial lines. The original group, Summerhill Neighborhood Incorporated, was led by Dean with the support of other African Americans who had strong roots in Summerhill. The other organization, Summerhill Neighborhood Development Corporation, had neighborhood representatives on its board but was in fact run by white businessmen, who lived in Atlanta's booming, north-side Buckhead area. The real estate men earnestly wanted to redevelop Summerhill but gave little thought to strengthening local organizations or training African Americans to carry out projects themselves.[67]

Summerhill's redevelopers, black and white, dreamed big dreams. They envisioned the Olympics as an engine that would fuel the rebuilding of Summerhill as a thriving, mixed-income community. Facing the new Olympics stadium would be Greenlea Commons—tree-shaded commercial-residential buildings and 259 townhouses grouped around an open square. Rents from leasing the townhouses to Olympic visitors would fill the coffers of the Summerhill NDC and subsidize the purchase of these homes by low-income homebuyers after the games ended. To further preserve Summerhill as a home for low- and moderate-income people, Charis Community Housing would build 200 low-cost homes and rebuild a public housing project called Martin Street Plaza, with plans to sell it to its tenants. Across the street, Summerhill NDC would develop a subdivision of more than fifty single-family houses called The Orchards. The main commercial drag, Georgia Avenue, would be restored with new businesses.[68]

Sensing the possibilities, Atlanta's civic leaders and newspaper editorialists ballyhooed Summerhill as a future showcase for neighborhood revitalization in the city. Atlanta's government agencies, philanthropists, and businesses shelled out large sums of money to rebuild the neighborhood. The state agency that handled Olympic properties acquired land across from the Olympic Stadium to be used by the Summerhill Neighborhood Development Corporation to build Greenlea Commons. The city's development agency, the Urban Residential Finance Authority, issued $17 million worth of bonds backed by the First Union National Bank to pay for 200 new homes in four projects, including Greenlea Commons. By his own account, Lupton brought to Summerhill several local philanthropies—including the prestigious Woodruff Foundation—and big businesses such as Home Depot and AMOCO. NationsBank agreed to finance 50 percent of land acquisition in five proposed housing developments at a cost of $600,000, and the Fleet Finance Company put up nearly $3 million in tax credits and grants for operating expenses, land acquisition, and real estate development.[69]

Billy Mitchell was wheeling and dealing like a true Atlanta real estate developer. He and Lupton talked foundation officers into deals based only on a handshake, the kinds of arrangements that work as long as no one asks questions. The Summerhill NDC sometimes cut corners by not securing loans, filing property titles, or handing over warranty deeds to its lenders. Officers from different foundations thought that Mitchell had given them title to the same properties. There were many deals and time was short, but Mitchell had faith that if he could start the revenues flowing, he would make everything right in the long run.[70]

While they frantically tried to cash in on the Olympics for the Summerhill neighborhood, however, the white do-gooders unwittingly destroyed the trust of the local black residents. Pressed by deadlines, they abandoned the strategy meetings of twenty or thirty people and let a small group of white financial experts make decisions and then inform the Summerhill leaders and residents. "If we had a two- or three-year period of time to get things done, it would have worked itself out," Mitchell recalled. "But there was so much happening so fast, it was very hard to go through and debate each and every issue."[71]

The local blacks did not always appreciate the whites' good intentions, especially when the businessmen hired their white friends instead of finding qualified African Americans. Mitchell chose Chuck LeCraw, the nephew of another prominent white real estate developer and a member of Mitchell's church, to help run the Summerhill Neighborhood Development Corporation. Because the parent organization shared the same office and needed executive help, LeCraw ended up making business decisions for Summerhill Neighborhood Incorporated. His decisions to trim operations, however, alienated Dean and the local Summerhill board members who scorned him as "Billy's Buckhead boy."[72]

The Carter Hall project brought the resentment and distrust to a head. The fifteen-story former Ramada Hotel, located a block from the proposed Olympic stadium, had become a hangout for prostitutes and homeless people and a roadblock to any revival of Summerhill. Mitchell hired two of his and

Lupton's friends, Chris Humphreys and Cecil Phillips, to develop the defunct hotel into private residences for college students and earn large sums for the Summerhill NDC. The developers bought the building for the nonprofit organization—which qualified the project for tax-exempt funding, including $11.2 million in bonds from the Urban Residential Finance Authority. Because real estate loans were hard to come by, it took the real estate dealers nine months of "conniving, convincing, leveraging, and layering" to put together a complicated financial package. They then secured contracts from Payne's ACOG and Olympic sponsors to lease the rooms, roof, and grounds of the former hotel.[73]

For their labors, Humphreys and Phillips stood to gain considerable fees and an entree to the downtown housing market, something they had been trying for years to obtain. They saw the dormitory project as a lucrative deal for both themselves and the neighborhood group. Lupton sympathized with his "bleary eyed, emotionally drained developer friends" whose efforts he considered "a fine example of men of faith employing their best market-place talents to promote the work of the Kingdom."[74]

The Summerhill folks saw things differently. They were offended when Humphreys and Phillips promptly named the dormitory after Jimmy Carter, as a way of recasting its image, without bothering to consult the neighborhood people. "We probably would have argued about which dead preacher to name it after," said one resident, "but at least we would have been asked." When Phillips and Humphreys negotiated a $250,000 deal with Coca-Cola to rent the side of the building for an enormous advertisement, the board members from Summerhill discomfited Mitchell and the corporate attorneys by insisting on going over the contract line by line and changing anything that did not sound right to them.[75]

It did not help when deals in Summerhill soured. Rising land prices and construction costs forced the Summerhill NDC to scale back its plan for Greenlea Commons from 259 townhouses—whose sale was supposed to subsidize costs for low-income home purchasers—to 76 units. Even with an emergency infusion of funds from the Atlanta City Council, the Greenlea Commons houses had to be priced well above the reach of Summerhill's low-income population, and its builder, John Weiland, says he lost more than a half million dollars on the venture. At the Orchards middle-income housing project, Summerhill NDC built only five of the planned seventeen homes, and these were done so hurriedly that the facades had to be rebuilt and drainage and soil problems had to be remedied to prevent the foundations from cracking. Nothing came of the proposed revival of the Georgia Avenue commercial strip, and the attempt to transfer ownership of the Martin Street public housing project to the residents fell apart after years of delays and squabbles.[76]

Even worse, the Olympics never created the bonanza that Dean and Mitchell had counted on to pay for their projects and loans. Houses did not sell quickly, and fewer college students rented Carter Hall dorm rooms than expected. Dean's doubts turned to alarm when he learned that Humphreys and Phillips stood to make $1 to $2 million in deferred commissions from developing Carter Hall and that Mitchell was running Summerhill NDC by borrowing large sums of money with Carter Hall as collateral. Dean was convinced that the developers were earning handsome profits while leaving the organization high and dry.[77]

Dean and disgruntled Summerhill NDC board members voted not to renew the organization's management contract with Humphreys and Phillips in February 1996. Billy Mitchell protested the removal of Phillips and Humphreys whom he felt were the only people skilled enough to extract money from Carter Hall. By then Dean's faction on the Summerhill board was fed up with the white businessmen and at the next meeting fired Mitchell. Joe Martin then resigned from the board and Lupton followed, but not before sending a letter to the foundation officers explaining that he had no confidence that the organization could repay its loans. The businessmen felt hurt and angry, and they concluded that blind greed had prevented Dean from letting them do the real estate development job that only they could perform.[78]

The upheaval led the foundations that had sent more than $3 million in grants and loans to investigate their investments in Summerhill. They discovered that the finances were a mess and that Summerhill NDC had few prospects for success in the future. The foundations decided not to send any more money to either of the Summerhill organizations until their outstanding loans were repaid.[79]

The "partnerships" with white businessmen and Christian workers had done little or nothing to increase the abilities of the Summerhill organization or its leaders to carry out projects on their own. Lacking anyone with expertise in real estate and business, Summerhill NDC's financial house of cards collapsed. Carter Hall lost so much money that Dean closed it. By 1998 Summerhill NDC was $2 million in debt. It failed to meet the deadline for completing three of its housing projects and was forced to return $8 million of its Urban Residential Finance Authority loan. Dean adopted a cavalier attitude toward returning loans to foundations, figuring they had gambled on big returns coming from the Olympics and lost. He could not ignore the telephone company, however, when it cut service to Summerhill NDC's office.[80]

To keep Summerhill NDC alive, Dean sold off its properties. After Carter Hall had been on the market for years, he sold it—the building will be turned back into a hotel. The community development department of NationsBank purchased lots at the Orchards and another project site and built houses for professionals on them. Dean has sold to for-profit developers lots that the Summerhill NDC had bought for a song. In one subdivision, named Dean's Village after the Summerhill leader, the price of the houses range from $289,000 to $400,000, far more than the old residents can afford. Dean celebrates the rampant gentrification as a great success.[81]

Others are not so happy about what happened in Summerhill. Phil Edwards, a Summerhill native who served on the Summerhill board, objected to the division between the increasingly expensive northern Summerhill and the still dilapidated southern portion of the neighborhood. "We just don't have the intermingling a community should possess," observed Edwards. "The older residents are somewhat leery and frightened by the repercussions." Indeed, if it were not for the hundred or so houses that Bob Lupton's Charis Commu-

The new Summerhill emerges next to the old, January 2001. Courtesy of Glenna Lang.

nity Housing built in the renewal area of Summerhill, few people of low or moderate income would be left.[82]

Atlanta's foundation officers, many of whom are owed hundreds of thousands of dollars, were chastened by their experience. They swear they will not lend again without keeping track of their agreements. The white businessmen too learned painful lessons in Summerhill. "There were a lot of great things coming out of Summerhill, but there were also a lot of terrible experiences and ruptured relationships," Joe Martin recalled ruefully. "At the end of the day," commented Cecil Phillips, one of the ousted Carter Hall developers who unsuccessfully sued Summerhill NDC to recover his developer's fees, "I was less chagrined about the money than the fact that it was an opportunity lost. Summerhill is no longer the leader, in anyone's mind, in the idea of neighborhood reclamation."[83]

Showpiece Urban Renewal

If Atlanta's business community failed to turn Summerhill into a model neighborhood, it was able to place its stamp on the remaking of public housing projects. Working under an unusually effective director, the Atlanta Housing Authority, long known for ineptitude, produced a series of showpiece housing projects during the 1990s. The agency's policy in these efforts was to demolish entire existing public housing projects and, with the help of private investment and developers, build new mixed-income apartment complexes on the same sites. This approach, which aims as much to upgrade neighborhoods as it does to help low-income people, appeals to the booster ethos of the town's business and civic elite.

Reflecting the indifference to historical buildings and artifacts that typifies boomtowns such as Atlanta, the city's public housing agency began the work of renewing public housing by destroying Techwood Homes, the first public housing project to be built in the United States.

There is a certain irony in this history. Atlanta's business and political elite has long taken an interest in the site of Techwood Homes—a tract west of downtown and immediately south of two of the city's icons: the Coca-Cola company headquarters and the Georgia Institute of Technology—and has been responsible, one way or another, for two slum clearance and housing projects there. In the early twentieth century, the area, known as Techwood Flats, was a slum inhabited by poor whites, and the town's chiefs considered it an eyesore. One of their number, Charles Palmer, a prominent real estate developer and owner of numerous downtown office buildings, decided to do something about it.[84]

Palmer discovered in 1933 that the newly created federal Public Works Administration—one of President Franklin D. Roosevelt's many efforts to combat the Depression—had started a program to fund limited-dividend corporations to clear slums and build low-cost housing, and he concocted a scheme to demolish Techwood Flats and build a new housing project. Palmer promoted the plan as a civic project, but it would also boost the values of his downtown real estate holdings. He enlisted a large group of influential Atlantans—including the mayor, the president of Georgia Institute of Technology, the head of the Atlanta Chamber of Commerce, and Clark Howell, the publisher of the *Atlanta Constitution* and friend of F.D.R.—to form Techwood Inc. The purpose of the organization was to finance the reconstruction of the flats, but the federal limited-dividend program was canceled. When the Public Works Administration announced it would build low-income housing projects itself, Palmer and Clark pushed the agency to build Techwood Homes for white residents and another project for African Americans, and they successfully petitioned Roosevelt to approve both.

The New Deal administrators and the Atlanta architects who had drawn up the proposal took great care in creating the inaugural project of the federal government's novel public housing program. Besides a 189-room dormitory for Georgia Tech students, Techwood Homes provided 604 apartments in two-story row houses and three-story garden apartment buildings. Its architects combined the flat-roofs and rectilinear shape of the new modernist architectural style with traditional brick facades. They built Techwood to last, employing modern construction materials such as poured and reinforced concrete. The kitchens included the latest appliances, and the laundry rooms were equipped with free washing machines. Techwood's developers even provided automobile garages for the tenants. Even more exceptional was the project's landscape, composed of sweeping green lawns, common gardens, and tennis courts, playgrounds, and a wading pool. Techwood was a small community that boasted medical and dental care facilities and small stores to serve its tenants. Public housing would never have it so good again.

Techwood Homes thrived for decades. Next to it, in 1940, the housing authority built Clark Howell Homes, adding 630 dwellings in fifty-eight tradi-

The cupola building at Techwood Homes, June 2000. Courtesy of author.

tional-looking townhouses to the original project. The housing authority maintained both projects for whites only until the Civil Rights Act of 1968 led to their integration. Techwood was placed on the National Register of Historic Landmarks in 1976, by which time its population was about 50 percent black.

The same type of business interest that had created Techwood Homes now began to threaten it. The changing population and rising crime rates at Techwood frightened Paul Austin, the president of nearby Coca-Cola, who enlisted John Portman, Atlanta's high-powered architect and inventor of the giant atrium-style hotel, in a scheme to demolish Techwood, disperse its residents, and build a fancy office and retail complex on its site. Austin's scheme might have been carried out, but the recently elected African American mayor, Maynard Jackson, backed away from the plan when it became public. It smacked too much of the kind of urban renewal that had hurt black residents in the recent past.[85]

By then Techwood was beginning to suffer from the Atlanta Housing Authority's decision to loosen the criteria for admitting residents into their projects. As in other large American public housing projects, falling rents and poor management afflicted the historic housing project with a host of plagues. A succession of housing authority directors did little or nothing to stop the downward spiral. In the early 1980s, housing code inspections revealed some 10,000 code violations in Techwood and Clark Howell, a finding that Mayor

Jackson used to obtain federal funds to renovate the projects. The Atlanta Housing Authority spent more than $17 million of U.S. Department of Housing and Urban Development (HUD) money to improve the kitchens and bathrooms, replace the roofs, floors, and windows, and modernize the heating, plumbing, and electrical systems. Unfortunately, a wave of inner-city drug dealing and the failure of the agency to address its admission and management problems all but canceled out the benefits of the home improvements. In the late 1980s, crack cocaine transactions and territorial fights between rival gangs of dealers precipitated an outbreak of crimes in the housing projects.[86]

Even so, it was not crime but the announcement in 1990 that Atlanta would host the Olympics that inspired the city's movers and shakers to take action on Techwood and Clark Howell Homes. The public housing projects, after all, stood between the Georgia Tech stadium where many of the games were to be held, the towering Coca-Cola headquarters building, and eventually Billy Payne's Centennial Olympic Park, which would be a centerpiece of Olympian Atlanta.

Suddenly Atlanta's powers were proposing plans to usurp the housing project for the Olympics. At the outset, the Olympic bid committee called for replacing Georgia Tech's three-story dormitory with a multistory tower that would be used to lodge Olympic athletes. (Payne's ACOG organization would develop a dormitory for athletes that was later rented to college students.) Georgia Tech, one of the Olympic planners, proposed that a private entity buy the Techwood land, disperse most of the residents, and keep less than 10 percent of the area for public housing. The president of the Atlanta City Council suggested demolishing Techwood and Clark Howell and building an Olympic Village that would later house students and some low-income families.

This last proposal particularly enraged Margie Smith, president of the Techwood tenants' association, who snapped, "Tell him to go build it on his own house." Despite the problems, occupancy rates at Techwood and Clark Howell Homes stood above 90 percent, and surveys showed that a large number of the residents of the housing projects wanted to stay put. They liked the affordability and location of the projects—and they resisted the idea of changing the character of their community. Until their ranks were thinned almost to nothing, the public housing residents and their leaders held firm in their resistance.[87]

Mayor Jackson publicly agreed that demolition of a sound and historically significant property was unnecessary and in 1991 formed an advisory committee to devise a viable redevelopment plan for Techwood and Clark Howell. The committee then hired a consortium of four firms (including a construction company) to act as consultants, but the consultants deceived the public housing residents and tried to engineer their removal from the premises. According to Larry Keating, a professor of planning at Georgia Tech who has studied the history of Techwood, the consultants dangled the idea of homeownership before the tenants without explaining that most of them would not be able to afford it. The housing agency blatantly discouraged the tenants' organizations from buying the housing projects, although the policy of the federal Department of Housing and Urban Development at the time favored such sales of public housing. Without bothering to analyze their own survey of tenants' opinions, the consultants proposed sharply reducing the 1,195 public housing apartments at Techwood and Clark Howell to 800 units for households with a range of incomes. The consortium made no effort to find public housing apartments to replace those that were demolished and presented only vague ideas for relocating the displaced residents. So sloppy was the plan that in February 1992, HUD, which the housing authority called on to pay $90 million to redevelop the projects, rejected it in the harshest terms.[88]

The campaign to reconstitute Techwood and Clark Howell Homes got back on track, thanks to a $300 million appropriation passed by the U.S. Congress in October 1992 to revitalize the nation's worst public housing projects. The Atlanta Housing Authority pursued the federal money with a new rehabilitation scheme that respected the desire of the tenants to remain in a public housing community. The plan would have preserved historic Techwood by enlarging the apartments to create duplex townhouses on the upper two stories of the existing buildings.[89]

The plan to preserve and restore the nation's first public housing project to its former glory was doomed. Atlanta's powers-that-be, ever conscious of the approaching Olympic games, were determined that Techwood would fall to the bulldozer and wrecking ball. Bill Campbell, the man who took over the mayor's chair from Maynard Jackson in November 1993, was committed to both neighborhood revitalization and good relations with Atlanta's business leaders. Campbell took control of the housing authority's board of commissioners, which in September 1994 named Renée Glover, one of its members and a former Campbell campaign aide, as executive director of the agency.[90]

Glover was aghast at the Atlanta Housing Authority and the projects it purported to run. Incompetence and mismanagement, Glover knew as a member of the board, riddled the department. As director, Glover overhauled the operations and got the housing authority taken off HUD's list of troubled agencies. With its incompetence, the agency had been unable to make a dent in the problems that overwhelmed housing projects such as Techwood Homes and East Lake Meadows. Taking note of the crime and the seemingly hopeless condition of many residents, Glover concluded that massing poor people in public housing was a recipe for disaster and so she set about reducing the concentration of poverty in the projects.[91]

But Glover also thought about public housing in Atlanta from the business perspective. The housing agency director was a lawyer who, as a partner in New York and Atlanta law firms, had specialized in business transactions and corporate finance. An effective and dedicated manager, Glover was one of a cadre of African American women in Atlanta who helped operate the city from behind the scenes. She proudly presented her public housing redevelopment projects as civic showpieces and declared to Central Atlanta Progress that the redevelopment of Techwood had to be "part of the downtown agenda."[92]

Glover rejected the renovation schemes of her predecessor, Earl Phillips, as much too gradual. In each of the projects to be renovated, the housing authority began by renovating a single building as a model of what was to come. The process perplexed Glover who could not understand why the agency had done nothing about the infrastructure problems and size of small apartments. In one embarrassing moment, sewage backed into the model building apartment in one of Atlanta's public housing projects just as a tenant leader was moving in and forced her to remove her furniture and belongings. "Oftentimes it was all cosmetic," Glover recalls, "and they weren't really getting into the root cause. It really didn't make a lot of sense."[93]

The problems of Atlanta's public housing, Glover believed, were fundamental. To solve them, the agency must start over by demolishing entire projects and carefully screening those who were allowed in the new buildings. Glover never seriously considered the possibility of reviving the Techwood community by restoring it as a historic monument. Instead, she swept away the old proposals to fix Techwood and drew up plans to wreck it and build a new mixed-income housing project called Centennial Place. The 1,081 public housing units surviving in Techwood and Clark Howell (about 100 had been sacrificed for Olympic athlete housing) were to be replaced at Centennial Place with three-story suburban-style townhouses containing 900 dwelling units. Of these units, 40 percent would be reserved for families with public housing level incomes, 20 percent would go to somewhat better-off low- and moderate-income families, and the remaining 40 percent would rent at market rates.[94]

In her campaign to replace Techwood, Glover benefited from good luck. The state government's long-time preservation officer, who had steadfastly opposed the demolition of Techwood, retired and was replaced by a more acquiescent official. The tenants' influence, always tenuous at best, had all but disappeared because the tenants had all but disappeared. Glover's predecessor (whether from incompetence or deviousness is not clear) had not filled the vacant apartments, thus shrinking the population of Techwood and Clark Howell Homes from 93 percent occupancy in 1990 to less than 6 percent by the end of 1994. At a meeting held just before the residents' vote on Glover's plan, housing authority staff members and consultants outnumbered the eight tenants who attended.[95]

Finally, to Glover's delight, Bill Clinton's secretary of HUD, Henry Cisneros, launched a campaign to demolish and rebuild old public housing projects throughout the country. In practice, this meant that HUD relaxed important restrictions that had inhibited such demolition in the past. Now instead of having to build a new apartment for every public housing unit they destroyed, the housing authority could give a large number of displaced tenants rental (Section 8) vouchers for use in private apartment buildings.

By arguing that the upcoming Olympic games imposed a critical deadline, Glover persuaded HUD officials to support her plan to demolish Techwood and Clark Howell Homes. Her scheme acquired a sense of inevitability. At meetings held to prepare a report to the federal government justifying their plan to destroy historic structures, Atlanta Housing Authority officials ignored any suggestions for saving the landmark public housing buildings. "It was such a done deal," recalls Karen Huebner, the city's urban design commissioner who attended the meetings, "you knew it was all over." The housing authority

Centennial Place, on the site of the former Techwood Homes, with Coca-Cola company headquarters looming in the background, January 2001. Courtesy of Glenna Lang.

even persuaded the handful of tenants who remained—some of whom said they would miss Techwood's communal gardens—that the only way they would ever have good homes again was to start afresh. The agency convinced them that the historic preservationists who objected were trying to deprive them of a better home.[96]

The housing authority successfully pushed through the demolition of Techwood and Clark Howell Homes and developed Centennial Place. Today the new complex has 738 rental apartments and about a hundred houses that are scheduled to be sold. The attractive clapboard and brick complexes fulfilled the long-standing aspirations of the city's corporate elite to create a downtown studded with monuments. Centennial Place stands as a testament to the ideal of civic progress that has long ruled Atlanta. Fittingly, the only remaining structure of historic Techwood Homes, the cupola building, is slated to be converted into corporate suites.[97]

Under Glover's sure-handed leadership, the new projects are well run and applicants carefully scrutinized before being allowed to occupy the new apartments. Whether Centennial Place is a *structural* improvement on Techwood Homes is another question. Recently a class at Georgia State University studied the decisions that led to the demolition of the sturdy, sixty-seven-year-old Techwood buildings and the construction of Centennial Place. John Carlston, an architect who had worked on the project, came to the class as an invited guest. One of the students asked him how long he thought the new buildings at Centennial Place would last. "Twenty-five years," Carlston replied.[98]

Revival Through Golf and God

If Centennial Place exemplifies public housing as civic showpiece, the housing authority's other pride and joy, Villages at East Lake, might suggest public housing as country club. At any rate, it is safe to say that the East Lake neighborhood is the nation's only urban area to be redeveloped through the game of golf.

Atlanta's East Lake neighborhood is somewhat unusual for an inner-city community in that it was originally developed as a resort area for wealthy whites. It is located four and a half miles east of downtown but sits in two counties: Fulton, which contains most of Atlanta, and DeKalb, a suburban and rural jurisdiction which the locals refer to as "Dee-Cab." In the early 1900s, the son and heir of the founder of the Coca-Cola company, Asa Candler Jr., helped promote East Lake as a fashionable place by building the East Lake golf course. A few years later, in 1913, the renowned golf course landscape architect, Donald Ross, redesigned the East Lake course and turned it into a masterpiece of the genre.

The neighborhood became a breeding ground for great golfers in the 1920s and 1930s. A neighborhood youth who became golf's Babe Ruth, Bobby Jones, learned to play on the East Lake course and ensured its fame by bringing home tournament trophies. The greatest amateur player in golf history, Jones won thirteen major golf titles, including four U.S. Opens, three British Opens, a British Amateur, and an unprecedented Grand Slam in 1930, before retiring at age thirty. Alexa Stirling, the three-time U.S. Women's Amateur champion and a friend of Jones, grew up across the street from the East Lake club. Charlie Yates, winner of the 1938 British Amateur, and two winners of the Southern Amateur tournaments also made East Lake their home course. So popular was the game that the Atlanta Athletic Club added a second golf course to meet the demand.[99]

For decades following its golf heyday, East Lake prospered. The postwar growth of the suburbs, however, siphoned off its affluent population. Beginning in the 1960s, working- and middle-class black families bought houses in East Lake, well-to-do whites sold out and left, and property values plummeted.

The neighborhood prestige suffered a blow in 1968 when the Atlanta Athletic Club sold the second golf course to the Atlanta public housing agency and departed for Atlanta's prosperous north side, leaving the East Lake Golf Club to manage the older golf course. On the site of the second golf course, the housing authority built East Lake Meadows, which was planned as a community of garden apartments that included a city park, shopping center, social and medical services, and elementary school. Because it straddled jurisdictions, however, East Lake Meadows was orphaned by local governments that should have taken responsibility for the housing development. The park was never completed, the shopping center never built, and the social services and clinics either did not get started or did not stay long.[100]

East Lake Meadows, rear view, before demolition.
Courtesy of Atlanta Housing Authority.

Bereft of grocery stores or children's recreational areas, East Lake Meadows gradually became a classic troubled public housing project. By 1991, the drug trade had taken firm hold, and crack cocaine and drive-by shootings had become part of everyday life. The majority of the project's population were young people who grew up, the *Atlanta Journal-Constitution* reported, in a world dominated by "policemen, danger, guns, and food stamps." So violent was East Lake Meadows that people now referred to it as Little Vietnam.[101]

The Atlanta Housing Authority—at the time directed by Earl Phillips—responded feebly to the deplorable conditions at East Lake Meadows. It proposed to spend almost a half million dollars to build a security fence around East Lake Meadows, ostensibly to prevent bad people from entering the premises. The project's residents angrily rejected the fence and instead demanded improvements in services and protection from drug dealers. "We won't let them box us in, or fence us in, or house us in, with nothing but red dirt, rats, and roaches," said Eva Davis, the long-time president of the East Lake Meadows tenant association. "If they won't give us something we want first," she added, displaying the belligerence for which she was known, "then to hell with their fence."[102]

Former president Jimmy Carter did better than the Atlanta Housing Authority. Moved by the plight of the East Lake Meadows residents, in 1991 he adopted the housing project and held it up as a symbol of the problems the Atlanta Project would attack. The next year Carter personally lobbied HUD Secretary Jack Kemp and persuaded him to award the Atlanta Housing Authority $33.5 million to renovate all 650 apartments and physically overhaul the poorly constructed, aging housing project. Eva Davis exulted, "Thank God for a miracle!" The miracle, however, would not come quickly. The housing authority, which intended to spend a year meeting with residents and architects before commencing renovations, planned to take four years to fix East Lake Meadows.[103]

As the number of African Americans in the East Lake neighborhood increased, the East Lake Golf Club grew isolated as a bastion of white privilege. Although not hard-core racists, the club's aging white directors shared the racial and class prejudices common to their ilk. The eighty-year-old director of the 750-member all-white club said in 1991 that he would not object to having as many as ten or fifteen black members "if we could get the ones I want." Despite its exclusiveness, the East Lake Golf Club fell on financial hard times. In 1993 its officers put the links up for sale, and members tried to purchase the course but failed to raise enough money.[104]

It was then that one of Atlanta's larger-than-life figures, real estate tycoon Tom Cousins, stepped in and offered to purchase the golf course, demonstrating that under certain circumstances even real estate developers will support historic preservation.

It is said around town that author Tom Wolfe used Cousins as a model for Charlie Croker, the flamboyant real estate developer in Wolfe's best-selling novel, *A Man in Full*. As a young man, Cousins married the daughter of the president of Auburn University and started a real estate business with his father and a small stake. He gradually made a fortune in Atlanta suburban real estate and, like Charlie Croker, gained a reputation for developing daring projects beyond the line of dense settlement—first building residential subdivisions in remote sections of DeKalb and Cobb Counties and later, shopping centers and office parks—including the Wildwood office complex overlooking the Chattahoochee River National Recreation Area. In the 1960s he began to play with downtown Atlanta real estate. Among his other projects, Cousins financed the Omni coliseum stadium, developed the Georgia World Congress Center, brought basketball and hockey teams to Atlanta, and in 1992 built what was said to be the ninth tallest building in the world, the NationsBank Plaza.[105]

Cousins particularly likes bird hunting, and he indulges this whim on a grand scale. Like Charlie Croker, Cousins owns what is called a plantation—in his case, a 6,900-acre estate named Nonami outside Albany, Georgia. In the rural plantation belt, where Nonami is located, wealthy Atlantans gratify their appetite for hunting bobwhite quail, turkey, deer, and the occasional bobcat.[106]

Cousins's other passion is golf. He had grown up near the links and played on them in his youth. He dreamed of restoring the golf course to its glory and making it a monument to the legendary Bobby Jones. In November 1993 Cousins dipped into his personal fortune and purchased the East Lake golf course—all 177 acres of it including three lakes and the much-altered, threadbare old clubhouse—for $4.5 million. He then set about a complete restoration of the historic landscaping and a luxurious recreation of the Tudor-style clubhouse. As for the club, Cousins announced he would boost membership fees (they were eventually pegged at $250,000 plus links fees) and reconstitute it for corporations and wealthy executives. Some members of the old East Lake Golf

Club objected that they would no longer be able to afford to play on the course, which was ironic in that the club's fees had long excluded local African Americans.[107]

The next year Cousins gave the club in its entirety to the C.F. Foundation, the family philanthropic organization run by his wife, and began to talk of establishing a golf academy to introduce children from the East Lake Meadows housing project to the game. His scheme was to direct $200,000 of each membership fee to the foundation's community development efforts. An article in the *Atlanta Journal-Constitution* cast aspersions on Cousins's motives, suggesting that he gave the golf course to his nonprofit foundation to gain a large tax write-off. Cousins only thought of helping the community, the paper reported, when he realized that the presence of "Little Vietnam" threatened his dream of turning the golf course into a memorial to Bobby Jones. According to Cousins and his family members, however, the real estate magnate for some time had wanted the C. F. Foundation to take a new approach to philanthropy, concentrating on a single program rather than giving many small grants. The task of rescuing East Lake Meadows and restoring the East Lake golf course, Cousins felt, presented a happy but coincidental convergence of opportunity.[108]

Another happy convergence occurred when Renée Glover assumed the directorship of the Atlanta public housing agency. Cousins, who had been unable to persuade Earl Phillips to let him help redo East Lake Meadows, found a willing collaborator in Glover. Instead of using the money the federal government had granted for renovating East Lake Meadows, Glover wanted to do what she had done at Techwood Homes: demolish the project and start over.[109]

Sure enough, the Atlanta Housing Authority and the C. F. Foundation announced in June 1995 that they had formed a partnership to demolish fifty acres of streets and brick-and-cinder block apartments and build a residential and recreation area, which would include a new eighteen-hole public golf course. They proposed replacing the East Lake Meadows' 650 units with 406 new dwellings, only half of which would go to public housing residents. Tenant leader Eva Davis commented, "A lot of residents feel like this is a sneaky way to get rid of us." Unlike what had happened at Techwood, in East Lake the tenants were going to have their say.[110]

In January 1996, after eight months of arduous negotiations, the East Lake Meadows residents, Atlanta housing officials, and Jimmy Carter (who had made it his and the Atlanta Project's cause five years earlier) signed an agreement on a plan for a $52 million country club residential subdivision. At the ceremony held at the Carter Center, Jimmy Carter compared the agreement to the breakthrough in the Middle East political world in which Palestinians had held elections. "We're going to have the best community in the country and the world," Renée Glover declared. "I feel like we're going somewhere," said Davis. "It's been a long, drawn-out process. But I thank God we made it."[111]

The agreement called for using a combination of government and private funds to build a new mixed-income 170-acre subdivision. It would contain 498 townhouses, garden apartments, and duplexes—the number would later

*Eva Davis (left), Renée Glover, and Atlanta mayor William Campbell,
jointly announcing the redevelopment of East Lake Meadows.
Courtesy of Atlanta Housing Authority.*

rise to 542—half of which would be reserved for public housing families. The
C. F. Foundation, owner of the nearby East Lake Golf Club, would put up
$20 million to pay for junior tennis and golf academies and the creation of a
new eighteen-hole public golf course. At the same time, Gregory Giornelli,
Tom Cousins's son-in-law and the executive director of the C. F. Foundation,
announced the formation of a new Cousins philanthropy, the East Lake Community Foundation, to oversee the real estate development and run the recreational facilities and programs at East Lake. (The real estate developer wanted
to put more distance between his private company and the East Lake project.)[112]

The road to the newly dubbed Villages of East Lake had been rocky, and it
would get rockier still. The agreement had taken months of difficult negotiations among the Cousins foundation, the public housing authority, and the
tenants of East Lake Meadows, led by the mercurial and tempestuous Eva
Davis. In fact, Jimmy Carter told Cousins he doubted the East Lake project
could succeed because in his long experience of negotiating with leaders
around the world, he had never encountered anyone as impossible as Eva
Davis.[113]

Davis drove a hard bargain, but she and the tenants had cause to be anxious. Hundreds of families who for years had endured terrible conditions in
East Lake Meadows were now to lose their homes. When Cousins originally
proposed building houses for sale, the tenants knew they would not be able to
afford them and demanded rental units. Cousins acceded to this request but
proposed to reduce the total number of dwellings by more than 200, and fol-

lowing the usual practice in mixed-income housing projects, reserve only 25 percent of these for public housing residents. Davis demanded that half of the dwellings be reserved for public housing families, and the housing authority and the Cousins foundation again acceded. The nervous tenants insisted that before any units were bulldozed, the foundation must build off-site housing for returning families.[114]

Even so, two hundred families stood to be evicted. The Atlanta Housing Authority assured the tenants it took their concerns seriously. Agency officials promised to provide these families with Section 8 rental vouchers and help relocate them in housing that met their approval.[115]

The Cousins family foundation officers felt they bent over backward to assuage Eva Davis and her followers—even taking tenants to Home Depot to help choose linoleum for the apartments—but some of the demands seemed to them unreasonable, even irrational. The tenants were adamant, for example, that the developers save the duplex houses, which had always been the most desirable residences in East Lake Meadows. The foundation officers, who wanted to replace the duplexes with a lake and part of the new golf course, could not understand why the tenants clung to these structures when the new apartments would be so much better. The tenants asked for brick exteriors instead of synthetic siding, and preferred gas to electric ranges. The foundation officers drew the line, however, at the tenants' demand that they build a fishing pond next to the senior citizens' high-rise.[116]

Davis faced, in the words of one reporter, "a Goliath with what amounts to a rock and a slingshot," and despite her ultimate defeat, achieved significant victories for her constituents. She was able to get more than twice the number of public housing units in the new community than the number in the original plan. Davis and the tenants convinced the developers to use partial brick facades and build new duplexes, both of which enhanced the appearance of the new development.[117]

In the end, nobody, not even Eva Davis, could overcome the combined power and determination of Tom Cousins and Renée Glover to create a completely new community. The first phase of the project—construction of the first third of new units—went smoothly enough. During the second phase, however, Eva Davis and the tenants decided that they had been betrayed and held a symbolic vote to oust the East Lake Foundation as developer. Renée Glover of the Atlanta Housing Authority and Greg Giornelli of the East Lake Community Foundation tried to soothe the tenants, but to no avail. In October 1998, the tenants' group sued the housing authority for breach of contract and asked to halt the project. Two months later, a judge ruled in favor of the housing agency and ordered Eva Davis and twenty-seven other tenant families to move out of East Lake Meadows to make way for the second phase of demolition and construction. Eva Davis's power was broken forever.[118]

Frank Alexander, the former housing advocate for the Jimmy Carter Center and the Atlanta Project, believes the Cousins foundation and the housing authority violated their agreement. Alexander had tried to mediate among the three parties but observed that the tenants were utterly overmatched and volunteered to help them negotiate the final agreement. He charges that the foundation and housing agency broke their promise to build replacement housing before they demolished on-site units. They also demolished the duplexes and community center they were supposed to preserve, according to Alexander, and never rebuilt the community center.[119]

The tenants had asked the housing authority to lobby to preserve the local elementary school, Alexander recounts, and had convinced the chair of the Atlanta school board to write a letter promising not to penalize the school for declining enrollments during the East Lake redevelopment. Nonetheless, the school board reversed course. In the face of the residents' opposition, it cut a deal to close the school, sell the land to the East Lake Community Foundation, and allow the Foundation to construct a charter school there. Foundation officers, for their part, felt that the foundation's efforts to create a high-quality school in East Lake was a matter to be settled by the foundation and the Atlanta public school department. Alexander credits the housing authority for doing a good job of finding accommodations for the families who did not return to East Lake, but he also points out that the new expense of paying for utilities—including air conditioning—raises the costs for the new homes to a level above what many of the previous tenants could afford.[120]

Although Cousins and Glover may have rammed their plan through, even their critics admit that the transformation of East Lake is remarkable. The apartments at the Villages of East Lake, designed with the potential market-rate tenants in mind, are large and lavish. Ranging from two to four bedrooms, they include walk-in closets, plush carpets, modern kitchens complete with

Villages of East Lake, duplex units with brick facades, January 2001.
Courtesy of Glenna Lang.

ceramic tiles on the counter tops, and bathrooms with tubs large enough to fit two people. The landscape is alluring. Besides the new golf course around which dwellings are grouped, the Villages development has a swimming pool and tennis courts. Across the street from the development is the restored historic East Lake course and clubhouse.

Against all odds, the East Lake Community Foundation has made the after-school golf academy popular among the black children of East Lake. When the foundation staff members first went door-to-door to enlist children for the academy, Tiger Woods had not become the world's most famous golfer, and the mothers told them, "Our kids don't play golf—they like basketball." The foundation persisted, however, and today about eighty-five children, ages seven through fifteen, are enrolled. Golf has become a recreational lure for the foundation's other after-school activities, including reading, science instruction, homework, ballet lessons, and trips to museums and dance concerts. The foundation officers encourage local students interested in golf to apply for sports scholarships to college because historically black schools frequently do not have enough athletes to fill their golf teams.[121]

The older youths of the neighborhood can enroll in the caddy program at the East Lake golf course. Staff members of the East Lake Community Foundation point out that caddying is a lucrative job, teaches necessary social skills, and offers opportunities for playing golf or befriending influential people. Cousins dictated that the players at the East Lake golf course must use caddies—carts were prohibited. The caddies' pay could reach $40 for carrying eighteen holes, about $8 to $10 an hour, far better than minimum wage. Cousins also placed caddies on the payroll. "Why shouldn't a caddie have health insurance," Cousins asked, "like any other employee?"[122]

Greg Giornelli and his non-golf-playing lieutenant, Janet Stratigos, declare that golf is only a means to the social, economic, and spiritual uplift that is the ultimate end of the East Lake Community Foundation. The most important program the foundation administers, they feel, is a Welfare to Work program, which trains people in job behavior and skills. The public housing residents are required to enroll in this program, which by 2001 had successfully placed fifteen residents in jobs. The foundation also emphasizes education and spent four years negotiating with the Atlanta Board of Education to open a new charter school at East Lake, the first charter school in the city of Atlanta. Some of the delay was caused by the controversy over the East Lake Community Foundation's decision to engage the for-profit Edison Project to run the school. By 2001, 240 students were attending the new school with its Back to Basics curriculum.[123]

The East Lake Community Foundation also employs missionaries to help the poor families who live in the Villages of East Lake. When the complex was being planned, Renée Glover envisioned the market-rate tenants as passive role models for the public housing tenants, but Tom Cousins wanted more interaction between the residents. Cousins also doubted that the complex that housed public housing families would attract enough market-rate tenants to the Villages. In a characteristic combination of the practical and idealistic, Cousins found solutions to both problems.[124]

Cousins turned to Bob Lupton, a fellow church member whose works he had funded for twenty-five years and who believes in bringing socially committed Christians to live in inner-city neighborhoods. As a part-time employee of the East Lake Community Foundation, Lupton recruited middle-class tenants from churches and seminaries to be what he called Strategic Neighbors. In return for a reduction of $200 in the rent, the missionaries organized Bible study groups, ran after-school programs, held teas for the seniors, printed a newsletter, and helped whoever needed assistance, whether it be new arrivals or elderly sick people. Fortunately, Lupton has enjoyed greater success working with Cousins in East Lake than he had working with Billy Mitchell and Douglas Dean in Summerhill.[125]

Christopher and Rebecca Gray, the young interracial couple hired to be the head chaplains at the Villages at East Lake, became immersed in the lives of their neighbors—children drop by their home constantly and they recently took two neighborhood girls with them on a vacation to Colorado. Both graduates of the Air Force Academy and five years' service in the military, the Grays at times have felt overwhelmed by their responsibilities. They wrote of their attempts to run a basketball team for the children:

> Our efforts seem shoddy and disorganized. What business do a "has been" springboard diver and football player have coaching basketball, anyway? . . . The next day we passed one of our girls in school. . . . As 9-year-old Latasha beamed, she pointed at us and told her teacher, "Look, Mrs. Felder! There's my basketball coach." We then remembered that these girls have never been on a sports team. They haven't played tee ball or Little League. . . . They were simply thrilled to be part of a team.[126]

The mission to assimilate the poor to middle-class behavior patterns is not always a happy one, especially when it means separating family members. Public housing residents often allow grown children, lovers, and relatives to live with them, which is technically against the rules but rarely enforced. Since police suspect these unofficial tenants of committing crimes, however, the managers of the Villages have enforced the housing authority rule that restricts the length of visits by relatives of public housing tenants. "Recently, E. was told she couldn't have her family spending so much time in her apartment," the Grays wrote regretfully:

> To Mary, the head of the Leasing Office, success is having a safe community. She also wants to make the middle-income folks happy . . . so they will renew their lease. To her, if the Leasing Office does not keep an eye on our neighbor E., then economically this community will not survive. . . . The friends and family who visit, or who are allowed to live off of the resident, are often responsible for the crimes that occur. . . . Mary's decision might hurt E. but the entire community will thrive without E.'s family.[127]

In effect, the Grays have had to watch as the managers obstructed the kinship networks the poor often rely on to survive.

The Cousins campaign to transform East Lake reached into the neighborhood as well. Lupton and Charis Community Housing, with the help of Cousins Foundation money, launched an attack on what Lupton calls the northern and southern "beachheads" of the East Lake neighborhood. They bought crack houses and either rehabilitated them or demolished the structures and built anew. One result of this effort was a large co-housing project, built in rambling village pattern (by John Weiland, the builder who had lost money in Summerhill), which was the first private new construction in East Lake in thirty years.[128]

One can criticize the efforts at East Lake for a paternalistic attitude or, like other recent public housing redevelopment, for only re-housing and aiding the few who have been lucky enough to get in. Yet Tom Cousins, Greg Giornelli, and their employees and associates are earnestly dedicated to helping public housing tenants climb out of poverty, and despite the inevitable setbacks, they have made progress. One woman, Anniquinnette Ross, who was unemployed while living in the old East Lake Meadows, completed the job training and got a job at a food services company. Recently a family "graduated" from public housing and, with the help of the East Lake Community Foundation, bought its first house located nearby in the neighborhood, an event that Foundation staff members and former East Lake neighbors celebrated by throwing a house-warming party for the family in the new home. Since East Lake Meadows was demolished, crime has dropped by 90 percent within the gated community of Villages of East Lake and by 60 percent in East Lake proper. In the real estate market, Tom Cousins's renovation of the golf course and reconstruction of public housing has clearly succeeded. Prices have boomed as the affluent are returning to East Lake and its golden golf course.[129]

Neighborhoods Without Golf Courses

Whether they succeeded or failed, believed in democracy or hierarchy, helped the woeful poor or replaced them with folks who toed the line, Atlanta leaders—Jimmy Carter, Clara Axam, Maynard Jackson, Billy Mitchell, Renée Glover, and Tom Cousins—attracted attention to the plight of Atlanta's depressed neighborhoods as no one had done before. For years national organizations such as the Ford Foundation shunned Atlanta because local business leaders would not support community development. The efforts that the Olympics stimulated helped change the way Atlantans thought about their city and the well-being of the inner-city neighborhoods and their residents. Partly as a result, Atlanta began to develop what older eastern cities have had in place for years, a system of funding nonprofit community development organizations.

Atlanta's United Way, for example, was a conventional, if large, umbrella charitable organization that the city's corporations generously supported. In the mid-1990s it signed on to community development. A notorious mismanagement scandal in the national United Way organization provoked the director of the Atlanta affiliate, Mark O'Connell, to reexamine the local branch's entire approach to giving. In the early days of the Atlanta Project, Jimmy Carter also inspired O'Connell by challenging all the city's leaders to ask themselves what they could do to change the intolerably ineffective way of dealing with the poor and afflicted. After several months of consultation and discussion, O'Connell came up with a startling concept. The United Way would fund projects aimed at the most pressing problems rather than automatically contributing to a roster of social service agencies. The agencies and their regular contributors naturally resisted at first, but O'Connell eventually persuaded them to accept the change. The United Way hired a specialist in community affairs who began a number of innovations including supporting local CDCs and helping to start a program of "individual development accounts" in which banks and corporations provided very poor people with $200 for every $50 they saved toward an education or buying a home.[130]

One of the recipients of the new United Way funds was the Atlanta Neighborhood Development Partnership (ANDP), Atlanta's home-grown financial intermediary. Its founder is Hattie Dorsey, a native Atlantan who had pursued a career with foundations in San Francisco and New York. On returning to Atlanta, Dorsey was appalled to see what had happened to the old neighborhoods and the apathy of the business elite to their plight. In 1991, with the encouragement of Dan Sweat and other civic leaders, she started a local group that, like the Enterprise Foundation and LISC, would raise corporate and foundation money to give to viable CDCs. Local nonprofit groups that were accustomed to receiving crumbs now became eligible for major grants that would cover much of their operating expenses—a crucial element for a success.[131]

A few years after Dorsey started the Atlanta Neighborhood Development Partnership, the Enterprise Foundation opened a local office. The local chapter tapped the National Community Development Initiative—a fund-raising drive spearheaded by a group of large foundations and a corporation that from 1991 to 1994 raised $62.5 million for Enterprise and LISC to distribute to local nonprofit groups. With this money, Enterprise's Atlanta office gave selected Atlanta CDCs support over a few years, allowing the CDCs time to develop the staff and expertise to earn revenues. Enterprise in Atlanta also provided national experts to local training institutes run by ANDP and with the United Way gave grants to neighborhood groups that ran safety programs, ranging from neighborhood security patrols to after-school and summer programs for young people. Although some civic leaders in Atlanta still do not support community development, enough have come around to build a system of institutions to support neighborhood organizations.[132]

Funding network aside, most Atlanta neighborhoods lack billionaires, golf courses, and Olympic stadiums that bring investors, grants, and new residents raining down like manna from heaven. Without valuable resources, the local organizations must use whatever resources they have and go about the hard work of consulting with and educating residents to raise pride and a sense of possibility. It is in the benighted neighborhoods that you can measure Atlanta's progress during the 1990s. Although some neighborhoods continue to stagnate, others show signs of life.

The Auburn Avenue section of the Old Fourth Ward had no Olympic arenas, but it did contain one natural resource. Here was the birthplace and childhood home of Martin Luther King Jr., America's foremost civil rights leader and a winner of the Nobel prize for peace. Like the families of many respected ministers, the King family dwelt in "Sweet Auburn" during the time it was the preeminent residential area for African Americans in Atlanta. It was the home of the great churches, including Ebenezer Baptist, and their pastors, who lived on Bishops Row, as well as the leading business owners, the high school principal, large contractors, and porters—who once held jobs considered highly respectable. In segregation days, maids, janitors, and laborers also lived in the Auburn Avenue district, occupying modest cottages of the type known in the South as "shotgun houses" (so called because the rooms were aligned in a row in such a way that a shot fired through the front entrance could fly out the back door without ever hitting a wall).

When Mtamanika Youngblood, a manager with Bell South, and her husband, an attorney, left the suburbs in 1985 to move into an old house near the King birthplace—which became a National Park Service Historic Site—they thought the revitalization of such a historic neighborhood near downtown was a sure thing. Soon they noticed, however, that even though they had lovingly restored their own house, other properties were deteriorating, burning, and being torn down. They joined the Historic District Development Corporation, a group originally aimed at restoring the King birthplace block, to prevent the Auburn Avenue district from becoming a neighborhood of vacant lots and empty houses. Eventually Youngblood put in so much time and effort that when the organization began to receive operating funds—courtesy of ANDP and the Enterprise Foundation—she became the organization's executive director and first paid staff member. She then persuaded the planners at CODA to include her neighborhood among the Olympic neighborhoods that CODA would assist, on the grounds that out-of-town spectators would be visiting one of Atlanta's few genuine tourist attractions.[133]

Dilapidated shotgun house, near the birthplace of Martin Luther King Jr. in Atlanta's Old Fourth Ward, before and after renovation. Courtesy of Historic District Development Corporation.

Realizing from her own experience that fixing up one house would not attract new people to the neighborhood, Youngblood helped develop an approach she called the "block by block strategy,"—restoring an entire block all at once by renovating existing homes and building new ones. To test the strategy, the Historic District Development Corporation chose a block that was run down and pockmarked with vacant lots but still had a few homeowners who wanted to save it. The community group rehabbed the deteriorated houses and supported the homeowners' efforts while its partner, NationsBank Community Development Corporation, built new houses on the empty lots. To Youngblood's delight, it worked.

The Historic District Development Corporation worked with private developers, government agencies, and philanthropies to create a new mixed-income community by preserving the historic housing stock. Using federal tax credits, a state tax assessment freeze for historic properties, and even the assistance of the National Trust for Historic Preservation, the group tried to maintain a mix of both types of housing stock, simultaneously renovating shotgun houses and developing large homes. As a result, much of the housing remained affordable for the area's long-time residents even as the affluent moved in. The regulations, which restricted the kinds of development allowed in historic districts, scared off speculators and allowed Youngblood's group time to control redevelopment. Now the newfound popularity of city living in Atlanta has begun to bring artists and professionals into Sweet Auburn.[134]

Then there is Reynoldstown, located well beyond Atlanta's gentrification zone and literally on the other side of the tracks. A low-lying rolling area with small bungalows tucked in among the trees, Reynoldstown was originally settled after the Civil War by emancipated slaves. The railroad and later lumber and sawmills provided jobs for African American workers. Working-class whites lived here and there intermingled with blacks or in the colorfully named Cabbagetown area nearby. Like so many other neighborhoods, Reynoldstown in the 1950s and 1960s lost population, and by the 1980s it experienced an influx of poor, single mothers and drug and crime problems.[135]

To combat the deterioration in community life, the elders of Reynoldstown organized the Reynoldstown Revitalization Corporation in 1989. To head the new group, they chose Young Hughley Jr., who had no background in community development but had roots in the neighborhood. His father, a janitor and garbage man, had moved the family to Reynoldstown in 1964. Some years later Young Hughley Jr. left Atlanta for a career in management, eventually moving to New York where he worked as a manager in the fields of theater, music, and art. Eventually Hughley returned to Atlanta as an art consultant. When Hattie Dorsey first began to stir up interest in forming neighborhood organizations, she contacted Young Hughley Sr., who had been the director of a Reynoldstown civic association back in the 1960s. Dorsey and Hughley's father, among others, asked if the younger Hughley would tackle the mission of rebuilding Reynoldstown with funds from Dorsey's Atlanta Neighborhood Development Partnership.

Hughley agreed, but he had to start almost from scratch. The neighborhood had few community resources besides the group of committed older residents.

"How do you make people feel good," Hughley wondered, "about where they stay and who they are?"[136]

Hughley consulted Reynoldstown residents about the neighborhood's most pressing problems and tried what he calls a "holistic approach" to solving them. To help restore the housing stock, Hughley obtained money from a variety of sources including the Atlanta Neighborhood Development Partnership, the Enterprise Foundation, community development block grants, and the Federal Home Loan Bank. He also received in-kind help from volunteer groups such as Christmas in April, Hands on Atlanta, and a Georgia Tech program, Teen Buzz. The Reynoldstown Revitalization Corporation helped elderly home owners rehabilitate their houses—more than 270 at last count. The organization also acquired the empty lots that created holes in the urban fabric and built new houses to sell at market or subsidized rates depending on the buyer's income. Recruitment of young homebuyers has been difficult because Reynoldstown lacks the cachet of other neighborhoods and Hughley tells his prospects he wants them to attend community meetings and help him revitalize the neighborhood.[137]

Young Hughley Jr. (center) at event held by the Reynoldstown Revitalization Corporation. Courtesy of Reynoldstown Revitalization Corporation.

To enrich the lives of the residents, the Reynoldstown Revitalization Corporation launched a battery of undertakings other than housing. The group runs family planning and parenting classes, art projects, General Educational Development (GED) classes for high school dropouts, and an anti-drug program.[138]

The centerpiece of the Reynoldstown Revitalization Corporation and the neighborhood's major event is the Wheelbarrow Summer Theater. A combination of community gathering, arts festival, and fundraiser, the Wheelbarrow Theater happened almost by accident. A retired architect visited Hughley to share his ideas about new kinds of housing for depressed neighborhoods and on the way out happened to notice the covered basketball court behind the community center that houses the Reynoldstown Revitalization Corporation. The architect said it would be natural to convert the space into a theater for the community. With his theater background, Hughley agreed it would be a great idea but set it aside to deal with more pressing matters. A month later the architect returned with a crew of architectural students to build the stage area as a school project.

Since 1996 the organization's staff members and neighborhood volunteers have organized the Wheelbarrow Summer Theater as a festival of gospel, blues, jazz, dance, and theater performances; handicrafts and visual arts; and fund-raising activities such as auctions. Atlanta corporations—including Coca-Cola—arts councils, radio stations, foundations—including Enterprise and Hattie Dorsey's Atlanta Neighborhood Development Partnership—sponsor the event. It takes a great effort to mount the festival, from converting the basket-ball court into an amphitheater with stage to bringing together all the events, and Hughley hovers over the endeavor like a nervous mother hen.

A few years after it started, Wheelbarrow Theater had a crisis. The lighting control panel, an expensive piece of electronic equipment, was missing. Hughley was greatly distressed. All the funds and volunteer effort he had scraped together for months were in jeopardy if the show itself could not be staged. He went to the basketball court and asked the boys who always hung out there if they knew where the lighting board was. They knew nothing about it. Hughley continued to search. A little later, one of the boys approached him and asked, "Does that mean you can't have the show?" The director of the Reynoldstown Revitalization Corporation told him, yes, there would be no show without the board. The boy said he thought he knew who had it. An hour later the lighting board mysteriously appeared. After a great collective sigh of relief, the show went on.[139]

It was a small victory for Reynoldstown. It was not a golf course or a fancy housing complex, but it was something. A sign, perhaps, that the people had begun to feel good about their community and themselves. Perhaps, too, it signified that after a decade of effort, inner-city Atlanta was at last getting reli-gion about community development and inner-city revival.

Rebirth in Boomtown

The experiences of Atlanta during the last decade reveal the forces that can drive and hinder urban rebirth in the rapidly growing cities of the South and West.

In Sunbelt boomtowns, business executives hold sway, free enterprise is seen as the solution to most problems, and the nonprofit sector has trouble getting a strong foothold. At the same time, religious beliefs, especially related to Christian missionary impulses, often provide a counterweight to the laissez-faire ideology. The hard-driving business executive in the Sunbelt who might not support the idea of nonprofits in theory may well contribute to, support, or even lead nonprofit organizations out of a sense of pious devotion and duty.

When business leaders, especially self-made ones, get involved in commu-nity development, they may introduce a more competitive approach to busi-ness deals than that taken by people used to philanthropy and government programs. Although this competitive edge breathes fresh air from the world of private enterprise, it can also conflict with the social goals of nonprofit com-munity development—including the informed participation of those who are supposed to benefit from the deals carried out in their name. Working out such conflicts takes time, but in Atlanta the impending Olympic games cre-ated a sense of urgency that left little time for communication.

The Olympics inspired Atlanta's leaders to attempt to revive the inner city as they had never tried before. Indeed, the unique political opportunity for urban projects created by the Olympics tempted leaders, such as Jimmy Carter and Maynard Jackson, to set impossible goals and take on too much at one time—a hazard of large projects. The city's leaders dreamed wonderful dreams, but their followers lacked either the time or the mechanism to make the great dreams come true. An event of the size and importance of the Olympics is rare, however, so most cities should be able to emulate the vision of Atlanta's projects but take a more measured approach, thereby avoiding the pitfall of overreaching.

As a southern city, Atlanta has had to deal with the issue of race and therefore has lessons to teach other American cities, which, regardless of region, all have racial troubles to one degree or another. In Atlanta, as elsewhere, it is sometimes difficult for affluent whites to act as equal partners with low-income members of racial minority groups. Given the memory and legacy of racism, bitter misunderstandings—such as occurred in Atlanta's Summerhill neighborhood—can easily crop up on both sides. No matter how well-meaning they may be, do-gooders must be sensitive to the dignity and feelings of those they would assist. Fortunately, Atlanta possesses a cadre of talented African American community development professionals—including not only directors of CDCs but also representatives of the financial intermediaries (such as the Atlanta Neighborhood Development Partnership and the Enterprise Foundation)—who can work with both white civic leaders and black neighborhood residents until the day Martin Luther King Jr. preached about finally arrives.

The city of Atlanta came late to the game of community development, but it went a long way in a short time. To make the city ready for the Olympics and the thousands of out-of-towners the games would bring, the city's leaders got the process of urban revival under way, even if they felt they had to rush it. Their urban improvements and programs helped to resuscitate long-neglected communities and increase the small but steady flow of middle-class artists and professionals to the central city. The ultimate lesson of Atlanta's brief encounter with community development is that even at the core of America's booming, sprawling, fast-growth cities—Phoenix, Jacksonville, and others—rebirth is possible.

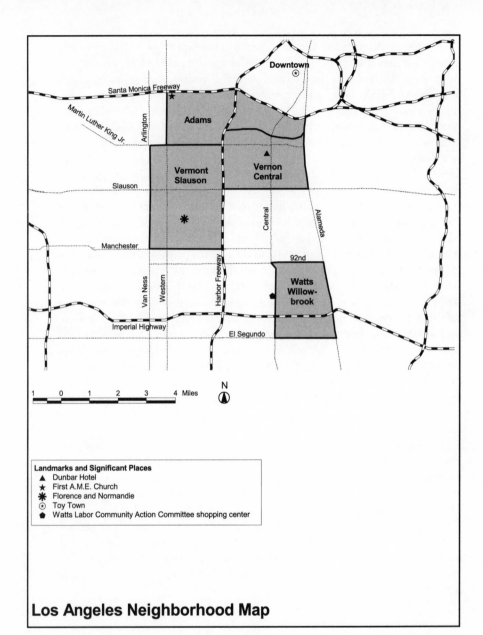

Santa Monica Freeway

Martin Luther King Jr.

Arlington

Downtown

Adams

Vermont
Slauson

Vernon
Central

Slauson

Central

Alameda

Manchester

Van Ness

Western

Harbor Freeway

92nd

Watts
Willow-
brook

Imperial Highway

El Segundo

| 1 | 0 | 1 | 2 | 3 | 4 | Miles |

N

Landmarks and Significant Places
▲ Dunbar Hotel
★ First A.M.E. Church
✳ Florence and Normandie
⊙ Toy Town
⬟ Watts Labor Community Action Committee shopping center

Los Angeles Neighborhood Map

NEW IMMIGRANTS
TRANSFORM THE OLD CITY

6

On a late spring afternoon in the West's most sprawling metropolis, a golden sun beams on Pueblo de Los Angeles, an incongruous collection of ancient structures—a Spanish mission church, an open-air market, and a row of adobe houses—tucked behind the glistening downtown of modern Los Angeles. A stream of people pushes down historic Olvera Street against the tide of home-bound office workers. In ones and twos and threes, the men and women enter the mission-style confines of El Paseo Restaurant, passing under the dark wooden ceiling beams until they reach a stuccoed room off the main dining hall. Here they drop their business cards in a large fish bowl and pick up margueritas and plates of enchiladas. As they nibble and sip, the thirty or so people at the semi-annual social mixer of the Food Industry Business Roundtable, or FIBR, chat cheerfully with one another, at times exchanging business cards or scribbling the names and phone numbers of people and companies.

Even in polyglot Los Angeles, the assembled members of FIBR form an intriguing assortment of people. Two of FIBR's officers, Kenny Yee, the voluble heir apparent to the Wing Hing Noodle Company, and Gina Harpur, the charming general manager of Juanita's Foods, circulate through the crowd and welcome the guests. Ozabe Banks, sole proprietor of a soul-food sausage company located in the heart of South Central Los Angeles, arrives with his baby in a stroller and attracts several friends who greet him and coo at the little one. Two men in cowboy boots and hats, the owners of Cacique Cheese over in City of Industry, will later in the evening win giant baskets of food, the grand prizes for the business card drawing. Sherman Loo, an officer of the City National Bank and appropriately dressed in a banker's dark suit, will give a talk on the year 2000 problems that business computers may encounter. And from L.A.'s bustling Toy Town district has come May Cheung, the gracious manager of the Toystar division of Tai Tung International and member of FIBR's sister organization, Toy Association of Southern California (or TASC). She is here to participate in the evening's main event, a farewell to Linda Yeung, who as director for economic development for the much-maligned riot-recovery agency, Rebuild Los Angeles, helped start FIBR and TASC and launch a new approach to local economic development.

Denise Fairchild, at left, and Linda Yeung, at Food Industry Business Roundtable Mixer honoring Yeung, El Paseo Restaurant, March 1999. Courtesy of Community Development Technologies Center.

Welcome to the western frontier of the inner-city revival. Here community development folks try to harness prevailing economic forces to help the urban poor.

Like their counterparts in eastern and midwestern cities, community development leaders in Los Angeles face problems arising from poverty of both the low-wage and underemployment varieties, which were symbolized by vacant lots and empty buildings conspicuous along the commercial corridors of the inner city. They fought these problems like others back east did— by creating organizations rooted in communities and building housing, for example. The practitioners of community development, however, quickly realized that the West had its own unique character. Poverty here did not appear in hulking tenements as in the Bronx; instead, it hid behind streets of small single-family houses and little yards. Unlike the tightly bounded, close-knit communities of Boston and Chicago, neighborhoods spread out in seemingly endless grids demarcated only by heavily trafficked boulevards and highways. Here a disparate array of racial and ethnic minority groups made up a majority of the population, and small manufacturers operated in shuttered buildings out of sight and out of mind. In such a landscape, the leaders in community development would discover that ethnic and economic networks as much as geographic ties could help uplift the inner city.

Two cataclysmic events shook the leaders of nonprofit community development in Los Angeles out of their conventional approaches to helping people in the inner city and led them into creative unorthodoxy. The first was the flood of immigrants, which since the 1980s has been transforming Los Angeles. Large parts of South Central Los Angeles, a vast area long known as an African American domain, became a region largely populated by Latinos. In some places the newcomers arrived so quickly that there were too few agencies to help them overcome the problems of poverty and unfamiliarity with a new culture. In other places, black leaders found themselves in the unusual situation of having to minister to foreign newcomers of extremely different backgrounds.

The second event was the worst riot in the United States in the twentieth century. It came in 1992 after the verdicts in the Rodney King police brutality case, killed more than fifty people, and destroyed hundreds of businesses and stores in inner-city L.A. Former baseball commissioner Peter Ueberroth was appointed head of Rebuild Los Angeles to save the inner city after the Rodney King riots but quit the job under a hail of criticism little more than a year later.

As the press turned its attention elsewhere, Ueberroth's little-known successor, Linda Griego, quietly retooled the organization. Meanwhile, her researchers made the startling discovery that South Central's neighborhoods, which were supposed to be economically prostrate, were actually industrial beehives growing jobs and churning out scalpels, designer chairs, sunglasses, tortillas, dolls, bicycling outfits, you-name-it.

The two events forced community development leaders to rethink their assumptions. In the South Central neighborhoods, the directors of nonprofits tackled the problem of working with the immigrants, trying to understand their cultural differences, helping them assimilate to American ways, but also teaching them about the history of the civil rights movement and of the African Americans who preceded them in L.A.'s inner city. The community development leaders also hit on a new economic strategy: help the independent-minded mom-and-pop urban manufacturers they had long ignored and, by so doing, increase the number of jobs in the inner city and improve the well-being of its residents.

The Peopling of Los Angeles

A great wave of foreign immigration has inundated America's cities over the last twenty years. More than fourteen million people moved to the United States between 1980 and 1997, and most of them moved to one of eleven urban regions in the East, Midwest, and West—Los Angeles, New York, San Francisco, Miami, Chicago, Washington (D.C.), Houston, San Diego, Boston, Dallas, and Philadelphia. In these metropolitan areas, immigrants have revived flagging inner-city housing markets, generated entirely new business sectors, and imbued once-desperate neighborhoods with an air of industriousness and aspiration. So obvious is the correlation between the presence of immigrants and economic vitality that local officials from Pennsylvania to Iowa have proposed measures to attract immigrants in the hopes of revitalizing their stagnant communities.[1]

Of all the immigrant gateways to the United States, no city has been transformed more than Los Angeles. The City of Angels has long been home to immigrants, especially Mexicans, but in recent years the influx of Latins and Asians has reshaped the social geography of Los Angeles and its sprawling metropolitan surroundings.

Unbeknownst to the world outside L.A. and to many Angelenos, the immigrants are profoundly changing the city's historically black ghettos—Watts and the neighborhoods of South Central Los Angeles. Immigrants from Mexico and Central America are redefining African American neighborhoods as Latin domains. The transition is taking place so quickly that there are few Latino leaders or institutions in South Central L.A. to serve the newcomers.

A look at the geography and history helps us to understand what is happening to Los Angeles's neighborhoods. The Los Angeles most of us know—through touring, movies, and TV—is located in the northern and western sections of the city. To the northwest are Hollywood with its famous movie landmarks, the enormous nature preserve of Griffith Park, and Laurel Canyon, where film and music celebrities drive their sports cars at breakneck speed along winding roads. Traveling due west from downtown, you encounter diverse middle-class neighborhoods and shopping areas, luxurious Beverly Hills, and finally the trendy beach towns of Santa Monica and Venice.

Less familiar is southern and eastern Los Angeles, although it is home to well over a million people and a good share of southern California's manufacturing muscle. To the east of downtown is Boyle Heights and East Los Angeles, the oldest of the current Mexican barrios. To the south is South Central Los Angeles, an ill-defined region of about forty square miles that includes the old black neighborhoods of Adams, Vernon Central, and Vermont Slauson. Far to the southeast—some seven miles from downtown—lies Watts. Industrial areas spill over the boundaries between these neighborhoods and adjacent towns such as Commerce, Vernon, and Huntington Park.

In fact, despite the image of L.A. as a southern California paradise, its industry and port were the engines that built Los Angeles into a great metropolis. More than the glamorous film industry, the gritty businesses of shipping, oil drilling, and airplane, automobile, and rubber manufacturing propelled the expansion of the city and nearby towns from the 1930s and especially during World War II. After the war, the aerospace industry developed into another dominant industry of the region. Most manufacturing developed in a broad swath that started east of downtown and ran south through Los Angeles and neighboring towns to the port of Los Angeles and the city of Long Beach. At the core of this manufacturing belt was the mighty Alameda Corridor— miles and miles of factory buildings lining Alameda Street and a network of railroad tracks—which, despite the closing of some of its largest factories during the 1960s and 1970s, retains its manufacturing strength today.

As the city grew, hundreds of thousands of African Americans, immigrants from south of the border and Asia, and American whites from the Midwest and South came to the L.A. region in search of the abundant service, construction, and manufacturing jobs.

The first African Americans to arrive dispersed in small colonies, but soon much of the growing black population congregated along Central Avenue, which begins downtown and runs parallel to the Alameda Corridor. The center of the black community moved progressively south on "The Avenue," from 9th Street in the 1910s to 12th Street in the 1920s. By 1930 most African Americans lived in a thirty-block area between Central Avenue and the Alameda railroad tracks, including the Adams Boulevard (26th Street) neighborhood, home to the city's influential and oldest African American congregation, the First African Methodist Episcopal (A.M.E.) Church. During the 1940s, a surge of African Americans from the South jumped the black population from 64,000 and 4 percent of the city's total population to 171,000 and 9 percent. As the original Central Avenue area became overcrowded, blacks pushed southward against hostile whites and started a settlement far south in Watts, where houses were small and inexpensive. From these neighborhoods close to the Alameda corridor, some blacks were able to overcome white prejudice and crack the manufacturing jobs barrier.[2]

From the 1920s to the 1950s, black L.A. developed as a lively cultural, literary, and musical center of African American life, a West Coast version of New York's

Harlem. The Vernon Central neighborhood, which extended to Slauson Boulevard, was its heart. Vernon Central contained the childhood home of Ralph Bunche, the Nobel Prize-winning diplomat, and the office building headquarters of the black-owned Golden State Mutual Life Company. At 42nd Street and Central Avenue stood the Dunbar Hotel, named after the African American poet Paul Lawrence Dunbar and frequented by such celebrities as W. E. B. DuBois and Lena Horne. In its handsome Art Deco lobby great jazz musicians—such as Duke Ellington and Billie Holiday—held court and sometimes got a jam session going. Around the hotel and all along Central Avenue a colorful array of dance halls, theaters, and shops catered to the black community.

During the 1960s the African American population of Los Angeles continued to grow and expand into new territories. The number of African Americans rose to a half million, or about 18 percent of the city's total population, by 1970. Blacks moved in large numbers into Watts and south of Slauson Boulevard into the South Central neighborhoods of Vermont Slauson and Crenshaw, and by 1970 they made up 80 percent of the population of South Central and Watts. In the African American enclaves, as in most of Los Angeles, the typical house was a one-story single-family residence (of varying sizes), and homeownership rates were high.[3]

The 1965 Watts riot, in which thirty-four people died, reinforced the impression that the city's African Americans were mired in East Coast–style ghettos, but in fact many were moving upward economically and out of the old neighborhoods. The black population stagnated in L.A. proper after 1970 but rose in nearby neighborhoods and towns—the posh neighborhood of Baldwin Hills and the middle-class suburb of Inglewood, for example—as well as in the more distant communities of Orange County and the Inland Empire centered on Riverside and San Bernadino. This exodus left both poor and middle-class African Americans in South Central and Watts, but as a group black homeowners aged as young people failed to replenish their numbers.[4]

Mexicans also came to Los Angeles seeking work during the early and mid-twentieth century and endured even greater hostility from Anglo-Californians than did blacks. Many Mexican immigrants originally migrated to southern California as agricultural workers and were treated as if they belonged to a low caste. Partly because of discrimination by employers, Mexican immigrants were less able than African Americans to find manufacturing jobs and were forced to take low-paying unskilled work.

And despite their relatively small numbers—in 1950 Latinos made up less than 7 percent of the population of Los Angeles County—signs of assertiveness, especially by young men, incensed many whites. During World War II, Los Angeles newspapers whipped up hysteria about the threat posed by Mexican street gangs. Following an East Los Angeles murder in 1942, which the tabloids dubbed the Sleepy Lagoon case, no fewer than thirty-four Mexican youths were arrested and charged with the crime. The next year off-duty sailors rampaged and attacked Mexicans wearing zoot suits, that era's baggy uniform of urban youth. In the 1950s police continued to conduct brutal crackdowns; one of the most notorious was portrayed in the James Ellroy novel and 1997 film, *L.A. Confidential*.

Immigrants from Asia also suffered from discrimination and persecution. The Chinese who came to Los Angeles worked primarily at low-wage service jobs, and during World War II, more than 40,000 of the city's Japanese-Americans had their property confiscated and were sent to internment camps.[5]

From Ghetto to Barrio

Yet California still held out the possibility of a better life, and after the United States enacted a liberal immigration law in 1965, the stream of immigrants coming to southern California turned into a mighty river. The number of Asian immigrants from Japan, China, Korea, Vietnam, and the Philippines increased dramatically—pushing out the boundaries of the old central city neighborhoods of Little Tokyo, Chinatown, and Koreatown and creating new settlements in suburban locales around Los Angeles County.

Even more impressive was the massive influx of people from south of the border. Between 1970 and 1990 the Latino population of Los Angeles County swelled to 3,306,000, an increase of more than two million people. The 2000 census reported that the number of Hispanics in the county had leaped still higher to 4,240,000. Of these, the great majority were Mexican immigrants, but by the 1980s Central Americans from such countries as El Salvador and Guatemala had joined the procession into Los Angeles.[6]

During the 1940s and 1950s, while blacks moved south, Mexican immigrants and their descendants marched east and made the region known as East Los Angeles their own. Branching eastward from Olvera Street downtown, they redefined the old Jewish and Italian neighborhoods of Boyle Heights and Lincoln Heights as colorful Mexican American communities and then expanded Latino L.A. as far east as unincorporated Belvedere.

After 1970, however, the huge numbers of new immigrants could not be contained in the old east-side communities. During the 1970s and 1980s Latino immigrants created new enclaves in neighborhoods scattered all over Los Angeles—west in Pico Union, northeast in Pacoima in the San Fernando Valley, but most noticeably in the historic black areas of south L.A. The newcomers—mainly Mexican but also Central American—first settled southeast of downtown and in the industrial towns, such as Vernon and Huntington Park, along the Alameda Corridor; then they began moving west into the old African American neighborhoods of South Central Los Angeles and Watts. During the 1990s, Mexicans and Central Americans continued to move to South Central and Watts. During the 1990s about two-thirds of home buyers who took out mortgages in South Central and about three-quarters of those in Watts were Hispanic. (See Appendix I.)

The ethnic transition was dramatic. In 1980 African Americans still made up 70 percent of the total population of southeast Los Angeles (including Watts) and 68 percent of the population of South Central. Twenty years later the black population of southeast Los Angeles had shrunk to only 25 percent; in South Central the figure had fallen to 38 percent. Meanwhile, the Hispanic share of the population had swelled to 73 percent of southeast L.A. and 54 percent of South Central.[7]

The Latinization of South Central Los Angeles, block of 4800 South Central Avenue near Vernon Avenue. Courtesy of Community Development Technologies Center.

You can see the change in the old black districts by visiting south L.A. The change is less visible on the residential streets—the pastel-colored stucco bungalows rarely indicate the ethnicity of their owners—than on the commercial corridors where the storefronts reflect the Latino culture. The Latinization begins in the southern section of downtown, which has become a *mercado* district of low-cost shops with hand-lettered signs in Spanish and sidewalk merchandise, especially cheap clothes and electronic gadgets. Traveling south through South Central and Watts, there are more such shops as well as appliance and furniture stores, butchers, taquerillas, used-car and junk-part lots, and even the occasional professional such as a notary public, all announcing themselves in Spanish. What is not so evident on a quick tour is the turmoil and struggle that has accompanied these symbols of ethnic transition.

Market, with signs in Spanish and hand-painted mural of Our Lady of Guadalupe, 4212 South Central Avenue, August 2002. Courtesy of Fred Stafford.

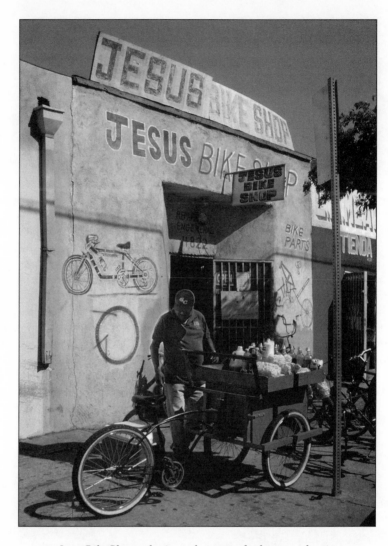

Jesus Bike Shop, a business that serves food cart vendors in
South Central Los Angeles, August 2002. Courtesy of Fred Stafford.

Who Helps the Newcomers?

The rapid dispersal of large numbers of immigrants throughout Los Angeles
has posed perplexing problems to the community development movement.
In response, some groups abandoned the conventional practice of working
only in a single neighborhood and instead focused attention on particular
ethnic groups at widely scattered sites across the region. One innovative group
called New Economics for Women specializes in helping poor Hispanic working parents, particularly single women and their children. The organization is
based in the inner-city neighborhood of Pico Union just west of downtown

where it has built a series of housing projects that were unusual for their social services. The first was Casa Loma, a 110-apartment complex for single mothers, that provides such programs as infant and child care, after-school classes, and a computer learning center for adults and children. Recently, however, New Economics for Women has expanded the types of projects and areas in which it works, taking on elderly housing, single-family homes, and townhouse developments in Canoga Park and North Hollywood in the San Fernando Valley and San Pedro far to the south near Los Angeles Harbor.[8]

Responding to the dispersal of new Asian immigrants, the Little Tokyo Service Center instituted "satellite programs" to serve some fifteen different ethnic groups—ranging from Taiwanese to Thai—each with different needs and cultures, in both the historically Japanese district downtown and other neighborhoods and towns. In Little Tokyo itself, the organization's CDC put studio apartments and commercial spaces into an old office building, turned a former church into an arts center (whose theater accommodates the leading and perhaps the oldest Asian American theater company in the country), and built Casa Heiwa, which shelters 100 households of ten ethnicities speaking eleven languages. At the same time, the Little Tokyo Service Center developed an eighty-two-unit apartment building for very low-income families west of downtown and a home for developmentally disabled adults out in the eastern suburb of Monterey Park.[9]

The ethnic transformation of southern Los Angeles happened so quickly, however, that this enormous territory as yet has few organizations dedicated to helping Latin immigrants make the transition to the life of the metropolis. The churches, especially the Catholic Church, help, but the church is hard pressed in an era when fewer people are becoming nuns and priests. The large network of Catholic community centers that existed in the 1950s has shriveled to only a handful.

In all of south Los Angeles, the only community development organization actually run by immigrants themselves is the Watts Century Latino Organization, located far to the south in Watts, and it is quite small and unprepossessing. To get an idea of the lowly status of Latinos in south L.A., you need only compare Watts Century Latino Organization to a comparable institution in East Los Angeles, the oldest and most developed area of Mexican settlement. In East Los Angeles, where Mexicans have migrated since the 1940s, the East Los Angeles Community Union, or TELACU, has built a shiny modern glass office building, complete with landscaped parking lot, as a headquarters for an empire of financial, real estate, construction, and education enterprises that spread throughout L.A. County and the San Gabriel valley.

In contrast, Watts Century Latino Organization occupies a squat building that used to be a liquor store on a street of small houses, a school, and a junk auto-parts yard. A visitor one day in April 1999 passed by the building several times before identifying it as the home of the organization. Nothing indicated its presence: an old rusting sign with the liquor store's name on it stood in the front yard; the building was boarded up with a grate over the door.

Inside, Watts Century Latino Organization gave every evidence of being a mom-and-pop operation—literally. Among the boxes piled around the recently

Arturo Ybarra (in cap) with neighborhood youth in front of the Watts Towers.
Courtesy of Watts Century Latino Organization.

renovated large room and adjacent office, director Arturo Ybarra held meetings and made phone calls while his wife sat at a long table stuffing envelopes with informational flyers. Their little child alternately clung to her mother and wandered under the tables.

Ybarra has struggled to expand Watts Century Latino Organization, but so far neither Latinos nor non-Latinos have responded much. Most Mexican and Central American newcomers are preoccupied with surviving in the new world of southern California. Many have either experienced political oppression in their home countries or feel the threat of deportation from the Immigration and Naturalization Service in the new land and are afraid to participate in public meetings. While sympathetic to some of Ybarra's ideas, the district's black political leaders are not overly concerned with what is, after all, a different constituency from the one that elected them. The city government and the foundations have not opened their coffers to Ybarra either.[10]

Ybarra is a stubborn idealist, however. He first came to live with an aunt in a small town in California to escape political trouble in Mexico where, as a student in social work during the 1960s, he was jailed for protesting against the government. In the United States, he joined practically every left-liberal movement of the 1970s and 1980s—to help migrant farmworkers, stop the Vietnam War, end U.S. intervention in Central America, fight apartheid in South Africa, promote immigrants' rights, and organize workers—before moving to Watts.

Ybarra swung into action in Watts in 1989 when he saw that although Latinos comprised half the district's population, only a handful showed up at meetings to discuss a large project the city's redevelopment agency was planning for their community. With the planning agency's support, Ybarra wrote and distributed a flyer in Spanish, which brought out hundreds of local Latinos to the meetings. Then he helped the residents launch a permanent organization in 1990 to represent the interests of Mexicans and Central Americans.

Soon Watts Century Latino Organization began to address the conflicts that Mexicans faced when they moved to black neighborhoods. Some African Americans resented their new Latino neighbors, and neighborhood toughs robbed, raped, and harassed the newcomers, especially those who lived in public housing projects. To help the people of Watts get along with one another, Ybarra organized a Watts Annual Latino/African American Cinco de Mayo celebration—complete with a parade and multi-ethnic carnival. Los Angeles's infamous street gangs posed another threat to the newcomers, especially the youth. Ybarra also designed programs for high school students and their parents to cut down gang violence, reduce the number of school dropouts, and improve the schools.[11]

Ironically, the Watts Century Latino Organization's most successful new programs—the high school workshops, for example—are carried out in conjunction with the African American-run CDCs of South Central and Watts. Without sizable grants of money from the large foundations and nonprofit intermediaries, the organization is restricted to partnerships and community relations work. Ybarra notes that California's recent anti-immigrant initiatives—aimed at preventing illegal aliens from receiving government welfare benefits

Hispanic and African American youth at a gathering held by the
Watts Century Latino Organization to stop violence in Watts.
Courtesy of Watts Century Latino Organization. 217

and schooling—are spurring Latino immigrants to become American citizens, and he hopes that will make them more politically active. Until they are, the only indigenous Mexican American community organization in all of southern Los Angeles remains a shoestring operation that derives support from black political leaders and community organizations.

Far from Watts, at the north end of South Central Los Angeles, the Esperanza Community Housing Corporation also works to help the immigrants. The Adams neighborhood, where Esperanza operates, was until the 1970s one of the oldest predominantly black areas of Los Angeles—it is home to the California Afro-American Museum. By the mid-1990s, however, Latinos made up two-thirds of the district's 138,000 people, and blacks only a quarter. While most of the members of the historic Ward African Methodist Episcopal church commute in from outside the district, the congregations of the area's Catholic churches are swelling. After masses on a recent Ash Wednesday, the local priests gave out a card with a list of religious services and times to parishioners and were astonished to discover that they had distributed 18,000 cards.[12]

The problems of the Adams neighborhood are daunting. Not far from the handsome campuses of the University of Southern California and Mount St. Mary's College are apartment buildings crowded with newly arrived immigrants. To the east side of the Harbor Freeway that divides the neighborhood are blocks and blocks of garment factories, warehouses, squat houses, and more dingy apartment buildings. The newspapers have run stories about appalling conditions in the Adams neighborhood slums—families inhabiting basements with gas leaks and apartments without toilets.

The immigrants who arrive from Mexico or central America often know very little English, and sometimes they can barely read Spanish. They work, but at jobs which by American standards pay little. That means they must pay much of their income for rent, often making up the shortage of cash by sharing apartments in run-down buildings. Parents, who often work more than two jobs, have trouble keeping their boys out of gangs and the drug trade.

The Esperanza Community Housing Corporation grew out of an effort to protect people from such conditions. In 1985 six families who were members of St. Vincent De Paul, the largest parish in the neighborhood, were evicted when the site of their homes was purchased to develop a garment factory in a neighborhood teeming with them. The church, and more specifically, Sister Diane Donoghue, led a drive to stop the sweat shop and instead create more homes to alleviate the chronic overcrowding in this immigrant port of arrival.[13]

Although many Americans are not aware of it, the Catholic Church, in its many forms and affiliated organizations, is one of the most important forces for helping the poor and downtrodden in the United States. Catholic Charities, for example, raises millions of dollars every year from government and private contributions and expends the money for a wide variety of social services ranging from emergency shelters to alcohol and drug treatment.

The president and driving force of Esperanza Community Housing Corporation is Sister Diane, a member of the Sisters of Social Service, a Hungarian order whose members first arrived in Los Angeles in 1926. Sister Diane, as she is known by one and all, began her work in South Central Los Angeles in the early

1970s at one of the community centers run by the Catholic Youth Organization. Since then she has developed a network of extensive contacts with community organizers, such as the Industrial Areas Foundation's Ernesto Cortes, and leaders of community development groups. Sister Diane's friendly face, bright blue eyes, and pleasant manner belie the formidable energy she brings to the task of helping the immigrants of South Central's Adams neighborhood.

Sister Diane and a crew of lay women run a battery of programs to stabilize the lives of the new immigrants. They have lobbied the city to crack down on the worst slum buildings, rehabilitated three run-down buildings, and recently acquired four others on one street. They also have built two new apartment buildings — including the organization's flagship building, Villa Esperanza, completed in 1994 with its thirty-three large apartments and child and community centers. Esperanza runs a day care from 6:30 A.M. to 5:30 P.M. — "working-class hours" Sister Diane calls them — so parents can get to the factories at seven in the morning.[14]

Immigrants from the Adams neighborhood take Esperanza's evening classes. For the most part, the women come to learn English. Esperanza's staff first organized English classes but then added a basic literacy course when it became clear that some women had difficulty learning English because they could not even read Spanish. The men, mainly garment and other factory workers, attend the computer lab. Again the staff members discovered that their adult students lacked what most of us might consider a basic skill and added a typing program to their computer class.

The Senderos, an apartment building rehabilitated by
Esperanza Community Housing Corporation. Courtesy of Ed Callahan.

The Villafana family in front of their apartment in Villa Esperanza, May 1995.
Courtesy of Janet Delaney.

"But they were so afraid, their hands and fingers were so stiff from factory work," observes Yadira Arévalo, a political refugee from El Salvador who coordinates education programs for Esperanza, "I used to say, well, probably they'll never learn. But it's amazing. The instructor gives them four to six weeks of typing lessons, which they have to do—otherwise they can't advance. And they do it. It is fascinating because you may think that some of them will never learn, but they do."

"I've seen people here who came with no typing skills, and at the end of six months, they know how to type. They know Microsoft Word, they have explored spreadsheets in Excel, and they can make presentations through PowerPoint."[15]

Not every class is practical, however. Esperanza also offers children and teenagers culture in the form of art and theater classes.

Sister Diane and Yadira are awed by the immigrants' drive to improve their lot in life. "The people don't fly by airplane to get here," Sister Diane explains. "They walk. They are very hard working. They want to make it."[16]

The Villafana family, who came from Guadalajara and reside in Villa Esperanza, exemplify the struggles, aspirations, and tragedies that are common among the Mexican and Central American immigrants of South Central. José Villafana supported his four children by working construction. When he wasn't working ten- or twelve-hour days, he and his crew traveled to sites outside Los Angeles for days at a time, building gas stations, car washes, and convenience stores. Teresa Villafana worked in a sewing sweat shop until her youngest son was born. Then she bought an industrial sewing machine and began to take in sewing—earning 50 cents a skirt, rarely more than $12–14 a day. Before they moved to Villa Esperanza, the Villafanas rented a small two-bedroom house where all four kids slept in one room.[17]

Like generations of immigrants to the United States before them, the Villafanas often contemplated moving back to the old country, but they decided to stay to give their children a better education and opportunity than they had. The Esperanza Community Housing Corporation eased some of the heavy burden the Villafanas carried. The organization charged the family only $525 a month for their four-bedroom apartment in Villa Esperanza, where the children found the building to be a safe haven from neighborhood gangs and used the community center after school to take computer classes or do homework. Then terrible misfortune struck. In 1996 José Villafana died after being hit by a forklift at work; he gave his life to help his kids improve theirs. After her husband died, Teresa turned to Esperanza for help in translating and negotiating with lawyers to settle his affairs.

Despite everything, the Villafana family persevered. The oldest daughter, Karen, won a scholarship to Occidental College. The next oldest, Nadia, attended the University of California at Santa Barbara, where she studied international relations. Nathalie turned down a scholarship to an exclusive private high school to be closer to her family and went on to attend Claremont McKenna College, and the youngest, Erik, attends a magnet school for gifted children. In 2001, the Villafanas moved from Villa Esperanza to a new house Teresa purchased with her savings in the growing inland town of Chino, California.[18]

The hundreds of people in Esperanza's housing and education programs are but a tiny proportion of the hundreds of thousands of Latino immigrants struggling to make it in the Adams neighborhood. Even the indefatigable Sister Diane admits that her organization can only make a dent in the overwhelming problems. Despite their emergence as a majority in southern Los Angeles, the Latino immigrants as yet are underserved.

African Americans and the New Ethnic Reality

In contrast to most newly arrived Mexican and Central American immigrants, the African American residents of South Central L.A. and Watts who need help have plentiful resources. Over the decades African Americans have built an impressive political and institutional infrastructure. Blacks in southern Los Angeles have captured important government offices—in the U.S. Congress, the state legislature, and the L.A. district council. They have many churches as well, including the powerhouse First African Methodist Episcopal Church, led by the Reverend Cecil Murray. Both the First and Ward A.M.E. Churches sponsor their own housing and economic development groups, two of several productive community development organizations started, run, and staffed by African Americans in southern L.A.

The black leaders of South Central and Watts had the disconcerting experience during the 1980s and 1990s of watching the population of the areas they serve shift from African American to Latino. The ethnic transition of south L.A. has reversed the historic role of blacks in America's urban neighborhoods. Like the whites they once displaced, they are now the stakeholders — homeowners, power brokers, and keepers of local institutions — who must somehow cope with a poorer racial minority group arising in their midst. Since most recent immigrants, so far, don't vote — either because they are not naturalized citizens or are not motivated to — African American politicians have not had to adjust their behavior. But community institutions operating close to the ground could not ignore the new reality.

Three of the leading community development corporations in Los Angeles are located on the front line of ethnic change in South Central and Watts. The Watts Labor Community Action Committee, Concerned Citizens of South Central Los Angeles, and Dunbar Economic Development Corporation were founded by African Americans, and their boards of directors and staffs are predominantly black. But now more Mexicans than blacks inhabit the neighborhoods where they operate, and these organizations must try to serve both their traditional African American constituency and the ever-increasing number of Latinos.

Concerned Citizens of South Central Los Angeles in Vernon Central, the old heart of African American L.A., has been the most aggressive in reaching out to its Latino neighbors. This is not surprising. Concerned Citizens' director, Juanita Tate, is an assertive and tough-minded leader. "Hey," she joked in 1995 about the drop in crime and gang activity, "my neighborhood isn't the hellhole it was even two years ago!"[19]

A native of Philadelphia, Tate retired from the Bell Telephone Company in 1985 to head Concerned Citizens when the organization was formed to halt the construction of a large municipal waste incinerator in Vernon Central, even though the state legislature had already approved a $535 million bond issue to fund it. After the incinerator project was defeated, Concerned Citizens developed four apartment complexes containing 115 units. When young troublemakers threatened the housing projects, the ever-resourceful Tate stopped them by hiring their older brothers as maintenance men. After the Rodney King riots, Tate exploited anxiety about South Central to persuade federal regulators to reverse policy and let Concerned Citizens start a neighborhood credit union. Concerned Citizens continues to tackle environmental issues as it runs a variety of community programs cleverly named by Tate: afternoon child care is called After School Nanny; the tutoring program is Study Buddy.[20]

When the service area of Concerned Citizens of South Central changed from two-thirds black to three-quarters Latino — in only six years according to staff members — Tate declared that the group would serve anyone, regardless of race or ethnicity. But she went further. Tate contacted Arturo Ybarra and arranged to assign a Latino woman she had hired to educate first-time home buyers for the Watts Century Latino Organization. She incorporated Latino churches and organizations into her neighborhood coalitions. And Concerned

The Gwen Bolden Manor housing complex, developed by the Concerned Citizens of South Central Los Angeles, East 41st Street near Hooper Avenue. Courtesy of Local Initiatives Support Corporation, Los Angeles.

Citizens sent community organizers to mobilize both the black and brown population into block clubs.[21]

"Well, we learned a lot about our neighbors," Tate comments on the experience of organizing Latinos in Vernon Central. Concerned Citizens' African American staff members found that Latinos were by no means a monolithic group—that Salvadorans felt insulted if they were called Mexican, while other Latino groups looked down on the Salvadorans. They also discovered Belizians, who were both black and Hispanic. "Of course, I don't speak the language," explains Concerned Citizens' organizing director, Melody Dove, "so we have a Spanish-speaking young person who works with me as a kind of partner to organize the Latino population and reach across the language barrier."[22]

Like Ybarra in Watts, Concerned Citizens' organizers found it difficult to organize Latinos partly because many adults stay in the area for only a few months—parking at a relative's house—before moving on, and partly because some older Latinos fear government reprisals if they step forward. Dove has had greater success organizing Latino teenagers, who make up virtually the entire student body of Vernon Central's high schools. (When bilingual programs were substituted for extracurricular programs such as music and art, black kids switched to schools outside the neighborhood.) She has hired several Spanish-speaking youth organizers, but young people are frequently more assimilated into American culture—Dove estimates fewer than half speak only Spanish—and often respond well to the Concerned Citizens' environmental campaigns, such as cleaning up the contaminated grounds of a local school.[23]

Five blocks north of Concerned Citizens at the corner of 42nd Street and Central Avenue, the Dunbar Economic Development Corporation, a product of a black historical preservation effort, faces the same Latinization of the population. In 1975, back when Vernon Central was almost completely black, a group of local residents campaigned to keep the wrecking ball away from a landmark of the golden age of black South Central, the Dunbar Hotel. The preservationists created a corporation to turn the hotel, which had been rendered useless as a residence by an earthquake the year before, into a black cultural historical museum.

The effort moved slowly, however, and in 1988 the group took a different tack by founding the Dunbar Economic Development Corporation to preserve and develop the Dunbar Hotel. Noting the aging black population of Vernon Central, the new organization retained the African American historical and cultural center on the ground floor and developed the upper floors into seventy-three small apartments for low-income elderly people. Two years later, they hired a director, Anthony Scott, a recent graduate of the Graduate School of Architecture and Urban Planning department at the University of California at Los Angeles, who had become interested in community development as a student intern in the city's economic development department.[24]

When he first came to Dunbar EDC, Scott noticed that Vernon Central contained many boarded-up buildings but was changing rapidly—an impression confirmed by the 1990 census figures that showed the district had become majority Latino. Seeing that the newcomers were stimulating the housing market, Scott and the Dunbar EDC developed residential buildings on either side of the Dunbar Hotel with family-size apartments.

Today Dunbar EDC's main ambition is to create a "historic renaissance district" that will revive a ten-block stretch of Central Avenue between Martin Luther King Boulevard and Vernon Avenue by celebrating the golden age of black L.A. With the restored Dunbar Hotel setting the tone, Scott aims to preserve the existing historic buildings that are abandoned or deteriorated and build new structures on vacant lots. He has begun with the Dunbar Hotel block to give a "historic feel" to the district: the neo-Californian Art Deco design of Dunbar EDC's new apartment building harks back to the era when Vernon Central was jumping with jazz clubs, dance parlors, and restaurants.[25]

The Watts Labor Community Action Committee (WLCAC) is also steeped in African American history, albeit of a more recent date. The tale of the organization and its founder, Ted Watkins, is an inspirational story of African Ameri-

The Dunbar Hotel, site of an African American historical and cultural center and apartments for low-income elderly people, redeveloped by the Dunbar Economic Development Corporation, at 42nd Street and South Central Avenue, August 2002. Courtesy of Ed Callahan.

can success in the face of discrimination and deprivation. Watkins was a pioneer who overcame adversity and racism. At age fourteen, he came alone from Meridian, Mississippi, to Los Angeles and eventually landed a job on the assembly line at the Ford Motor Company. Watkins rose through the ranks of the United Auto Workers and in 1949 became chairman of the bargaining committee. In 1965, just a few months before the area exploded in violent rage, he founded WLCAC to help the poor people of Watts. So successful and celebrated was WLCAC that after riots broke out in London's black suburbs in the 1980s, the British government hired Watkins to open an office in London and consult with community groups there. WLCAC's founder died in 1993, but since then his children have led the organization and kept his memory alive.[26]

Like TELACU in East Los Angeles, WLCAC was an early community development organization that blended social protest and social programs, which were often part of the federal government's War on Poverty. And like TELACU, WLCAC used government monies to run a battery of programs—including those that offered summer jobs for youth, manpower training, child care, and meals and recreation for the elderly. The organization's real estate department has developed more than 500 houses and apartments since 1971, when it began by moving condemned houses and apartment buildings to vacant lands for renovation, and includes a subsidiary nonprofit contracting company. Over the years, WLCAC has opened its own supermarket, restaurant, gas station, youth-run laundromat, and toy and furniture stores.[27]

WLCAC's showpiece is the seven-acre newly rebuilt shopping center at 109th and Central Avenue. Here WLCAC has its main headquarters, youth center, and the Ted Watkins Center for Communication, which includes a theater, galleries, exhibition spaces, and civil rights history museum. The museum is a testament to the civil rights movement. One exhibit of photographs displays civil rights leaders in action during the 1950s and 1960s; another exhibit is a life-size replica of a Mississippi delta road complete with swamps where civil rights workers were killed.

Like other organizations, WLCAC has been forced to deal with the Latinization of its base area. If the group's leaders were not aware of the ethnic transition, the 1992 Rodney King upheavals brought it home with a vengeance. During the chaos, rioters looted WLCAC's shopping center and burned down its headquarters. Disaffected Mexican youths were suspected of destroying this symbol of African American achievement.

Both the Dunbar EDC and the Watts Labor Community Action Committee have recognized the emergent Latino population by collaborating with immigrant organizations. Anthony Scott believes he has convinced Latino merchants that the Dunbar EDC's redevelopment plan based on black history can help revitalize the neighborhood. Scott made a deal with the Central American Resource Center, or CARECEN, a refugee service organization in Pico Union (an immigrant neighborhood located west of downtown). CARECEN's organizers helped Dunbar encourage Latino merchants to join the newly formed Vernon Central chamber of commerce, while Dunbar's staff advised CARECEN on ways of becoming a community development organization. WLCAC teamed up with Watts Century Latino Organization to hold the annual Latino/African American Cinco de Mayo festivities and carry out the anti-gang and racial harmony programs in the Watts schools.[28]

Nonetheless, both Dunbar EDC and WLCAC are in the anomalous position of celebrating black history and culture in environments that are increasingly dominated by others. Both organizations are trying to teach the newcomers about the black heritage of their new neighborhoods, much as the schools and settlement houses run by white Anglo-Americans tried to inculcate American values in European immigrants a century ago. Here, in south Los Angeles, African Americans, members of a group long unassimilated, worry about assimilating Central Americans into African American society.

The WLCAC civil rights museum, for example, tries to appeal to Hispanics with photography exhibits of the working and living conditions of Mexican immigrants in California, an "African-American and Chicana Women Artists Exhibit," and portraits of Latino as well African American youths. The flier for the display of a slave ship sunk in 1700 and recently discovered off the Florida coast is printed in Spanish as well as English.

But will African American history ever be important to Mexican and Central American newcomers? As part of its effort to revive Vernon Central by celebrating the black culture, Dunbar EDC holds an annual jazz festival at the Dunbar Hotel. Scott reports that each year more locals attend the festival. When asked if Mexicans played jazz—perhaps a south-of-the-border equivalent of Afro-Cuban music or Brazilian bossa nova — Scott replied wistfully, no, there was no such music, and, in fact, most young people, both black and Latino, preferred hip-hop music to the older African American art form, jazz.[29]

Hence, black reformers of southern Los Angeles at the end of the twentieth century discovered what white reformers on New York's Lower East Side learned a century before. When it comes to assimilating foreigners, historic legacies and values pale in comparison to American popular culture.

To Rebuild a Fallen City

At the height of the great ethnic transition, Los Angeles was hit by one of the worst upheavals an American city experienced during the twentieth century. The riots that started on April 29, 1992, in South Central Los Angeles at the corner of Florence and Normandie Avenues left fifty-four persons dead, more than two thousand injured, and more than one thousand buildings damaged or destroyed at an estimated cost of $1 billion.[30]

At first glance, the riots appeared to be solely a massive expression of black rage over miscarriages of justice. The disorders began immediately after the policemen charged with assaulting an African American, Rodney King, in a videotaped beating shown repeatedly on television, were found not guilty. African American anger at the police and the courts had been simmering for months since the acquittal of a Korean shopkeeper who shot a fifteen-year-old girl, Latasha Hawkins, in the back of the head at point blank range as she was walking out of the store.

But the Rodney King riots were not a replay of the 1965 Watts riot. Unlike Watts, the 1992 rampages expressed African American hostility to the immigrants who were transforming Los Angeles. The mobs pillaged the Korean-owned liquor and convenience stores scattered across South Central Los Angeles. African American rioters attacked Latinos and Asians — in one of the most vicious incidents, young black men beat Fidel Lopez senseless, pulled down his pants, and sprayed black paint over the bleeding, unconscious man's genitals and body. (Many African Americans heroically saved mob victims during the riot, however, and most blacks did not participate at all.)[31]

The riots, like other aspects of L.A. life in the 1990s, were Latinized. After twenty-four hours, the riots evolved into a general looting spree throughout the city. In the port-of-arrival neighborhoods of South Central and mid-city Los Angeles, poor young immigrants from Central America and Mexico took over the looting and helped themselves to food, furniture, and household items.

The Rodney King riots brought to a climax a series of misfortunes that badly shattered the sunny self-confidence of Angelenos. California had enjoyed years of glorious boom times during the 1980s. In 1988 a blue-ribbon committee issued an optimistic report, LA 2000, which assumed that the Los Angeles economy was recessionproof. Almost immediately, California's economy crashed, its aerospace industry and real estate market collapsed, and Los Angeles County shed about 200,000 jobs. Los Angeles, which had long been depicted in books and films as a city of sun, wealth, and play, now appeared in films such as *Grand Canyon* as a symbol of urban woes. And the riots left many wondering if the city could ever fully recover.[32]

Beyond the tragedy of deaths and personal injuries, the violent disturbances dealt a direct blow to community development efforts by taking out numerous stores and services in neighborhoods that were already underserved. For years community groups such as the Vermont-Slauson Economic Development Corporation had been redeveloping empty lots and storefronts along the commercial corridors of South Central Los Angeles—always time-consuming work. Now newly burned out and boarded up stores scarred the inner-city boulevards, clearly visible to the commuters who sped by. Many observers interpreted the breakdown of South Central's retail sector as a direct or indirect result of economic woes such as low wages and high unemployment rates. How then to revive the area's economy?

Within days after the upheavals ended, Los Angeles Mayor Tom Bradley and Governor Pete Wilson acted to save the battered City of Angels. The Democratic mayor and Republican governor looked to Peter Ueberroth, a celebrated businessman and civic leader, to lead the largest community and economic development effort undertaken in a city since the days of Lyndon Johnson's Model Cities program. Ueberroth had organized the 1984 Olympics held in Los Angeles, one of the great successes of Bradley's long tenure as mayor. Afterward Ueberroth served as the commissioner of major league baseball for five years. A businessman with a sense of public duty, he seemed the perfect candidate to coordinate the rejuvenation of Los Angeles's poor and riot-torn neighborhoods.

Ueberroth and Mayor Bradley encouraged Angelenos to hold high expectations for recovery from the riot. Their optimism at the initial press conference and the name of the new agency, Rebuild Los Angeles, suggested that soon money would flow to owners of damaged properties and every destroyed building would be replaced. Ueberroth's actual plan was to enlist businesses—and to him that meant large corporations—to work with government and neighborhood groups to revive the economy of the afflicted areas. Ueberroth planned to use his considerable skills to influence the heads of corporations to donate money, people, and equipment to Rebuild Los Angeles and persuade large businesses, especially chain retail outlets, to open branches in South Central and other inner-city areas. He also hoped to coordinate large amounts of government funds. Both Governor Wilson and President George Bush had come to South Central immediately after the riot and promised to provide money to help the riots' victims.

Although little appreciated and soon forgotten, Ueberroth's accomplishments at Rebuild Los Angeles were considerable. In the long run, he extracted about $500 million in commitments and contributions for rebuilding projects. During his tenure, Chief Auto Parts announced it would reopen twenty-eight stores and build fifteen new ones in inner-city Los Angeles; Shell Oil agreed to reconstruct a service station as a mini-mart and job-training center; Vons, a giant supermarket chain, declared it would build up to a dozen new stores at a cost of $100 million (eventually nineteen new supermarkets were built); and the Toyota car company joined with the local Urban League to open a $3 million training center in the black suburb of Crenshaw.[33]

Yet the effort to rebuild inner-city L.A. proved far more difficult than Ueberroth or anyone else imagined. Despite Ueberroth's repeated attempts to lobby for money, government leaders reneged on their promises to put up big sums to help rescue Los Angeles's poor neighborhoods. When Governor Pete Wilson discovered a large deficit in the California budget, he cut spending for existing programs and refused to undertake any new efforts. For similar reasons, President Bush never followed through either. After Bill Clinton was elected, his administration created an Enterprise Zone program to fund inner cities, but even though government officials called it the Rodney King Zone because it was designed to help South Central Los Angeles, they rejected Los Angeles's application. (As a consolation prize, Washington later set up a Community Development Bank, but it was slow to make loans.) Even some city officials would not cooperate, perhaps because Ueberroth at times treated them cavalierly.[34]

From the outset, Rebuild Los Angeles was battered with criticism. On the streets of South Central, community development workers were livid that a high-rolling agency led by someone from suburban Orange County would take on their work without even consulting them. "The whole idea of rebuilding L.A. is a joke," scoffed Anthony Scott. "What have we been doing all these years?"

"I was pissed," recalled Denise Fairchild, the director of LISC's Los Angeles office at the time. "We were out there working with community groups, and all of a sudden this riot repair agency came on board with all these people from Orange County and everywhere else." Politicians, including congresswoman Maxine Waters, and Jesse Jackson, who was not even a Los Angeles resident, blasted Ueberroth for being a fat-cat white executive unfamiliar with inner-city L.A.[35]

Ueberroth responded to the criticism by expanding the agency, and faster than you could say "War on Poverty," Rebuild Los Angeles mushroomed into an ungainly bureaucracy. When members of L.A.'s major ethnic nationalities protested that they deserved a voice, Ueberroth added four co-chairpersons, one for each ethnicity. When interest groups clamored to get in on the action, he invited them to join the board. The board eventually expanded to more than eighty people—ranging from State Treasurer Kathleen Brown, the sister of former governor Jerry Brown, to Danny Bakewell, an activist who had shut down post-riot demolition work crews in South Central to get jobs for blacks. Ueberroth set up eleven volunteer task forces on subjects ranging from affordable housing to racial harmony. Some of the board members and task forces were productive, but the Olympic size of the operation was too great to be efficient. Meanwhile, as the months rolled by, neighborhood residents could see no results.[36]

Ueberroth's initial corporate strategy was also flawed. Inserting large corporate facilities into low-income neighborhoods has rarely succeeded, and the recession and cuts in defense spending undermined the top-down approach at the outset. Furthermore, the barons of oil, aerospace, and Hollywood who ruled corporate L.A. in the 1980s when Ueberroth ran the Olympics had by and large been replaced. Outside investors had taken over Hollywood, and a new set of entrepreneurs had risen in emergent technology industries such as biotechnology, health care, and environmental engineering. Although he connected well with the CEOs and board members of major corporations, Ueberroth was slow to adjust to the city's changing economy.[37]

Sensing the organizational and strategic problems, Ueberroth attempted to change the focus of Rebuild Los Angeles in the spring of 1993. To redefine the agency's image and convey a sense of common purpose, the directors and staff of Rebuild L.A. now called their organization RLA, as in "Our L.A." Seeing the limits of big business, RLA's directors began to think about studying small businesses (here defined as companies with 100 or fewer employees).[38]

But by then Ueberroth had lost the public relations war. Reflecting the gloomy outlook prevailing in the city, the local news media ignored achievements and seized on every shortcoming of Rebuild Los Angeles. RLA unintentionally fueled the negativity by exaggerating its accomplishments—an announcement that it had received $585 million in corporate commitments was off by $87.7 million, and an RLA list of sixty-eight companies that promised to invest in the inner city, the *Los Angeles Times* reported, contained nineteen companies with no such plans. The press obtained a private RLA study—the sort that corporations undertake in secrecy—which suggested that no less than $6 billion and 75,000 new jobs would solve the problems of inner-city Los Angeles and interpreted it to mean that anything short of these impossible numbers spelled failure.[39]

Finally, on May 21, 1993, the man who was supposed to save the city resigned from Rebuild Los Angeles. Ueberroth said the reasons were personal, but he probably had tired of functioning as a lightning rod for criticism. In the following months, Rebuild L.A. drifted under the direction of its remaining co-chairs, demonstrating that whatever Ueberroth's faults, he had been a strong leader. After a new mayor, Republican Richard Riordan, was elected, RLA abandoned its clumsy system of co-chairs and sought a single chief. Several prominent executives were offered the position of chair of the executive committee, but—mindful of what happened to Ueberroth and the difficulties of saving the organization—turned it down.[40]

Griego Takes Over

At last, the first person who had been offered the job of board chair of Rebuild Los Angeles changed his mind and accepted the post. Lodwrick M. Cook, the chief executive officer of ARCO and an RLA board member, was planning to retire but decided that too many Los Angeles citizens had placed their hope in RLA to let it fall apart. He insisted that Rebuild Los Angeles hire a full-time executive director and that it be Linda Griego, the former deputy mayor for economic development, restaurant owner, and fifth-place finisher in the recent mayoral race. In February 1994 Cook and Griego took over what remained of Rebuild Los Angeles. With Griego installed as director, Cook reaffirmed his committment to RLA—even after he underwent coronary bypass surgery.[41]

To many Angelenos, Griego was a strange choice to recharge the faltering agency. Some thought her appointment itself symbolized the failure of Rebuild L.A. "From restaurateur to deputy mayor to RLA president makes an interesting profile," a former co-worker in the Bradley administration sniffed, "but . . . besides putting together a menu with meatloaf on it, what do you have to say for yourself?"[42]

True enough, Linda Griego seemed the polar opposite of Peter Ueberroth, a square-jawed corporate celebrity whose personal Rolodex was stuffed with the names of Fortune 500 CEOs. She was a thin and unassuming woman who had been raised by a working-class Mexican American family in a small town in New Mexico, and before her stint as deputy mayor, she had worked in obscurity. Her eclectic resume included running a chili stand and a flower stall, working as a legislative aide to Senator Alan Cranston, and managing a successful restaurant in the downtown financial district.

But some of the differences between herself and her famous predecessor turned out to be pluses. Whereas Ueberroth lived in Orange County, Griego had resided for a number of years in the Baldwin Hills neighborhood, known as home to affluent blacks. She had intimate knowledge of the city and delighted in figuring out ways to improve it. The time she spent in city hall and her run for mayor had produced numerous contacts in government and politics.

And unlike the lordly manager who chews out subordinates, Griego believes in keeping staff morale high. In turn, she earns the devoted loyalty of the people who work for her. Back when Griego operated her chili stand, she struck up a conversation with a fifteen-year old girl named Yvette Nunez and offered her a job. For years after, Nunez followed Griego, working for her in Senator Alan Cranston's office, in the city government, and RLA. On joining RLA, Griego immediately noticed the timidity of the staff members. If you called out one of their names, it seemed to her, the person would flinch, as if about to be hit. Griego immediately went to work to overcome the fear of being yelled at for taking initiative. She needed to instill a new psychology for the new program.[43]

New Thinking: Bottom-Up Development

Griego and Cook were determined to make effective use of what money remained at RLA—only about two of approximately ten million dollars Ueberroth had raised for operating expenses remained. The lavish budget for operations was slashed. No longer would RLA freely hand out grants to any group calling itself a community organization. Griego eliminated the task forces on affordable housing, racial harmony, and urban planning. She freely admitted she did not know how to solve problems such as gangs and bad schools so, even if other organizations weren't already grappling with these issues, she wouldn't try.[44]

Instead RLA adopted what Griego called a "bottom-up" strategy of economic development to alleviate the problems of poverty and lack of services in Los Angeles's inner city. The primary goals were to assist small and medium-size businesses—by creating networks of inner-city manufacturers for exchanging business information—and to rebuild the vacant lots with retail stores, especially supermarkets, in low-income neighborhoods. As deputy mayor, Griego had begun to pursue similar objectives, but now she could expand the scope of her mission. For instance, RLA targeted any neighborhood with 20 percent of its population below the poverty line, thus extending its operations beyond the worst riot-damaged districts to what the staff dubbed "economically neglected areas." She didn't realize it, but Linda Griego was about to pioneer a new and creative approach to community development.

Helping small businesses, however, was a hard sell. In 1993 Ueberroth had dismissed Griego's plans for small businesses, telling her, "They don't amount to anything, they're five jobs here, five jobs there." He was not alone. Most economists, politicians, and journalists still believed the large corporations that had sustained southern California in the past were the only means to its future prosperity. When they saw that large defense contractors and oil companies were not returning, they concluded that City of Angels was doomed. They interpreted everything from the 1994 Northridge earthquake to Ueberroth's resignation from of RLA as a symbol of failure.[45]

Furthermore, even in the world of nonprofit community development, housing had eclipsed business development as the most popular way to uplift communities. In the early days of community development, governments and philanthropies had poured money into businesses and watched their investments go up in smoke. As we have seen, during the late 1970s and early 1980s in the South Bronx and in Boston's Codman Square neighborhood, the efforts of nonprofits to manage new industries and supermarkets ended in failure, and there were many more such collapses across the country. Small business is risky under any circumstances—the majority of all new enterprises fail within a few years—but these inner-city enterprises operated in areas that many business owners shunned because they feared they could not turn a profit there. Nor did it help when nonprofit entrepreneurs thought that social commitment was more important than knowing what it takes to run a business. Successes in funding and carrying out housing programs convinced most practitioners in the community development field to use housing renovation and development as its primary tool for improving neighborhoods.[46]

Griego remained undeterred, nonetheless. She knew that L.A. was still alive and kicking, and small businesses were the reason.

Fortunately for RLA, two iconoclastic intellectuals agreed with Griego and argued in newspaper opinion columns and research reports that Los Angeles was not going down the tubes. Infuriating the doomsayers, journalist Joel Kotkin and economist David Friedman asserted that L.A.'s crises were temporary and did not threaten the city's basic assets.

Friedman, whom Griego had hired to do research for Los Angeles's economic development department, was one of a small group of theorists investigating economic "sticky regions." Sticky regions was the odd name the economists conferred on places, such as remote Gifu, Japan, and northeastern and central Italy, which retained industries despite the incentives in a global economy to move away. The manufacturers of sticky regions were not large mass-production industries, but small flexible industries—aerospace and machine shop technology in Gifu; traditional products such as shoes, leather handbags, and knitwear in Italy—that emphasized value over volume. Friedman had found similar industries in southern California including Los Angeles textile firms that computerized printing and weaving operations to design and deliver their products faster than their foreign competitors. The key to the success of these flexible industries was collaborative networks to exchange business information, access to capital, and governmental encouragement.[47]

To save South Central, Kotkin and Friedman rejected as ineffective both the traditional liberal solution—massive government subsidies for jobs and social programs—and the conservative panacea—tax-free enterprise zones to attract outside businesses. Kotkin and Friedman urged that Los Angeles give up trying to entice corporations, which they saw as lumbering dinosaurs of the past. Instead those who would save L.A.'s inner city, they argued, should first focus their efforts on creating a vital economy that would assist "the vast majority of African Americans, Latinos, Asians, and Anglos" who believed in self-help and were looking for jobs but were in danger of falling further into poverty, and second, build the resources to tackle the special problems of the chronically alienated members of the underclass. Take the necessary steps, Kotkin and Friedman urged, to create a sticky region for Los Angeles's small and medium-size flexible manufacturing firms.[48]

So much for the theory. Friedman and Griego knew that RLA staff needed to understand the situation in South Central and the other neglected areas more precisely before taking action. The first step was research, and thanks to Peter Ueberroth, RLA had research tools to die for. Corporations had donated tens of thousands of dollars worth of technological equipment—IBM computers, comprehensive databases from Dun and Bradstreet and Dow Jones, and sophisticated Geographic Information Systems programs for mapping their findings.

When they saw RLA's capabilities, the veterans of L.A.'s economic development department exclaimed, "This is unbelievable!" At the old agency, where budgets and time away from answering constituents requests were limited, it took months to study one industry. Often the statistics were out-of date by the time the staff finished the research. At RLA, they could collect up-to-the-minute information on several industries simultaneously. RLA's researchers tackled the most difficult and time-consuming investigations: examining neighborhoods, census tract by census tract, to learn the identity of all the manufacturing companies within them and how many people they employed, and find out how many more workers they might hire.[49]

Despite the press's conviction that few properties destroyed in the riots had been restored, RLA research on vacant lots found that by the end of 1996 more than 85 percent of all damaged buildings were repaired or rebuilt, including 149 gas stations and thirty-five supermarkets. About 150 riot-damaged buildings remained vacant, but most of these had been liquor stores, which activists in South Central campaigned vigorously to keep closed.[50]

RLA researchers compiled an extensive database on more than two hundred vacant lots and underutilized buildings, interviewed property owners, and visited sites. They found that most of the properties that had not been rebuilt were, like existing vacant lots, too small to interest retail store owners. Developers generally insist on a five-acre lot to build a supermarket, but most of South Central's empty parcels occupied less than a quarter acre. Lack of parking and access to capital also hampered commercial development of vacant lots.

RLA staff mapped two approaches to the vacant lot problem. First, they would seek to fill vacant properties that spread along already existing shopping corridors. Second, they would attempt to assemble parcels of land in order to attract shopping centers. For now, developing the remaining vacant lots is difficult, but at least the nature of the problem has been identified.[51]

But, most important, while studying vacant lots, RLA found remarkable information about economic conditions in inner-city Los Angeles.

A Golden Ghetto?

RLA's high-powered research effort produced the shocking news that South Central Los Angeles was, in its own way, thriving.

For years most people who didn't live there believed South Central to be a dying ghetto inhabited by a hopeless underclass. Professor Tom Larson, an economist at California State University in Los Angeles, was originally one such pessimist. When Griego was deputy mayor, she hired Larson to assess the economic needs of South Central, and after she took over RLA, she provided him with more funds to continue his research. Larson fit the stereotype of a baby-boomer academic: he wore his hair long and expounded conventional liberal ideas in his research. When he began his work on South Central Los Angeles, he pictured a bleak region of growing poverty, unemployment, and misery.

And at first Larson found relatively few businesses in South Central. His method of counting was to go to city hall and tally the number of licenses granted to operate businesses in South Central. "You will never find businesses in South Central that way," Griego admonished the professor. "Most of them don't have licenses. You have to go door-to-door." Sure enough, when Larson organized a team of multilingual graduate students to canvass the neighborhood, he was shocked by what they found. Not only were there many businesses in L.A.'s inner city, but the number of enterprises *was growing*.[52]

Larson made other startling discoveries. South Central, Larson found, contained no large and growing underclass. It had far fewer poor and far more working-class families than he or most others expected. Nor were African Americans in South Central particularly poor: their poverty rate was far lower than the national average and had dropped in the late 1980s. Nor were poverty rates and the concentration of the poor—two key indicators of distress for academics and activists—high compared with those of other cities. There was poverty in South Central, but it arose from low wages, not welfare-style unemployment.[53]

*Worker in underwear and shirt factory and outlet, Santee Alley,
Los Angeles fashion district, 1999. Courtesy of Fred Stafford.*

Larson's research exploded so many myths about South Central that it hardly seemed that he was talking about the same place everybody else was. Contradicting the stereotype that South Central had no jobs because the old manufacturing facilities had closed, Larson found that most of the area's adults were employed, many families had more than one breadwinner, and manufacturing jobs abounded. While a lot of these jobs—especially those in textile and apparel factories—paid low wages, others paid well above the minimum wage. The residents of South Central were not trapped; they were constantly coming and going. As some left for better housing in more affluent areas, others arrived to occupy the district's inexpensive homes. Even the old chestnut about the poor being isolated from suburban jobs did not hold for South Central: its residents were served by north-south and east-west bus lines, metropolitan train service, and three major freeways.

South Central had problems for sure. Low wages made it difficult for immigrant families to get ahead. Some African Americans, especially the elderly, had not been able to climb up and out of the old neighborhoods. And it clearly lacked enough retail stores for its population, a situation aggravated by the destruction wrought by the rioters in April 1992. "I like it here," one South Central resident declared in comparing his neighborhood to other southern California locales. "I like that we don't have floods and our houses don't fall down the cliff. What I'd like in my neighborhood is a nice salad bar."[54]

Worker in a Chinese noodle factory. Courtesy of Community Development Technologies Center.

It might not have had a salad bar, but South Central was making plenty of salad. RLA researchers counted 1,100 food processors operating in Los Angeles County, some 60 percent of them in South Central and the rest of Los Angeles County's "economically neglected areas."[55]

Los Angeles's neighborhoods were producing much more than food. The City of Angels is the largest manufacturer of clothing, largest toy distribution center, and second largest furniture builder in the United States—for many reasons including its access to southern California's large consumer market, the area's well-known identification with leisure lifestyles and Hollywood glamour, and the large number of immigrants who boost the economy as entrepreneurs and workers. South Central and the other neglected areas, according to RLA, held more than 70 percent of Los Angeles County's apparel and textile firms and 80 percent of their employees; more than 50 percent of the toy companies and their workers; and a third of the furniture manufacturers and a fifth of their workers. In addition, much of L.A. County's metalworking and plastics manufacturing took place in these neighborhoods, and a significant portion of the lucrative biomedical, entertainment, and electronics firms operated in and around them. All in all, Los Angeles's neglected areas contained 15,000 manufacturers who employed more than 360,000 people (with an average of 24 hands per firm) and each year generated more than $54 billion in sales.[56]

Even Griego was surprised at the size of the revenues some small factories generated. Some did not just assemble parts—a process that adds relatively little value to the product—but actually manufactured the product itself. One plastic plant, she learned, produced molds for making fashionable sunglasses.[57]

Building Industries to Build Neighborhoods

While Griego and her colleagues compiled information, a Harvard Business School professor shook up conventional thinking about the economy of the inner city and affirmed the small-business-oriented approach of RLA. In a groundbreaking article published in the *Harvard Business Review*, Michael E.

Porter argued that although entitlement programs such as food stamps were necessary, the inner cities would never revive until government replaced irrational and piecemeal economic subsidies with a rational and effective program that exploited "the competitive advantage of the inner city." Countering beliefs that inner-city neighborhoods were awful places where only drug dealers conducted business, Porter argued that its central location, large and underestimated local markets, eager work force, and—shades of Friedman's sticky regions—proximity to regional clusters of related companies made the inner city an excellent place to do business. Porter founded his own organization, Initiative for a Competitive Inner City, and called on businesses, governments, and nonprofits to improve the business climate and strengthen existing companies in the inner city.[58]

As it turned out, this is just what RLA staff members were about. They had begun to formulate ways to build up the industries that clustered within the neglected areas and turn L.A.'s inner city into a sticky region. They zeroed in on the most important industries in inner-city Los Angeles—biomedical products, food processing, toys, apparel and textiles, furniture, metalworking, and plastics manufacturing. RLA researchers went into the field to interview more than 250 companies, trade associations, and industry experts to find their common interests and most pressing needs.[59]

At first Griego and her lieutenants believed that a series of workshops and meetings would suffice, but they discovered that the small business leaders in the areas of biomedicine, food production, and toys wished to develop permanent trade organizations to carry on the work that RLA had begun.[60]

The biomedical industry, RLA's researchers found, was an emerging economic giant. They uncovered some 800 biomedical companies, which developed and manufactured pharmaceutical drugs and medical devices ranging from surgical blades to wheelchairs. About a quarter of the firms operated in or near the areas with more than 20 percent of the population below the poverty line, and these companies employed more than 10,000 people and earned more than $1 billion in annual revenues. The biomedical industry paid above-market wages, exported to Asia, Canada, and Europe, and was likely to grow dramatically in the future. And by buying the products of metalworking, plastics, glass, electronics, and computer software companies, the biomedical firms stimulated the growth of local companies in other fields.

Yet the biomedical companies of Los Angeles lacked the means to pursue their common interests and expand their own industry. In November 1995, RLA helped fill this gap by convening a conference of representatives of companies who organized the Southern California Biomedical Council (SCBC) as a nonprofit, mutual benefit corporation. With many prosperous members and the great potential of biotechnology, the new organization soon stood on its own feet. It has sponsored industry conferences on topics such as improving manufacturing practices, started a newsletter, and set up a sophisticated site on the Internet that includes a home page, programs of future conferences, discussion forum, and reprints of recently published articles on the field.[61]

Today the SCBC has grown to a force to be reckoned with. It counts as members more than sixty medical firms, who pay dues of up to $3,000 based on the number of employees; several large medical schools and educational departments; several law firms and investor firms, including Smith Barney; and in an honorary capacity, a U.S. congressman. SCBC has an executive director, issues press releases, and has been successful in getting its point of view reported in the *Los Angeles Times*. Lately, SCBC has been campaigning to get government support and investments from venture capital firms to build up the field's biotechnology sector.[62]

RLA also went to Toy Town, one of Los Angeles's hidden hives of business activity and a parable for the sticky region economists. In the 1970s, southern California's toy industry was dominated by large toy manufacturers, especially Mattel, the largest toy company in the world. In the early 1980s, Asian immigrants started their own toy companies, and soon some of these entrepreneurs opened toy import businesses in an unlikely area, the skid row and mission district of downtown Los Angeles. Working people came to the warehouses, bought toys at wholesale, and resold them at weekend flea markets.

From these humble beginnings grew Toy Town, a general distribution center of more than one hundred wholesale businesses, most of which are owned and operated by immigrants from China, Hong Kong, Korea, and Vietnam. Most of Toy Town's outlets are small, one-room warehouses whose garage doors roll up to show all the available merchandise wrapped in clear plastic.[63]

Some Toy Town operations, however, are large. Take Toy Star, for example. It occupies a three-story warehouse and a parking lot with a half-dozen loading docks where trucks line up four or five deep during busy seasons. At Toy Star, buyers choose their orders in the two large showrooms filled mainly with hundreds of different size dolls, but also a few remote-controlled toy cars, balls, and other small toys. Behind the showrooms and offices are the cavernous warehouse floors, in the middle of which are conveyor ramps equipped with rollers to move the goods from floor to floor for storage, packaging, and shipping. Toy Star, a division of Tai Tung International, is truly international. The company's factories in Hong Kong and China make its dolls—interestingly, almost all of them are versions of classic European dolls with light skin and blonde hair—which buyers will sell primarily in Central America. Appropriately, Toy Star's thirty-some employees are Asian and Latino.[64]

May Cheung holding a doll in the showroom of Toy Star, a division of Tai Tung International. Courtesy of Community Development Technologies Center.

To galvanize the diverse entrepreneurs of Los Angeles's toy industry, RLA sponsored a series of eighteen conferences and workshops, beginning in 1994. More than one hundred toy companies attended the gatherings to learn about such issues as the North American Free Trade Agreement, product safety, toy design, and expansion of domestic and international markets. Faced with the end of both RLA and its sponsorship of the workshops, twenty-five toy companies—including Mattel, which was interested in keeping toy manufacturing standards high—organized a permanent industry group, Toy Association of Southern California (TASC) in early 1996.[65]

TASC, now assisted by Community Development Technologies Center (CD Tech), follows the precedent set by RLA of helping the toy entrepreneurs by disseminating industry information and encouraging business connections. TASC continues to hold forums on issues and trends in the toy industry. In a meeting in 1999, for example, the group discussed the use of polyvinyl-chloride in toy products and the recent discovery that a substance in this plastic may harm young infants. TASC has recruited members of different fields allied to the toy industry, such as retailers, accountants, and lawyers. At the social mixers, the entrepreneurs—hard-nosed and independent like many small-business owners—meet their business rivals, whom they ignored in years past, and talk over common interests. May Cheung, the manager of Toy Star, likes to attend because she can hear what toy products are popular or sellable now and the latest from the trade shows. At a recent TASC mixer Cheung met a woman from Hong Kong whose company sold radio-controlled cars and had just set up an office in the United States; Cheung ended up buying her goods to sell from the Toy Star showrooms.[66]

Organizing ethnic food producers posed a more difficult challenge to Linda Griego's operatives. The food manufacturers—often family members—as well as their customers were divided by ethnic culture. By tradition, company directors operated independently of one another and worked long hours, leaving little time for extracurricular activities. Even entrepreneurs from the same ethnic group considered the owners of similar food companies to be competition and never spoke to them.[67]

RLA tried to demonstrate to the managers of the food companies that they faced similar business problems and government regulations. In September 1995 RLA began a series of meetings for the ethnic food processors by holding a workshop on trends in the supermarket business and how food manufacturers could take advantage of tax credits. In December, economist David Friedman spoke to the food processors about the advantages of trade networks for small businesses. In February 1996 RLA organized focus groups for Asian noodle companies and tortilla manufacturers to allow the owners and managers of

Gina Harpur sitting in Juanita's Foods factory atop cans of menudo. Courtesy of Community Development Technologies Center.

the two industry subgroups to meet each other and discuss their common interests.[68]

Then in the fall of 1996, with RLA and its sponsorship of such activities due to expire the following year, the leaders of two dozen food producers—primarily Asian and Mexican food companies—decided to form their own permanent nonprofit trade association, the Food Industry Business Roundtable or FIBR. With the help of RLA and the Southern California Edison (electric) Company, FIBR held an opening celebration at Southern California Edison's Customer Technology Application Center, which drew more than seventy companies. FIBR has grown to a core of thirty-four member companies—an achievement in a fragmented industry with independent traditions—but maintains contact with 600 companies, whose names were originally gleaned from the RLA business database. FIBR has already succeeded in gaining recognition of the food industry's contributions to the local economy: in March 1998 Los Angeles Mayor Richard Riordan invited FIBR's officers to accompany him on a trade mission to China. On the visit the Angelenos found a Mexican restaurant whose food they deemed inferior to similar fusion products made in L.A. "There were won ton tacos!" Gina Harpur, the FIBR president and general manager of Juanita's Foods, declared, "They can do much better!"[69]

Like the members of RLA's other manufacturing networks, the leaders of FIBR enthusiastically believe that building their industry helps both their small businesses and their home base of Los Angeles. Kenny Yee is the vice president of the Wing Hing Noodle Company and the third generation in his family to be in the business. A cheerful energetic man in his thirties—the kind of enthusiastic guy you would like to have on your softball or basketball team—Yee became involved in FIBR when he realized that however small and isolated his company was, it was affected by the world around it. Wing Hing is located just inside the northeastern boundaries of South Central (at 23rd Street and the Alameda Corridor) and has about thirty employees. After the 1992 riots his family might have decided to move the business away from South Central. But even if Wing Hing moved, Yee reasoned, it would still remain in southern California where recessions, earthquakes, or riots would hurt business. Yee joined the effort to bolster the small-scale entrepreneurs and was elected vice president of FIBR.[70]

Kenny Yee calls FIBR a loosely organized full-service consulting group. The managers of small businesses do not have the time, knowledge, or sometimes even the courage to track down the many agents such as accountants, bankers, or equipment suppliers, who can help them in their business. "You can try to call your public utility all day long," Yee explains, "but their agents don't really know who you are, or you don't really know how to deal with them. Yet through organizations (such as FIBR and TASC), we get to know and work with them."[71]

After a local television news program exposé led local health inspectors to crack down on unsanitary conditions in L.A.'s restaurants, FIBR conducted programs on food safety for entrepreneurs who reasoned that their operations soon might fall under similar scrutiny. One hundred fifty people came in June 1998 to the half-day forum on food safety regulations organized by FIBR,

L.A. County Supervisor Yvonne Brathwaite Burke (one of southern California's important elected officers), and the county's health departments. It was the first time that local food processors were able to meet the county health officials and exchange information in friendly circumstances. The forum was such a success that FIBR, this time working with U.S. congresswoman Lucille Royball-Allard, organized a similar workshop with officials from the Food and Drug Administration and the U.S. Department of Agriculture.[72]

At such sessions, FIBR and its members opened channels to county and federal safety regulators. Such connections have proved important. Recently a county inspector found sixty violations at a tortilla company in East Los Angeles and ordered the company to cease operations until a reinspection a few days later. The company's owners eliminated the violations and naively decided they could reopen before the follow-up inspection. When the county officials found out, they shut the business down for two weeks, a devastating blow to this small company.

A manager of the company called Yvette Nunez, who coordinated FIBR activities for RLA's successor, Community Development Technologies Center, and frantically asked for help. The company would go out of business if it remained closed for so long, and its twenty-some employees would lose their jobs. Nunez scolded the tortilla company managers for not following the rules, but called the L.A. County Health Department to plead their case. More phone calls, visits by the inspectors, and meetings between the managers and the inspectors followed, and eventually the health department relented and allowed the tortilla company to reopen long before the end of the two-week period.[73]

The people at RLA and CD Tech who assist small businesspeople have been excited to see the entrepreneurs develop untapped potential and become leaders. Denise Fairchild, the director of Community Development Technologies Center, is impressed with Gina Harpur. Harpur had never chaired a meeting in her life, but when she became president of FIBR, she studied and mastered Robert's Rules of Order. Fairchild reports, "She started taking classes at Toastmasters to learn public speaking, and now marches into legislative offices to deal with USDA and FDA issues. The experience with FIBR really paid off."[74]

Los Angeles's food manufacturers used to be oblivious to politics, but now through FIBR they have developed political clout. When legislators in the state assembly introduced a measure that would have tripled state inspection fees for food manufacturers and eliminated inspections by local inspectors—who understood the field well and had personal relationships with the small manufacturers—the FIBR board objected strenuously. The board members argued that the increase in fees would create a hardship for small businesses and allow unscrupulous manufacturers to avoid state inspection, perhaps endangering the reputation of the state's food industry by selling unsafe food. After they discovered that the impetus for the legislation came from giant companies—such as Del Monte—that operated in northern California under different conditions, FIBR's members worked with the city and county officials to revise the plan, testified at a hearing in the state assembly, and won a compromise that was much more beneficial to the small operators in southern California.[75]

Aside from immediate practical business issues, FIBR encourages the ethnic food manufacturers to collaborate with one another, and the results can be surprising. Among its members, FIBR counts a man who manufactures noodles and a woman who makes Asian sauces and salad dressings. They have started to package his crunchy noodles and her salad dressing together as an item.

Some FIBR members are crossing cultural boundaries in the search for new foods and customers. Kenny Yee, for one, is excited about the prospects for cultural food "crossovers." His Wing Hing Noodle Company sells the sheets used to wrap Chinese appetizers such as egg rolls and won tons to ethnic Chinese and other Asian stores but also to retail outlets, institutions, and national chain restaurants with Asian items on the menu. The company has begun to sell sheets of wheat dough — similar to that used in preparing won tons — to upscale restaurants where the chefs use them to make ravioli.[76]

For Yee this is just a beginning. He points out that California food fashions have influenced national eating habits. Working together through FIBR, he believes L.A.'s ethnic food producers will be able to fuse distinct traditional cuisines and come up with new products that will catch on in the national food market.

Ozabe Banks, FIBR's pioneer of crossover foods, might well be the one to popularize L.A.-style ethnic food fusion. Banks is an African American who grew up in South Central Los Angeles and runs a sausage company at Florence Avenue and Crenshaw Boulevard, just two miles from Florence and Normandie Avenues, the famous flash point of the King riots. Banks took pre-medical training in biology in college but abandoned the idea of becoming a doctor and instead, in the mid-1980s, accepted the offer of a family friend to assist in his meat-cutting business by making chicken sausage. Five years later, the man died, and Ozabe and his father, a chef in his own right, took over the operation and began selling under the company name, Money Saver's Meats. Banks calls his flagship product "the best chicken sausage in town" and others concur. The commanders of District 77, the main police station in South Central, buy hundreds of pounds of Banks's chicken links for their neighborhood barbecues every year.[77]

Henry Leong, at left, and Ozabe Banks at Food Industry Business Roundtable event. Courtesy of Community Development Technologies Center.

Ozabe Banks wants to expand his neighborhood operation, and to do so he is ready to travel beyond the usual ethnic barriers of local food makers. Most of his customers are African Americans who live in or near South Central, but since joining FIBR, Banks has been investigating ways to market Money Saver's Meats to Chinese Americans. Banks is a good friend of Henry Leong, a leader of FIBR and owner of the Quon Yick Noodle Company (started by Leong's father). Together the two men have visited Chinese-owned stores and restaurants in L.A.'s Chinatown and the neighboring cities of Monterey Park and Alhambra where many Asians have settled. In 1999 Banks sold his chicken sausages at a Chinese New Year's celebration in the neighborhood of Roland Heights. He consulted with the staff of a local Chinese newspaper to determine the best way of telling the paper's readers about his product. Banks recently opened a new manufacturing plant for his sausages, making it possible to carry out his strategy of persuading the Chinese of Los Angeles to dine on soul-food chicken sausages. If that works, who knows what may follow?[78]

An End and a Beginning

One of the many ironies in the story of RLA is that when the agency was about to go out of business, most of its operations were taken over by a small untested organization led by Denise Fairchild, who had been one of its severe critics. In 1997 when RLA was due to expire, its work was nowhere near complete. The agency had just started the efforts to develop vacant lots and open more stores in South Central. RLA had midwifed the birth of trade associations for the biomedical industry, the merchants of Toy Town, and the ethnic food producers, but these organizations were still young. The agency had only begun to teach textile and apparel firms about modernizing their equipment and methods, and upgrading their workforce. And RLA's treasure trove of databases, information maps, and business and community surveys was useless unless someone could exploit it.

To ensure that RLA's work would continue, Linda Griego held an auction of its programs and assets. Seventeen organizations submitted proposals to carry on RLA's endeavors. Among them were heavy hitters: the University of California at Los Angeles, the University of Southern California, and Los Angeles LISC. In the end, however, the leaders of RLA bypassed the large and prestigious institutions and chose to put most of their programs for building manufacturing networks and developing vacant lots into a two-year-old nonprofit organization, Community Development Technologies Center, affiliated with a community college trade school and directed by Denise Fairchild, who had once bitterly condemned RLA.[79]

Maybe the choice made sense. RLA had become an unorthodox urban agency, and Fairchild's vision of social activism and organizing was broader than simply developing housing, the approach taken by most in the community development field. A tall woman who looks younger than her age, Fairchild is very much a child of the 1960s. After graduating in 1971 from Fisk University, a well-known traditionally African American college in Nashville, Tennessee, Fairchild worked for War on Poverty Community Action agencies and welfare rights groups in Newark, New Jersey. She helped convert an apartment building into a cooperative in the South Bronx and started two nonprofit organizations in Los Angeles.

In 1989 Fairchild became program director of L.A. LISC where she encouraged local CDCs to try other strategies in addition to developing housing. She was especially interested in creating jobs for low-income people: she convened a committee of experts and CDC officers to find a way to exploit the vital regional economy of southern California to find well-paying and career-track jobs for low-income people. Out of this came a health services project—in which Esperanza Community Housing Corporation participated—to bring medical clinics and training to the inner-city neighborhoods as a way of promoting both employment and health. Having been involved with long-standing indigenous organizations such as Esperanza and Concerned Citizens of South Central Los Angeles, Fairchild resented the outsider Ueberroth's early attempts to revitalize inner-city L.A. without recognizing others working in the field.[80]

Despite the health industry project, Fairchild felt constrained by LISC's emphasis on real estate development and in 1995 left to start a new organization. She named it Community Development Technologies Center or CD Tech. Its purpose was to train organizers and staff members for nonprofit community organizations and help the poor obtain jobs and start businesses. She set up CD Tech at the Los Angeles Trade Technical College, a vocational school located in the factory district of South Central, a place she felt was well-situated for her new work on jobs.

Before leaving LISC, Fairchild got to know Linda Griego through their mutual interest in developing inner-city vacant lots and replacing the liquor stores destroyed during the riots with facilities more beneficial to the communities. During the last months of RLA, they had worked together in a large consortium of federal and local government agencies, banks, companies, and nonprofit groups. Coordinated by the Urban Land Institute and RLA, the consortium aimed to increase the number of retail businesses in South Central L.A. Both resourceful problem solvers, the business woman and the activist got along well.[81]

As Denise Fairchild learned about RLA's work with the small manufacturers that blanketed South Central and the rest of inner-city L.A., a lightbulb went on in her head. People in the community development field talked a lot about exploiting "local assets"—usually meaning hospitals, government agencies, or large real estate development projects—to help neighborhoods obtain jobs or money for programs. Fairchild realized that the small businesses were as much an asset as any large institution and that helping their owners could create more and better jobs for inner-city residents. She decided to enter the bidding for RLA's operations.[82]

Despite the small size and youth of her organization, Fairchild had some advantages over her better-known and better-financed rivals. From working with Linda Griego, she knew that Griego wanted to keep RLA's projects operating together and avoid selling off the retail or manufacturing programs to different agents—and this suited her plans for CD Tech. Fairchild also appealed to Griego's practical side: she proposed that CD Tech and Trade Tech College would give neighborhood people and organizations more access to RLA's valuable database than the ivory towers of the universities. When she persuaded the chancellor of the district community colleges to join CD Tech in its application to take over RLA, Fairchild's proposal acquired the institutional weight that her young operation lacked. Griego and the RLA board awarded RLA's successor, named LA PROSPER Partners, to CD Tech and Los Angeles Trade Technical College. Denise Fairchild finds it a little embarrassing, but she now rules the agency she once castigated.[83]

Under Fairchild, CD Tech has continued and extended RLA's innovative work in supporting manufacturing networks. Staff members coordinated and consulted with the textile and apparel, furniture, and plastics industry organizations and the associations of food processors, biomedical firms, and toy companies that RLA helped found.

In 1999 Merrill Lynch signed up to help. The powerful financial management company had already provided an analysis of the toy industry and competitive factors to TASC and set about to do the same for the FIBR, SCBC, furniture, and plastics industries. The firm's West Coast managers also promised to lend up to $20 million and invest $5 million in small businesses in Los Angeles and Orange Counties, but seeing a profitable trade, three years later they had raised their commitment to $120 million and by February 2002 had loaned $110 million of the total sum. At the same time Merrill Lynch also lowered the amount of its minimum loans from $300,000 to $100,000, which enabled smaller businesses to get in on the action.[84]

CD Tech also enlisted small manufacturing companies in an experimental worker program designed to retain workers while teaching them vital skills. Suss Design, a knitwear manufacturer; Matteo Home, a home furniture manufacturer; and El Burrito Mexican Food Products gave their employees time off to take classes in English, math, computer skills, nutrition, and financial planning. At the same time, if the workers saved at least $20 each month for two years, the sum was doubled by a group of private institutions up to a total grant of $2000. The workers could use their nest egg to help buy a house, obtain more education, or start their own business. As the experiment bore fruit— with workers regularly putting money aside and reaching the $2000 level— companies, such as American Apparel, M and M Jeans, Uncle Darrow's restaurant, and two Chinese noodle manufacturers, joined the program, and the funders made it more flexible so that workers could use their savings for health insurance or home computers.[85]

Tackling the large and dynamic textile and apparel industry is a difficult task, made more so by the reluctance of the government agencies and foundations to aid in the effort. CD Tech has proposed low-cost health insurance and on-site childcare (which apparel manufacturers asked CD Tech for help in obtaining) for workers in the textile and garment industry, but officials of philanthropic and public agencies have turned down these opportunities to help the working poor probably because they are afraid of being criticized for helping sweatshop operators.

Under the guidance of Linda Wong, CD Tech continues to study the fast-changing textile and apparel industry—its wage and occupation structures, vital sectors such as sportswear products, and the impact of the North American Free Trade Agreement (NAFTA)—so that local entrepreneurs can chart a successful path for employees.[86]

Thanks in part to the innovative work of RLA and CD Tech, the government of Los Angeles incorporated inner-city economic development into the city's economic development policy. Mayor Richard J. Riordan appointed Rocky Delgadillo, a lawyer whom Peter Ueberroth had recruited to RLA to foster business growth, to take over Linda Griego's old job as deputy mayor for economic development, and Delgadillo was able to build on his experience gained at RLA. In 1999 Delgadillo helped institute Genesis L.A., a central part of the mayor's economic plan, to develop fifteen—later the number rose to twenty-two—large blighted industrial and commercial sites. Genesis L.A. was a high-profile project that combined the government's resources with funds from large banks; its five member board included the CEO of Washington Mutual and retired basketball star and entrepreneur, Earvin "Magic" Johnson. Besides trying to lure or retain companies, the city's economic development office, under Delgadillo, also sponsored trade associations. It promoted groups organized by Rebuild LA and CD Tech and helped start new roundtables, including one for new entertainment media. By the time the administration changed—in 2001 Delgadillo was elected city attorney and James K. Hahn became mayor—the government had accepted the importance of inner-city small-scale manufacturing to the health of the city's economy as an incontrovertible fact.

Back in the neighborhoods of South Central Los Angeles, the CDCs tapped the surging economic energy of the City of Angels. Esperanza Community Housing Corporation in February 2001 opened a large *mercado*, or market, for low-income people to make and sell hand-made goods and services. Concerned Citizens of South Central Los Angeles operates its own business, the On Time Printing and Computer Center, where neighborhood residents learn and work at graphic design, layout, typesetting, copying, and postscript imaging. Under the capable hands of director Marva Smith Battle-Bey, the Vermont-Slauson Economic Development Corporation has been helping businesses for many years, offering businesses money through a revolving loan fund and advice about capital, marketing, business plans, accounting, and management. Recently the organization opened a small business incubator with offices and services. Similarly FAME Renaissance, the economic development wing of the First African Methodist Episcopal Church, runs three loan programs for working capital, equipment, and technical assistance and has opened its own incubator for minority-owned small businesses.[87]

Trailblazing

Los Angeles has blazed new trails in the efforts to revive the inner city. Much of the innovation has come from attempts to grapple with two potent and at times related trends: the massive influx of immigrants and the growth of the business sector, particularly small manufacturers. These trends, powerful in Los Angeles, have also been at work in other American cities. Immigrants have poured into many cities and spurred different approaches to community development, and efforts to cultivate small businesses in inner-city neighborhoods have blossomed into a national movement.

Immigrants have revitalized inner-city neighborhoods in Los Angeles by increasing the population, augmenting the local labor force, and stimulating local housing and retail markets. Since California is home to one-third of the nation's foreign-born population, it is natural that Los Angeles would benefit from their presence, but new arrivals have boosted the population and invigorated the markets in cities as diverse as Houston, Washington, and Newark.

However hardworking they may be, newly arrived immigrants are often beset by low wages, lack of skills, and overcrowded housing conditions. Just as the Esperanza Community Housing Corporation tries to ameliorate the conditions in the Adams neighborhood in Los Angeles, service and community development organizations struggle to solve overwhelming problems in poor immigrant quarters across the country. In Miami, the East Little Havana neighborhood is a densely packed landing place, at first for people from Cuba, but in the 1990s also from Nicaragua, El Salvador, Honduras, and Guatemala. The transient and impoverished nature of the population has inspired the East Little Havana Community Development Corporation to develop low-cost condominiums to give some of the new Floridians a chance to build some equity. As in South Central L.A., however, in places such as the industrial towns of New Jersey and Connecticut, poor immigrants can arrive so rapidly that social service and community development agencies cannot move in quickly enough to address the needs of the newcomers.

The experience with immigrants in Los Angeles teaches that community development organizations sometimes must alter their usual practices if they wish to serve these population groups. The strong ethnic identities and dispersed settlement patterns of the newcomers led TELACU, Little Tokyo Service Center CDC, and New Economics for Women to serve Hispanic and Asian immigrants in territories far from their neighborhood headquarters. Community development groups elsewhere have adopted similar approaches. In Oakland, California, for example, the East Bay Asian Local Development Corporation started in Oakland's Chinatown, carried out projects in other neighborhoods such as West Oakland and the neighboring town of Emoryville, and recently expanded into Contra Costa and Alameda Counties. On the other coast, Viet-AID, an organization founded in 1995, works with Vietnamese immigrants in an immigrant section of Dorchester but also throughout the Boston area. Community development work must be tailored to the special characteristics of immigrants.

Immigrants have also forced community development groups to adapt to the changing ethnic character of neighborhoods. In Los Angeles, predominantly African American groups have broadened their clientele to include Hispanics of diverse origins. The projects of the Japanese American organization, Little Tokyo Service Center, are pan-Asian, with a bit of Hispanic thrown in. Similarly, the changing demographics of Oakland has led the East Bay Asian Local Development Corporation to serve a population that is 41 percent African American, 36 percent Asian and Pacific Islander, 11 percent Hispanic, and the rest white, Native American, and other ethnicities.[88] Organizations

247

Garment and leather manufacturing and wholesale outlets, block of 8300 Vermont Avenue. Courtesy of Community Development Technologies Center.

that serve changing or polyglot neighborhoods have to keep up with their new population or risk becoming irrelevant.

The small business sector of Los Angeles's economy, in which immigrants are workers, entrepreneurs, and consumers, also helped lift inner-city neighborhoods. Business activity in L.A.'s inner-city neighborhoods grew so much that Rocky Delgadillo declared it to be "the next frontier for development, period. Not just inner-city development." [89] When they realized that small-time manufacturers, the disrespected Rodney Dangerfields of economic policy, were generating wealth and jobs in the inner city and beyond, Los Angeles's nonprofit and government leaders began to fashion ways to strengthen the companies and raise the skills and wages of their employees.

As the government and nonprofit agencies avidly encouraged mom-and-pop manufacturers in L.A., the idea of nurturing small businesses once again became a central part of urban policy. Across the country, CDCs have been lending money—often made available by local banks and corporations—to small local businesses and offering technical assistance and training to neighborhood entrepreneurs. Like CD Tech in Los Angeles, CDCs began to assist local companies to form trade associations. [90]

One of the reasons for the resurgence of economic development was that governments were pushing it. States—including California, New York, New Jersey, and Arizona—and federal agencies, such as the Department of Commerce's Economic Development Administration, the Small Business Administration, and the Department of Housing and Urban Development, administered a variety of loan and assistance programs for small and micro-businesses in areas of low income or high unemployment. The Clinton administration organized a large interagency workgroup to advertise and coordinate the many departments that ran programs geared to promoting inner-city businesses. It also helped establish the Community Development Financial Institution Fund, which gave grants to institutions such as credit unions, venture capital funds, and micro-enterprise funds that lent money to community and economic development projects.

Much fanfare accompanied the creation of another Clinton program, Enterprise and Empowerment Zones, which give tax abatements, loans, and grants to expand businesses and employment in low-income areas. Although employment has grown in many of the areas where the program has been carried out, relatively few businesses in the zones used the federal tax incentives and hardly any owners were influenced by the incentives to hire workers or invest more heavily.[91] Despite incentives, business managers tend to decide where to situate their companies based on access to transportation and proximity to materials, parts, and markets, a point often made by Michael Porter.

Porter himself has contributed to the resurgence of economic development as a tool for urban rebirth. His Initiative for a Competitive Inner City has been hired by several municipalities, including Oakland, Louisville, and St. Louis, to assess the opportunities and recommend business strategies for inner-city neighborhoods. The Initiative also produces reports on such subjects as retail opportunities in inner cities and best practices in employing inner-city workers; it advises inner-city business managers directly as well. To publicize the business advantages and vitality of markets in the inner city, the Initiative has teamed with *Inc.* magazine since 1999 to compile an annual list of the 100 fastest-growing private companies in America's inner cities. The Inner City 100 includes enterprises from such far-flung and seemingly unlikely locales as El Paso, Detroit, Buffalo, Philadelphia, Hartford, and so, like Porter's other efforts, advertises the economic viability of the urban core.[92]

It should not surprise anyone to discover that firms from South Central Los Angeles regularly find their way to the list of top inner-city businesses. Nor should it surprise anyone that the anchor tenant of a $10 million shopping center at the corner of Vermont and Slauson Avenues, developed by the Vermont-Slauson Economic Development Corporation with the assistance of Genesis L.A. and the mayor's office, is a branch of one of the largest supermarket chains in Mexico. Nor that when the Merrill Lynch Foundation sponsored CD Tech to assemble a Southern California Minority Business Atlas of some 70,000 firms of six main national backgrounds, the guide was so popular that the foundation asked the nonprofit to follow up with another.[93]

After all, who can predict what Los Angeles's bubbling cauldron of people, ethnic groups, and businesses will produce next?

*The bustle of life in the new South Bronx, Brook Avenue and
East 161st Street, July 2001. Courtesy of Glenna Lang.*

CONCLUSION

7

The revival of the inner city is under way across the United States. The changes taking place in New York, Boston, Chicago, Los Angeles, and Atlanta also have been occurring in Washington, D.C., Miami, Kansas City, San Antonio, Denver, San Francisco, Portland, Seattle, and elsewhere. In some cities the revival has just begun or is progressing slowly. Revitalization in Philadelphia and Detroit, for example, has been limited to a relatively small number of neighborhoods. Unlike other large cities, Philadelphia and Detroit are still evolving away from the original industrial economies that made them grow. As a result they continue to shed population, slowing the redevelopment of the neighborhoods. Yet even these lagging metropolises show signs of inner-city revival.

The revival reflects historic shifts in the functions of American inner-city neighborhoods. In the recent past, American inner cities were made up of ghetto neighborhoods for racial minorities, many of which later became depopulated districts for the elderly and families on welfare. Some neighborhoods still remain as they were, but most have evolved toward becoming either working-class immigrant districts or gentrified neighborhoods. (In this regard, some American cities are coming to resemble traditional European cities, such as Paris, in which the wealthy inhabited the core and the working classes lived on the periphery.)

Districts such as the South Bronx and South Central Los Angeles exemplify bedroom communities for ethnic, usually immigrant, working-class people. They resemble earlier immigrant quarters of the late nineteenth century, except that their inhabitants usually do not have the opportunity to work, as their predecessors did, in centrally located port and large-scale industrial jobs. They are just as likely to work in service occupations—as orderlies in hospitals, office cleaners, receptionists—and to work in the suburbs. Presumably, with sufficient economic opportunity, the immigrants will move out to new areas and suburbs. If more immigrants arrive to replace the current occupants, the inner-city districts will remain ethnic neighborhoods. Otherwise they will begin to change again.

The recent movement of educated, upper-middle-class people to the central city has also affected the character of the inner city. Attracted by the nightlife, stores, and cultural entertainments that contemporary downtowns offer, artists, bohemians, singles, gays, retirees, and professional families have taken up residence in downtown office districts and nearby neighborhoods. Some work downtown and enjoy both the urbane culture and living close to their jobs. Many old slum districts in the inner city are well located for those who want to be near downtown and the sophisticated urban life; in addition, they contain historic buildings, which are highly prized by the new urbanites.

As the inner-city evolves, it mixes old and new types of residents. A few neighborhoods stabilize as diverse communities, but most are in transition to either working-class or cosmopolitan elite districts.

If the inner cities are slowly being repopulated, where have the former residents of the inner city gone? As William Julius Wilson has noted, middle-class and professional blacks departed the old ghettos for the outer city neighborhoods and suburbs. African Americans in Los Angeles, for example, have migrated to the far reaches of the metropolitan area, to northern Los Angeles county, and to San Bernardino and Riverside counties. Migration from Washington, D.C., has redefined Prince George's County in Maryland as a middle-class black suburban district.

Just as significant is the migration of the poor—African American but also Hispanic, Asian, and white—out of the central cities. The number of poor people in the inner cities has shrunk, while the number in outer-city neighborhoods, small to medium-size cities, and towns has grown or held steady. Economically stagnant industrial towns—Buffalo, New York, is a good example—or inner-belt suburbs whose housing stock is aging and whose population has declined offer low-income households relatively inexpensive places to live.

In short, the physical and social problems that once undermined inner-city neighborhoods are moving further out within our sprawling metropolitan areas. Certain outlying cities and towns already have or will soon develop the deterioration of buildings, drug dealing, crime, and delinquency long associated with inner-city poverty. Such increasingly impoverished and troubled places deserve attention. They provide fertile fields for new community development efforts.

Even as inner-city neighborhoods revive, we will need to apply the lessons of the revival elsewhere: in inner-city neighborhoods still in need of improvement, industrial cities, and suburban slums. Those lessons, drawn from the cities and neighborhoods examined in this book, are summed up in the following general observations.

To launch successful and sustained renewal, communities need a cadre of people—leaders—who can change the perceptions or actual conditions that will affect the perceptions of their neighborhoods. Some of these catalytic agents are survivors, such as Genevieve Brooks in the South Bronx, who witnessed the downfall of their communities but refused to accept it. Others are like Leonard McGee of the Gap Community Organization on Chicago's South

Side: urban pioneers who made their new neighborhoods a full-time cause. Still others, including Sister Diane Donoghue in South Central Los Angeles, are outsiders who are profoundly committed to the poor and downtrodden. Whoever they are, these leaders combine perceptiveness, persistence, and a belief that the people are capable of making a different future for themselves.

Although they are idealistic, good community development leaders are practical and even demanding. They run programs to educate young people and keep them out of trouble and work to get relief from property taxes and home improvement grants and loans into the hands of low-income elderly homeowners. Yet they also set clear standards of behavior for tenants in their housing and evict those who fall short. The local leaders strike a balance between the needs of current and new residents and between serving the poor and redeveloping the neighborhood.

The most successful practitioners of community development cultivate close relationships with their neighbors. Earnest Gates and Wilma Ward particularly revered the elders of their neighborhood on Chicago's West Side, turning to them for advice and moral support, but the common bond among all the diverse personalities who led community development groups was respect for the people in their communities. Community development leaders meet frequently with local residents, ministers, school principals, and anybody else who cares to learn what people feel are the most pressing needs of the community and how their group intends to fulfill them. Some check local opinion by holding annual festivals or even passing out questionnaires. However they interact with their neighbors, the best in the community development game listen well and respond.

To move from discussion to action in community development, organization is key. The local institutions dedicated to revitalization—church groups, community organizations of the Industrial Areas Foundation type, community development corporations, business associations, and improvement associations—bring different types of people together for different purposes. Many effective community development organizations, such as the Mid-Bronx Desperados, are in fact federations of such block clubs, tenant associations, churches, and other local institutions. Yet whatever form these organizations or alliances take, their success depends on their ability to mobilize and coordinate the actions of local residents and leaders.

Successful community development also requires collaboration. No single entity—even government—is strong or clever enough to uplift a neighborhood on its own. The experience of the Boston Housing Partnership demonstrated that local groups that built relationships with private agents and public agencies gained access to money, expertise, and authority to carry out community development projects. On Chicago's Near West Side, small community leaders made serious headway once they teamed up with a large institution such as the Chicago Bulls basketball club.

Government counts, and counts a lot. When inner-city neighborhoods hit the skids, governments officials accelerated the decay by looking the other way. Conversely, most community development projects have depended on either cooperation or financial aid of government agencies, or both. Whether it is a matter of donating land or supplying funds for housing development, clearing projects through regulatory hurdles, or sending policemen to shut down a criminal hangout, the support of elected officials, department heads, and staff is needed. In many cities, federal programs, such as the community development block grant, provide desperately needed operating funds to community development organizations.

Therefore, local groups have to enlist government officials in the cause of their community's redevelopment. Fortunately for the local groups, federal, state, and municipal governments have earmarked money and programs for community development. In many cases all that is required is filling out the government forms and demonstrating the ability to carry out projects with "due diligence." In other circumstances, however, community groups such as the Nehemiah church groups in New York had to resort to private persuasion or large noisy public protests to get government officials to cooperate. During the late 1980s, however, a group of enlightened government officials transformed New York City's Department of Housing Development and Preservation from an ineffectual agency into one dedicated to carrying out projects with neighborhood organizations. Similarly, in Boston, police officers and personnel from the criminal justice agencies joined with community groups to create one of the most innovative anti-crime campaigns in the country. In Chicago, the mayor, Richard M. Daley, has offered timely help to citizens' groups and thrown the weight of his administration behind community development efforts. The government of Los Angeles embraced and assisted the city's innovative nonprofit economic development programs.

Government officials can become too involved, however, and interfere with community renewal. When local government officials in Harlem and Chicago attempted to control community development projects by choosing housing contractors and developers, little was accomplished. Politicians who impose their own schemes and insist on patronage distort or stultify community development. By the same token, not all community organizations have been immune to greed, incompetence, and the lust for power.

Despite its temptations, money is vital to community development. Local groups needed money not only to run their projects but also to pay rent and salaries. Besides government agencies, religious denominations and philanthropic foundations—too numerous to list—were willing to back sound community development schemes and help pay overhead. National financial intermediaries such as the Neighborhood Reinvestment Corporation, LISC, and the Enterprise Foundation as well as local intermediaries, such as Hattie Dorsey's Atlanta Neighborhood Development Partnership, also provided money to run the storefront operations. Entrepreneurial community development organizations, like Father Gigante's SEBCO, also found ways—such as real estate development fees—to earn revenue from their projects. The federal Community Reinvestment Act spurred banks to make loans for inner-city development projects.

Philanthropic institutions support community development in other ways besides providing cash. Intermediaries and foundations either provided or paid community development groups to obtain essential business and management expertise. The Neighborhood Reinvestment Corporation, LISC, and the Enterprise Foundation pride themselves on the training and information that they give to local community development leaders. Local intermediaries also made it their business to build up the storefront operations. In addition, national and local intermediaries function as a conduit between corporate executives and the small local organizations.

Large campaigns that set ambitious goals but lack a well-thought-out plan for realizing them fail, often loudly. Despite raising awesome sums, Peter Ueberroth's Rebuild Los Angeles and Jimmy Carter's Atlanta Project promised too much before anyone had a clear idea of the ways to fulfill the promises. In both cases, much time and money was expended at the outset as the officials of the umbrella organizations tried to determine the identities and methods of the local organizations that would carry out the mission. The inability of these crusades to meet the announced goals led many to overlook their accomplishments and dismiss them as failures. These experiences suggest that it is better to start wide-reaching programs on a small scale and gradually expand them or—as in the case of Edward Koch's Ten Year Plan for housing in New York City—have a specific set of programs in place at the beginning.

Community development, like urban renewal before, suffers when authority flows too much from the top down. Government authorities or outsiders with money have tried to impose their ideas on areas that lacked self-sufficient local organizations, a situation that prevailed in Atlanta, which until recently lacked a tradition of politically strong neighborhoods and community development organizations. Showing it is possible for outside agencies to help and gain the trust of inner-city communities, the Corporation for Olympic Development in Atlanta painstakingly worked with local residents to develop plans to improve their neighborhoods. In contrast, in Atlanta's Summerhill, a lop-sided partnership between strong-willed downtown businessmen and a neighborhood leader inexperienced in the ways of community development cracked under the pressure of trying to rush a revival and left bitterness on all sides. The danger of top-down schemes is that they will produce flashy real estate projects that serve primarily middle- or upper-middle-class households, excellent programs that reach only a limited number of people, or unhappy fiascoes.

The most successful community development programs allowed many autonomous parties to carry them out. Again a notable example is New York's Ten Year Plan. Flexible federal programs include community development block grants, which subsidize a wide variety of organizations and projects, and the low-income housing tax credit, which enables many organizations and developers to develop homes. Not all projects have succeeded, but that is one of the advantages of the current community development system. Even as some projects fail, others will work. Some organizations will falter, but others will learn through trial and error. Experienced groups set an example for the novices.

Generally speaking, community development efforts that tapped the power of capitalism had the widest impact. Private individuals, not nonprofit or government agencies, develop and operate the vast majority of businesses and homes in this country. As we have seen, local landlords, storeowners, and

255

manufacturers invest in local real estate, fix up homes, and hire workers, all of which directly affect the well-being of inner-city residents. Philanthropies and government agencies would do well to emulate the Community Preservation Corporation building rehabilitation program in New York City and the small business programs of RLA and CD Tech in Los Angeles. Assisting the owners of small properties and businesses and engaging them in community activities hold great potential for the community development field.

Finally, those who have emerged as leaders of community development know it is a slow and gradual process, more trial-and-error than tried-and-true. Even the most impressive practitioners—including Father Gigante and Genevieve Brooks in the Bronx, Bill Jones and Bill Walczak in Codman Square in Boston, Earnest Gates and Wilma Ward on Chicago's Near West Side, Juanita Tate of Concerned Citizens of South Central Los Angeles, and Mtamanika Youngblood and Young Hughley on Atlanta's east side, and many, many more across America—experienced setbacks, sometimes even crushing defeats. Yet they persevered. The leaders of community development understand intuitively that the work of transforming neighborhoods goes step by step, house by house, block by block.

APPENDIX I

INNER-CITY MORTGAGE
BORROWERS

New York City, South Bronx

	1994	1997	2000
Black (%)	39	41	34
Hispanic (%)	47	42	48
White (%)	7	6	5
Less than 50% of median income (%)	1	2	7
50–80% of median income (%)	21	21	25
80–120% of MSA income (%)	52	49	31
Greater than 120% of MSA income (%)	26	28	37
Number of loans	390	169	331

Census tracts in South Bronx   11, 15, 17, 23, 25, 27.01, 27.02, 31, 33, 35, 37, 39, 41, 43, 47, 49, 57, 59.01, 59.02, 61, 65, 67, 69, 71, 73, 75, 77, 79, 81, 83, 85, 87, 89, 91, 97, 99, 105, 115.01, 115.02, 119, 121.01, 121.02, 123, 125, 127.01, 127.02, 129.01, 129.02, 131, 133, 135, 137, 139, 141, 143, 145, 147, 149, 151, 153, 155, 157, 161, 163, 165, 167, 169, 171, 173, 175, 177, 179, 181, 183, 187, 189, 193, 195, 197, 199, 201, 211, 213.02, 217.02, 219, 221, 223, 225, 227.02, 227.03, 229.02, 367, 369.02

Boston

	Roxbury			Dorchester		
	1994	1997	2000	1994	1997	2000
Black (%)	65	58	48	58	44	42
Hispanic (%)	20	14	17	13	12	11
White (%)	8	22	25	13	24	30
Less than 50% of median income (%)	23	19	8	22	16	4
50–80% of median income (%)	43	38	26	36	37	25
80–120% of MSA income (%)	23	24	33	28	28	34
Greater than 120% of MSA income (%)	11	19	33	14	19	38
Number of loans	181	233	306	350	319	352

Census tracts in Roxbury   801–804, 807, 813–817, 819–821, 901–906, 924, 1101.01, 1203
Census tracts in Dorchester   912–920, 922, 923, 1004, 1005

Chicago

	Near South Side			Douglas		
	1994	1997	2000	1994	1997	2000
Black (%)	27	26	17	62	80	64
Hispanic (%)	1	5	3	10	0	2
White (%)	58	55	63	24	10	15
Less than 50% of median income (%)	1	2	2	0	2	13
50–80% of median income (%)	5	8	13	38	8	33
80–120% of MSA income (%)	18	21	30	19	35	25
Greater than 120% of MSA income (%)	76	69	55	43	55	29
Number of loans	153	132	576	21	49	312

	Grand Boulevard			Kenwood and Oakland		
	1994	1997	2000	1994	1997	2000
Black (%)	85	84	67	65	70	63
Hispanic (%)	0	2	3	3	1	2
White (%)	6	10	13	19	21	22
Less than 50% of median income (%)	12	2	4	4	4	7
50–80% of median income (%)	15	20	25	16	18	16
80–120% of MSA income (%)	52	45	37	29	33	35
Greater than 120% of MSA income (%)	21	33	34	52	46	42
Number of loans	33	49	146	112	140	255

Census tracts in Near South Side, Douglas, Grand Boulevard, Kenwood, and Oakland: see list in Appendix II.

Atlanta

	Mechanicsville, Summerhill, Peoplestown, Pittsburgh			Old Fourth Ward, Butler St., Bedford Pine		
	1994	1997	2000	1994	1997	2000
Black (%)	37	48	48	39	27	24
Hispanic (%)	0	5	1	2	2	3
White (%)	57	27	31	47	65	59
Less than 50% of median income (%)	7	14	11	2	7	6
50–80% of median income (%)	33	20	24	23	36	31
80–120% of MSA income (%)	20	39	34	42	23	30
Greater than 120% of MSA income (%)	40	27	31	33	34	34
Number of loans	30	44	139	64	128	381

Census tracts in Mechanicsville, Summerhill, Peoplestown, and Pittsburgh 44, 48, 55.01, 56, 57, 63
Census tracts in Old Fourth Ward, Butler St., and Bedford Pine 17, 18, 28, 29

Los Angeles

	South Central (south)			South Central (north)		
	1994	1997	2000	1994	1997	2000
Black (%)	22	24	27	18	14	18
Hispanic (%)	71	68	63	67	68	59
White (%)	4	5	6	10	12	12
Less than 50% of median income (%)	2	2	2	2	1	0
50–80% of median income (%)	28	27	27	20	14	14
80–120% of MSA income (%)	48	43	45	42	42	40
Greater than 120% of MSA income (%)	22	28	25	35	43	46
Number of loans	1472	1892	2553	235	300	420

	Watts		
	1994	1997	2000
Black (%)	8	15	12
Hispanic (%)	85	77	74
White (%)	4	5	7
Less than 50% of median income (%)	3	1	3
50–80% of median income (%)	33	40	41
80–120% of MSA income (%)	43	39	40
Greater than 120% of MSA income (%)	22	20	16
Number of loans	167	211	263

Census tracts in South Central (south) 2281–2289, 2291–2294, 2315–2319, 2321–2328, 2371–2384, 2392–2393, 2395–2398, 2400, 2402–2414

Census tracts in South Central (north) 2211–2212, 2213.01, 2213.02, 2214–2219, 2220, 2222, 2225–2227, 2247, 2312–2314

Census tracts in Watts 2420, 2422–2423, 2426–2427, 2430–2431

Source: Joint Center for Housing Studies Enhanced Home Mortgage Disclosure Act Database

PROFILE OF NEIGHBORHOOD POPULATIONS, 1970–2000

NEW YORK NEIGHBORHOODS

Hunt's Point	1970	1980	1990	2000
Total population	15,272	9,510	8,817	11,365
Percent change in population since previous census		−37.7	−7.3	28.9
Percent Hispanic	58.9	73.9	75.7	71.1
Percent White	8.5	2.9	2.5	1.4
Percent Black	32.5	22.9	20.8	26.6
Percent Asian and Pacific	n.a.	0.1	0.4	0.3
Percent foreign-born	12.0	16.7	14.3	21.1
Percent below poverty level	29.6	40.9	47.4	48.4
Average family income (in 1999 dollars)	$31,948	$23,747	$27,160	$23,787
Percent attended or completed college	6.1	9.5	15.2	19.9
Number of housing units	4,830	3,597	2,762	3,816
Percent housing units vacant	4.6	16.0	5.5	9.9

Crotona Park East	1970	1980	1990	2000
Total population	61,433	13,352	16,243	22,135
Percent change in population since previous census		−78.3	21.7	36.3
Percent Hispanic	58.4	59.6	61.6	63.3
Percent White	5.0	0.6	1.4	1.1
Percent Black	36.4	39.2	35.5	34.2
Percent Asian and Pacific	n.a.	0.2	1.0	0.7
Percent foreign-born	6.4	11.7	17.0	23.4
Percent below poverty level	41.2	48.3	45.6	39.6
Average family income (in 1999 dollars)	$26,150	$21,079	$26,453	$34,417
Percent attended or completed college	3.1	9.3	13.7	24.4
Number of housing units	18,767	6,221	5,610	8,022
Percent housing units vacant	4.5	20.9	3.7	9.4

Morrisania	1970	1980	1990	2000
Total population	37,388	16,348	17,621	21,763
Percent change in population since previous census		−56.3	7.8	23.5
Percent Hispanic	18.6	19.2	32.6	47.5
Percent White	2.4	0.8	0.4	0.9
Percent Black	78.5	79.3	66.3	50.6
Percent Asian and Pacific	n.a.	0.2	0.2	0.3
Percent foreign-born	5.4	8.3	8.9	18.7
Percent below poverty level	32.9	47.5	46.8	43.2
Average family income (in 1999 dollars)	$31,147	$24,272	$27,276	$31,217
Percent attended or completed college	5.3	11.0	18.2	23.8
Number of housing units	11,669	6,720	6,203	8,111
Percent housing units vacant	3.9	12.7	6.9	10.2

Melrose	1970	1980	1990	2000
Total population	64,357	31,103	31,358	35,404
Percent change in population since previous census		−51.7	0.8	12.9
Percent Hispanic	58.1	58.8	63.1	68.6
Percent White	12.7	5.6	2.3	1.7
Percent Black	29.0	34.6	33.8	28.1
Percent Asian and Pacific	n.a.	0.5	0.3	0.8
Percent foreign-born	8.2	10.8	12.8	23.6
Percent below poverty level	34.4	44.4	49.7	44.0
Average family income (in 1999 dollars)	$28,910	$25,152	$24,644	$28,654
Percent attended or completed college	3.8	10.9	14.5	19.0
Number of housing units	20,139	11,425	10,342	12,467
Percent housing units vacant	5.1	6.1	3.2	6.5

Longwood	1970	1980	1990	2000
Total population	68,190	21,496	26,564	30,447
Percent change in population since previous census		−68.5	23.6	14.6
Percent Hispanic	66.2	76.3	76.4	77.1
Percent White	5.3	1.6	1.7	1.2
Percent Black	28.2	21.6	20.8	20.7
Percent Asian and Pacific	n.a.	0.2	0.3	0.5
Percent foreign-born	5.9	15.6	19.0	29.4
Percent below poverty level	40.8	49.4	53.4	44.6
Average family income (in 1999 dollars)	$28,203	$21,921	$24,520	$31,556
Percent attended or completed college	3.2	8.3	11.9	19.2
Number of housing units	20,430	8,218	8,526	10,246
Percent housing units vacant	4.1	13.4	4.6	7.6

APPENDIX II

NEW YORK NEIGHBORHOODS *(continued)*

Morris Heights	1970	1980	1990	2000
Total population	45,697	35,105	42,104	46,163
Percent change in population since previous census		−23.2	19.9	9.6
Percent Hispanic	29.8	36.7	49.0	56.2
Percent White	40.1	3.1	1.6	1.1
Percent Black	29.2	58.9	48.9	41.4
Percent Asian and Pacific	n.a.	0.4	0.1	0.5
Percent foreign-born	18.7	13.8	21.1	30.5
Percent below poverty level	16.9	43.7	45.2	41.8
Average family income (in 1999 dollars)	$41,197	$25,373	$27,677	$31,180
Percent attended or completed college	12.5	16.2	22.4	24.4
Number of housing units	16,736	13,093	13,911	15,954
Percent housing units vacant	1.3	7.9	4.4	7.5

The following tracts (2000 Census) were used to delineate the New York neighborhoods:

Hunt's Point   91, 97, 99, 105, 115.01, 115.02
Corona Park East   121.01, 123, 125, 153, 155, 157, 161
Morrisania   133, 135, 137, 149, 151
Melrose   65, 67, 69, 71, 73, 75, 77, 79, 141
Longwood   83, 85, 87, 89, 127.01, 127.02, 129.01, 129.02, 131
Morris Heights   53.02, 205, 213.01, 215.01, 215.02, 217.01, 243, 245, 247

Source: United States census, derived from data prepared by GeoLytics, E. Brunswick, N.J.

BOSTON NEIGHBORHOODS

South End	1970	1980	1990	2000
Total population	18,503	20,916	22,467	22,586
Percent change in population since previous census		13.0	7.4	0.5
Percent Hispanic	8.3	13.6	14.7	15.6
Percent White	40.8	38.1	43.0	47.3
Percent Black	36.2	33.4	26.9	21.6
Percent Asian and Pacific	n.a.	14.2	14.8	14.1
Percent foreign-born	15.8	20.3	19.2	20.3
Percent below poverty level	32.1	21.2	21.1	23.0
Average family income (in 1999 dollars)	$34,281	$40,405	$59,894	$69,987
Percent attended or completed college	16.9	41.2	57.2	61.9
Number of housing units	8,709	10,812	11,907	12,230
Percent housing units vacant	16.4	13.0	12.0	4.9

Upham's Corner, Dorchester	1970	1980	1990	2000
Total population	15,346	12,541	12,588	13,102
Percent change in population since previous census		−18.3	0.4	4.1
Percent Hispanic	6.6	23.8	25.6	21.0
Percent White	78.6	43.4	25.5	14.3
Percent Black	13.6	26.4	32.6	45.7
Percent Asian and Pacific	n.a.	0.5	2.8	4.5
Percent foreign-born	11.8	24.5	31.4	34.5
Percent below poverty level	19.5	27.5	24.4	24.9
Average family income (in 1999 dollars)	$41,624	$34,382	$47,043	$44,183
Percent attended or completed college	10.2	18.6	28.4	29.6
Number of housing units	5,096	4,446	4,234	4,367
Percent housing units vacant	6.7	8.7	9.0	5.4

Codman Square, Dorchester	1970	1980	1990	2000
Total population	27,226	22,202	23,020	23,881
Percent change in population since previous census		−18.5	3.7	3.7
Percent Hispanic	1.9	8.8	10.4	11.7
Percent White	86.3	43.5	24.2	12.2
Percent Black	11.4	46.2	60.4	65.8
Percent Asian and Pacific	n.a.	0.6	2.7	7.3
Percent foreign-born	12.1	19.4	27.9	34.3
Percent below poverty level	11.6	22.5	17.6	19.6
Average family income (in 1999 dollars)	$48,495	$42,552	$56,448	$50,197
Percent attended or completed college	13.2	28.1	36.5	37.4
Number of housing units	8,470	7,702	7,853	8,049
Percent housing units vacant	4.7	9.5	8.6	5.3

BOSTON NEIGHBORHOODS (*continued*)

Dudley Square, Roxbury	1970	1980	1990	2000
Total population	30,598	24,685	26,098	26,457
Percent change in population since previous census		−19.3	5.7	1.4
Percent Hispanic	8.0	14.5	19.3	23.2
Percent White	20.1	7.7	4.9	6.8
Percent Black	71.4	74.3	68.8	62.5
Percent Asian and Pacific	n.a.	0.3	1.0	1.3
Percent foreign-born	9.2	12.0	15.6	19.6
Percent below poverty level	30.4	30.4	32.9	29.0
Average family income (in 1999 dollars)	$32,422	$32,699	$36,177	$39,691
Percent attended or completed college	8.5	18.3	26.2	29.2
Number of housing units	11,286	10,640	10,545	10,205
Percent housing units vacant	14.5	17.6	11.4	10.3

The following tracts (2000 Census) were used to delineate the Boston neighborhoods:

South End   704–709, 711, 712
Upham's Corner, Dorchester   912–915
Codman Square, Dorchester   920, 922, 923, 1004, 1005
Dudley Square, Roxbury   801, 803–806, 814, 817, 818, 904, 906

Source: United States census, derived from data prepared by GeoLytics, E. Brunswick, N.J.

CHICAGO NEIGHBORHOODS

Near South Side	1970	1980	1990	2000
Total population	8,752	7,243	6,828	9,509
Percent change in population since previous census		−17.2	−5.7	39.3
Percent Hispanic	1.4	1.6	0.6	4.0
Percent White	11.1	3.9	5.4	25.2
Percent Black	81.5	93.4	93.6	64.4
Percent Asian and Pacific	n.a.	1.2	1.2	5.9
Percent foreign-born	2.6	4.6	1.7	5.8
Percent below poverty level	37.3	43.3	61.0	32.3
Average family income (in 1999 dollars)	$28,307	$25,573	$19,822	$70,835
Percent attended or completed college	11.9	23.6	27.7	62.7
Number of housing units	3,223	2,488	3,123	5,578
Percent housing units vacant	9.6	2.7	7.0	16.0

Near West Side	1970	1980	1990	2000
Total population	79,224	57,560	46,197	46,419
Percent change in population since previous census		−27.3	−19.7	0.5
Percent Hispanic	8.7	9.8	9.3	9.5
Percent White	25.1	12.8	18.8	25.3
Percent Black	69.3	74.2	66.8	53.3
Percent Asian and Pacific	n.a.	2.3	5.0	11.1
Percent foreign-born	6.7	9.0	9.8	12.6
Percent below poverty level	36.5	51.1	51.1	37.5
Average family income (in 1999 dollars)	$32,953	$28,640	$32,242	$56,325
Percent attended or completed college	8.7	22.2	35.1	52.0
Number of housing units	23,829	20,140	21,543	21,408
Percent housing units vacant	8.5	8.5	23.6	15.1

Douglas	1970	1980	1990	2000
Total population	43,044	35,157	30,652	26,470
Percent change in population since previous census		−18.3	−12.8	−13.6
Percent Hispanic	1.3	1.4	0.8	1.1
Percent White	11.6	9.0	5.2	6.6
Percent Black	85.8	86.6	90.9	86.2
Percent Asian and Pacific	n.a.	3.1	2.6	5.6
Percent foreign-born	2.7	4.4	3.7	5.5
Percent below poverty level	33.3	41.6	46.3	41.2
Average family income (in 1999 dollars)	$36,229	$33,268	$32,178	$39,978
Percent attended or completed college	25.7	37.8	40.4	47.3
Number of housing units	15,738	15,173	14,964	13,604
Percent housing units vacant	5.2	5.4	15.9	20.5

CHICAGO NEIGHBORHOODS *(continued)*

Grand Boulevard	1970	1980	1990	2000
Total population	80,125	53,741	35,897	28,006
Percent change in population since previous census		−32.9	−33.2	−22.0
Percent Hispanic	0.5	0.2	0.5	0.8
Percent White	0.5	0.3	0.1	0.6
Percent Black	95.6	99.0	99.1	98.2
Percent Asian and Pacific	n.a.	0.1	0.1	0.1
Percent foreign-born	0.2	0.8	0.3	0.7
Percent below poverty level	39.4	55.6	63.9	46.9
Average family income (in 1999 dollars)	$29,948	$23,608	$19,959	$32,063
Percent attended or completed college	6.3	12.5	18.1	28.5
Number of housing units	25,948	20,863	16,409	13,744
Percent housing units vacant	8.0	10.4	22.1	27.4

Kenwood and Oakland	1970	1980	1990	2000
Total population	45,188	38,722	26,375	24,473
Percent change in population since previous census		−14.3	−31.9	−7.2
Percent Hispanic	0.9	1.1	1.1	1.5
Percent White	11.9	11.8	13.5	12.1
Percent Black	83.2	86.2	83.4	82.4
Percent Asian and Pacific	n.a.	0.9	1.6	3.5
Percent foreign-born	2.3	3.3	3.8	7.2
Percent below poverty level	32.5	42.8	40.3	31.1
Average family income (in 1999 dollars)	$45,507	$40,445	$55,998	$59,765
Percent attended or completed college	18.8	38.6	47.2	56.9
Number of housing units	17,283	16,471	14,462	12,823
Percent housing units vacant	9.8	9.5	20.6	12.7

The following tracts (2000 Census) were used to delineate the Chicago neighborhoods:

Near South Side   3301–3305
Near West Side   2801–2843
Douglas   3501–3515
Grand Boulevard   3801–3820
Kenwood and Oakland   3901–3907, 3601–3605

Source: United States census, derived from data prepared by GeoLytics, E. Brunswick, N.J.

Old Fourth Ward and Butler (incl. Auburn Ave.)	1970	1980	1990	2000
Total population	10,931	6,919	5,959	6,698
Percent change in population since previous census		−36.7	−13.9	12.4
Percent Hispanic	0.3	0.2	0.9	9.0
Percent White	8.8	10.3	6.8	12.2
Percent Black	90.7	88.9	92.2	77.8
Percent Asian and Pacific	n.a.	0.5	0.2	0.5
Percent foreign-born	0.1	1.2	2.5	11.8
Percent below poverty level	35.5	45.7	42.9	33.4
Average family income (in 1999 dollars)	$29,753	$21,674	$23,719	$36,124
Percent attended or completed college	8.1	13.2	18.8	42.3
Number of housing units	3,792	3,601	3,490	3,486
Percent housing units vacant	6.6	14.2	19.8	14.6

Summerhill	1970	1980	1990	2000
Total population	7,270	3,971	3,991	4,300
Percent change in population since previous census		−45.4	0.5	7.7
Percent Hispanic	0.0	3.5	0.7	1.7
Percent White	35.3	22.7	22.1	23.7
Percent Black	64.2	73.2	77.2	73.4
Percent Asian and Pacific	n.a.	0.2	0.1	0.6
Percent foreign-born	0.6	4.2	1.8	1.9
Percent below poverty level	47.1	50.6	53.1	44.2
Average family income (in 1999 dollars)	$23,200	$18,696	$26,282	$35,330
Percent attended or completed college	1.7	12.7	35.1	52.5
Number of housing units	2,904	1,889	1,694	1,956
Percent housing units vacant	16.2	14.2	11.5	5.2

Mechanicsville and Peoplestown	1970	1980	1990	2000
Total population	14,643	8,748	7,566	6,915
Percent change in population since previous census		−40.3	−13.5	−8.6
Percent Hispanic	0.3	0.4	1.5	2.0
Percent White	1.0	1.2	2.7	2.2
Percent Black	98.6	98.3	94.6	93.5
Percent Asian and Pacific	n.a.	0.1	1.1	1.9
Percent foreign-born	0.0	0.4	2.2	5.2
Percent below poverty level	47.8	57.8	59.9	48.6
Average family income (in 1999 dollars)	$23,025	$19,924	$18,043	$25,643
Percent attended or completed college	3.9	5.0	11.3	16.8
Number of housing units	4,552	3,868	3,524	3,512
Percent housing units vacant	9.6	19.0	24.0	14.7

APPENDIX II

267

ATLANTA NEIGHBORHOODS *(continued)*

Reynoldstown	1970	1980	1990	2000
Total population	3,267	2,108	1,721	1,626
Percent change in population since previous census		−35.5	−18.4	−5.5
Percent Hispanic	0.5	0.3	0.7	3.8
Percent White	7.7	6.1	3.3	11.1
Percent Black	91.9	93.6	95.5	83.1
Percent Asian and Pacific	n.a.	0.3	0.5	1.2
Percent foreign-born	0.0	0.0	2.3	11.3
Percent below poverty level	25.5	36.5	26.2	20.0
Average family income (in 1999 dollars)	$33,094	$25,010	$33,944	$39,844
Percent attended or completed college	4.9	6.8	17.4	36.2
Number of housing units	908	804	791	769
Percent housing units vacant	4.7	12.4	19.0	13.3

East Lake	1970	1980	1990	2000
Total population	7,415	7,728	6,453	3,560
Percent change in population since previous census		4.2	−16.5	−44.8
Percent Hispanic	0.0	0.5	0.1	2.4
Percent White	11.8	5.3	4.6	13.9
Percent Black	89.1	93.5	94.9	83.3
Percent Asian and Pacific	n.a.	0.1	0.0	0.1
Percent foreign-born	0.0	0.9	0.6	5.2
Percent below poverty level	16.6	35.6	42.7	16.2
Average family income (in 1999 dollars)	$41,211	$31,855	$31,141	$47,612
Percent attended or completed college	9.8	13.2	14.0	36.4
Number of housing units	1,760	2,242	2,179	1,498
Percent housing units vacant	3.2	5.8	11.8	8.9

The following tracts (2000 Census) were used to delineate the Atlanta neighborhoods:

Old Fourth Ward   17, 28, 29 (Fulton County)
Summerhill   48, 49 (Fulton County)
Mechanicsville and Peoplestown   44, 46, 55, 56 (Fulton County)
Reynoldstown   31 (Fulton County)
East Lake Meadows   208.02 (De Kalb County)

Source: United States census, derived from data prepared by GeoLytics, E. Brunswick, N.J.

LOS ANGELES NEIGHBORHOODS

Adams (east and west)	1970	1980	1990	2000
Total population	70,654	82,722	99,016	96,823
Percent change in population since previous census		17.1	19.7	−2.2
Percent Hispanic	23.9	48.1	63.1	67.4
Percent White	14.2	11.0	8.3	8.2
Percent Black	56.9	36.2	23.9	17.2
Percent Asian and Pacific	n.a.	3.9	4.1	6.2
Percent foreign-born	15.8	39.4	49.4	49.1
Percent below poverty level	29.4	29.6	34.7	37.7
Average family income (in 1999 dollars)	$32,089	$30,577	$33,831	$36,160
Percent attended or completed college	16.0	19.0	17.4	20.1
Number of housing units	27,004	25,242	28,283	27,450
Percent housing units vacant	8.4	4.7	9.3	6.6

Vernon Central	1970	1980	1990	2000
Total population	57,663	62,422	89,439	92,619
Percent change in population since previous census		8.3	43.3	3.6
Percent Hispanic	6.6	34.0	68.7	81.9
Percent White	2.6	1.2	0.8	1.1
Percent Black	90.1	64.0	29.0	16.1
Percent Asian and Pacific	n.a.	0.4	1.1	0.5
Percent foreign-born	2.6	24.6	49.0	50.7
Percent below poverty level	37.1	37.3	37.4	41.5
Average family income (in 1999 dollars)	$28,197	$27,471	$31,464	$33,460
Percent attended or completed college	9.2	13.7	10.3	10.6
Number of housing units	22,754	21,938	22,715	22,790
Percent housing units vacant	7.5	6.2	6.5	9.1

Vermont Slauson	1970	1980	1990	2000
Total population	105,915	100,076	118,121	122,704
Percent change in population since previous census		−5.5	18.0	3.9
Percent Hispanic	7.4	12.5	37.9	51.5
Percent White	7.2	2.4	1.1	1.1
Percent Black	83.3	83.5	59.6	46.0
Percent Asian and Pacific	n.a.	1.1	0.8	0.6
Percent foreign-born	4.5	10.1	29.4	33.9
Percent below poverty level	21.4	28.1	29.9	33.8
Average family income (in 1999 dollars)	$37,832	$34,982	$37,988	$37,424
Percent attended or completed college	16.7	23.8	22.0	22.1
Number of housing units	37,503	36,904	38,462	39,180
Percent housing units vacant	5.4	4.4	7.6	9.3

LOS ANGELES NEIGHBORHOODS *(continued)*

Watts and Willowbrook	1970	1980	1990	2000
Total population	43,835	40,416	47,939	52,016
Percent change in population since previous census		−7.8	18.6	8.5
Percent Hispanic	9.8	16.5	43.8	62.3
Percent White	2.0	1.0	0.8	1.0
Percent Black	89.4	71.1	38.0	23.4
Percent Asian and Pacific	n.a.	0.3	0.1	0.4
Percent foreign-born	2.7	9.9	26.7	34.3
Percent below poverty level	44.4	46.5	44.2	44.2
Average family income (in 1999 dollars)	$27,581	$26,002	$27,513	$32,153
Percent attended or completed college	8.3	13.0	13.2	13.6
Number of housing units	12,419	11,556	12,323	13,316
Percent housing units vacant	7.4	5.0	5.1	9.3

The following tracts (2000 Census) were used to delineate the Los Angeles neighborhoods:

Adams (east and west) 2215, 2216, 2217.10, 2218.10, 2218.20, 2219, 2221, 2222, 2225–2227, 2240.20, 2244.10, 2244.20, 2246, 2247, 2264.10, 2264.20 , 2267, 2270.01, 2270.02, 2312.10, 2312.20, 2313

Vernon Central 2281, 2282.10, 2282.20, 2283.10, 2283.20, 2284.10, 2284.20, 2285, 2286, 2287.10, 2287.20, 2288, 2289, 2291–2293, 2294.10, 2294.20, 2311, 2318, 2319, 2328

Vermont Slauson 2315, 2316, 2317.10, 2317.20, 2321.10, 2321.20, 2322–2327, 2371–2376, 2377.10, 2377.20, 2378, 2379, 2381, 2382, 2383.10, 2383.20

Watts and Willowbrook 2420–2423, 2426, 2427, 2430, 2431, 5352, 5354, 5404, 5406, 5407

Source: United States census, derived from data prepared by GeoLytics, E. Brunswick, N.J.

NOTES

Introduction

1. Jill Jonnes, *South Bronx Rising: The Rise, Fall, and Resurrection of an American City* (New York: Fordham University Press, 2002), 333–36.
2. Pam Belluck, "Blighted Areas Are Revived," *New York Times*, May 30, 2000.
3. Brian J. Berry, "Islands of Renewal in Seas of Decay," in *The New Urban Reality*, ed. Paul E. Peterson (Washington, D.C.: The Brookings Institution, 1985), 69–96; Elvin K. Wyly and Daniel J. Hammel, "Islands of Decay in Seas of Renewal: Housing Policy and the Resurgence of Gentrification," *Housing Policy Debate* 10:4 (1999), 711–71.

Chapter 1

1. Jon C. Teaford, *The Rough Road to Renaissance — Urban Revitalization in America, 1940–1985* (Baltimore: Johns Hopkins University Press, 1990), 10–43; Robert A. Beauregard, *Voices of Decline: The Postwar Fate of US Cities* (Cambridge, Mass.: Blackwell Publishers, 1993), 79–157.
2. Herbert J. Gans, *The Urban Villagers, Group and Class in the Life of Italian-Americans* (New York: Free Press, 1962); Thomas Hines, "Housing, Baseball, and Creeping Socialism: The Battle of Chavez Ravine, Los Angeles, 1949–1959," *Journal of Urban History* 8:12 (February 1982), 123–44; Martin Anderson, *The Federal Bulldozer* (Cambridge, Mass.: MIT Press, 1964); Jane Jacobs, *The Death and Life of Great American Cities* (New York: Random House, 1961); John H. Mollenkopf, *The Contested City* (Princeton, N.J.: Princeton University Press, 1983); Marc A. Weiss, "The Origins and Legacy of Urban Renewal," in *Urban and Regional Planning in an Age of Austerity*, ed. Pierre Clavel, John Forester, and William W. Goldsmith (New York: Pergamon Press, 1980).
3. Harrison E. Salisbury, *The Shook-Up Generation* (New York: Harper & Brothers, 1958), 77.
4. *Report of the National Advisory Commission on Civil Disorders* (New York: Bantam Books, 1968); *Building the American City: Report of the National Commission on Urban Problems to the Congress and to the President of the United States* (Washington, D.C.: U.S. Government Printing Office, 1968), 1, 5.

5. These new programs were contained in Sections 235 and 236 of the Housing and Urban Development Act of 1968.

6. Charles M. Haar, *Between the Idea and the Reality: A Study in the Origin, Fate, and Legacy of the Model Cities Program* (Boston: Little, Brown, 1975).

7. Paulette V. Walker, "Stadium Area Links Survival to Olympics," *Atlanta Journal-Constitution*, December 27, 1990; Chicago Fact Book Consortium, eds., *Local Community Fact Book Chicago Metropolitan Area* (Chicago: University of Illinois, 1995), 125–26.

8. Ken Auletta, *The Underclass* (New York: Random House, 1982).

9. In addition, Congress created Neighborhood Housing Services of America to act as a secondary market for NeighborWorks loans. Louis Winnick, "Going to Scale: The Ascent of Neighborhood Housing Services," unpublished paper, n.d.; Phillip L. Clay, *Neighborhood Partnerships in Action* (Washington, D.C.: Neighborhood Reinvestment Corporation, 1981).

10. Avis C. Vidal, Arnold M. Howitt, and Kathleen P. Foster, *Stimulating Community Development: An Assessment of the Local Initiatives Support Corporation*, Research Report R86-2, John F. Kennedy School of Government, Harvard University, June 1986, II, 3–6; http://www.liscnet.org/whatwedo/facts/

11. For statistics and history, see http://www.enterprisefoundation.org.

12. The tax credit was predicated on the housing projects having for fifteen years either 20 percent of the units occupied by households at or below 50 percent of the area median income or 40 percent of the units occupied by households at or below 60 percent of the area median income (with incomes in both categories adjusted for household size).

13. Jean L. Cummings and Denise DiPasquale, *Building Affordable Rental Housing: An Analysis of the Low-Income Housing Tax Credit* (Boston: City Research, 1998), 39.

14. Manasi Bhargava and Stacey Gordon, "Supporting Communities: An Assessment of the Community Development Industry," Policy Analysis Exercise (Cambridge, Mass.: John F. Kennedy School of Government, 2002); National Congress for Community Economic Development (NCCED), *Against All Odds: The Achievements of Community-Based Development Organizations* (Washington D.C.: NCCED, 1989); Carol F. Steinbach, *Tying It All Together* (Washington D.C.: NCCED, 1995); Carol F. Steinbach, *Coming of Age: Trends and Achievements of Community-Based Development Organizations* (Washington D.C.: NCCED, 1999). Bhargava and Gordon derived the figure of 8,400 community development organizations from a sample of nonprofit respondents to IRS form 990. By extrapolating from results from a mail survey, the NCCED estimated the existence of 3,600 CDCs in 1998, about twice as many as it had estimated to exist a decade before.

Chapter 2

1. Yalman Onaran, "The Bronx," *Christian Science Monitor*, June 1, 1994.

2. Lloyd Ultan, *The Beautiful Bronx, 1920–1950* (New York: Arlington House Publishers, 1979); Evelyn Gonzalez, "From Suburb to City: The Development of the Bronx, 1890–1940," *Building a Borough: Architecture and Planning in the Bronx, 1890–1940* (Bronx, N.Y.: Bronx Museum of the Arts, 1986), 8–29.

3. Jill Jonnes, *South Bronx Rising: The Rise, Fall, and Resurrection of an American City* (New York: Fordham University Press, 2002), 223.

4. Jonnes, *South Bronx Rising*, 223–48.
5. Jonnes, *South Bronx Rising*, 191.
6. Jonnes, *South Bronx Rising*, 226.
7. Jonnes, *South Bronx Rising*, 227.
8. Jonnes, *South Bronx Rising*, 231, 233.
9. Jonnes, *South Bronx Rising*, 232–33.
10. Jonnes, *South Bronx Rising*, 251–52.
11. Jonnes, *South Bronx Rising*, 298–99.
12. Richard Manson, interview by author, tape recording, New York, March 8, 2001.
13. Father Louis R. Gigante, interview by author, tape recording, Bronx, New York, November 9, 2000.
14. Michael Goodwin, "Controversial Father Gigante Wins Applause," *New York Times*, July 15, 1981; Jonnes, *South Bronx Rising*, 169.
15. Jonnes, *South Bronx Rising*, 170 (quote); Gigante, interview.
16. Louis R. Gigante, "The History of SEBCO," typescript, n.d., Gigante file, Box 1, Jill Jonnes Papers, Harry T. Johnson Collection, Herbert H. Lehman College, City University of New York.
17. Jonnes, *South Bronx Rising*, 170–98.
18. Jonnes, *South Bronx Rising*, 189–91.
19. Francis X. Clines, "More Heavenly Pursuits Beckon a Pragmatist," About New York column, *New York Times*, August 30, 1977; Jonnes, *South Bronx Rising*, 302.
20. Clines, "More Heavenly Pursuits"; Pranay Gupte, "Colombo Is Eulogized as a Champion of Civil Rights," *New York Times*, May 27, 1978; Goodwin, "Controversial Father Gigante." For the last thirty years, newspapers have recorded the court prosecutions and alleged crimes of the Gigante brothers. For a tabloid-style account of a federal jury's 1997 conviction of Vincent Gigante on racketeering charges and Father Gigante's reaction, see Jerry Capeci, "Chin: Dazed, Confused, Guilty," This Week in Gang Land, World Wide Web page http://www.ganglandnews.com/column39 (April 26, 2001).
21. Gigante, interview.
22. Diane Winston, "Bronx Community Groups," Master's Project, Columbia Journalism School, 1982, 19; Gigante, interview.
23. Gigante, interview.
24. Gigante, interview; Gigante, "History of SEBCO"; Fact sheet, SEBCO Development Inc., 1989.
25. Gigante, "History;" SEBCO fact sheet; Keith Moore and Don Gentile, "5000 Seek 236 Apartments," *New York Daily News*, January 25, 1981.
26. Gigante, interview; Gigante, "History of SEBCO"; SEBCO fact sheet.
27. Winston, "Bronx Community Groups," 20; Jonnes, *South Bronx Rising*, 302–3.
28. Goodwin, "Controversial Father Gigante."
29. Felice Michetti, interview by author, tape recording, New York, March 9, 2001.
30. Anita Miller, interview by author, tape recording, Newtown, Pennsylvania, December 7, 2000.
31. Michetti, interview.
32. Jonnes, *South Bronx Rising*, 318.
33. Jonnes, *South Bronx Rising*, 300–301, 321–22.
34. Jonnes, *South Bronx Rising*, 318.
35. Patrick Breslin, "On These Sidewalks of New York, the Sun Is Shining Again," *Smithsonian Magazine*, April 1995, 110; Genevieve Brooks, interview by author, Bronx, New York, May 23, 1995.

36. Brooks, interview; Breslin, "On These Sidewalks," 106; Jonnes, *South Bronx Rising*, 250–52.
37. Jonnes, *South Bronx Rising*, 249–50.
38. Reverend Monsignor William Smith, interview by author, Bronx, New York, October 28, 2000.
39. Smith, interview.
40. Smith, interview.
41. Smith, interview.
42. Julie Sandorf, interview by author, tape recording, New York, November 9, 2000.
43. Sandorf, interview.
44. Sandorf, interview.
45. Smith, interview.
46. Sandorf, interview.
47. Jonnes, *South Bronx Rising*, 311–16.
48. Jonnes, *South Bronx Rising*, 318–19.
49. Edward J. Logue, interview by Jill Jonnes, typescript, Bronx, New York, May 18, 1983, Logue file, Box 1, Jill Jonnes Papers, Harry T. Johnson Collection, Herbert H. Lehman College, City University of New York; (quote) Edward I. Koch, interview by author, tape recording, New York, May 1, 2001.
50. Edward I. Koch with William Rauch, *Mayor* (New York: Simon and Schuster, 1984), 127–35; Jonnes, *South Bronx Rising*, 324–25. According to Jonnes, the White House proposed business loans, construction of a federal office building, a job training facility, a mental health center, and the renovation of a nearby public housing project.
51. Jonnes, *South Bronx Rising*, 342.
52. Jonnes, *South Bronx Rising*, 327, 384; Joel Kotkin, *Can the Cities Be Saved?* (Santa Monica, Calif.: Milken Institute, 1997), 22; "Industrial Developments," World Wide Web page http://www.panynj.gov/economic_development, May 30, 2002.
53. Miller, interview.
54. Miller, interview.
55. Jonnes, *South Bronx Rising*, 382; Logue, interview by Jonnes.
56. Alan S. Oser, "Lessons from One-Family Housing in the South Bronx," *New York Times*, April 21, 1985; Jonnes, *South Bronx Rising*, 376.
57. Oser, "Lessons."
58. Sandorf, interview.
59. Sandorf, interview. Peter Bray provided information about the Nighthawks.
60. Oser, "Lessons."
61. Oser, "Lessons"; Sandorf, interview.
62. Joe Klein, "The Last of the Big-Time Spenders," *New York*, June 18, 1984, 27.
63. Jonnes, *South Bronx Rising*, 345.
64. Jonnes, *South Bronx Rising*, 346–47.
65. Jonnes, *South Bronx Rising*, 346–47.
66. Jonnes, *South Bronx Rising*, 348–49; William Frey, interview by author, tape recording, New York, July 27, 2001.
67. Jonnes, *South Bronx Rising*, 356, 363.
68. Jonnes, *South Bronx Rising*, 354, 359.
69. Jonnes, *South Bronx Rising*, 356–59.
70. Frey, interview.
71. Jonnes, *South Bronx Rising*, 358.

72. Jonnes, *South Bronx Rising*, 360–62.
73. Jonnes, *South Bronx Rising*, 368–69.
74. Frey, interview.
75. "New York's Best Landlords," *New York Sunday News Magazine*, October 10, 1982.
76. Frey, interview.
77. Frey, interview; Frances A. McMorris, "He Likes His Job, Tenants Like Him," *Newsday*, February 24, 1985.
78. Frey, interview.
79. Jonnes, *South Bronx Rising*, 354–55.
80. Jonnes, *South Bronx Rising*, 308–10.
81. Frey, interview; Michetti, interview. Jonnes found that although the sole purpose of the West Tremont Neighborhood Preservation office was to process building repair loans, in the previous three years it had not approved a single loan. Jonnes, *South Bronx Rising*, 359.
82. Frey, interview; Miller, interview.
83. Jonnes, *South Bronx Rising*, 317; John Joseph O'Connor and Edward I. Koch, *His Eminence and Hizzoner: A Candid Exchange* (New York: William Morrow and Co., 1989), 194–98, 215–18.
84. Avis C. Vidal, Arnold M. Howitt, and Kathleen P. Foster, *Stimulating Community Development: An Assessment of the Local Initiatives Support Corporation*, Research Report R86-2, John F. Kennedy School of Government, Harvard University, June 1986, VI, 33–34.
85. Manson, interview.
86. Alan Finder, "New York Pledge to House Poor Works a Rare, Quiet Revolution," *New York Times*, April 30, 1995.
87. Michetti, interview.
88. Reminiscences of Paul A. Crotty, interviewed August–October 1992 by John Metzger, Koch Administration Project, Columbia Oral History Research Office Collection (hereafter CUOHROC), 58–60.
89. Crotty, Reminiscences, CUOHROC, 121–23.
90. Paul A. Crotty, interview by author, tape recording, New York, May 1, 2001.
91. Koch, interview; Crotty, interview; Charles J. Orlebeke, *New Life at Ground Zero: New York, Home Ownership, and the Future of America's Cities* (New York: Rockefeller Institute Press, 1997), 130.
92. Michetti, interview.
93. Crotty, Reminiscences, CUOHROC, 67.
94. Crotty, interview; Alex Schwartz, "New York City and Subsidized Housing: Impacts and Lessons of the City's $5 Billion Capital Budget Housing Plan," *Housing Policy Debate* 10:4 (1999), 843; Frank P. Braconi, "In Re *In Rem*: Innovation and Expediency in New York's Housing Policy," in *Housing and Community Development in New York City: Facing the Future*, ed. Michael H. Schill, (Albany: State University of New York Press, 1999), 93–118.
95. Sandorf, interview.
96. Koch, interview.
97. Mark A. Willis, interview by author, tape recording, New York City, New York, March 8, 2001.
98. Michael Lappin, telephone interview by author, tape recording, New York, May 10, 2001.
99. Lappin, interview.
100. Lappin, interview.

101. Lappin, interview.
102. Lappin, interview.
103. Lappin, interview.
104. Lappin, interview.
105. Crotty, interview.
106. Braconi, "In Re *In Rem*," 108–9.
107. Lappin, interview.
108. Willis, interview.
109. Paul Grogan, interview by author, Cambridge, Mass., May 4, 2001; Willis, interview.
110. Grogan, interview.
111. Grogan, interview; Brooks, interview; Marc Jahr to author, July 5, 2002.
112. Grogan, interview; Willis, interview.
113. Sandorf, interview.
114. Sandorf, interview; Grogan, interview.
115. Sandorf, interview.
116. Sandorf, interview.
117. Crotty, interview.
118. Frey, interview.
119. Frey, interview; U. S. House of Representatives, Hon. Jose E. Serrano of New York, "Tribute to Father Lloyd Springer," *Congressional Record Daily Digest*, 106th Cong., Monday, September 11, 2000; http://www.aafe.org/history.
120. Frey, interview.
121. Gigante believed that it was enough that his organization submitted its records to the IRS (which has never questioned his operations) and felt insulted that someone with his record of accomplishment would be subjected to such a request. Gigante, interview.
122. Michetti, interview.
123. Jack Newfield and Wayne Barrett, *City for Sale: Ed Koch and the Betrayal of New York* (New York: Harper & Row, 1988).
124. Crotty, Reminiscences, CUOHROC, 71–33; Grogan, interview.
125. Willis, interview.
126. Crotty, interview; Crotty, Reminiscences, CUOHROC, 72; Koch, interview.
127. Crotty, interview; Koch, interview; Crotty, Reminiscences, CUOHROC, 72.
128. Paul S. Grogan and Tony Proscio, *Comeback Cities: A Blueprint for Urban Neighborhood Revival* (Boulder, Colo.: Westview Press, 2000), 91.
129. Grogan, interview; Sandorf, interview.
130. Grogan, interview.
131. Sandorf, interview; Grogan and Proscio, *Comeback Cities*, 92.
132. Grogan and Proscio, *Comeback Cities*, 92.
133. Crotty, interview; Michetti, interview.
134. The Partnership reported that buyer income for its two-family homes in Melrose and Hunt's Point was $30,400 and $33,000, respectively, and for single-family houses at Salters Square in East Crotona Park from $34,700 to $42,000. These figures may be averages. New York City Housing Partnership, *Building Homes, Not Just Housing* (New York: New York City Housing Partnership, 1992), 10; Rachelle Garbarine, "South Bronx Sees Revival Causing Shift in Housing," *New York Times*, December 26, 1997.
135. Orlebeke, *New Life*, 42–48.
136. Orlebeke, *New Life*, 67–68, 76–77, 89–91.
137. Orlebeke, *New Life*, 98–99.

138. Orlebeke, *New Life*, 54; Crotty, interview.
139. Orlebeke, *New Life*, 139.
140. Orlebeke, *New Life*, 125; Grogan, interview.
141. Frank Braconi and Kristin Morse, *A Preliminary Assessment of the Community Redevelopment in the South Bronx* (New York: Citizens Housing and Planning Council, January 1998), 8; Crotty, interview; Orlebeke, *New Life*, 142, 145–46.
142. Samuel Freedman, *Upon This Rock: The Miracles of a Black Church* (New York: HarperCollins, 1993), 316–17.
143. Freedman, *Upon This Rock*, 323–26.
144. Crotty, Reminiscences, CUOHROC, 165.
145. Freedman, *Upon This Rock*, 333.
146. Freedman, *Upon This Rock*, 334.
147. Freedman, *Upon This Rock*, 319.
148. Freedman, *Upon This Rock*, 335–38.
149. Freedman, *Upon This Rock*, 339.
150. Meile Rockefeller, "Land Use, Housing, and Community Development in New York City, Melrose Court, Part A," Case Study, New York University School of Law, 6, 9.
151. Rockefeller, "Land Use, Housing, and Community Development," 5.
152. Koch, interview.
153. Jim Rooney, *Organizing the South Bronx* (Albany: State University of New York Press, 1995), 141, 146, 168.
154. Manuel Colon and Bert Bennett to Abraham Biderman, August 29, 1989, in Rockefeller, "Land Use, Housing, and Community Development," App. 11.
155. Rooney, *Organizing*, 179–80.
156. Rooney, *Organizing*, 180–81, 184–85.
157. Tom Jones, William Pettus, Michael Pyatok, *Good Neighbors: Affordable Family Housing* (Melbourne, Australia: Images Publishing Group, 1997), 188–89.
158. Rooney, *Organizing*, 190–91.
159. Lee Stuart, telephone interviews by author, Bronx, New York, July 31, 2001, August 5, 2002. For an authoritative summary of the South Bronx Churches Nehemiah program, see Lee Stuart, "'Come, Let Us Rebuild the Walls of Jerusalem': Broad-Based Organizing in the South Bronx," in *Signs of Hope in the City*, ed. Robert D. Carle and Louis A. DeCaro Jr. (Valley Forge, Penn.: Judson Press, 1999), 159–69.
160. Lee Stuart, "Redefining the Public Sphere: South Bronx Churches and Education Reform," in *Signs of Hope*, ed. Carle and DeCaro Jr., 170–82.
161. Xavier De Souza Briggs, Anita Miller, and John Shapiro, "Planning for Community Building: CCRP (Comprehensive Community Revitalization Program) in the South Bronx," *Planners' Casebook* 17 (Winter 1996), 1–6.
162. Miller, interview.
163. Juan Rodriguez, interview by author, May 23, 1995.
164. Bronx crime statistics from the New York Police Department, courtesy of Jill Jonnes. Clifford Krauss, "Murder Rate Plunges in New York City: A 25-Year Low in First Half This Year," *New York Times*, July 8, 1995.
165. Clifford J. Levy, "Walking the Beat, the Police Find Many Allies on the Street," *New York Times*, April 4, 1993; Fox Butterfield, "Many Cities in U.S. Show Sharp Drop in Homicide Rate," *New York Times*, August 13, 1995; Kevin Flynn, "Behind the Success Story, a Vulnerable Police Force," *New York Times*, November 25, 2000.

166. Fox Butterfield, "Reason for Dramatic Drop in Crime Puzzles the Experts," *New York Times*, March 29, 1998; Bernard E. Harcourt, *The Illusion of Order: The False Promise of Broken Windows Policing* (Cambridge, Mass.: Harvard University Press, 2001).

167. Braconi and Morse, *Preliminary Assessment*, 7–10, 14. Housing statistics are for Bronx Community Board Districts, 1, 2, and 3. The number of total houses built was 3,302, of which 2,790 houses were developed under the New York Housing Partnership New Homes program and 512 by the South Bronx Churches Nehemiah program. For property values near homeowner projects, see Ingrid Gould Ellen, Michael Schill, Scott Sussin, and Amy Ellen Schwartz, "Building Homes, Reviving Neighborhoods: Spillovers from Subsidized Construction of Owner-Occupied Housing in New York City," *Journal of Housing Research* 12: 2 (2001), 185–216; James Q. Wilson and George Kelling, "Broken Windows," *The Atlantic Monthly*, March 1989, 29–38.

168. Braconi and Morse, *Preliminary Assessment*, 36–38, 44; Community District Profiles for Community Districts 1, 2, and 3, City Planning Department, New York, World Wide Web page http://www.nyc.gov/html/dcp/html/bx1(2, 3)lu.html.

169. Jim Yardley, "Second Look at South Bronx's Revival," *New York Times*, December 13, 1997.

Chapter 3

1. Robert H. Haas, interview by author, tape recording, Dorchester, Mass., July 14, 1998; Dorchester Bay Economic Development Corporation, *Annual Report, 1997*.

2. U. S. Bureau of the Census; City of Boston, Boston Redevelopment Authority, *Neighborhood Profile, 1988: Roxbury*; *Neighborhood Profile, 1988: North Dorchester*; *Neighborhood Profile, 1988: South Dorchester*.

3. Rolf Goetze and Mark R. Johnson, *Roxbury Planning District: 1990 Population and Housing Tables*; *North Dorchester Planning District: 1990 Population and Housing Tables*; *South Dorchester Planning District: 1990 Population and Housing Tables*; Boston Redevelopment Authority, Policy Development and Research Department, January, 1992.

4. Margaret C. O'Brien, *Diversity and Change in Boston's Neighborhoods: A Comparison of Demographic, Social, and Economic Characteristics of Population and Housing, 1970–1980*, Boston Redevelopment Authority, Policy Development and Research Department, October 1985, Table 105, 168; Boston Persistent Poverty Project, *Perspectives on Poverty in Boston's Black Community* (Boston: The Boston Foundation, 1992), 38; Boston Persistent Poverty Project, *A Status Report on Boston, Its Families and Children* (Boston: The Boston Foundation, 1995), 134.

5. Haas, interview; Ada Focer, interview by author, tape recording, Boston, November 5, 1998.

6. William J. Walczak, interview by author, tape recording, Dorchester, Mass., July 23, 1998.

7. J. Anthony Lukas, *Common Ground: A Turbulent Decade in the Lives of Three American Families* (New York: Alfred A. Knopf, 1985).

8. Haas, interview.

9. Walczak, interview.

10. Mel King, *Chain of Change: Struggles for Black Community Development* (Boston: South End Press, 1981); John H. Mollenkopf, *The Contested City* (Princeton, N.J.: Princeton University Press, 1983); Robert Whittlesey, interview by author, tape recording, Cambridge, Mass., September 30, 1998; Greater Boston Community Development, Inc., *A Decade of Housing Services: 1970–1980* (Boston: GBCD, 1980).

11. Kenneth D. Wade, interview by author, tape recording, Boston, July 27, 1998.

12. Charlotte Kahn, interview by author, tape recording, Boston, July 17, 1998.

13. Walczak, interview.

14. Focer, interview.

15. William H. Jones, telephone interview by author, tape recording, Chicago, Ill., October 27, 1998.

16. Kimberly Blanton, "New Life in Codman Square," *Boston Globe*, March 26, 1995.

17. The agencies are the Community Development Finance Corporation (CDFC)—said to be the first state agency in the United States to finance community development projects—and the Community Economic Development Assistance Corp. (CEDAC). The Community Enterprise Economic Development Program provides operating support to CDCs. King, *Chains of Change*, 201–2; Matthew Thall to author, August 3, 2002; Langley Keyes, telephone communication to author, August 9, 2002. The author is grateful to Matthew Thall for bringing King's breakfast meetings to his attention.

18. Paul Grogan, interview by author, tape recording, Cambridge, Mass., October 19, 1998.

19. William Edgerly, interview by author, tape recording, Cambridge, Mass., November 10, 1998.

20. Grogan, interview.

21. Grogan, interview.

22. Whittlesey, interview.

23. Patrick E. Clancy, telephone interview by author, tape recording, Philadelphia, November 24, 1998.

24. Grogan, interview.

25. Boston Housing Partnership, Inc., "Request for Proposals," August 18, 1983; Harold Nassau, Metropolitan Boston Housing Partnership, telephone interview by author, Boston, November 5, 1998.

26. Katharine E. Bachman, interview by author, tape recording, Boston, November 17, 1998.

27. Bachman, interview; James P. Luckett, interview by author, tape recording, Cambridge, Mass., November 9, 1998.

28. Luckett, interview.

29. Luckett, interview.

30. Boston Redevelopment Authority, Neighborhood Planning Program, *Dorchester Uphams Corner: District Profile and Proposed 1979–1981 Neighborhood Improvement Program* (Boston: 1979), cited in Peter Medoff and Holly Sklar, *Streets of Hope: The Fall and Rise of an Urban Neighborhood* (Boston: South End Press, 1994), 32.

31. The following account is drawn from Medoff and Sklar, *Streets of Hope.*

32. Medoff and Sklar, *Streets of Hope*, 124–5.

33. Medoff and Sklar, *Streets of Hope*, 140.

34. Luckett, interview.

35. Except where noted, the following account of the Boston Rehabilitation Project and the Granite Properties is drawn from Hillel Levine and Lawrence Harmon, *Death of an American Jewish Community—A Tragedy of Good Intentions* (New York: Free Press, 1992) and Kay Gibbs, "Slumming It: How Millions Were Spent to Bring Drugs and Blight to Grove Hall," *Boston Observer* 4:3 (March 1985). The author acknowledges Lew Finfer for sharing the latter reference.

36. Levine and Harmon, *Death of an American Jewish Community*, 120.

37. Eleanor G. White, telephone interview by author, Boston, November 19, 1998. Whittlesey, interview; BHP II Limited Partnership Confidential Private Offering Memorandum, June 19, 1987, 93–94.

38. Luckett, interview.

39. Whittlesey, interview; BHP II Limited Partnership Confidential Private Offering Memorandum, June 19, 1987; Bachman, interview.

40. Sally Williams, telephone interview by author, tape recording, Dorchester, Mass., December 3, 1998.

41. Williams, interview.

42. James Ferris, interview by author, Dorchester, Mass., May 1, 1995.

43. Ferris, interview.

44. White, interview.

45. White, interview.

46. Ferris, interview; White, interview.

47. Bachman, interview.

48. Focer, interview.

49. Jones, interview.

50. Jones, interview.

51. Jones, interview.

52. Jones interview; Bachman interview.

53. Blanton, "New Life in Codman Square."

54. Walczak, interview.

55. John Buntin, *A Community Responds: Boston Confronts an Upsurge of Youth Violence*, Case Program, Kennedy School of Government, Harvard University, 1998, 2. The following account is drawn from Buntin's study, unless otherwise noted.

56. Matthew Brelis, "A Victim of Murder Recalled by Father," *Boston Globe*, November 3, 1990.

57. Buntin, *A Community Responds*, .

58. Buntin, *A Community Responds*, 8.

59. Buntin, *A Community Responds*, 9.

60. Buntin, *A Community Responds*, 13, 14.

61. For Eugene Rivers and the collaboration between clergy and police in Boston, see also Kenneth L. Woodward, "The New Holy War," *Newsweek*, June 1, 1998, 26–29, and Paul F. Evans, "Cops, Crime, Clergy," ibid., 25.

62. Buntin, *A Community Responds*, 36.

63. Richard Carlson, Director of Valuations, Boston Assessing Department, January 1999.

64. Dudley Street Neighborhood Initiative, "From the Bottom Up: The Dudley Street Neighborhood Initiative Strategy for Sustainable Economic Development" (December 1997); Department of Neighborhood Development, Press Release, "Mayor Menino Announces HUD Approval of $10.5 Million for Dudley Square," September 21, 1998; City of Boston Department of Neighborhood Development, *2001 Abandoned Building Survey* (Boston: City of Boston, 2001).

65. Charles Grigsby, interview by author, tape recording, Boston, October 23, 1998; Department of Neighborhood Development, Housing Development Program Summary, April 1998; Stephanie Ebbert, "Report Shows a 40% Drop in Abandoned Sites in City," *Boston Globe*, October 8, 1998.

66. DSNI, "From the Bottom Up"; Gregory Watson, interview by author, tape recording, Roxbury, Mass., July 22, 1998.

67. Ronald F. Ferguson and Sara E. Stoutland, "Reconceiving the Community Development Field," in *Urban Problems and Community Development*, ed. Ronald F. Ferguson and William T. Dickens (Washington, D.C.: Brookings Institution Press, 1999), 33–75.

68. Joe Flatley, president and CEO, Massachusetts Housing Investment Corporation, testimony before the Housing and Community Opportunity Subcommittee of the House Financial Services Committee, May 22, 2001.

69. Alexander von Hoffman, *Fuel Lines for the Engine of Urban Revival: Neighborhoods, Community Development Corporations, and Financial Intermediaries* (Washington, D.C.: Fannie Mae Foundation, 2001).

Chapter 4

1. Earnest Gates, interview by author, tape recording, Chicago, May 27, 1999.

2. Carl Sandburg, "Chicago" in *Chicago Poems* (New York: Henry Holt, 1916).

3. William Cronon, *Nature's Metropolis: Chicago and the Great West* (New York: W. W. Norton, 1991).

4. Nicholas Lemann, *The Promised Land: The Great Black Migration and How It Changed America* (New York: Knopf, 1991); population figures derived from U.S. Census by Arnold R. Hirsch, *Making the Second Ghetto, Race and Housing in Chicago, 1940–1960* (New York: Cambridge University Press, 1983), 17.

5. Allan H. Spear, *Black Chicago; the Making of a Negro Ghetto, 1890–1920* (Chicago: University of Chicago Press, 1967); St. Clair Drake and Horace Cayton, *Black Metropolis: A Study of Life in a Northern City*, rev. ed. (New York: Harper & Row, 1962).

6. William M. Tuttle Jr., *Race Riot: Chicago in the Red Summer of 1919* (New York: Atheneum, 1980), 98; Spear, *Black Chicago*, 78–79.

7. Harold M. Mayer and Richard C. Wade, *Chicago: Growth of a Metropolis* (Chicago: University of Chicago Press, 1969), 445.

8. Mayer and Wade, *Chicago*, 382–86; Hirsch, *Making the Second Ghetto*, 259.

9. Wendell Campbell Associates, Inc. and Applied Real Estate Analysis, *Mid-South Strategic Development Plan: Restoring Bronzeville* (Chicago: City of Chicago Department of Planning and Development and the Mid-South Planning Group, September 1993), 21.

10. Chicago Fact Book Consortium, eds., *Local Community Fact Book Chicago Metropolitan Area* (Chicago: University of Illinois, 1995), 123–24, 130–31.

11. Wendell Campbell Associates, *Mid-South Strategic Development Plan*, 30.

12. Sokoni Karanja, interview by author, Chicago, April 14, 1998.

13. Karanja, interview.

14. Karanja, interview.

15. Timothy Samuelson, telephone interview by author, Chicago, February 23, 2000.

16. Samuelson, interview.

17. [Timothy Samuelson] Commission on Chicago Landmarks, *Black Metropolis Historic District* (Chicago: Chicago Department of Planning and Development, 1994), 3, 35–36.

18. [Samuelson], *Black Metropolis Historic District*, 5–6.
19. [Samuelson], *Black Metropolis Historic District*, 9–14.
20. [Samuelson], *Black Metropolis Historic District*, 15–18.
21. Samuelson, interview.
22. Samuelson, interview.
23. Samuelson, interview.
24. Brian J. Berry, "Islands of Renewal in Seas of Decay," in *The New Urban Reality*, ed. Paul E. Peterson (Washington, D.C.: The Brookings Institution, 1985), 69–96.
25. Berry, "Islands of Renewal," 94; Elvin K. Wyly and Daniel J. Hammel, "Islands of Decay in Seas of Renewal: Housing Policy and the Resurgence of Gentrification, " in *Housing Policy Debate* 10:4 (1999), 711–71; Brian J. L. Berry, "Comment," *Housing Policy Debate* 10:4 (1999), 783–88; Kathryn P. Nelson, *Gentrification and Distressed Cities: An Assessment of Trends in Intrametropolitan Migration* (Madison: University of Wisconsin Press, 1988).
26. Mike Royko, quoted in Gerald D. Suttles, *The Man-Made City: The Land-Use Confidence Game in Chicago* (Chicago: University of Chicago Press, 1990), 232–33.
27. Kevin Jackson, interview by author, Chicago, April 14, 1998.
28. Cheryl Jenkins Richardson, "Historic Gap Fills in the Blanks," *Chicago Sun-Times*, Homelife section, September 13, 1992; Leroy E. Kennedy, interview by author, tape recording, Chicago, May 26, 1999; Leonard McGee, interview by author, Chicago, May 26, 1999.
29. Pamela Sherrod, "Urban Renewal: Pioneering Spirit Turning Gap Neighborhood Around," *Chicago Tribune*, August 30, 1992; Cornelius Goodwin, interview by author, Chicago, May 26, 1999.
30. Goodwin, interview.
31. Goodwin, interview.
32. Goodwin, interview.
33. Goodwin, interview; McGee, interview.
34. McGee, interview; Samuelson, interview.
35. Phillip Johnson, interview by author, Chicago, March 7, 2000.
36. Peter Bynoe, telephone interview with author, Chicago, April 11, 2000. The history of the decision to keep the White Sox baseball team in Chicago, build a new stadium, and build houses to replace those demolished by the project can be traced in various articles that appeared in the *Chicago Tribune* from May through December 1988. See, for example, John Kass and Kerry Luft, "Sox Neighbors Agree to Stadium Deal Relocation Set to Begin in October," *Chicago Tribune*, August 4, 1988.
37. Lois Wille, *At Home in the Loop: How Clout and Community Built Chicago's Dearborn Park* (Carbondale: Southern Illinois University Press, 1997), 1–10, (quotation) 9.
38. Wille, *At Home in the Loop*, 64.
39. Wille, *At Home in the Loop*, 172.
40. Larry Mayer, telephone interview by author, Boca Raton, Fla., May 9, 2000.
41. McGee, interview; Karanja, interview; (8,000 visitors) Stephen Rynkiewicz, "Urban Parade of Homes Shows Off Chicago Style," *Chicago Sun-Times*, January 29, 1993; Richardson, "Historic Gap Fills in the Blanks"; Judy Moore, "Homes on the March; Parade Aims for Young Couples Committed to City," *Chicago Sun-Times*, September 4, 1992.

42. For an academic's amusing observations of how the development game is played in the Windy City, see Suttles, *The Man-Made City*.

43. Kennedy, interview; Leonard McGee, telephone interview by author, May 12, 2000.

44. Kennedy, interview; Campbell Associates, Inc., *Mid-South Strategic Development Plan*.

45. Campbell Associates, *Mid-South Strategic Development Plan*.

46. David E. Baker, interview by author, tape recording, Chicago, April 21, 2000; Kennedy, interview.

47. Baker, interview.

48. Jane Gross, "Trinity College Leads Effort to Create Hartford Renewal," *New York Times*, April 14, 1997; David Holmstrom, "An Aloof University Learns How to Be a Good Neighbor," *Christian Science Monitor*, September 11, 1997; http://www.oup.org.

49. Baker, interview; Kennedy, interview.

50. Pat Dowell-Cerasoli, interview by author, Chicago, April 14, 1998.

51. "9 Bronzeville Sites to Get Landmark Status," *Chicago Tribune*, August 27, 1998; "Legislators Finagle Funds for ROTC School," *Chicago Tribune*, October 7, 1999; City of Chicago Department of Planning and Development, "Bronzeville Community Development Highlights," brochure, 1998.

52. Jeanette Almada, "Filling the Gap—Prices Affordable in Growing Douglas Neighborhood," *Chicago Tribune*, October 4, 1998; Karanja, interview; McGee, interview, May 26, 1999; Mid-South Planning and Development Commission, "Third Annual Bronzeville Historic House Tour, June 29, 1997," brochure, 6.

53. Karanja, interview.

54. Jeanette Almada, "Communities. At Home in Douglas," *Chicago Tribune*, September 28, 1998; Jeanette Almada, "Luxury Returns to 44th & King; Upscale Buyers Lured by History, Area's Possibility," *Chicago Tribune*, June 13, 1998.

55. Dorothy Tillman, interview by author, tape recording, Chicago, May 28, 1999.

56. "Lord of the Vacant Lots," *Chicago Tribune*, June 25, 1998; Tillman, interview; Raoul V. Mowatt, "Bronzeville Plan Features Homes by African-American Builders," *Chicago Tribune*, February 26, 2000.

57. Andrew Martin, "Blues District Plan Off-Key, Critics Say," *Chicago Tribune*, February 22, 1998; Dowell-Cerasoli, interview; Tillman, interview.

58. Dowell-Cerasoli, interview; Martin, "Blues District Plan Off-Key"; Tillman, interview.

59. Tillman, interview; Howard Reich, "Breaking Old Ground Rising Where Bronzeville's Regal Once Reigned, Lou Rawls' Namesake Theater Is . . . ," *Chicago Tribune*, April 7, 1999; Andrew Martin, "At Long Last, Lou Rawls Center Gets Off Ground," *Chicago Tribune*, May 14, 1998; Quincy Jones, *Q: The Autobiography of Quincy Jones* (New York: Doubleday, 2001), 13.

60. Martin, "Blues District Plan Off-Key."

61. Patrick T. Reardon, "Can Bronzeville Reclaim Its Soul? After Redevelopment, The Name May Be All That's Left of the Community's Rich Heritage," *Chicago Tribune*, May 21, 2000; Celeste Garrett and Kevin Lynch, "Center Delay Pits Rawls, Tillman—Singer Retreats from Support of Bronzeville Site," *Chicago Tribune*, July 20, 2001.

62. John Carpenter, "1.5 Billion Public Housing Deal Is Signed," *Chicago Sun-Times*, February 6, 2000; Lynn Sweet, "CHA Negotiations Marked by Distrust," *Chicago Sun-Times*, February 6, 2000.

63. Hirsch, *Making the Second Ghetto*, 234–38; Arnold R. Hirsch, "Massive Resistance in the Urban North: Trumbull Park, Chicago, 1953–1966," *Journal of Urban History* 82:2 (September 1995), 522–50.

64. Devereaux Bowly, *The Poorhouse: Subsidized Housing in Chicago, 1895–1976* (Carbondale and Edwardsville: Southern Illinois University Press, 1978).

65. Bowly, *The Poorhouse*, 122, 123, 132; Suttles, *The Man-Made City*, 62, 66, 134–37, 197–98; Gary Rivlin, *Fire on the Prairie: Chicago's Harold Washington and the Politics of Race* (New York: Henry Holt, 1992), 71–74, 216, 238.

66. Suttles, *The Man-Made City*, 63–65.

67. For a unique close-up account of life in Robert Taylor Homes, see Sudhir Alladi Venkatesh, *American Project: The Rise and Fall of a Modern Ghetto* (Cambridge, Mass.: Harvard University Press, 2000).

68. Connie Jones, interview with author, Chicago, April 20, 2000.

69. Patricia Titus, interview by author, Chicago, April 20, 2000. According to Tyrone Galtney (interview, Chicago, April 20, 2000), however, the harsh conditions at Robert Taylor Homes were exaggerated.

70. Joseph Shuldiner, interview by author, Chicago, April 15, 1998.

71. Melita Marie Garza and Gary Washburn, "Jackson Leaving Top Post at CHA," *Chicago Tribune*, May 4, 2000; Sarah Downey and John McCormick, "Razing the Vertical Ghettos," *Newsweek*, May 15, 2000; Francine Washington, interview by author, Chicago, May 2, 2000.

72. From 1993 to 2001, HUD awarded 165 Revitalization Grants totaling more than $4.5 billion to 146 Housing Authorities to demolish more than 115,000 severely distressed public housing units and develop close to 66,000 better quality dwellings. http://www.hud.gov/offices/pih/programs/ph/hope6/about/, content updated April 3, 2002; Phillip Jackson, interview by author, tape recording, Chicago, April 20, 2000.

73. Garza and Washburn, "Jackson Leaving Top Post"; Curtis Lawrence and Fran Spielman, "Alderman Chosen as New CHA Chief," *Chicago Tribune*, May 4, 2000; Melita Marie Garza and Andrew Zajac, "Overhaul of CHA Hinges on Investors," *Chicago Tribune*, February 12, 2000; Melita Marie Garza, "CHA Finance Chief Quits as Bond Sale Nears," *Chicago Tribune*, April 22, 2000; Gary Washburn, "New Top Exec Takes CHA Reins," *Chicago Tribune*, May 5, 2000.

74. Curtis Lawrence, "The Peterson Principle," *Chicago Sun-Times*, March 26, 2001.

75. The other part of the Gautreaux decision that ordered the building of new public housing units at scattered sites in Chicago's non-black neighborhoods moved even more slowly than the voucher program. Kate N. Grossman, "Neighborhoods Fear Influx of Poor Renters," *Chicago Sun-Times*, March 27, 2001; Robin Snyderman and Steven D. Dailey II, *Public Housing in the Public Interest: Examining the Chicago Housing Authority's Relocation Efforts* (Chicago: Metropolitan Planning Council, February 2002); Flynn McRoberts, "Gautreaux Housing Program Nears End," *Chicago Tribune*, January 12, 1996.

76. "CHA's Bold 'Plan for Transformation' Seeks to Improve Living Conditions for Residents," *Chicago Housing Authority Times*, December 1999, 1, 4; Kate N. Grossman and Curtis Lawrence, "CHA's Big Gamble," *Chicago Sun-Times* March 25, 2001; Kate N. Grossman, "CHA 'fesses Up: It Lacks Funds for Building Plan," *Chicago Sun-Times*, December 31, 2001.

77. Chicago Fact Book Consortium, *Local Community Fact Book*, 103–6.

78. Gates, interview.
79. Gates, interview.
80. John McCarron and Terry Wilson, "West Side Gets Look at Stadium Plan," *Chicago Tribune*, April 22, 1987.
81. John McCarron and Terry Wilson, "Bears Stadium Proposal Splitting Up West Side," *Chicago Tribune*, April 16, 1987.
82. Terry Wilson, "West Side Residents Using a Blitz against Bears Stadium Plan," *Chicago Tribune*, April 14, 1987; Mary Schmich, "Land War Turns to Mutual Respect," *Chicago Tribune*, June 24, 1992; Gates, interview.
83. Wilma Ward, telephone interview by author, Chicago, April 28, 2000; Gates, interview.
84. Ward, interview; Gates, interview; John McCarron, "Slum Owner's Brother Tries to Sack Bears Stadium," *Chicago Tribune*, August 29, 1988.
85. Gates, interview; Ward, interview.
86. McCarron, "Slum Owner's Brother"; Gates, interview.
87. John McCarron, "Stadium Moguls Go One-on-One but It's No Playground Battle for Wirtz and McCaskey," *Chicago Tribune*, October 16, 1988; John McCarron, "Deadlock Stifles All West Side Stadium Plans," November 20, 1988; James Strong, "Daley Cool to a Bears-Only Stadium," *Chicago Tribune*, August 10, 1989.
88. John McCarron, "Daley Blows a Whistle on Plans by Hawks, Bulls for New Arena," Chicago Tribune, May 23, 1989.
89. Mike Kiley and John McCarron, "Wirtz Blames City for Impasse over Arena," *Chicago Tribune*, April 6, 1990.
90. Ben Joravsky, "Reinsdorf's Secret Weapon," *Chicago Reader*, September 20, 1996.
91. Ward, interview; Joravsky, "Reinsdorf's Secret Weapon;" Gates, interview.
92. Howard Pizer, telephone interview by author, Chicago, April 21, 2000; Joravsky, "Reinsdorf's Secret Weapon"; Gates, interview.
93. Gates, interview.
94. Gates, interview; Joravsky, "Reinsdorf's Secret Weapon."
95. Gates, interview; Joravsky, "Reinsdorf's Secret Weapon."
96. Pizer, interview.
97. Gates, interview.
98. Joravsky, "Reinsdorf's Secret Weapon."
99. Joravsky, "Reinsdorf's Secret Weapon"; Pizer, interview.
100. Pizer, interview.
101. Joravsky, "Reinsdorf's Secret Weapon."
102. Pizer, interview; Gates, interview; Joravsky, "Reinsdorf's Secret Weapon."
103. Gates, interview; Ron Grossman and Flynn McRoberts, "Near West Side Rebounds Like Its Bullish Neighbors, Community Thriving," *Chicago Tribune*, June 7, 1998.
104. Pizer, interview.
105. Grossman and McRoberts, "Near West Side Rebounds"; Gates, interview.
106. Patrick Barry, *Rebuilding the Walls: A Nuts and Bolts Guide to the Community Development Methods of Bethel New Life, Inc. in Chicago* (Chicago: Bethel New Life, Inc., 1989); Mary Nelson, interview by author, Chicago, April 16, 1998; Bethel New Life, Inc., miscellaneous documents and brochures.
107. Richard Townsell, interview by author, Chicago, April 16, 1998.
108. http://www.lcdc.net/, June 10, 2002; Lawndale Christian Development Corporation, *You're Home in North Lawndale*, n.d.; LCDC Fact Sheet, 1998.

109. The Resurrection Project, Fact Sheet, March 26, 1998; The Resurrection Project, Annual Report, 1996–1997; Susana Vasquez, "The Mexican Folkloric Dance Company of Chicago," *Nueva Vida* 18 (Fall 1998), 3; http://www.resurrectionproject.org, June 11, 2002.

110. David Skidmore, "Chicago Parish Providing Signs of Hope on Urban Landscape," *Episcopal News Service*, October 15, 2001 (http://www.episcopalchurch.org/ens/2001-207.html); Richard Tolliver, interview by author, Chicago, April 14, 1998; Ron Stodghill, "Bringing Hope Back to the 'Hood," *Business Week*, August 19, 1996, 70–73; David Broder, opinion column, *Washington Post*, April 23, 1997.

111. John Easton, "Here Goes the Neighborhood," *University of Chicago Magazine* 92:5 (June 2000); William H. Jones, interview by author, Chicago, April 15, 1998; Fund for Community Redevelopment and Revitalization, Fact Sheet, n.d.; Jeanette Almada, "North Kenwood/Oakland Enjoying an Influx of the Middle Class," *ChicagoTribune*, April 26, 1998.

112. Chicago Rehab Network, *Network Builder*, Fall–Winter 1997 (Twentieth Anniversary Issue); http://www.chicagorehab.org; Jackson, interview.

113. Neighborhood Housing Services of Chicago (NHSC), "Nonprofit Group Celebrates 25 Years and $1 Billion in Chicago Neighborhood Investments," press release, March 2000; NHSC, "Fact Sheet"; http://www.nhschicago.org, June 12, 2002; David Listokin, Elvin K. Wly, Larry Keating, Kristopher M. Rengert, and Barbara Listokin, *Making New Mortgage Markets: Case Studies of Institutions, Home Buyers, and Communities* (Washington, D.C.: Fannie Mae Foundation, 2000), 401–16; Bruce Gottschall, telephone interview by author, May 27, 1998.

114. Ronald Grzywinski, "The New Old-Fashioned Banking," *Harvard Business Review* 69:3 (May–June 1991), 87–98; David Osborne, "A Poverty Program That Works: Success Comes to South Shore, Chicago," *The New Republic* 200:19 (May 8 1989), 22–25; Richard P. Taub, *Community Capitalism* (Boston: Harvard Business School Press, 1988, 1992).

115. Grzywinski, "New Old-Fashioned Banking," 96.

116. Ronald Grzywinski, interview by author, Boston, April 6, 1998; Shorebank 1996 Annual Report; http://www.sbk.com/livesite/aboutssb/ab_misshistory.cfm, June 12, 2002.12, 2002.

Chapter 5

1. "Cousins Asks Developers to Duplicate East Lake," *Atlanta Business Chronicle*, December 8, 1997; Ellen Rand, "A Winning Strategy for Growth: Diversify, Maximize Value, Give Back to the Community," *Development Magazine*, Fall 1997; Monica K. Gummig, "Florida Developer Gathers Inspiration from Cousins," *Atlanta Business Chronicle*, October 5, 1998.

2. "Cousins Asks Developers," *Atlanta Business Chronicle*.

3. Gummig, "Florida Developer."

4. Frederick Allen, *Atlanta Rising* (Marietta, Ga.: Longstreet Press, 1996), 240.

5. Allen, *Atlanta Rising*, 238–39, 246; Melissa Turner, "Report Acknowledges 'many gifts,'" *Atlanta Journal and Constitution* (hereafter *AJC*), September 17, 1999; Melissa Turner, "Payne: We Made Mistakes," *AJC*, October 15, 1999; Melissa

Turner, "Billy Payne: Hero of the Hard Sell," Inside the '96 Olympics series, *AJC*, August 6, 2000.

6. Melissa Turner, "The Mayor and the Man," Inside the '96 Olympics series, *AJC*, August 7, 2000; Turner, "Billy Payne."

7. Jim Newton, "Olympic Bid: $1 Billion for Facilities," *AJC*, July 28, 1989.

8. Clarence N. Stone, *Regime Politics: Governing Atlanta, 1946–1988* (Lawrence: University Press of Kansas, 1989), 32, 63–65.

9. Allen, *Atlanta Rising*, passim; Stone, *Regime Politics*, 83–108.

10. Allen, *Atlanta Rising*, 220; Stone, *Regime Politics*, 108–34.

11. Elizabeth Kurylo, "Carter Plans Project to Aid City's Needy: 'All-Out Effort' to Use Volunteers in Tackling Various Social Issues," *AJC*, October 25, 1991; "Goal: Minimum Funds, Maximum Volunteers," *AJC*, October 25, 1991.

12. Douglas Greenwell, interview by author, tape recording, Atlanta, August 2, 2000.

13. Mark O'Connell, telephone interview by author, Atlanta, September 22, 2000; John Blake, "Carter: Atlanta Project Must Focus on Families," *AJC*, October 19, 1995.

14. Scott Bronstein, "A Pound of Despair: The Baby That Moved President Carter to Tears," *AJC*, October 26, 1991.

15. Douglas A. Blackmon, "Carter Hits the Streets for Solutions: Enormity of City's Woes Shows Need for Ongoing Effort, He Says," *AJC*, November 26, 1991.

16. Chet Fuller, "Carter Goes to the People for Atlanta Project Ideas: Starting to Focus 2-week-old Plan to Help Inner City," *AJC*, November 8, 1991.

17. Fuller, "Carter Goes to the People."

18. Chet Fuller, "A Guide to the Atlanta Project: Jimmy Carter's Newest Project Aims to Help Atlanta's Neediest," *AJC*, March 7, 1992.

19. O'Connell, interview.

20. Michael W. Giles, *Evaluation of the Atlanta Project, Part 2: Analysis and Findings* (Atlanta: Carter Collaboration Center, January 1995), 56; Chet Fuller, "Atlanta Project Attracting Big Donors," *AJC*, July 16, 1992; Gary Pomerantz, "The Atlanta Project: Five Years Later: Great Expectations, Humbling Reality," *AJC*, September 9, 1996; Peter Scott, "Service Groups Feel Threatened by Atlanta Project: Carter Clout Cited as Donations Fall," *AJC*, October 17, 1992.

21. Maria Saporta and Chet Fuller, "Carter Picks a Chief for City Project: Noted Civic Leader to Tackle Social Ills," *AJC*, November 12, 1991.

22. Saporta and Fuller, "Carter Picks a Chief"; Greenwell, interview.

23. Greenwell, interview; Fuller, "A Guide to the Atlanta Project."

24. Douglas A. Blackmon, "Crowd at Fair Shows Atlanta Project Is on the Move: 132 Groups Show Services Available for Poor Families," *AJC*, August 23, 1992.

25. Giles, *Evaluation, Part 2*, 30–32, Appendix A.

26. Giles, *Evaluation, Part 2*, (Appendix A) 67, 69, 70, 72; (Appendix B) 80, 90.

27. Giles, *Evaluation, Part 2*, 43–45.

28. Giles, *Evaluation, Part 2*, 41–42.

29. Frank S. Alexander, telephone interview by author, tape recording, Atlanta, September 25, 2000; Giles, *Evaluation, Part 2*, 36–38; Frank S. Alexander, "The Atlanta Project: Building Foundations through Initiatives in Housing," draft report, December 28, 1995 (author's copy courtesy of Frank S. Alexander).

30. Atlanta won this sizable award—$100 million in direct payments and an additional $150 million in tax incentives—from the Department of Housing and Urban Development, but as with the Atlanta Project, it has produced few enduring results.

31. Giles, *Evaluation, Part 2*, 34–36; Greenwell, interview.

32. Gary Pomerantz, "Atlanta Project Official Quits, Alleging Racism," *AJC*, September 17, 1992; Peter Scott, "Sweat Denies Ex-Adviser's Charge of Racism within Atlanta Project," *AJC*, October 21, 1992; Peter Scott, "Coordinator Criticizes Atlanta Project: Input from Blacks Called Insufficient," *AJC*, July 8, 1993.

33. Peter Scott, "Panel to Examine Charges against the Atlanta Project," *AJC*, July 9, 1993; Peter Scott, "Carter Wants More Black Execs in the Atlanta Project," *AJC*, July 14, 1993; Peter Scott, "King Center Exec Tapped for Atlanta Project Job," *AJC*, September 1, 1993.

34. Gary Pomerantz, "Dan Sweat: His Last Hurrah?" *AJC*, December 26, 1992; Hattie Dorsey, interview by author, tape recording, Atlanta, August 3, 2000.

35. Pomerantz, "Dan Sweat"; Alexander, interview.

36. Michael W. Giles, telephone interview by author, Atlanta, September 20, 2000.

37. Giles, *Evaluation, Part* 2; Jill Vejnoska, "Group Has Abandoned Mission, Report Finds," *AJC*, February 16, 1995; Jill Vejnoska, "Atlanta Project's Vision Dims: Internal Report Criticizes Group's Ability to Aid Poor," *AJC*, February 16, 1995.

38. Giles, *Evaluation, Part* 2, 23–26.

39. Vejnoska, "Group Has Abandoned Mission"; Patti Puckett, Richard Bono, and Jill Vejnoska, "Coordinators Hail Critique of Atlanta Project," *AJC*, February 16, 1995; John Blake, "Four Clusters Declare Independence; Carter Asks Others to Hold Off," *AJC*, September 21, 1995.

40. John Blake, "Carter: Atlanta Project Must Focus on Families," *AJC*, October 19, 1995; John Blake, "Atlanta Project Lowers Its Goals: Five Years Later: Effort to Help Poor May Have Tried to Do Too Much, Trims Budget for Streamlined Second Phase," *AJC*, August 27, 1996; Greenwell, interview.

41. Leon Eplan, interview by author, tape recording, Atlanta, August 1, 2000.

42. City of Atlanta, "An Olympic Development Program for Atlanta," report presented by Maynard Jackson, Mayor of the City of Atlanta, 99th Session of the International Olympic Committee, Barcelona, Spain, July 22, 1992; Alma E. Hill and Bert Roughton Jr., "New City Board Will Plan, Guide '96 Renovations," *AJC*, October 10, 1992.

43. Bert Roughton Jr., "No Agreement between Mayor, Aderhold on CODA Job," *AJC*, December 17, 1992; Alma E. Hill, "Jackson Picks Exec to Co-Chair CODA," *AJC*, December 29, 1992.

44. Bert Roughton Jr., "CODA President Stepping Down for New Games Job: Exit Raises Questions about City's Plans," May 11, 1993; Alma E. Hill, "Martin Mentioned as a 'Possibility' for CODA Post," May 15, 1993.

45. Clara Axam, interview by author, tape recording, Atlanta, August 1, 2000.

46. Clara Axam, interview; Randall Roark, interview by author, tape recording, Atlanta, August 2, 2000.

47. Axam, interview.

48. Axam, interview; Maria Saporta, "$6 Million Goal Met, CODA To Announce at Meeting Today," *AJC*, February 20, 1996; Lyle V. Harris, "Spruce-up Projects Progressing According to Plan, Officials Say," *AJC*, June 16, 1995.

49. Roark, interview; Alma E. Hill, "At CODA'S Helm, Axam Must Steer Neighborhoods through Revitalization," *AJC*, July 17, 1993; Harris, "Spruce-up Projects."

50. Roark, interview; Saporta, "$6 Million Goal Met"; Corporation for Olympic Development in Atlanta (hereafter CODA), *The Civic Trust: CODA Public Spaces Program* (Atlanta: CODA, 1996); CODA, *Master Development Program: Public Spaces and Olympic Ring Neighborhoods* (Atlanta: City of Atlanta De-

partment of Planning and Development, n.d.); CODA, Public Spaces Program, CODA projects plan map, 1996.

51. David A. Crane, telephone interview by author, tape recording, Tampa Bay, Fla., September 23, 2000; Robert Begle, interview by author, tape recording, Atlanta, August 3, 2000.

52. CODA, *Olympic Ring Neighborhoods Survey Summary Report* (Atlanta: CODA, September 1993).

53. City of Atlanta Department of Planning and Development and CODA, *Master Olympic Development Program for City of Atlanta* (Atlanta: City of Atlanta and CODA, October 1993); Alma E. Hill, "Neighborhood Plan Unveiled; Will Cost $220 Million," *AJC*, October 20, 1993; Alma E. Hill, "Despite Great Expectations for Redevelopment of Inner-City Neighborhoods, Not Much Improvement Has Been Made," *AJC*, June, 9, 1996.

54. Begle, interview.

55. Crane, interview; Alma E. Hill, "Communities Raise a Ruckus over CODA: Residents Question Revitalization Plan, Express Concern over Slum Designation," *AJC*, November 11, 1993; Begle, interview.

56. Hill, "Despite Great Expectations"; Crane, interview.

57. Roark, interview; Axam, interview; William McFarland, interview by author, tape recording, Atlanta, August 2, 2000. For a comprehensive list of neighborhood improvement projects in Atlanta's inner-city neighborhoods on the eve of the Olympic games, see Renee Kemp-Rotan, *Atlanta: Urban Renaissance* (Atlanta: City of Atlanta Department of Housing and Community Development, 1996).

58. Hill, "Despite Great Expectations"; http://www.atlanta-habitat.org. For the origins of Habitat for Humanity, see Millard Fuller and Diane Scott, *Love in the Mortar Joints* (Chicago: Follett Publishing, 1980) and Millard Fuller with Diane Scott, *No More Shacks* (Waco, Tex.: Word Books, 1986).

59. Estimates of Summerhill's population in 1990 vary. A writer for the *Atlanta Journal-Constitution* found fewer than 3,000 people in December 1990. A report done for the Summerhill Neighborhood Development Corporation and the City of Atlanta put the lowest population figure at 3,500. The city used census data to find 4,201 people in Summerhill, but as another report in 1993 explained, the boundaries used in this calculation covered a larger area than planners customarily used to define Summerhill. Quotation and population estimate, Paulette V. Walker, "Stadium Area Links Survival to Olympics," *AJC*, December 27, 1990; Urban Collage, Inc., Summerhill Prospectus (Atlanta: Summerhill Neighborhood Development Corporation, Atlanta Development Authority, and City of Atlanta, November 1997), 1; "Summerhill Urban Redevelopment Plan," approved by the Council of the City of Atlanta and by the Mayor of Atlanta, October 18, 1993, 3; Urban Land Institute, *Summerhill, Atlanta, Georgia: An Evaluation of Development and Redevelopment Strategies for Central Atlanta Progress, Sumerhill Neighborhood, Inc., and the City of Atlanta*. A Panel Advisory Services Report (Washington, D.C.: Urban Land Institute, 1991), 11–16.

60. Walker, "Stadium Area"; Douglas Dean, interview by author, tape recording, Atlanta, August 4, 2000.

61. Matt Kempner, "Summerhill Neighbors Fight for Financial Life," *AJC*, April 19, 1998.

62. Dean, interview; Urban Land Institute, *Summerhill*, 7–8.

63. Jim Newton, "Olympic Bid: $1 Billion for Facilities: New Stadium Is Part of Vast Building Plan," *AJC*, July 28, 1989; Lorri Denise Booker and Cynthia

Durcanin, "What Are the Risks? Leery Advocates Worry City's Poor Neighborhoods Will Be 1996's Big Losers," *AJC*, September 23, 1990; Bert Roughton Jr., "Fight Vowed over '96 Stadium Site," *AJC*, November 29, 1990; Walker, "Stadium Area."

64. Robert Lupton, telephone interview by author, Atlanta, October 4, 2000; Robert Lupton, "On Owning a Vision," *Urban Perspectives*, newsletter, Family Counseling Services Ministries, June 15, 1993.

65. Lupton, interview.

66. Melissa Turner, "Unrealized Dream—Summerhill's Olympic Rebirth Started with Visions of a Mixed-Income Community," *AJC*, January 14, 2001.

67. Michelle Hiskey, "SNDC Leader Doesn't Equate Profit, Reward," *AJC*, August 26, 1991; Turner, "Unrealized Dream"; Lupton, interview.

68. CODA, *Olympic Ring Neighborhoods Survey Summary Report*, 147–49; Michelle Hiskey, "Summerhill Moves Closer to Facelift for 1996 Games," *AJC*, August 26, 1994; Bert Roughton Jr. and Michelle Hiskey, "Olympic Dream in Danger?" *AJC*, April 5, 1992; Michelle Hiskey, "Residents Near Stadium Site Win Corporate Support for Renovation," *AJC*, January 7, 1993; Michelle Hiskey, "Much to Celebrate in Summerhill," *AJC*, June 20, 1992.

69. Kempner, "Summerhill Neighbors Fight for Financial Life"; Lupton, interview; Alma E. Hill, "Revitalization to Help Summerhill the Most," *AJC*, May 14, 1994.

70. Turner, "Unrealized Dream"; Lupton, interview; Ann Carrns, "Rebellious Summerhill's Plunge into Future," *Atlanta Business Chronicle*, August 5, 1996.

71. Turner, "Unrealized Dream."

72. Hiskey, "SNDC Leader"; Lupton, interview.

73. Kempner, "Summerhill Neighbors"; Turner, "Unrealized Dream"; (quotation) Robert Lupton, "Reflections on a Done Deal," *Urban Perspectives*, October 20, 1992.

74. Maria Saporta, "Inn at Stadium Being Converted to Student Dorm," *AJC*, August 20, 1992; Carrns, "Rebellious Summerhill's Plunge"; Lupton, "Reflections on a Done Deal."

75. Carrns, "Rebellious Summerhill's Plunge"; Robert Lupton, "A Deal Done Well," *Urban Perspectives*, February 15, 1994.

76. Lyle V. Harris, "City Approves Funds to Build Housing for Lease," *AJC*, March 19, 1996; Alma E. Hill, "Developers Scale Back Project," *AJC*, January 12, 1996; Turner, "Unrealized Dream"; Alma E. Hill, "Redevelopment of Inner City Falling Short," *AJC*, June 9, 1996.

77. Turner, "Unrealized Dream"; Melissa Turner, "Summerhill," draft, December 2000; Kempner, "Summerhill Neighbors."

78. Turner, "Summerhill"; Alma E. Hill, "Development Decisions Are Power Struggle," June 9, 1996; Carrns, "Rebellious Summerhill's Plunge."

79. Turner, "Unrealized Dream."

80. Kempner, "Summerhill Neighbors."

81. Turner, "Unrealized Dream"; Dean, interview.

82. Turner, "Unrealized Dream."

83. Turner, "Unrealized Dream."

84. The following account of the history of Techwood Homes is drawn from Larry Keating and Carol Flores, "Sixty and Out: Techwood Homes Transformed by Enemies and Friends," *Journal of Urban History* 26:3 (March 2000), 275–311; and Carol A. Flores, "US Public Housing in the 1930s: The First Projects in Atlanta, Georgia," *Planning Perspectives* 9:4 (October 1994), 405–30.

85. Keating and Flores, "Sixty and Out," 284–85; Allen, *Atlanta Rising*, 186.

86. Flores, "US Public Housing," 424; Keating and Flores, "Sixty and Out," 286–87.

87. Keating and Flores, "Sixty and Out," 287–91, (quotation) 289.

88. Larry Keating, "Redeveloping Public Housing: Relearning Urban Renewal's Immutable Lessons," *Journal of the American Planning Association* 66:4 (Autumn 2000); Keating and Flores, "Sixty and Out," 290–95.

89. Keating and Flores, "Sixty and Out," 296.

90. Keating and Flores, "Sixty and Out," 297; Allen, *Atlanta Rising*, 247.

91. Renée Lewis Glover, interview by author, tape recording, Atlanta, August 2, 2000.

92. Roark, interview; Keating and Flores, "Sixty and Out," 297.

93. Glover, interview.

94. Keating and Flores, "Sixty and Out," 299.

95. Keating and Flores, "Sixty and Out," 295; Karen Huebner, telephone interview by author, Atlanta, November 30, 2000.

96. Keating and Flores, "Sixty and Out," 299–300; Glover, interview; Huebner, interview.

97. Atlanta Housing Authority, www.atlantahousingauth.org, Property Profiles, September 2000; Richard White, public relations officer, Atlanta Housing Authority, private communication.

98. Huebner, interview.

99. H. M. Cauley, "East Lake: Atlanta Community Working to Make the Future Brighter," *AJC*, April 10, 1994; Joe Strauss, "Restoring East Lake's Splendor: Cousins Wants to Turn Bobby Jones' Old Course into a Living Memorial," June 11, 1994.

100. Douglas A. Blackmon, "East Lake: Can Gulf Between Two Worlds Be Bridged?" *AJC*, December 22, 1991.

101. Blackmon, "East Lake."

102. Blackmon, "East Lake."

103. Lyle V. Harris, "$33.5 Million for East Lake Meadows," *AJC*, October 29, 1992.

104. Blackmon, "East Lake"; Tom McCollister, "East Lake Will Be Preserved," *AJC*, November 16, 1993.

105. Ernest Holsendolph, "Cousins Spends Life Building a Reputation for Integrity," *AJC*, July 23, 1995; Tammy Joyner, "Atlanta's Cousins a Towering Success," *AJC*, October 6, 1998; Allen, *Atlanta Rising*, 154–55, 169–72, 196–97.

106. Dan Chapman, "A Ruffling of Feathers: South Georgia's Quail Plantations, Playgrounds for Atlanta's Rich, Are Bracing against Environmentalists and Outsiders," *AJC*, June 23, 2000.

107. Joe Strauss, "Restoring East Lake's Splendor," *AJC*, June 11, 1994; Tom McCollister, "Cousins Buys East Lake Country Club, Plans Renovation," *AJC*, November 16, 1993; McCollister, "East Lake Will Be Preserved"; Mary Louise Kelly, "Fraud Alleged in East Lake Golf Club Suit," *AJC*, January 24, 1994.

108. Maria Saporta, "Cousins Dreams of Revitalizing East Lake Area," *AJC*, November 15, 1995; S. A. Reid and Glenn Sheeley, "Bringing Golf to Public Housing," *AJC*, June 18, 1995; Gregory J. Giornelli, interview by author, Atlanta, January 3, 2001.

109. Giornelli, interview.

110. Macon Morehouse, "Mixed-Income Housing Proposed for East Lake Meadows," *AJC*, June 1, 1995; Darryl Fears and Charmagne Helton, "East Lake Redevelopment: 'Where Are We Going?'" *AJC*, June 2, 1995.

111. S. A. Reid, "East Lake Parties Near Agreement on Redelopment Project," *AJC*,

August 27, 1995; S. A. Reid, "East Lake Pact: A 'Great Step Forward,'" *AJC*, January 26, 1996.

112. Reid, "East Lake Pact."

113. Giornelli, interview.

114. Macon Morehouse, "Revised Plan Pushed for East Lake," *AJC*, June 14, 1995; Reid, "East Lake Parties Near Agreement"; Reid, "East Lake Pact"; Alexander, interview; Giornelli, interview.

115. Fears and Helton, "East Lake Redevelopment"; Alexander, interview.

116. Giornelli, interview; Morehouse, "Revised Plan"; Hollis R. Towns, "Rebuilding Dispute: East Lake Residents Seek to Oust Developers," *AJC*, March 5, 1998.

117. Fears and Helton, "East Lake Redevelopment"; Alexander, interview; Giornelli, interview.

118. Towns, "Rebuilding Dispute"; Hollis R. Towns, "East Lake Residents Sue Housing Agency," *AJC*, October 30, 1998; Hollis R. Towns, "East Lake Residents Dealt Legal Setback," *AJC*, December 17, 1998.

119. Alexander, interview.

120. Alexander, interview; Giornelli, interview; Hollis R. Towns, "East Lake's Unique Experiment," *AJC*, September 15, 1997.

121. Robert Lupton, interview by author, Atlanta, January 3, 2001; Jane J. Stratigos, telephone interview by author, Atlanta, September 12, 2000 and interview by author, Atlanta, January 3, 2001; Giornelli, interview.

122. Stratigos, interviews; Gironelli, interview; (quotation) Lorne Rubenstein, "East Lake Making 'Golf with a Purpose' Work," *Golfweb*, April 2, 1996; http://services.golfweb.com.

123. Giornelli, interview; Stratigos, interviews.

124. Cynthia Tucker, "The Villages of East Lake: Hope from the Ground Up," *AJC*, October 17, 1999.

125. Lupton, interview, January 3, 2001; Tucker, "Villages of East Lake."

126. Tucker, "Villages of East Lake."

127. Tucker, "Villages of East Lake."

128. Lupton, interview, January 3, 2001.

129. Tucker, "Villages of East Lake"; Stratigos, interviews; Lupton, interview, January 3, 2001.

130. O'Connell, interview; Jeralyn Sheehan, telephone interview by author, Atlanta, September 18, 2000.

131. Dorsey, interview.

132. Kate Little, interview by author, tape recording, Atlanta, June 21, 2000.

133. Mtamanika Youngblood, interview by author, tape recording, Atlanta, June 21, 2000.

134. David Listokin and Barbara Listokin, "Historic Preservation and Affordable Housing: Leveraging Old Resources for New Opportunities," *Housing Facts & Findings* 3:2 (2001), 1, 6–14.

135. Reynoldstown Revitalization Corporation, "History of Reynoldstown," *Reynoldstown 130 years . . . "A Collective Spirit*," Souvenir Program, Wheelbarrow Summer Theater, June 24–26, 1999, 9–10; Young T. Hughley Jr., interview by author, tape recording, Atlanta, June 21, 2000.

136. Hughley, interview.

137. Hughley, interview.

138. Reynoldstown Revitalization Corporation, *Reynoldstown on the Rise—A Strategy for Rebuilding Our Families and Our Community*, brochure, n.d.

139. Hughley, interview.

Chapter 6

1. U. S. Census Bureau, *Profile of the Foreign-Born Population in the United States: 1997*, Current Population Reports Special Studies, P23–195, 9, Fig. 1-2, 17; Benjamin Chinitz, "Urban Growth Patterns—Trends, Forces, Policy Issues, Prospects, Research Needs," paper delivered at the Lincoln Land Institute, December 16, 1992; Laurent Belsie, "An Iowa Debate over Newcomers," *Christian Science Monitor*, July 27, 2001; Monica Rhor, "Planning a Strategy to Lure Immigrants," *Philadelphia Inquirer*, May 20, 2001; Linda K. Harris, "Phila. Seeks to Attract More Immigrants," *Philadelphia Inquirer*, October 18, 2000.

2. John H. M. Laslett, "Historical Perspectives: Immigration and the Rise of Distinctive Urban Regions, 1900–1970," in *Ethnic Los Angeles*, ed. Roger Waldinger and Mehdi Bozorgmehr (New York: Russell Sage Foundation, 1996), 43–45, 55–56, 58; Keith E. Collins, *Black Los Angeles: The Maturing of the Ghetto, 1940–1950* (Saratoga, Calif.: Century Twenty One Publishing, 1980); Lynell George, *No Crystal Stair: African-Americans in the City of Angels* (London and New York: Verso, 1992).

3. Bayrd Still, *Urban America: A History with Documents* (Boston: Little, Brown, 1974), 406–7; David M. Grant, Melvin L. Oliver, and Angela D. James, "African-Americans: Social and Economic Bifurcation," *Ethnic Los Angeles* in ed. Roger Waldinger and Mehdi Bozorgmehr (New York: Russell Sage Foundation, 1996), 382; Tom Larson, "An Economic View of South Central Los Angeles," *Cities* 15:3 (1998), 199.

4. Grant, Oliver, and James, "African-Americans," 400–402.

5. Laslett, "Historical Perspectives," 54–58.

6. Los Angeles County Children's Planning Council, *Ethnic Community Profiles: Planning for a New Los Angeles* (Los Angeles: Los Angeles County Children's Planning Council, 1996), Table 35, 81; U.S. Census Bureau, 1990 U.S. Census Data, Database: C90STF3A; U.S. Census Bureau, DP-1 Profile of General Demographic Characteristics: 2000.

7. City of Los Angeles Department of City Planning, *Community Plan Profiles of City of Los Angeles* (December 1996); City of Los Angeles Department of City Planning, Demographics Research Unit Statistical Reports, Census 2000: "City of Los Angeles, Population Statistics from the 2000 Census, City Planning Areas, Population and Race/Ethnicity" (http://www.ci.la.ca.us/pln/C2K).

8. New Economics for Women, Fact Sheet, n.d.; See also Web site http://www.neweconomicsforwomen.org, July 23, 2002.

9. Little Tokyo Service Center Community Development Corporation, *1997 Annual Report*; http://www.ltsc.org/cdc/index.html, July 23, 2002.

10. Arturo Ybarra, interview by author, tape recording, Los Angeles, March 22, 1999.

11. Ybarra, interview; "Watts Century Latino Organization Background" fact sheet.

12. Coalition of Neighborhood Developers, *From the Ground Up: Neighbors Planning Neighborhoods* (Los Angeles, 1994), 33; Sister Diane Donoghue, interview by author, tape recording, Los Angeles, March 22, 1999.

13. Donoghue, interview.

14. Donoghue, interview.

15. Yadira Arévalo, interview by author, tape recording, Los Angeles, March 2, 1999.

16. Donoghue, interview.

17. Arévalo, interview; Tom Jones, William Pettus, Michael Pyatok, *Good Neighbors: Affordable Family Housing* (Melbourne, Australia: Images Publishing Group, 1997), 27.

18. Arévalo, interview, 1999, and telephone interview by author, Los Angeles, July 23, 2002.
19. Juanita Tate, interview by author, Washington, D. C., May 10, 1995.
20. Concerned Citizens of South Central Los Angeles, *Fact Sheet—December 18, 1996*; Tate, interview, 1995.
21. Juanita Tate, interview by author, Los Angeles, April 23, 1998.
22. Tate, interview, 1998; Melody Dove, interview by author, tape recording, Los Angeles, March 19, 1999.
23. Dove, interview; Nevada Dove and Debra Parra, joint interview by author, tape recording, Los Angeles, March 19, 1999.
24. Dunbar Economic Development Corporation, Organizational History, http://www.dunbaredc.org; Anthony Scott, interview by author, Los Angeles, April 23, 1998.
25. Scott, interview.
26. Watts Labor Community Action Committee, *Working Together to Build a Better Los Angeles* (Los Angeles: WLCAC, 1994).
27. Watts Labor Community Action Committee, *Working Together*.
28. Scott, interview; Haya El Nasser, "Changing Face of Watts: Hispanics Find Home in Black Neighborhood," *USA Today*, May 4, 1991; Watts Century Latino Organization, flyers, Cinco de Mayo Celebration, assorted years.
29. Scott, interview.
30. "Charting the Hours of Chaos," *Los Angeles Times*, April 29, 2002; Don Lee, "5 Years Later, a Mixed Legacy of Rebuilding," *Los Angeles Times*, April 22, 1997.
31. For a definitive account of the riots, the events that triggered them, and governmental policies that contributed to them, see Lou Cannon, *Official Negligence: How Rodney King and the Riots Changed Los Angeles and the LAPD* (New York: Times Books, 1997).
32. Fred Siegel, *The Future Once Happened Here: New York, D.C., L.A., and the Fate of America's Big Cities* (New York: Free Press, 1997), 117–18; Joel Kotkin, *Can the Cities Be Saved?* (Santa Monica, Calif.: Milken Institute, 1997), 79.
33. William Hamilton, "Ueberroth's Pitch Falls Short in L. A.; 'Rebuild' Is Beset by Critics," *Washington Post*, April 11, 1993; Rebuild LA (RLA), *Rebuilding LA's Urban Communities: A Final Report from RLA* (Santa Monica, Calif.: Milken Institute, 1997), 16.
34. "Exit, Disgusted," *The Economist* (London), May 29, 1993.
35. William Fulton, "In Los Angeles, the Healing Begins," *Planning* 59:1 (January 1993), 23–25; Denise G. Fairchild, interview by author, tape recording, Los Angeles, February 9, 1999.
36. Fulton, "In Los Angeles"; Linda Griego, telephone interview by author, Los Angeles, February 12, 1999.
37. Robert A. Beauregard, "The Unavoidable Presence of Space," *The American Behavioral Scientist* 40:3 (Jan. 1997), 365–74; "Exit, Disgusted"; Joel Kotkin and David Friedman, "The Los Angeles Riots: Causes, Myths, and Solutions," *Progressive Policy Institute Commentary* 2 (February 1993), 14–20; Kotkin, *Can the Cities Be Saved?*, 37–40.
38. Hamilton, "Ueberroth's Pitch Falls Short." The official definitions of a small business vary. For regulatory purposes, the U.S. Small Business Administration designates small business for each type of industry by a particular level of annual revenue or number of employees. For research purposes, the Office of Advocacy U.S. Small Business Administration adopts the general definition of a small business as an independently owned and operated firm with fewer than

500 employees. In 1999, the State of California defined a small business as an independently owned and operated firm operating solely or principally in California and that was either a service, construction, or nonmanufacturer with 100 or fewer employees, and average annual gross receipts of ten million dollars ($10,000,000) or less over the previous three years, or a manufacturer with 100 or fewer employees.

39. "Exit, Disgusted"; Haya El Nasser, "Skepticism High Over 'Rebuild L. A.' Project," *USA Today*, November 19, 1992.
40. "Ueberroth Quits L.A. Job," *Washington Post*, May 22, 1993; "Exit, Disgusted"; Paul Feldman, "Great Expectations; as Head of RLA, Linda Griego Has Definite Ideas about Getting Things Done," *Los Angeles Times*, June 5, 1994; Paul Feldman, "Griego and Cook Take RLA Helm," *Los Angeles Times*, February 16, 1994.
41. Steve Proffit, "Linda Griego, Lodwrick Cook; Redefining RLA as an Engine of Economic Development," *Los Angeles Times*, February 27, 1994; Paul Feldman, "RLA Board Chairman to Stay Through 1995," *Los Angeles Times*, May 24, 1995.
42. Feldman, "Great Expectations."
43. Linda Griego, telephone interview by author, Los Angeles, February 12, 1999; Linda Griego, interview by author, Santa Monica, Calif., March 25, 1999.
44. Griego, interview, February 12, 1999; Feldman, "Griego and Cook Take RLA Helm."
45. Griego, interview, February 12, 1999.
46. Avis C. Vidal, *Rebuilding Communities: A National Study of Urban Community Development Corporations* (New York: Community Development Research Center, 1992), 64, 71.
47. Griego, interview, February 12, 1999; David Friedman, "Getting Industry to Stick: Creating High Value Added Production Regions in the United States," MITJP (Series), 93–02 (Cambridge, Mass.: The MIT Japan Program, Massachusetts Institute of Technology, 1993); David Friedman, *The Misunderstood Miracle: Industrial Development and Political Change in Japan* (Ithaca, N.Y.: Cornell University Press, 1988).
48. Kotkin and Friedman, "Los Angeles Riots," 13 (quotation), 14–30.
49. Griego, interview, February 12, 1999; *Rebuilding LA's Urban Communities*, 44.
50. *Rebuilding LA's Urban Communities*, 45.
51. *Rebuilding LA's Urban Communities*, 45–51; Virginia Oaxaca, interview by author, March 20, 1999.
52. Griego, interview, Feb. 12, 1999; Tom Larson, telephone interview by author, April 20, 1999.
53. Tom Larson, "An Economic View of South Central Los Angeles," *Cities* 15:3 (1998), 193–208.
54. Larson, "An Economic View," 202.
55. *Rebuilding LA's Urban Communities*, 27–28.
56. *Rebuilding LA's Urban Communities*, 63, appendix C.
57. Griego, interview, February 12, 1999.
58. Michael E. Porter, "The Competitive Advantage of the Inner City," *Harvard Business Review*, May–June 1995, 55–71.
59. *Rebuilding LA's Urban Communities*, 23–24.
60. Griego, interview, March 25, 1999; Linda Yeung, interview by author, tape recording, Los Angeles, March 24, 1999.
61. *Rebuilding LA's Urban Communities*, 26–27.
62. http://www.socalbio.org.

63. *Rebuilding LA's Urban Communities*, 38.
64. May Cheung, interview by author, tape recording, Los Angeles, March 24, 1999.
65. *Rebuilding LA's Urban Communities*, 39.
66. Cheung, interview.
67. Yeung, interview.
68. Yvette Nunez, telephone interview by author, Los Angeles, September 14, 1999.
69. *Rebuilding LA's Urban Communities*, 30–31; Yvette Nunez, interview by author, tape recording, Los Angeles, March 24, 1999; "Food Industry Business Roundtable," *CD Tech News* 1 (Fall 1998).
70. Kenneth Yee, interview by author, tape recording, Los Angeles, March 24, 1999.
71. Yee, interview.
72. Nunez, interview, March 24, 1999.
73. Nunez, interview, March 24, 1999.
74. Nunez, interview, March 24, 1999; Fairchild, interview.
75. Nunez, interview, September 14, 1999.
76. Yee, interview.
77. Ozabe Banks, interview by author, tape recording, Los Angeles, March 24, 1999.
78. Banks, interview.
79. Denise G. Fairchild, telephone interview by author, September 22, 1999; Griego, interview, March 25, 1999.
80. Fairchild, interview, March 25, 1999.
81. Fairchild, interview, September 22, 1999.
82. Fairchild, interview, September 22, 1999.
83. Fairchild, interview, September 22, 1999.
84. "Merrill Lynch Is Bullish on LAMNI," *CD Tech News*, 2 (Spring 1999); Linda Wong, telephone interview by author, Los Angeles, June 21, 2002.
85. Fairchild, interview, September 22, 1999; Nunez, interview, March 24, 1999; Community Development Technologies Center, "Worker Income Security Program (WISP)," brochure, n.d; Wong, interview, June 21, 2002.
86. Linda Wong, interview by author, September 15, 1999.
87. Lisa Mascaro, "Business Rises from the Ashes," *Los Angeles Daily News*, April 29, 2002.
88. http://www.ebaldc.org/organization/mission.htm
89. Rocky Delgadillo, interview by author, tape recording, Los Angeles, March 24, 1999.
90. Carol F. Steinbach, *Coming of Age: Trends and Achievements of Community-Based Development Organizations* (Washington, D.C.: National Congress for Community Economic Development, 1999), 13–14.
91. Scott Hebert, Avis Vidal, Greg Mills, Franklin James, and Debbie Gruenstein, "Interim Assessment of the Empowerment Zones and Enterprise Communities (EZ/EC) Program: A Progress Report," prepared for U.S. Department of Housing and Urban Development, November 2001.
92. George Gendron, "FYI"; Michael Porter and Anne Habiby, "A Window on the New Economy," and related articles, *Inc.* (May 1999); http://www.icic.org.
93. Elena Gaona, "Gigante Breaks New Ground," *Los Angeles Times*, April 30, 2002. April 30, 2002.

INDEX

Note: Italicized page numbers refer to illustrations.